Husserl's Transcendental ~~Phenomenology~~

Edmund Husserl (1859–1938) is regarded as the founder of transcendental phenomenology, one of the major traditions to emerge in twentieth-century philosophy. In this book Andrea Staiti unearths and examines the deep theoretical links between Husserl's phenomenology and the philosophical debates of his time, showing how his thought developed in response to the conflicting demands of Neo-Kantianism and life-philosophy. Drawing on the work of thinkers including Heinrich Rickert, Wilhelm Dilthey, and Georg Simmel, as well as Husserl's writings on the natural and human sciences that are not available in English translation, Staiti illuminates a crucial chapter in the history of twentieth-century philosophy and enriches our understanding of Husserl's thought. His book will interest scholars and students of Husserl, phenomenology, and twentieth-century philosophy more generally.

ANDREA STAITI is Assistant Professor of Philosophy at Boston College. He has published many articles in journals such as *Husserl Studies*, *Continental Philosophy Review*, *Philosophy and Social Criticism*, and *Research in Phenomenology*. He is the author and co-editor of several books, including *New Approaches to Neo-Kantianism* (Cambridge, forthcoming 2015) and *Geistigkeit, Leben und geschichtliche Welt in der Transzendentalphänomenologie Husserls* (2010).

Husserl's Transcendental Phenomenology

Nature, Spirit, and Life

ANDREA STAITI

CAMBRIDGE
UNIVERSITY PRESS

CAMBRIDGE
UNIVERSITY PRESS

University Printing House, Cambridge CB2 8BS, United Kingdom

One Liberty Plaza, 20th Floor, New York, NY 10006, USA

477 Williamstown Road, Port Melbourne, VIC 3207, Australia

314-321, 3rd Floor, Plot 3, Splendor Forum, Jasola District Centre, New Delhi-110025, India

79 Anson Road, #06-04/06, Singapore 079906

Cambridge University Press is part of the University of Cambridge.

It furthers the University's mission by disseminating knowledge in the pursuit of education, learning and research at the highest international levels of excellence.

www.cambridge.org
Information on this title: www.cambridge.org/9781107638679

First published 2014
First paperback edition 2018

A catalogue record for this publication is available from the British Library

Library of Congress Cataloging in Publication data
Staiti, Andrea Sebastiano, 1981–
Husserl's transcendental phenomenology : nature, spirit, and life / Andrea Staiti.
    pages   cm
Includes bibliographical references and index.
ISBN 978-1-107-06630-4
1. Husserl, Edmund, 1859–1938. 2. Phenomenology. I. Title.
B3279.H94S6955   2014
142′.7–dc23

                                                        2014004975

ISBN 978-1-107-06630-4 Hardback
ISBN 978-1-107-63867-9 Paperback

A mia moglie Sara,
con amore e gratitudine

Contents

Acknowledgments

This book crowns a line of research that I started pursuing over ten years ago with my MA thesis at the Università degli Studi di Milano in Italy. It would be hard to acknowledge each and every person whose support, care, and intellectual generosity made my research possible and my life livable. However, it would also be hard *not* to acknowledge at least those to whom I owe my passion for philosophy, and those who graciously enabled me to cultivate it. First, I want to express my gratitude to my colleagues at the Boston College philosophy department for providing an ideal intellectual home. In particular, I would like to thank our chairman Arthur Madigan, S. J. and the Dean of the College of Arts and Sciences David Quigley for granting me a research leave in the fall of 2012, which allowed me to complete the typescript.

During these years I was lucky to meet extraordinary scholars of phenomenology, whose spoken and written words shaped the way I think about Husserl and his ambitious project. Elio Franzini, Carmine Di Martino, and Vincenzo Costa provided invaluable insight when I was a student, and to this day I know I can always rely on their generous feedback. Beatrice Centi, Costantino Esposito, Faustino Fabbianelli, and Massimo Ferrari have been wonderful interlocutors and I can only be thankful that they were willing to follow my work from afar and get me involved in many great initiatives. A special word of thanks goes to my *Doktorvater* Hans-Helmuth Gander, to whom I owe four unforgettable years in Freiburg and pretty much everything I know about Husserl's *Nachlaß*.

I can hardly express how much indebted I am to Nicolas De Warren and Claudio Majolino for being wonderful friends, effective critics, careful readers, and just admirable scholars. I would also like to thank all the members and participants of the Husserl Circle, which has been the perfect venue to present and discuss my work. In particular, I learned a lot from Burt Hopkins, John Drummond, Steve Galt Crowell, James Dodd, Tom Nenon, Sebastian Luft, and Thane Naberhaus.

A heartfelt word of thanks goes to Prof. Ullrich Melle and Dr. Thomas Vongehr at the Husserl Archive in Leuven for sharing with me Husserl's notes on Simmel and granting permission to quote from them.

Last but not least, let me thank my students Evan Clarke, Andrea Cimino, Karen Kovaka, Chris Sheridan, and Ben Martin for all the intellectual stimuli they provide and for reading ample sections of this book. Brian Tracz, Kevin Marren, and Daniel Cattolica have been the most accurate and dependable copy editors. Any mistakes or stylistic problems that the reader may still find are entirely my responsibility.

This book is dedicated to my wife Sara, for her angelic patience and her loving support. It is said that behind every great man there is a great woman. If this is true, then the fact that I am married to Sara proves what I always suspected: great women outnumber great men.

Abbreviations

Franz Böhm

OG   *Ontologie der Geschichte* (Tübingen: Mohr Siebeck, 1933)

Wilhelm Dilthey

GS I–XXVI   *Gesammelte Schriften* (Göttingen: Vandenhoeck &
Ruprecht, 1914–2005)
SW 1–5   *Selected Works* (Princeton University Press, 1985–2010)

Edmund Husserl

BW I–X   *Briefwechsel* (Dordrecht: Springer, 1994)
Crisis   *The Crisis of the European Sciences and Transcendental
Phenomenology: An Introduction to Phenomenological
Philosophy* (Evanston, IL: Northwestern University Press,
1970)
Hua I–XLI   *Husserliana – Gesammelte Werke* (Dordrecht: Springer,
1950–2010)
Ideas I   *Ideas Pertaining to a Pure Phenomenology and to a
Phenomenological Philosophy. First Book: General
Introduction to a Pure Phenomenology, Collected Works*, vol.
2 (Dordrecht: Kluwer, 1982)
Ideas II   *Ideas Pertaining to a Pure Phenomenology and to a
Phenomenological Philosophy. Second Book: Studies in the
Phenomenology of Constitution, Collected Works*, vol. 3
(Dordrecht: Kluwer, 1989)
Mat I–VIII   *Husserliana – Materialien* (Dordrecht: Springer, 2001–)
Phen. P.   *Phenomenological Psychology: Lectures Summer Semester
1925*, trans. J. Scanlon (The Hague: Nijhoff, 1977)
PRS   *Philosophy as a Rigorous Science*, in E. Husserl, *Shorter
Works* (University of Notre Dame Press, 1981)

Emil Lask

LP   *Die Logik der Philosophie und die Kategorienlehre*, in E. Lask,
        Gesammelte Schriften, vol. 2 (Tübingen: Mohr Siebeck, 1923)
NEW   *Notizen zur Einteilung der Wissenschaften*, in E. Lask, *Gesammelte
        Schriften*, vol. 3 (Tübingen: Mohr Siebeck, 1924)
SW   *Zum System der Wissenschaften*, in E. Lask, *Gesammelte Schriften*,
        vol. 3 (Tübingen: Mohr Siebeck, 1924)

Heinrich Rickert

LCF   *The Limits of Concept Formation in Natural Science* (Cambridge
        University Press, 1986)
MPU   "Die Methode der Philosophie und das Unmittelbare," in
        H. Rickert, *Philosophische Aufsätze* (Tübingen: Mohr Siebeck,
        1999)
SH   *Science and History: A Critique of Positivist Epistemology*
        (Princeton, NJ: Van Nostrand, 1962)
WPW   *Wissenschaftliche Philosophie und Weltanschauung*, in
        H. Rickert, *Philosophische Aufsätze* (Tübingen: Mohr Siebeck,
        1999)

Georg Simmel

K   *Kant. Sechzehn Vorlesungen gehalten an der Berliner Universität*, in
        G. Simmel, *Gesamtausgabe*, vol. 9 (Frankfurt am Main: Suhrkamp,
        1997)
PGP   *Die Probleme der Geschichtsphilosophie. Eine
        erkenntnistheoretische Studie*, in G. Simmel, *Gesamtausgabe*, vol. 9
        (Frankfurt am Main: Suhrkamp, 1997)
PHT   *The Problem of Historical Time*, in G. Simmel, *Essays on
        Interpretation in Social Science* (Totowa, NJ: Rowman & Littlefield,
        1980)
PPH   *The Problems of the Philosophy of History: An Epistemological
        Essay* (New York: The Free Press, 1977)
VL   *The View of Life: Four Metaphysical Essays with Journal Aphorisms*
        (University of Chicago Press, 2010)
WuK   *Was ist uns Kant?*, in G. Simmel, *Gesamtausgabe*, vol. 5 (Frankfurt
        am Main: Suhrkamp, 1997)

Wilhelm Windelband

GN   "Geschichte und Naturwissenschaft," in W. Windelband,
       *Präludien: Aufsätze und Reden zur Philosophie und ihrer
       Geschichte*, vol. 2 (Tübingen: Mohr Siebeck, 1915)

Introduction

This book has a double purpose. First, it is an essay in the history of European philosophy. Its goal is to present to Anglophone readers a hitherto largely ignored chapter in nineteenth- and early twentieth-century German thought: the dispute about the foundations of the natural and human sciences involving the Neo-Kantians and the so-called life-philosophers, or *Lebensphilosophen*. Second, it is a critical study of Husserl's late work. As such, its goal is also to advance our understanding of transcendental phenomenology by locating it in the philosophical context of its time. In this second respect, it can be considered an essay in what the German philosopher Dieter Heinrich termed *Konstellationsforschung*, or constellation analysis. This historical–philosophical method prioritizes intellectual spaces [*Denkräume*] over individual figures and is designed to shed light on complex ideas that developed in the context of ongoing philosophical exchanges among multiple thinkers.[1]

Not infrequently, Husserl is presented as an isolated thinker, too engrossed in his own project to engage productively with the great philosophers of the past, let alone his contemporaries. Moreover, post-Husserlian phenomenologists such as Heidegger or Derrida often projected back on their putative father their own theoretical concerns, thus encouraging generations of scholars to explore Husserl's work from an extremely idiosyncratic point of view. For decades, it was

---

[1] Martin Muslow provides the following definition of a philosophical constellation: "A philosophical constellation can be defined as the strong connection of people, ideas, theories, problems or documents that influenced one another in such a way that only the analysis of this connection (and not the analysis of its isolated components) enables the understanding of the philosophical import and development of said people, ideas and theories." M. Muslow, "Zum Methodenprofil der Konstellationsforschung," in M. Muslow and M. Stamm (eds.), *Konstellationsforschung* (Frankfurt am Main: Suhrkamp, 2005), 74–97. Here 74.

customary to read Husserl hunting for the latent seeds of subsequent
existential hermeneutics and deconstruction, attempting to expose pur-
ported *aporiae* that only later practitioners of phenomenology were
able to fully acknowledge. In effect, in the wake of post-Husserlian
phenomenology, scholars often compelled Husserl himself to join in a
rather artificial dialogue with the likes of Heidegger, Merleau-Ponty,
Sartre, Gadamer, and Derrida. Admittedly, reading Husserl as part of
this dialogue proved fecund for the development of postwar European
thought, but as far as Husserl himself is concerned, this is a dialogue
that never actually occurred. The historical Husserl took part in very
different conversations, and, in particular, from the 1910s onward, he
actively contributed to the aforementioned dispute concerning the philosophical foundations of the natural and human sciences. This dispute
had been going on virtually since the demise of Hegelian idealism in the
second half of the nineteenth century, and its roots reach deep into
Kant's transcendental philosophy. In light of Husserl's contribution to
the debate on the foundations of the natural and human sciences, the
twofold purpose of this book finds its theoretical justification. More
specifically, I intend to show that this debate was an incubator for the
development of Husserl's mature thought.

As the chapters unfold, it will become increasingly clear that from
roughly the beginning of the 1910s until his death in 1938 Husserl
understood himself explicitly as a contributor to this debate. He avidly
read the works of leading philosophers such as Rickert, Simmel, and
Dilthey and responded to them, in part overtly and in part implicitly, in
both his published and unpublished writings. Stated more boldly, transcendental phenomenology could only gain its distinctive contours in
the context of Husserl's thoughtful confrontation with his contemporaries, who, in turn, carried forward a philosophical legacy dating back
to Kant. While it has been shown convincingly that Husserl's *Logical
Investigations* developed within the context of a fruitful conversation
within the Brentano school,[2] the fact that his work *after* the *Logical
Investigations* was carried out in ongoing intellectual exchange with the
Neo-Kantians and the life-philosophers has been mentioned here and
there, but it has never been the object of a thorough study. This book
intends to fill this gap in the existing Husserlian scholarship and to

---

[2] See, for instance, R. Rollinger, *Husserl's Position in the School of Brentano*
(Dordrecht: Kluwer, 1999).

situate Husserl's transcendental phenomenology (back) in its authentic philosophical lineage: Kant's critical philosophy in its specific connotation as a transcendental theory of knowledge.

The acclaimed British historian Eric Hobsbawm (1917–2012) famously called the nineteenth century a long century, because, in his narrative, it started with the French Revolution in 1789 and ended with the outbreak of World War I in 1914. An argument could be made that the nineteenth century was even longer in philosophy, starting with Kant's *Critique of Pure Reason* in 1781 and ending symbolically with Husserl's death in 1938.[3] This is, at least, the hypothesis I would recommend the reader to keep in mind while reading this book: Husserl is not so much the initiator of a twentieth-century trend generically called 'phenomenology,' but the last philosopher of the nineteenth century, whose work condenses some of the most interesting aspects of this fertile age of thought while, at the same time, developing an absolutely original project. Needless to say, the groundbreaking achievements of Husserl's project carried over into the next century, which, at least philosophically, is probably not over yet.

The perspective I am delineating, again, is neither intended to downplay Husserl's impact on many of the greatest minds in twentieth-century European philosophy, nor to suggest that Husserl's philosophical achievements are conclusive or definitive in any sense of these terms. Husserl's phenomenology is a working philosophy, one that is designed to carry out increasingly sophisticated descriptions of what is essential to our experiences in their multifarious variety and to our experience as a whole. The process of constant refinement and revision in which this work unfolds makes Husserlian phenomenology impervious to a definitive systematization and immune to the illusion that it can exhaust the possibilities of philosophy once and for all. Husserl's own failure to produce a system of phenomenology bears witness to the intrinsically open-ended nature of his work. Accordingly, the claim contained in the reading hypothesis suggested above is not that Husserl is the last nineteenth-century philosopher because he somehow concluded or completed the historical trajectory of transcendental thought. He is the last nineteenth-century philosopher 'just' because

---

[3] In this sense, it was a felicitous decision to devote the final chapter to Husserl in the newly published D. Moyar (ed.), *Routledge Companion to Nineteenth Century Philosophy* (New York: Routledge, 2010).

after his death, and probably already during the last years of his life, philosophy switched topics. The rise of Heidegger's existentialism on the one hand and of logical positivism on the other decreed the end of transcendental thinking and redefined almost from scratch what the true goals of philosophy ought to be.[4] Eventually, while Husserl was still read as a forerunner of Heidegger in some circles and as a polemical counterpart in other circles, most great thinkers surrounding him during his lifetime faded into oblivion. The nascent existentialist movement had its reasons not to read the Neo-Kantians and the life-philosophers anymore. Purportedly, their debate about the transcendental foundations of the sciences did not reach the desired level of radicalism set by the master of Messkirch, that is, it failed to ask the only question worth asking in philosophy: what is the meaning of "Being" overall? In turn, the nascent movement of analytic philosophy felt exempt from engaging with the weighty tomes on the philosophical foundations of the natural and the human sciences for a different set of reasons: these works dealt with allegedly intractable pseudo-problems preempted by empiricism and the logical analysis of language.

In the Anglophone world, some scant interest for Neo-Kantianism and *Lebensphilosophie*, which inflamed the philosophical scene in pre-war Germany, seemed to linger on among theorists of the social sciences in the 1960s and the 1970s.[5] As regards the theory of the natural sciences, on the contrary, transcendental questions about the possibility of nature as a theoretical construct had been long replaced by questions about the so-called logic of scientific discovery. In spite of this marginal attention among social scientists, the overwhelming bulk of primary texts by the Neo-Kantians and the *Lebensphilosophen* remained untranslated, and the few scholars who touched on them did so with a very selective focus, given that their primary interest lay elsewhere. Full restitution of the debate's philosophical meaning was simply not part of their agenda. Questions about the foundations of the sciences remained at best methodological questions asked by practicing social scientists in their spare time.

---

[4] Note that merely decreeing that a certain idea is over does not amount to refuting or disproving the idea in question. It is more an act of the will than an act of the intellect.

[5] Guy Oakes' abridged translations of Simmel and Rickert, along with his helpful introductory essays, are the main example of this trend. See the list of sources at the end of this book for full references.

Fortunately, this past decade witnessed encouraging signs of resurgent interest in Neo-Kantianism and *Lebensphilosophie*, as well as growing awareness that these movements were of paramount importance for the development of mainstream currents in twentieth-century philosophy. As for Neo-Kantianism, Michael Friedman blazed the trail for this recent trend with his rightly acclaimed book *A Parting of the Ways: Carnap, Cassirer and Heidegger.*[6] Through a sharp examination of the famous Davos conference in 1929 featuring Cassirer versus Heidegger on the interpretation of Kant, Friedman shows convincingly that Cassirer's brand of Neo-Kantianism had a profound impact on Carnap and the ensuing Anglo-Austrian philosophy of science up to Thomas Kuhn. Moreover, Friedman suggests that the debate between Cassirer and Heidegger foreshadows in significant ways the (in)famous rift between analytic and continental philosophy that characterized the discipline after World War II. More recently, Peter Gordon published a monumental study of the Davos debate,[7] which expands considerably our understanding of the philosophical disagreement between Heidegger and Cassirer and confirms beyond reasonable doubt that Neo-Kantianism is worth careful consideration for those interested in twentieth-century intellectual history. Among other things, Gordon unearths a tension between 'thrownness' and 'spontaneity' underlying Heidegger's and Cassirer's interpretation of Kant and argues that this tension is a helpful foil for looking at further ramifications for philosophy after Davos. Just one year after the appearance of Gordon's book, Fredrick Beiser published a thorough study of the German historicist tradition,[8] which includes illuminating chapters on Dilthey, Windelband, Rickert, Lask, and Simmel and argues that their work is decisive for a complete understanding of the characteristically German preoccupation with history in philosophy. Additionally, Sebastian Luft co-edited together with Rudolf Makkreel an excellent collection of essays on Neo-Kantianism and contemporary philosophy,[9] and he is

---

[6] M. Friedman, *A Parting of the Ways: Carnap, Cassirer and Heidegger* (La Salle, IL: Open Court, 2000).

[7] P. Gordon, *Continental Divide: Heidegger – Cassirer – Davos* (Cambridge, MA and London: Harvard University Press, 2010).

[8] F. Beiser, *The German Historicist Tradition* (Oxford University Press, 2011).

[9] S. Luft and R. Makkreel (eds.), *Neo-Kantianism in Contemporary Philosophy* (Bloomington: Indiana University Press, 2010).

about to publish a much-needed reader on the Neo-Kantian movement as a whole.

This very recent trend was to some extent pre-dated in Heidegger studies. In the wake of the ongoing publication of Heidegger's earlier works, a few years ago, Heidegger scholars started looking at the works of Neo-Kantians and life-philosophers mentioned in Heidegger's lectures. This led them to the conclusion that these thinkers are in fact worth reading and that they played an important role in the genesis of Heidegger's project of a fundamental ontology via the existential analytic in *Being and Time* (1927).[10]

In the wake of growing intellectual ferment surrounding Neo-Kantianism, *Lebensphilosophie* and their cultural milieu, the present book is intended to contribute a further perspective on this rich chapter of German philosophy. There are at least two respects in which this book occupies a distinctive venue among existing and developing studies on Neo-Kantianism, *Lebensphilosophie*, and their connections to phenomenology. First, to my knowledge, Husserl's position in this complicated tangle of philosophical ideas has never been adequately discussed.[11] In this regard, this book sets out to accomplish for Husserl what other scholars have already accomplished successfully for Heidegger. Second, the present book has a rather unusual focus: it deals exclusively with the Southwestern school of Neo-Kantianism and, to some extent, prioritizes Georg Simmel over Wilhelm Dilthey in the discussion of *Lebensphilosophie*. This is because, on the one hand, as I will discuss in Chapter 6, Husserl's appropriation of Simmel is more ramified and interesting than Husserl's initial dismissal and subsequent

---

[10] See D. Farrell Krell, *Daimon Life: Heidegger and Life-Philosophy* (Bloomington: Indiana University Press, 1992); C. Bambach, *Heidegger, Dilthey and the Crisis of Historicism* (Ithaca, NY and London: Cornell University Press, 1995); and most recently S. Campbell, *The Early Heidegger's Philosophy of Life: Facticity, Being, and Language* (New York: Fordham University Press, 2012).

[11] There are, of course, a few exceptions, which convinced me that a book-length study would be a desideratum. See, for instance: R. D'Amico, "Husserl on the Foundational Structures of Natural and Cultural Sciences," *Philosophy and Phenomenological Research* 42 (1981): 5–22; J. E. Jalbert, "Husserl's Position between Dilthey and the Windelband-Rickert School of Neo-Kantianism," *Journal of the History of Philosophy* 26 (1988): 279–296; and the set of papers devoted to Simmel and phenomenology in *Human Studies* 26/2 (2003). Bob Sandmeyer's recent book *Husserl's Constitutive Phenomenology: Its Problem and Promise* (New York: Routledge, 2009) includes one chapter on Husserl and Dilthey.

reappraisal of Dilthey. Similarly, on the other hand, while Husserl always maintained a polite and at times even obsequious attitude towards the so-called Marburg school[12] (the current of Neo-Kantianism starting with Cohen and culminating with Cassirer's philosophy of symbolic forms), he engaged actively only with the Southwestern school, and in particular with the work of his predecessor at the University of Freiburg, Heinrich Rickert. The Southwestern Neo-Kantian insistence on the necessity to *demarcate* different fields of scientific inquiry, rather than focusing chiefly on the natural sciences (Cohen) or on the dynamics of symbolization common to all human activities (Cassirer), was naturally appealing to Husserl, since it seemed to lead straight to fundamental questions that only phenomenology could adequately address.

In fact, asking about the correct demarcation of different fields of knowledge lies at the heart of philosophical thinking from its very inception. In Plato's dialogues, Socrates struggles with his interlocutors to establish who is competent to speak meaningfully about various topics. This often involves attempts to define the sphere of competence of various 'arts' and to keep them separate from one another. In the early dialogue *Ion*, for instance, Socrates ridicules the rhapsodes for believing that they can speak meaningfully of things lying outside their own sphere of competence, which is restricted to poetic declamation. In the *Republic*, Socrates' famous refutation of Thrasymachus similarly revolves around the sophist's conflation of two different 'arts': money-making and politics. Knowledge of the Forms, for Plato, would grant the philosopher the capacity to distinguish sharply between spheres of knowledge that need to be kept distinct.

---

[12] In a footnote to his lectures on *Natur und Geist* in 1919 (which will be discussed at length in Chapter 5) Husserl remarks in passing that "only the Marburg Neo-Kantianism was able to avoid a trivialization [*Verflachung*] of Kant's powerful intuitions." E. Husserl, *Natur und Geist. Vorlesungen Sommersemester 1919, Husserliana Materialien*, vol. 4 (Dordrecht: Springer, 2002), 193 n. Hereafter Mat IV. In any case, Husserl does not expand on this laudatory remark, and he rather hastens to add: "However, in Marburg Neo-Kantianism, too, it is not the whole Kant who lives on. The whole Kant can only be drawn out of Kant's own writings" (*ibid.*). Husserl would often pay homage to the Marburg school, and he was certainly positively impressed by their philosophical achievements. However, with the exception of Paul Natorp's transcendental psychology, Husserl *de facto* never felt compelled to deepen his understanding of the Marburg school beyond the basics.

In a similar vein, Aristotle often defers discussion of certain topics with the explanation that they belong in a different discipline, thus defending the necessity to organize the universe of knowledge in a way that keeps conflations and equivocations at bay. The very thrust of his *Metaphysics* is in the definition and demarcation of a new, fundamental philosophical discipline. Disquisitions about the distinctions and hierarchic order of different fields of knowledge cut across the whole Middle Ages and were still paramount to Descartes. The situation slowly changed after the scientific revolution, which seemingly imposed the universal adoption of the *mos geometricus* for whatever subject matter was under scrutiny. As we shall see in Chapter 7 of this book, it was not until Kant's Copernican turn that the sphere of validity of naturalistic methods was relativized, thus reopening an intellectual space for a pluralistic conception of knowledge and for a debate that had lain dormant for most of the foregoing two centuries. As the preface to the second edition of the *Critique of Pure Reason* evidences, Kant bestowed great importance on the philosophical demarcation of different fields of inquiry and considered this a necessary presupposition in order for any discipline to stop "groping about"[13] and set itself on "the secure path of a science."[14]

In the second half of the nineteenth century, the impressive flourishing of historical, literary, political, and economic studies, whose high standards of rigor could hardly be disputed, called for philosophical elucidation. Previously, such disciplines either did not have scientific status or had been overshadowed by the dominance of naturalistic research. Their rapid flourishing in the spirit of rigor bore witness to reason's capacity to understand empirical reality well beyond the limited scope of nature. In particular, the common trait of virtually all the humanistic disciplines coming to fruition in the nineteenth century was that they dealt in some way with human cultural achievements. Unlike the subject matter of physics, the subject matter of history, literary studies, and political economics, to mention but some, is undeniably shaped by subjective activity. Accordingly, thinkers in the tradition of *Lebensphilosophie*, such as Dilthey and Simmel, worked to articulate a transcendental foundation of these disciplines by reference

[13] I. Kant, *Critique of Pure Reason* (Cambridge University Press, 1998), 106 (B vii).
[14] *Ibid.*, 107 (B x).

to historically living subjects whose activity is at the origin of both cultural objects and the methods for their cognition. In the human sciences, as Dilthey famously puts it, "life grasps life,"[15] therefore these disciplines should be sharply distinguished from the natural sciences.

The major challenge to this view stemmed from the consideration of the newly born discipline of experimental psychology. Grounding their work on the hypothesis of psychophysical parallelism, researchers in this novel field, such as Wundt and Fechner, proved that the psychic life of human subjects can be fruitfully investigated relying on the very same methods employed to discover laws in other provinces of nature. Psychology, on this account, is just another natural science. Rickert and most Neo-Kantians rejected Dilthey and Simmel's criteria for a demarcation of the sciences precisely in consideration of the explanatory power of experimental psychology. Granted that psychology is a natural science, they opposed the idea that references to psychic life can be sufficient to clarify what is distinctive about the human sciences. These sciences, in Rickert's view, do not deal with psyche but with culture, that is, with objects bearing an ostensible relationship with significant, culturally acknowledged values. Without anticipating too much, it is important to underscore that late nineteenth-century psychology and its philosophically ambiguous status were a battlefield of endless controversies in almost the same sense in which Kant spoke about metaphysics roughly one century earlier. It is revealing that over three decades into the twentieth century, in his unfinished work *The Crisis of the European Sciences and Transcendental Phenomenology* (1935–1936) Husserl claims emphatically that psychology is still "the truly decisive field,"[16] that is, the field whose correct demarcation and

---

[15] W. Dilthey, "Der Aufbau der geschichtlichen Welt in den Geisteswissenschaften," in W. Dilthey, *Der Aufbau der geschichtlichen Welt in den Geisteswissenschaften, Gesammelte Schriften*, vol. 7 (Göttingen: Vandenhoeck & Ruprecht, 1927), 79–291. Here 136. Hereafter GS VII. English trans. by R. Makkreel and J. Scanlon, *The Formation of the Historical World in the Human Sciences*, in W. Dilthey, *Selected Works*, vol. 3 (Princeton University Press, 2002), 100–311. Here 157, translation modified. Hereafter SW 3.

[16] E. Husserl, *Die Krisis der europäischen Wissenschaften und die transzendentale Phänomenologie. Eine Einführung in die phänomenologische Philosophie*, *Husserliana*, vol. 6 (The Hague: Nijhoff, 1954). Hereafter Hua VI. English translation by D. Carr, *The Crisis of the European Sciences and Transcendental Phenomenology: An Introduction to Phenomenological Philosophy* (Evanston, IL: Northwestern University Press, 1970), 208. Hereafter *Crisis*.

investigation have the most bearing on the future of philosophy and of Western civilization as such. For nineteenth-century thinkers, including Husserl, therefore, questions about the demarcations of different scientific fields and in particular about the correct classification of psychology were anything but otiose academic undertakings: they stood at the vital core of philosophical inquiry. Reviving the genuine philosophical impetus behind these questions is one of the main goals of this book.

As far as Husserl is concerned, the importance of his work on nature, psychic life, and the different spheres of scientific inquiry are certainly not unknown. What has been mostly overlooked is rather the central meaning of these topics for a correct understanding of transcendental phenomenology as a whole and for a full grasp of its intersections with other philosophical trends in Husserl's time. It is noteworthy that none of the numerous introductions to Husserl's phenomenology that appeared in English in recent years presents Husserl's position on the natural and the human sciences, let alone the broader debate in which his position took shape. Presumably, this issue has been deemed marginal to the actual core of Husserl's work and thus dispensable for introductory purposes. While there is some truth to the fact that Husserl's phenomenological analyses of nature, psyche, and culture are rather advanced and that they presuppose at least some basic familiarity with the phenomenological method in general, they cannot be considered as dealing with a delimited sphere of problems that can be safely isolated and left out of consideration. On the contrary, these analyses are crucial to understanding both the import and the scope of Husserl's transcendental-phenomenological philosophy as such. To give just one example, the rationale behind the performance of the phenomenological *epoché* and reduction is bound to remain obscure if the burning questions about the ontological status of psyche and the scientificity of psychology are not adequately understood.[17] Perhaps it was insufficient appreciation of this point that led various post-Husserlian thinkers to believe that they could harmlessly drop the *epoché* and the reduction as mere relics of an embarrassing Cartesian past and still continue to do phenomenology. In this regard, I believe that the reactivation of the debate on the philosophical foundations of the natural and the human sciences attempted in this book, among other

---

[17] This point will be discussed at length in Chapter 6.

things, will shed much needed light on the meaning and the indispens-
ability of two of phenomenology's pillars: the *epoché* and the reduction.

Before I proceed to outline the structure of this book, I would like to
add three brief yet important remarks.

(1) One valuable thing I have learned from some of the thinkers I
    discuss is that no theoretical work is possible without relying on
    some principle for the selection and organization of the materials
    under scrutiny. This is especially true of historically oriented
    writing. In this sense, I am fully aware that the historical narrative
    offered in this book is largely determined by my own philosophical
    commitments. I understand myself as a practicing phenomenolo-
    gist and consider Husserl's work a viable source for philosophy in
    the present. From this perspective, I look at the development of the
    debate on the foundations of the natural and the human sciences as
    somehow 'teleologically' oriented towards Husserl's discovery of a
    transcendental (i.e., non-naturalistic) dimension of subjectivity,
    which seems to me an enduring achievement of his life's work
    and a major progress toward a correct description of said founda-
    tions. This book, however, is not meant to be a defense of Husserl
    or yet another introduction to phenomenology. Therefore, I expect
    that on average my readers are likely to have at least some previous
    understanding of transcendental phenomenology, that they are
    already convinced of its value and that they will thus be able
    at least to empathize (if not sympathize) with the Husserlian
    standpoint I consistently maintain throughout the book without
    feeling that I am omitting too many preliminary explanations
    and justifications. Moreover, there is something distinctively
    Husserlian to letting both the meaning and the significance of
    philosophical terms or methods emerge progressively over the
    course of the analysis, rather than defining or justifying them
    univocally from the outset. Contrary to dominant trends in con-
    temporary philosophy, definitions and justifications in phenomen-
    ology are given, if needed, at the end of a philosophical analysis,
    not at the beginning. Likewise, the justification of a certain line of
    description is not to be provided in advance, but it should emerge
    alongside the actual pursuit of phenomenological insights.
    Considering that this is a work in the history of philosophy con-
    ducted from a phenomenological perspective, and in order to show

important features of transcendental phenomenology, it was mandatory to respect the style of thinking that characterizes this philosophical discipline. This being said, I want to emphasize that the debate I present in this book could be addressed in equally meaningful ways from different standpoints, and this would probably bring to light aspects of it that remained at the margins of my own presentation. I can only wish that reading this book will prompt other scholars in the history of philosophy to study the same materials from different standpoints and to produce new reconstructions, even dramatically divergent from the one I offer here.

(2) In 2010, I published a revised version of my dissertation under the title *Geistigkeit, Leben und geschichtliche Welt in der Transzendentalphänomenologie Husserls.*[18] While the topics of the present book largely overlap with the topics I discuss there, I have since changed my mind on a number of important things and significantly broadened the focus of my research. To give just one example, in my previous book I limited the presentation of Southwestern Neo-Kantianism to the early phase of Rickert's philosophy and (partly misled by Husserl) interpreted it as being exclusively focused on methodological questions. Here, on the contrary, I argue that for Rickert and Southwestern Neo-Kantianism, questions of method are a doorway into ontological questions, and I show this through a discussion of the entire historical trajectory of the school. Moreover, while the gist of the previous book is an examination of Husserl's theory of the historical world *per se*, and the overwhelming bulk of it is devoted to a close reading of Husserlian texts, here I am primarily focused on the debate between Husserl and his contemporaries, which there served merely as a foil. In short, while I believe that *Geistigkeit, Leben und geschichtliche Welt in der Transzendentalphänomenologie Husserls* is still worth reading for those who are interested in a detailed examination of Husserl's texts on the historical world and related issues, the present book is much more comprehensive and ambitious. Nothing in this book is a mere repetition of what I had already accomplished, and, in turn, there is nothing valuable about my previous book that has not been significantly rethought and deepened here.

---

[18] A. Staiti, *Geistigkeit, Leben und geschichtliche Welt in der Transzendentalphänomenologie Husserls* (Würzburg: Ergon Verlag, 2010).

(3) As I mentioned above, for most primary sources I discuss in this book there are no English translations available. Concerning Husserl, my work draws primarily on recently published manuscripts, both research notes and lectures. In spite of their often fragmented nature, these are the most fruitful and reliable texts to reconstruct Husserl's position. We know today that, for example, the second book of *Ideen*, which was considered the mandatory source for the themes we are about to explore, is actually spurious. It was heavily edited and rewritten by Edith Stein, who had her own original ideas on these issues and inevitably tended to build them into Husserl's typescript.[19] Given the centrality of currently untranslated texts for my interpretation, I considered part of my task in writing this book to let these texts speak for themselves and offer to my readers at least some of the most significant passages in translation. This is why, especially at crucial joints of my presentation, I generally favored full quotation over paraphrase at the expense of slightly hampering the fluency of my own text. Translating Husserl and his colleagues into English can be an excruciating task, and keeping the translations literal is frequently not an option due to the verbosity and grammatical awkwardness of the original prose. Therefore, here and there I took liberties that a professional translator would perhaps have pondered more thoroughly than I did. However, the translations in this book are a means to an end, and while I always consulted existing translations and translators for the most difficult passages my effort was to let the meaning of these texts come to light, even when this required a good deal of reshuffling their letter. I also deliberately chose not to follow strict rules of consistency for some of the key terms employed by the philosophers I discuss. Consider, for instance, the German word *Geist* as it occurs in the term *Geisteswissenschaften*. Translating this word with one and the same term ('mind,' or 'culture,' or the like) in each of its occurrences would be harmful, given that German philosophers often exploit its ambiguity in order to emphasize different facets of the complex reality that they call *Geist*. Accordingly, I translate *Geisteswissenschaften* in various ways, depending on the context: human sciences, humanities,

---

[19] An edition of the original manuscript of *Ideen II* is currently under preparation at the Husserl Archive.

cultural sciences, historical sciences, socio-historical sciences, sciences of subjectivity, sciences of psychic life, etc. For the English-speaking reader, it is particularly important to keep in mind that in late nineteenth-century Germany there was no distinction between the so-called humanities and the so-called social sciences, and *Geisteswissenschaften* is a term that embraces both fields. This is true in today's German academia as well, where the term *Geisteswissenschaften* is still current.

The opening chapter of this book, "Southwestern Neo-Kantianism in search of ontology," is devoted to a reconstruction of the historical trajectory of this philosophical school. I examine the works of Windelband, Rickert, Lask, and Böhm and argue that they are from the very start geared towards ontology. In particular, their goal is to clarify the ontological status of the objects investigated by the human sciences in contrast with the ontological status of the objects investigated by the natural sciences. The Southwestern Neo-Kantians attempt to do so without any reference to consciousness or psyche, which for them are natural objects studied by an empirical science: experimental psychology. I show that this consistent exclusion of subjectivity from the sphere of the human sciences ultimately leads to dire problems that cannot be solved within their theoretical framework.

Chapter 2, "Life-philosophical accounts of history and psyche: Simmel and Dilthey," presents the work of Georg Simmel and Wilhelm Dilthey. Arguably, they are the spearheads of *Lebensphilosophie*, at least as far as the debate on the demarcation of the sciences is concerned. Simmel and Dilthey both argue that a reference to psychic life is the distinctive trait of the subject matter of the human sciences. In this way, they solve the problem left open by the Neo-Kantians at the very beginning of their inquiry. 'Life' is the ontological marker of the human sciences, and prior to all theoretical inquiry 'life' is built into the fabric of human-scientific objects. This starting point presents a number of advantages, though it is likewise problematic upon closer scrutiny. Neither Simmel nor Dilthey succeeds in clarifying adequately the relationship that they think obtains between 'life' and nature. None of them is willing to defend any version of Cartesianism, but the affirmation of psychic life as a distinct ontological sphere ostensibly requires some clarification of how this distinct ontological sphere relates to the ontological sphere of nature. From Husserl's point of view, which is examined in detail in subsequent chapters, the life-philosophers' basic conviction is correct. However, their difficulties arise from a failure to distinguish between the empirical and the transcendental dimensions of subjectivity.

Chapter 3, "Standpoints and attitudes: scientificity between Neo-Kantianism and Husserlian phenomenology," moves to consider an issue common to both the Neo-Kantians and the life-philosopher: the description of different standpoints as the subjective sources for the theoretical categories characterizing different scientific fields. Sensitivity to the plurality of standpoints as the transcendental source for the multiple spheres of objects investigated scientifically is shown to be a common trait of the debate as a whole. After examining the notion of standpoint in Neo-Kantianism and Dilthey's distinction between inner and outer experience I introduce Husserl's key notion of "attitude," or *Einstellung*. I argue that the notion of attitude provides a strategic entry into the phenomenological perspective from within the debate presented in the first two chapters. The chief merit of Husserl's notion of attitude is to avoid the possible fragmentation of our picture of the world connected with the acknowledgment of equal value to divergent scientific standpoints. Introducing the notion of a living *transcendental ego* as the identical source of various attitudes and describing the constitutive meaning of the possibility of switching attitudes vis-à-vis one and the same object, Husserl maintains both a commendable theoretical pluralism and an anti-relativistic emphasis on the unitary life-source that underlies divergent stances on the world.

Chapter 4, "The reception of Husserl's *Ideen* among the Neo-Kantians," focuses on the work Husserl arguably wrote in order to engage the Neo-Kantians: *Ideas Pertaining to a Pure Phenomenology and to a Phenomenological Philosophy* (1913). Unfortunately for Husserl, this work had the effect of alienating his most devoted students in Göttingen, who read it as an inexplicable turn to idealism, and it did not produce the desired effect of winning the Neo-Kantians over to the cause of phenomenology. Rickert charges Husserl of being an intuitionist, that is, of diminishing the importance of conceptual and discursive thought and celebrating the alleged immediacy of intuition instead. This, for Rickert, is the hallmark of *Lebensphilosophie*, and, accordingly, he accuses Husserl of being an 'undercover' life-philosopher. In his review of *Ideas*, Natorp strengthens Rickert's charges with a broadly Platonist critique of Husserl's concept of essence and further criticizes the 'eidetic method' as unfit to grasp subjectivity as such. The eidetic method, so Natorp argues, turns subjectivity into precisely what it is not: an object. In this chapter, I provide responses to Rickert and Natorp from a Husserlian point of view and argue that their critiques are helpful to clarify the meaning of two crucial concepts in Husserl's phenomenology, that is, 'essence' and 'consciousness.' Clarifying these concepts is crucial for articulating Husserl's position in the following chapters.

Chapter 5, "Husserl's critique of Rickert's secretly naturalistic transcendentalism: The *Natur* und *Geist* lectures (1919–1927)," is a thorough examination of Husserl's critique of Rickert's demarcation of the natural and the human sciences. The two major sources for this chapter are Husserl's seminal lectures on *Natur und Geist*, which he delivered in two very different versions in 1919 and 1927. Here, Husserl argues for the necessity of multiple criteria in the demarcation of the sciences, distinguishing between both the formal-methodological structure of science and the material-ontological status of various fields on inquiry. His main charge against Rickert is that he has in no way clarified why the world of experience is amenable to scientific conceptualization. Rickert, in Husserl's critical characterization, replaced the difficult Kantian problem of a transcendental deduction of the categories with a vaguely pragmatic reference to the necessity of using concepts in order to master the overwhelming infinity of disconnected data streaming in from our senses. Rickert, on Husserl's account, did not provide a plausible description of 'the world of experience,' to which he nonetheless constantly refers. In the context of his critique of Rickert, Husserl crucially states that transcendental phenomenology is in fact a "*scientific* life-philosophy,"[20] thus providing an important clue about his self-understanding in the philosophical context of his time.

Chapter 6, "*Historia formaliter spectata*: Husserl and the life-philosophers," is meant to substantiate Husserl's aforementioned claim about phenomenology being a scientifically committed kind of life-philosophy. This includes both an appreciation of Dilthey's and Simmel's work and a critique of what he takes to be their weaknesses, the first of which is their inclination toward a kind of anti-rationalist historicism. This chapter draws from a variety of Husserl's manuscripts

---

[20] E. Husserl, *Natur und Geist. Vorlesungen 1927*, *Husserliana*, vol. 32 (Dordrecht: Springer, 2001), 240–241. Hereafter Hua XXXII.

and unpublished notes on his private copies of Simmel's books. First, Husserl's method of phenomenological *epoché* and reduction is intended to bring to light the overarching unity that characterizes subjectivity. In so doing, he intends to counteract a tendency common to *both* naturalistic psychology *and* life-philosophy to split apart subjectivity into a 'lower' natural stratum and an 'upper' spiritual stratum. Second, from within the new perspective on subjectivity as a self-contained sphere yielded by the reduction, Husserl proceeds to clarify the sense in which we can consider history itself a *world*. This includes a detailed description of *empathy* as the conscious act that enables the *communalization* of our experiences and allows us to understand ourselves as members of an indefinitely open community of transcendental subjects. Third, Husserl discusses in a close engagement with Simmel the meaning of *historical time* for the constitution of history as a scientifically accessible ontological sphere. Finally, Husserl clarifies a key dichotomy for the life-philosophers: psychic motivation as opposed to natural causality.

Chapter 7, "The life-world as the source of nature and culture: towards a transcendental-phenomenological worldview," introduces the theme of the life-world from the perspective of Husserl's confrontation with the Neo-Kantians and the life-philosophers. I argue that the 'life-world' theme should be interpreted in light of Husserl's attempt to articulate a humanistic worldview in continuity with what I call the Kantian liberation narrative, that is, an understanding of Kant's Copernican turn as liberation from naturalism. This includes a discussion of Husserl's deconstructive genealogy of naturalism in *Crisis*.

Chapter 8, "Ethical and cultural implications in Husserl's phenomenology of the life-world," concludes the book with a sketch of Husserl's transcendental-phenomenological worldview. I argue that Husserl sees a transformative power in the phenomenological attitude. Practicing phenomenology is a way for the individual to achieve a dignified sense of self, enabled by the discovery of the transcendental, non-naturalistic dimension of her subjectivity. Husserl's comes extremely close to the view of life presented by Fichte in his popular writings such as *The Vocation of Man* (1800), in which reality is interpreted as the raw material for moral action. At the intersubjective level, phenomenology is committed to clarifying intuitively the meaning of the key notion of 'humankind,' which plays a central role in the tradition of transcendental philosophy. Phenomenology's contribution to humankind is its work towards the elucidation of the historical teleology inherent in humankind and oriented towards the birth of a universal culture. In Husserl's ideal narrative universal culture is not a kind of monochrome globalization but rather a unity within a multiplicity of differences, in which local home-worlds are preserved while the awareness of partaking of the one world common to all humans increases.

1 | Southwestern Neo-Kantianism in search of ontology

Das beständige Wetzen der Messer ist [...]
langweilig wenn man Nichts zu scheiden vorhat

Herrman Lotze[1]

For the so-called Neo-Kantian thinkers, philosophy begins with the fact of science. Modern science represents for them freedom from groundless metaphysical speculation; it provides a model of rigor and objectivity for all human inquiry. Although philosophy addresses the transcendental rather than the empirical, it takes the existence of objectively intelligible, empirical knowledge, i.e., the fact of science, as its necessary point of departure.[2]

Despite this origin, however, it does not follow that Neo-Kantian philosophy must remain merely ancillary to empirical science. On the contrary, Neo-Kantianism is better understood, in general, as an effort to re-establish a distinctive theoretical space for philosophy in a time dominated by an unprecedented flourishing of empirical research, both natural and humanistic. In particular, through critical reflection on

---

[1] H. Lotzte, *System der Philosophie – Zweiter Theil: Drei Bücher der Metaphysik* (Leipzig: Hirzel, 1879), 15. Quoted in H. Rickert, "Die Methode der Philosophie und das Unmittelbare," in H. Rickert, *Philosophische Aufsätze* (Tübingen: Mohr Siebeck, 1999), 107–151. Here 107. Hereafter MPU. "The constant whetting of knives is boring, if one has nothing to cut."

[2] It was Hermann Cohen who coined the phrase "das Faktum der Wissenschaft." I will not discuss Hermann Cohen's brand of Neo-Kantianism (he founded the so-called Marburg School) in any detail in this book. I will only examine the main line of criticism raised by Paul Natorp against Husserl's *Ideen I* in Chapter 4, but only to the extent that Natorp's critique reinforces and clarifies Heinrich Rickert's own line of criticism. The reason for this omission is twofold: (1) The Southwestern school was involved in a much more lively exchange with Husserlian phenomenology than the Marburg school and is thus more relevant to the overall purpose of the book; (2) Whereas Cohen, Natorp, and his brilliant student Cassirer have been given some attention in recent years, there is virtually no scholarship devoted to the Southwestern school in English, which is regrettable given its philosophical importance.

procedures, goals, and achievements of empirical science, Neo-Kantian philosophy elaborated previously unknown *tasks* for philosophical work. To give but one example – and in so doing, to set the tone for this first chapter – Neo-Kantian thinkers hold that the practice of empirical science entails tacit operations of reason, operations bound to remain implicit for the practicing scientist and only disclosed via distinctive transcendental-philosophical analyses. Such tacit operations of reason constitute the object cognized, at a higher level, by proper scientific inquiry. The Kantian heritage of this conception is manifest. However, the Neo-Kantians set out to determine an 'a priori' more pluralistic than the a priori originally considered by Kant. This new conception of the a priori does not end with a few principles governing the experiential construction of natural phenomena, but extends to the spheres of culture and history as well; it does not merely shape inchoate sense data but entertains complex relations with the materials it structures.

In this chapter, I will follow one strand in the intellectual trajectory of Southwestern Neo-Kantianism along which the philosophical import of this school in creating a new space and new tasks for philosophy is particularly evident: the philosophical demarcation of natural and human science. I will argue that, standard interpretations notwithstanding, the Neo-Kantian treatment of the problems connected both to a classification of different forms of scientific activity and to the defense of the autonomy of the historical sciences as distinct from the natural sciences points toward the formulation of a *sui generis* ontology. In other words, if we follow the development of the problems tackled originally by Wilhelm Windelband and Heinrich Rickert, which were subsequently carried out by second-generation Southwestern thinkers such as Emil Lask and the virtually unknown Franz Böhm, we discover a unitary effort to employ epistemological and methodological analyses as a sort of lens in which the ontological structure of different objects of knowledge becomes visible. Thus, contrary to the conventional account, Neo-Kantianism does not provide merely the background out of which Husserlian phenomenology would develop but rather the intellectual space in which Husserlian phenomenology displays its own philosophical potential. The phenomenological ontology and, furthermore, the transcendental phenomenology envisioned by Husserl are theoretical projects deeply consonant with the preoccupations of the Southwestern thinkers.

In this chapter, I intend to show how Neo-Kantianism, and, in particular, Southwestern Neo-Kantianism, sets the theoretical stage for the kind of ontological investigations proper to Husserlian phenomenology. Only within the Neo-Kantian context does one discover the full meaning of Husserl's characterization of subjectivity as necessarily transcending its empirical dimension and his utilization of direct eidetic descriptions. Thus, these central features of Husserl's project require examination in light of the theoretical space created by Neo-Kantian transcendental philosophy.

Windelband's *Rektoratsrede* and its ontological implications

Arguably, the debate within the Southwestern School concerning different forms of scientificity began with Wilhelm Windelband's *Rektoratsrede*, delivered at the University of Strasbourg in 1894 under the title *History and Natural Science*.[3] This text develops a methodological opposition between *nomothetic* (viz. natural) and *idiographic* (viz. historical) science.[4] While nomothetic science seeks general laws – and in so doing moves away from particular facts – idiographic science aims precisely at a rigorous, but also lively and empathetic, restitution of particular facts.[5] Windelband distinguishes and assesses sciences according to the "formal characteristic of their theoretical goals",[6] rather than by the ontological realities (in Windelband's language, "materials") that they investigate. For this reason, critics have repeatedly raised charges of abstract methodologism and ontological indifference against Windelband's position and, with little hesitation, have extended these accusations to the whole of Southwestern Neo-Kantianism. However, and contrary to this opinion, Windelband's speech contains more nuance and sophistication than its critics concede. A closer look reveals that Windelband embeds his methodological distinction within a broader concern with the full scope of scientific activity, beyond the strictures of one-sided naturalism. Accordingly, Windelband proposes his distinction as the *beginning*,

---

[3] W. Windelband, "Geschichte und Naturwissenschaft," in W. Windelband, *Präludien: Aufsätze und Reden zur Philosophie und ihrer Geschichte*, vol. 2 (Tübingen: Mohr Siebeck, 1915), 136–160. Hereafter GN.
[4] GN, 145.   [5] GN, 150.   [6] GN, 144.

rather than the conclusion, of a transcendental-philosophical line of inquiry into what he later calls the logic of historical sciences.

First, it should be noted that Windelband's turn to a methodological distinction arises from his dissatisfaction with *one specific form* of ontological distinction of science and not with ontological distinctions in general. This particular distinction, the customary distinction between nature and spirit (*Geist*), divides the universe of scientific knowledge into *Naturwissenschaft* and *Geisteswissenschaft*. The reason behind Windelband's rejection of the nature/spirit distinction as a viable standpoint from which to understand scientific activity has multiple components. The distinction rests upon the unquestioned metaphysical assumption from early modern philosophy that *Natur* and *Geist* correspond to knowledge of the natural and knowledge of the psyche, which would mistakenly construe practitioners of human sciences (art history, sociology, political economy) as dealing either exclusively or primarily with psychic facts. Moreover, and most importantly, the newborn science of empirical psychology simply could not be brought under the same umbrella of existing *Geisteswissenschaften*.[7]

This last point deserves further attention. Empirical psychology exhibits an important trait often obscured by the object-oriented distinction of *Natur* and *Geist*: empirical psychology posits general laws that govern the unfolding of human psychic life, and in this respect it is aligned with traditional natural science. This intellectual habit of positing general laws distinguishes an entire province of science, which Windelband therefore labels "nomothetical" (law-positing).

Having identified the distinctive intellectual habit of natural science (not its concern with physical nature but its pursuit of general laws), we can, in a Kantian fashion, also establish its limit, by contrasting it with other existing forms of scientific thought. Furthermore, as Windelband specifies, making this trait explicit allows us to recognize the pervasiveness of nomothetical forms of thought as well as the fateful allegiance between these forms and traditional logic.[8] The exclusive focus of traditional logic on the *general* forms of correct reasoning makes it particularly useful for inquiries concerning general laws, but this predominance of law-positing forms of thought casts a distorting shadow over the other half of the scientific universe, namely the

---

[7] GN, 142–143.   [8] GN, 147.

idiographic or historical half, obscuring the scientificity of those sciences that concern singular, unrepeatable facts. Although both nomothetic and idiographic thought start by collecting facts, nomothetic thought treats facts as mere variables of fixed laws to be discovered, whereas idiographic thought moves towards a more precise determination of the singular fact at hand, such as a painting, a political party, or the life of a great writer.

Considering this opposition between nomothetical and idiographic forms of scientific thought, as Windelband did, we can see "why a struggle for the decisive influence on the general world- and life-view of mankind is bound to flare up and in fact did flare up between them."[9] To echo the famous phrase by C. P. Snow, the division of these "two cultures" does nothing more than manifest the intrinsic tension between two logically opposite forms of thought.[10] However – and this is the outcome of Windelband's analysis – these two forms of thought do not mutually exclude one another, but rather complement each other, as two parts of our total knowledge. Thus, the question of the primacy of one over the other does not arise. Rather, like intellect and sensibility for Kant, "these two components of human knowledge cannot be traced back to one common source"[11] and are therefore bound to remain heterogeneous.

This insight leads to the first ontological implication in Windelband's analysis: the tension between nomothetic and idiographic science recasts, at a more complex level, a basic tension that runs across all objectivity as such. Every object in the world includes a formal and a material component and can never be *simultaneously* cognized under both categories. Whereas natural scientific thought reduces the facticity of a given object to ever-recurring regularity and thus emphasizes its being structured by a certain 'form' (the law), historical thought highlights the dependence of its objects upon a particular context of meaning and tends to grasp the given fact in its absolute unrepeatability. In this way, historical thought turns to the material, factual component of objectivity; Windelband refers to this dimension of objectivity as its being an "event" (*Ereignis*).

---

[9] GN, 152.
[10] See C. P. Snow, *The Two Cultures* (Cambridge University Press, 1998).
[11] GN, 157.

An example will shed some light on these complicated and terminologically idiosyncratic analyses. A chemist understands a given lump of
gold as a sample of metal, with atomic number 79 and a melting point at
about 1064° C. This temperature, like a point on the Cartesian plane,
results from the intersection of a number of general laws. The historian
understands the same lump of gold, say, as a Roman coin minted under
Trajan and as celebrating the greatness of the Empire at the apex of its
geographical extension. It belongs to a unique and unrepeatable historical constellation. A general law determines the fact that gold melts at
1064° C and regulates the set of possible states of every atom of this
metal. However, that precisely *this* piece of gold, here and now, melts
at 1064° C cannot be deduced a priori from the natural law, for this is
an individual, about which, qua individual, the law has nothing to say.
The law does not prescribe the historical existence, the facticity, of gold
in the first place, neither in general nor in any specific place and time. It
does not prescribe the 'event' of this piece of gold and all that it entails in
terms of further possibilities. Natural scientific thought a priori excludes
from its purview everything that determines a given entity in its unrepeatable uniqueness (*Einmaligkeit*), for such thought concerns itself
only with the invariable (*das Immergleiche*), i.e., laws. Conversely,
history a priori excludes from its purview that which renders a given
entity a mere instance of a certain kind of reality, for it concerns itself
exclusively with what is unrepeatable about objects and situations.
Therefore, "the law and the event [*das Ereignis*] remain beside one
another as the fundamental, incommensurable magnitudes of our picture of the world"[12] and no philosophical speculation can ever plau-
sibly absorb one magnitude into the other.

This distinction between the unique (event) and the invariable (law),
which follows from the methodological classification of sciences, adumbrates the necessity of a fresh ontological, content-oriented distinction
after the old *Natur/Geist* distinction has been dismissed. Whereas every
conceivable object may serve as an example of its particular class (and
thus be subsumed under invariable laws), not every object deserves
treatment as a unique entity belonging to history. I can contemplate
the raindrop dripping down my windowpane as long as I wish, but in no
meaningful way will *this* particular drop of rain appear to me as a
unique entity in world-*history*. On the other hand, I can look at the

---

[12] GN, 160.

ruins of a Roman bridge and understand the stones as simply pieces of a very solid material standing according to strict natural laws, but the Roman bridge is also a unique historical item, embedded in a context of meaning open to historical-scientific inquiry. This, however, begs questions that Windelband's student, Heinrich Rickert, attempted to answer: how can we discriminate between unique objects suitable for historical research and mere natural objects instantiating general laws? Is this distinction completely arbitrary?

Rickert's concept of ontology – part 1

Whereas Windelband's *Rektoratsrede* ends with only a gesture toward a new, necessary, ontological distinction, Rickert moves much further in this direction. He devotes two major publications to this topic of a philosophical classification of the sciences: *Die Grenzen der naturwissenschaftlichen Begriffsbildung* and *Kulturwissenschaft und Naturwissenschaft*. In them, Rickert insists that a full understanding of scientific activity requires a supplementary object-oriented distinction between nature and culture in order to complete Windelband's methodological distinction between history and natural science.[13]

Although Rickert remains faithful to his teacher's emphasis on the *priority* of a methodological distinction in the classification of sciences,[14] he indicates that he does so chiefly because such a distinction

[13] Rudolf Makkreel misinterprets Rickert's position when he writes: "But for Rickert even the material distinction of nature and culture is inadequate and needs to be replaced by a more precise methodological distinction between generalizing and individualizing sciences." R. Makkreel, "Wilhelm Dilthey and the Neo-Kantians: On the Conceptual Distinction between *Geisteswissenschaften* and *Kulturwissenschaften*," in Luft and Makkreel, *Neo-Kantianism in Contemporary Philosophy*, 253–271. Here 255. Rickert does not intend to replace a material distinction with a formal distinction. Instead, he insists that the formal distinction between generalization and individualization *allows for* the replacement of a weak material distinction between *Geisteswissenschaft* and *Naturwissenschaft* with a much stronger one between cultural science and natural science. Thus, the formal distinction is the tool for articulating a superior material distinction.

[14] It should be noticed that Rickert is critical of the distinction between nomothetic and idiographic as proposed by his teacher Windelband. For a discussion of this point see A. Zijderveld, *Rickert's Relevance: The Ontological Nature and Epistemological Functions of Values* (Leiden and Boston, MA: Brill, 2006), 246–255. For a full-scale presentation of Rickert's philosophy see my entry "Heinrich Rickert," *Stanford Encyclopedia of Philosophy*: plato.stanford.edu/archives/win2013/entries/heinrich-rickert.

renders ontological commitments controllable and scientifically oriented; thus, he avoids borrowing such ontological commitments from
a pre-theoretical worldview without further reflection.[15] Following
Windelband, Rickert seeks not to dismiss ontological distinctions outright but to articulate them more accurately than the foregoing philosophical traditions. For Rickert, this requires taking a close look at
the way existing sciences actually work. Logically speaking, that is
with respect to their methods, there are only two groups of sciences:
the generalizing and the individualizing.[16] This is a difference in
Begriffsbildung, somewhat inadequately translated as "concept-
formation." Some sciences construe their concepts by moving *away
from* the merely individual; other sciences construe their concepts by
moving *closer to* individual contents of reality. As a simple fact about
the sciences, the philosopher must include this in her considerations at
her point of departure (but, again, not of arrival). Rickert praises Kant
for being the first philosopher, after the scientific revolution, who
grasped unambiguously this logical characteristic of natural scientific
inquiry. In fact, in his *Prolegomena to Any Future Metaphysics that will
be able to come forward as a Science* (1783), Kant provides an
extremely fruitful definition of the domain of reality investigated by
the natural sciences: "*Nature* is the *existence* of things, insofar as
[*sofern*] that existence is determined according to universal laws."[17]
With this brief definition Kant brings to light two important factors
about natural scientific research: (1) it aims at the determination of
universal laws; (2) it does not find its objects ('the existence of things')
already given, but rather it produces them through the choice of a
particular perspective from which to view experienced reality, in this

[15] On this point see A. Dewalque, "A quoi sert la logique des sciences historiques de
Rickert?," *Les Études philosophiques* 1 (2010): 44–66. Here 59–60. As the
author emphasizes, it is telling that Rickert entitles his book "cultural science and
natural science," thus making his *material-ontological* distinction prominent over
and above his methodological one between historical science and natural science.
Regrettably, the English version of the book conceals this fact by the arbitrary
translation of the original title, *Kulturwissenschaft und Naturwissenschaft* as
"Science and History."

[16] H. Rickert, *Science and History: A Critique of Positivist Epistemology*
(Princeton, NJ: Van Nostrand, 1962), 45. Hereafter SH.

[17] I. Kant, *Prolegomena to Any Future Metaphysics that will be able to come
forward as a Science* in I. Kant, *Theoretical Philosophy after 1781* (Cambridge
University Press, 2002), 50–169. Here 89.

case, that of universal laws.[18] This second point already entails the
possibility of choosing other points of view with respect to the world
of experience, other perspectives that would reveal the existence of
things in a different light than that of universal laws. Rickert thought
that Kant had not seen this possibility – a possibility that Kant himself
opened up – and so the task of its systematic development fell to the
Neo-Kantian movement:

> To be sure, by thus qualifying his definition with the words "insofar as
> [*sofern*] it is determined," Kant brought to an end the exclusive pre-eminence
> of the concept of nature, at least in philosophy if not in the individual sciences.
> In other words, the "world view" of the natural sciences [. . .] was reduced by
> Kant also *in theory* from one for which absolute validity was claimed to one
> that was to be regarded as only relatively valid; and the method of the natural
> sciences was concomitantly limited to a special field of investigation.[19]

Following Kant's definition, one can no longer dogmatically posit
nature as a metaphysical reality-in-itself. Rather, nature is grasped as
the counterpart of a specific way of looking at reality, namely, the one
interested in working out general laws. For Rickert, precisely this de-
absolutization of nature by means of philosophical criticism made room
for a new consideration of the historical world, otherwise doomed to
concealment by the naturalistic trend of pre-Kantian metaphysics. As
Rickert writes in a later work, "nature is no longer 'the world', but
rather an apprehension of sensible being carried out by the scientific
subject."[20] Even if "Kant himself did not produce a systematic critical
philosophy of history,"[21] a logical perspective on history in the same
spirit as his original perspective on nature appears desirable – one which
is thoroughly consistent with his critical philosophical agenda and made
possible by it. Furthermore, if our generalizing concept-formation alone
forms nature, then history arises exclusively from our view of empirical
reality in its *Einmaligkeit*, i.e., its unrepeatable contingency. As anticipated above, Rickert labels this sort of concept-formation, which grasps
reality in this capacity, "individualizing." By contrasting generalizing

---

[18] See Chapter 3 for a systematic treatment of the concept of standpoint in Neo-
Kantianism and its divergence from Husserl's concept of attitude.
[19] SH, 5–6, translation modified.
[20] H. Rickert, *Die Probleme der Geschichtsphilosophie. Eine Einführung*
(Heidelberg: Carl Winters, 1924), 139.
[21] *Ibid.*, 140.

and individualizing methods, Rickert reasserts in his own terms the dualistic opposition between law and event proposed by Windelband. However, in slight contrast with his teacher, Rickert holds that grasping reality in its *Einmaligkeit* requires a robust set of conceptual tools, so he cannot depend upon the softer, almost pictorial form of representation suggested by the word "idiographic." After all, historians are scientists, not poets or novelists. Thus, as Rickert summarizes, methodologically speaking, "*empirical reality becomes nature when we conceive it with reference to the general. It becomes history when we conceive it with reference to the distinctive and the individual.*"[22]

Contrary to shallow presentations of Rickert's thought, this methodological distinction does not embody a complete philosophical demarcation of the sciences. Rather, it represents a point of departure for an epistemologically informed investigation of the ontological side of both the natural-scientific and the historical method:

The circumstance that the same sensible world can be investigated scientifically according to two completely *different* logical standpoints must gain significance also for ontology, in particular, for the question concerning the being of reality as a whole.[23]

For this reason, one common characterization of Rickert's position appears inaccurate. It goes as follows: for Rickert, "in view of the formal distinction of Natural Science and Cultural Science as two different, yet correlated, mutually amplifying approaches or methods, the ontological distinction is superfluous";[24] accordingly, "in the end, ontology is epistemology."[25] Indeed, epistemology does have a methodological primacy, but only in order to make possible ontological inquiry, unburdened by unquestioned metaphysical assumptions such as the *Natur/Geist* distinction. For Rickert, ontology has a theoretical goal of its own. To contrast the two, epistemology (or in Rickert's language, methodology) investigates logical structures in different patterns of concept-formation; ontology, on the other hand, investigates the different kinds of objectivity grasped in scientific conceptuality. Thus, while Rickert does hold that "nothing exists except in

---

[22] H. Rickert, *The Limits of Concept Formation in Natural Science* (Cambridge University Press, 1986), 34. Hereafter LCF.

[23] H. Rickert, "Die Heidelberger Tradition und Kants Kritizismus (Systematische Selbstdarstellung)," *Philosophische Aufsätze*, 347–411. Here 374.

[24] Zijderveld, *Rickert's Relevance*, 243.   [25] *Ibid.*, 246.

judgment,"[26] he also upholds the complete legitimacy and even necessity of asking just *what* does not exist except in judgment. Because different judgments – different connections formed between concepts according to either the generalizing or individualizing method – correspond to different objects, each sort of judgment requires a separate investigation of the materials proper to it, and this task belongs to ontology.

In fact, the significant *asymmetry* in the applicability of the generalizing and individualizing methods demands attention to the ontological dimension. To reiterate the two poles of the asymmetry, every conceivable bit of reality (physical or psychic) admits of conception as determined by general laws and thus as an instance of a given province of nature; not all reality allows for investigation according to individualizing concept-formation. In response to this, Rickert argues that it is reality related to a *value* that deserves treatment as distinctive and individual. The Roman coin mentioned above allows for an understanding and investigation of itself as more than just a lump of gold because of its objective relation to a value (say, political grandeur). On the contrary, the raindrop on my windowpane does not exhibit such a relation. Although both the Roman coin and the raindrop are, following Windelband's suggestion, "events," only the first possesses the dignity of a *historical* event.[27] This explains why a competent numismatist will possess a set of technical concepts to talk about the Roman coin; with them, she will produce a thorough explication of the elements of meaning pertaining specifically to *this* coin. Even if every object could in principle receive a value-content, for Rickert not every object is a priori endowed with value in the same way in which every object stands a priori under natural laws.

In the investigation of any given object, value-relatedness is either present or absent. The historian, who does not arbitrarily assign value

---

[26] T. Willey, *Back to Kant: The Revival of Kantianism in German Social and Historical Thought (1860–1914)* (Detroit, MI: Wayne State University Press, 1978), 143.

[27] Of course, this does not in principle exclude the possibility of investing the raindrop on my windowpane with the dignity of historical value and thus of elevating it to the rank of historical event. A lover of pop music may argue that the raindrops that inspired Paul Simon to write his beautiful ballad *Kathy's Song* or those that kept falling on Burt Bacharach's head are, in fact, historical events. But then, again, the raindrops are viewed not simply as raindrops but as the carriers of an objective relatedness to the aesthetic values expressed in the two songs.

to objects but rather investigates value-relevant objects, can only acknowledge this "presence or absence"[28] of value-relatedness in the objects she sets out to investigate. Rickert does not take interest in the subjective dynamics of the concrete bestowals of value upon otherwise natural objects because he understands them as more historical and psychological rather than as resulting from robust material-ontological principles. Thus, he considers the intention of the Roman artisan who designed and minted the coin, thereby conferring value-relatedness on what otherwise would have been just a lump of gold, a fact, and not an ontological principle. One can sharply distinguish between two kinds of objects regardless of their empirical origin: those related to values (cultural objects) and those that are value-free (natural objects). Only when applied to value-related objects does the individualizing method of historical science generate meaningful scientific knowledge. We cannot arbitrarily attribute or remove this objective relatedness to values; that is, in some things, we find it already there, and in others, we do not. Therefore, we recognize it as a "material distinction" (*materiale Auszeichnung*), as found on the side of the object and not on the side of the theoretical activity of the historian.[29]

In neither *Die Grenzen der naturwissenschaftlichen Begriffsbildung* nor *Kulturwissenschaft und Naturwissenschaft* does Rickert expand further on the structure of the material side. He instead attempts to demonstrate that the concept of value is necessary for understanding culture and that positing values does not undermine scientificity in the practice of historical studies.[30] His insistence on the value-relatedness of the objects of cultural science does not in the slightest oppose the general scientific principle of making exclusively value-free judgments, for it is absolutely possible to make value-free judgments about value-related objects, such as simply acknowledging the given form of value-relatedness and spelling out its implications for the given historical context. Rickert so valued this idea, which among other things inspired

---

[28] SH, 19.

[29] However, as Dewalque points out, "even the material distinction is in a certain respect formal" (Dewalque, "A quoi sert la logique des sciences historiques de Rickert?," 62), so Rickert's direction of inquiry would be better characterized as "a formal ontology of history" (65). This means that Rickert does not take interest in this or that value-related object but in value-relatedness generally, as a form that innervates a certain kind of objectivity.

[30] SH, 90–91.

the great sociologist Max Weber, that he devoted long portions of his books to repeating it and warding off possible misunderstandings, though the details of these discussions need not occupy us further here.

Rickert's concept of ontology – part 2

The distinction between value-related (cultural) and value-free (natural) objects does not exhaust Rickert's preoccupation with ontology. Even though the bulk of Rickert's philosophy moves from the ontological-material *fact* of value-relatedness towards a theory of historical conceptualization and its validity, scholars have detected in his later works an "ontological turn."[31] I would argue, however, that while ontology occupies an increasingly central place in Rickert's later work, it is excessive to speak of a turn. As the foregoing section showed, Rickert is aware of the importance of the material side of cognition from the very beginning and he recognizes that it deserves a separate scrutiny. The matter of cognition cannot be reduced to its form.

'Ontology' becomes for Rickert the title of a *Problematik* encompassing the entire material side of knowledge and progressively acknowledging its complexity. In part, factors in the contemporary intellectual atmosphere of the Weimar Republic motivated this concentration on ontology. A general discontent with academic philosophy was growing among the younger generations exposed to the horrors of World War I. In particular, transcendental philosophy, with its distinct focus on the forms of cognition, fell in status due to its apparent distance from reality and concrete life. Knowledge and science generally – once counted among the highest achievements of humankind – now suffered accusations of veiling reality, hampering genuine access to it, and suffocating the spontaneity of life. It seemed that only Nietzsche (or perhaps a caricature of Nietzsche) and his epigone Oswald Spengler was wholeheartedly cherished by young German intellectuals of the period. This generation celebrated intuition and immediacy and set them against what they considered the cumbersome procedures of scientific thought. According to this trend, only the intuitionists promised to

---

[31] J. Farges, "Philosophie de l'histoire et système des valeurs chez Heinrich Rickert," *Les Études philosophiques* 1 (2010): 25–44. Here 26. A similar position is defended in L. Kuttig, *Konstitution und Gegebenheit bei H. Rickert: Zum Prozess der Ontologisierung in seinem Spätwerk, eine Analyse unter Berücksichtigung nachgelassener Texte* (Essen: Die Blaue Eule, 1987).

grant direct access to the 'truth' of reality, while the latter threatened to give rise to mental shackles and academic estrangement. Faced with this atmosphere, Rickert realized that the future of the Kantian tradition in German philosophy depended significantly on its ability to prove that an emphasis on the forms of cognition does not necessitate the subordination or neglect of material or ontological considerations. In other words, Rickert thought that the Kantian tradition did not need to marginalize the 'reality' sought by the younger generation. In order to accomplish this, proponents of Kantianism had to demonstrate that, contrary to superficial opinions of the time, the articulation of a strong ontology requires one to begin from the fact of cognition and its forms. Furthermore, only such a robust ontology, conducted along the lines of Kantian criticism, could dispel the false yet enticing hope in immediate intuitions among contemporaries in the practice of philosophy.

This intellectual atmosphere, however, does not represent the most interesting impetus behind Rickert's late emphasis on ontology. Rather, the move towards ontology appears intrinsic to Southwestern Neo-Kantianism as such, with the ontological problematic already entailed by Windelband's original formulation of the nature/history distinction. Thus, Rickert works within a connotation of transcendental philosophy distinguished from that of Kant by precisely this trend in the direction of the ontological. To contrast the two, Kant conceives of the material side of cognition as *fundamentally homogeneous*. In other words, Kant identifies one and only one ontological kind of material in experience that undergoes categorial formation: spatio-temporal sense data. In a significant paper entitled "The Method of Philosophy and the Immediate," which summarizes his late ventures into ontology, Rickert calls this position "hyletic sensualism,"[32] thereby purposefully echoing the Platonic/Aristotelian concept of the *prote hyle*. Certainly, in this context, the concept of *hyle* does not refer to dogmatically posited metaphysical 'prime matter' but to the raw material out of which we allegedly construe the objects of our experience, i.e., sense data. Hyletic sensualists like Kant and, in Rickert's interpretation, Husserl "believe that all they can observe in the pure content of their experiences is sensuous states [*sinnliche Zustände*], and accordingly they put all non-sensuous components on the account of the *form*."[33] Thus, by applying the traditional Kantian form/content scheme, hyletic

---

[32] MPU, 128.   [33] *Ibid.*

sensualists only admit of sensuous content in experience: the subjective side issues as a formal component to everything that transcends the sensuous sphere. Objects (*Gegenstände*) in a full-blown sense are considered sensuous states (*sinnliche Zustände*) after the infusion of categorial forms of objectivity. Rickert, however, calls for a more focused investigation of pure *Zustände* (material complexions of content-data before they undergo categorial formation) and seeks an elaboration of a "pure doctrine of states" (*reine Zustandslehre*), as a necessary ontological supplement to the traditional "theory of objects" (*Gegenstandstheorie*).[34] He saw that the *Zustandslehre* must investigate the materials of cognition before intellectual forms categorially structure them as objects, and "its task would be to make abstraction from all that is *co*-apprehended when the specialized sciences talk about their material."[35] If one consistently abstracts from all categorial formations, and so allows for an unprejudiced scrutiny of the unstructured contents of experience, then, as Rickert argues, one finds non-sensuous elements constantly given in experience alongside sensuous elements. He admits that all immediately given non-sensuous material components of experience are necessarily concomitant with sensuous components, though hyletic sensualists like Kant, he claims, wrongly interpret this concomitance as a form of identity. Rickert pinpoints the error in hyletic sensualism as follows: since non-sensuous components always and only appear as given alongside sensuous components, sensuous and non-sensuous components must be identical. However, this rests on the assumption "that sense-organs are the only path through which something 'from outside', i.e. without the mediation of thought, can reach consciousness."[36] While the reception of material for categorial formation depends upon some sort of activity of the sense-organs, we also have, in concomitance with sense-data, non-sensuous elements of meaning that stream into our field of experience, piggybacking, as it were, on the underlying sensuous elements.

[34] MPU, 121.
[35] *Ibid.* Rickert believes that a correctly executed *Zustandslehre* would have the resources to replace Husserlian phenomenology because of its superior awareness of the duality of form and matter in the constitution of every kind of objectivity. Whereas in Rickert's view phenomenology believes itself to have a direct, intuitive access to the objects of cognition, his Neo-Kantian *Zustandslehre* would be more aware of the careful distinctions and abstractions required in order to obtain the "material of science untouched by thought" (MPU, 126). For a detailed discussion of Rickert's charges of intuitionism against Husserl's phenomenology see Chapter 4.
[36] MPU, 128.

Rickert's favorite example for illustrating his position is our experience of written words. While reading a book, we clearly have more than just the sensuous experience of ink scribbles on the white paper. "Rather, together with the sensuous word-pictures something fundamentally different from these word-pictures comes about, something that we grasp as immediately as the sensuous component as soon as, in concomitance with the words, we 'think' something."[37] The non-sensuous component is the word's meaning. We experience this element of meaning as so 'real' and so distinct from the scribbles on paper that we grasp *one and the same meaning* in concomitance with different types of sense-data. For example, consider when we experience the acoustic data of the spoken word instead of the visual data of the written word. Rickert deems this example sufficient to reject hyletic sensualism. Word-meanings are immediately given, but they differ from, say, the visual data of black ink marks that we locate in space and time while reading. Similar analyses reveal similar results in the experience of artistic values grasped in concomitance with the visual experience of patches of color on canvas or the experience of an obligation in concomitance with the acoustic data produced by the voice of our superior. In all these cases "a fundamental duality [*Urdualität*] in the immediate experience-state [*im unmittelbaren rein Zuständliche*] comes to light."[38] This fundamental duality, for Rickert, has nothing to do with the shaping activity of categorial formation but is a basic ontological fact. This fact, however, only becomes visible through regressive inquiry that moves from a full-blown theory of objects – like the one articulated in Rickert's first works – to one that discloses the ontology of the ultimate materials undergirding all differences encountered at the level of categorially formed objects. In other words, if categorially formed objects appear as either value-free (nature) or value-laden (culture), this distinction exists because at a deeper level the world consists of two fundamentally different kinds of materials, both immediately given in experience. Contra Kant's ontological monism of sense-data, Rickert emphatically states that "only an *ontological pluralism* does justice to the richness of the world."[39]

---

[37] MPU, 129.   [38] MPU, 136.

[39] H. Rickert, "Thesen zum System der Philosophie," *Philosophische Aufsätze*, 319–324. Here 320.

Whereas the sensuous delimits the sphere of the perceivable, the non-sensuous delimits the sphere of the intelligible. The two spheres intermingle in concrete experiences, but each allows for independent observation, and, most importantly, each undergoes its own forms of categorialization and subsequent objectification. Rickert writes:

Accordingly, the domain of pure states [*das Gebiet des Zuständlichen*] should be divided into sensuous perceptions and non-sensuous partial acts of understanding [*Verstehungen*] so that these two realms, at least as regards their immediacy, stand beside one another in full coordination.[40]

The *intelligible* nature of non-sensuous components such as word-meanings is a critical element in order to understand correctly the full picture of Rickert's ontology. To restate his central distinction, sense-data grant us perceptions, while items like word-meanings grant us acts of understanding, or intellections. Rickert's choice of the neologism *Verstehungen* to designate the grasp of non-sensuous components of experience reveals his willingness to maintain a complete parallelism with *Wahrnehmungen* (perceptions) and, furthermore, to stress the fragmentary, nearly erratic nature of the items we find at this pre-objective, '*rein zuständlich*' level. Regarding *Verstehungen*, Rickert clarifies that grasping the meaning of a word does not amount to a full-blown act of understanding, but rather only a partial prefiguration of such – it does so only at a higher level thanks to the mediation of conceptual thought. In other words, isolated graspings of non-sensuous meaning-components does not reach the status of full-blown act-experiences of meaning, or intellections. This mimics the way in which an isolated sense-datum or even a complexion of sense-data, prior to all categorial formation, does not equal an object. An example will help unpack the meaning of Rickert's notion of *Verstehung*. Consider the experience of traveling in a foreign country and having only very basic skills in the local language. While sitting on a crowded bus in rush hour, one has a very abundant acoustic experience but can only grasp one word here or there. One only experiences scattered fragments of meaning. Rickert understands the intelligible sphere of *reine Zuständlichkeit* (which he holds one cannot experience directly but can only reconstruct regressively) as something like a

---

[40] MPU, 139.

hyperbolic version of just this experience. It is an endless kaleidoscope of meaning-fragments prior to their being woven together into an intelligible unity.[41] Thus, the task falls to us, as rational agents, to turn *both* the chaos of sensibility *and* the chaos of intelligibility into a proper sensible world of objects and a proper intelligible world of meaning-formations (*Sinngebilde*).

Rickert (and Windelband) had a favorite metaphor for our stance in experience prior to categorial structuring: a soldier assailed (*bestürmt*) from all sides by all kinds of experiential data. Only through categorial thought do we "become lords" (*Herr werden*) of the realm of experience, which for Rickert, prior to this appropriation, closely resembles a very rugged battlefield. With this account, resulting from his late work, Rickert opened up for Neo-Kantian philosophy an investigation into the pre-objective dimension of what is immediately given in experience and formulated a pluralistic ontology, extending beyond the strictures of Kant's original doctrine.

Emil Lask: categoriality and being

A presentation of Southwestern Neo-Kantianism and its move towards ontology cannot neglect the contribution of perhaps the most interesting and complex philosopher in its ranks: Emil Lask. Regrettably, his untimely death in World War I at the age of forty left his own philosophical project largely unfinished. However, unlike with other thinkers of the Southwestern school, scholars have explored Lask's thought in some depth in recent years, in part due to his influence on Martin Heidegger and the pertinence of his work to current debates on the so-called 'space of reasons.'[42] Given this situation, I will only present those elements of Lask's philosophy specifically relevant to the present

---

[41] Interestingly, Rickert comes very close to Gottlob Frege's famous argument that words do not have 'meaning' (*Bedeutung*) unless they are structured into a sentence. A further exploration of the issue, however, would exceed the scope of this chapter.

[42] Steven G. Crowell offers a thoughtful and engaging presentation of Lask's philosophy in *Husserl, Heidegger and the Space of Meaning: Paths toward Transcendental Phenomenology* (Evanston, IL: Northwestern University Press, 2001). On Lask and current philosophical debates see Steven G. Crowell, "Transcendental Logic and Minimal Empiricism: Lask and McDowell on the Unboundedness of the Conceptual," in Luft and Makkreel, *Neo-Kantianism in Contemporary Philosophy*, 150–174.

chapter. These appear scattered throughout Lask's major publication, *Die Logik der Philosophie und die Kategorienlehre*,[43] and his later notes for a *System der Wissenschaften*,[44] a work which scholarship has yet to give serious consideration. Although one generation younger than his teacher Rickert, Lask's *Kategorienlehre*, published in 1911, had a significant and indisputable influence on Rickert's late emphasis on ontology. In a certain sense, then, Lask precedes Rickert on the path towards ontology. However, from a purely theoretical point of view, Rickert's position is more cautious and less radical than Lask's. Understandably, the older and more accomplished philosopher accepted his student's challenges only with some reservations. In this respect, even if Lask's reflections on ontology came first historically, they constitute a further, innovative step beyond Rickert in the theoretical treatment of ontology in Southwestern Neo-Kantianism.

In his *Kategorienlehre*, Lask intends to revise Lotze's *Sein/Geltung* theory,[45] which examined the peculiar scientificity of philosophical thought. Lask seeks to overcome Lotze's view that *Sein* and *Geltung* correspond to two separate worlds by reconciling the divided spheres of the two concepts. At the same time, he sought to retain Lotze's groundbreaking insight into the dual nature of all cognition and being. As Rickert already pointed out, notions such as 'being' or 'reality' are not themselves 'real'; they belong in the realm of irreality (*Unwirklichkeit*) and validity (*Geltung*) rather than in that of empiricity. In this sense, *Sein* (being) itself is a kind of *Geltung* (validity). For this reason, Lask dismisses the idea of a realm of existing beings, on the one hand, and a realm of timeless validities on the other. For him, the two realms intersect one another in the notion of "being," which he defines as the specific form of validity of real existents. Thus, existing beings are what they are because they enjoy the mark of validity called "reality."

---

[43] Emil Lask, *Die Logik der Philosophie und die Kategorienlehre, Gesammelte Schriften*, vol. 2 (Tübingen: Mohr Siebeck, 1923), 1–282. Hereafter LP.

[44] Emil Lask, *Zum System der Wissenschaften, Gesammelte Schriften*, vol. 3 (Tübingen: Mohr Siebeck, 1924), 239–257. Hereafter SW.

[45] For an instructive discussion of Lotze's position and its impact on Lask's philosophy see Uwe B. Glatz, *Emil Lask: Philosophie im Verhältnis zu Weltanschauung, Leben und Erkenntnis* (Würzburg: Königshausen & Neumann, 2001), 54–63. Lotze introduced his distinction in order to clarify the status of Ideas in Plato's philosophy. He holds that Ideas should be understood as *validities* and not as existents. Accordingly, a distinction results between *Sein* (being) and *Geltung* (validity) which does not allow for further explanation.

In order to clarify the complex relationship between the spheres of *Sein* and *Geltung*, Lask suggests reforming such language and employing the Kantian distinction between matter and form, or category. Lask rejects the Kantian (and Rickertean) idea of universally valid forms that would 'descend' upon an amorphous material stratum, because it suggests a predominance of the formal/categorial over the material (of *Geltung* over *Sein*), a situation in which the material receives its differentiation and structure only thanks to the formal component. For Lask, this intellectualism tarnishes the Kantian tradition and undermines its full philosophical potential. Thus, he sets out to remove it.

Against the predominance of the formal, Lask embarks on what could be called an *apology of the material*, albeit conducted along a transcendental-critical line of thought. He acknowledges the success of thinkers such as Lotze and, even more so, Rickert in drawing a sharp distinction between validity/value and being/reality. However, for Lask, the real nature of the originary relation [*Urverhältnis*][46] between the sphere of valid categories and the sphere of materials has been overlooked:

If one looks at any determination whatsoever, e.g. a determination of logical content, one becomes aware of the fact that the validity-content [*Geltungsgehalt*] does not fulfill its meaning in itself, does not rest on itself, does not constitute a 'world' apart. On the contrary, validity-content [*Geltungsgehalt*] needs to nestle against something else, it craves for completion; it points beyond itself towards a foreign element lying outside of itself.[47]

This foreign element toward which all validity-content intrinsically points is the material. No validity, category, form, or logical content (a set of expressions that simply highlights different facets of the same function) holds valid prior to its 'commitment to' some material content. Conversely, no amorphous material exists which, in a second moment, receives its form from some intellectual operation. The two elements always appear together: hence, "the two-worlds theory must be transformed in a two-elements theory."[48]

The 'unity' of the categorial component and the material component constitutes objects in a full sense. Objects, considered as the unity of category and material, bear meaning: they are unities of meaning ready for further exploration in theoretical thought. Lask thus calls them

---

[46] LP, 32, *passim.*   [47] *Ibid.*   [48] LP, 45.

"theoretical meaning" (*theoretischer Sinn*).[49] The objects themselves endow our theoretical statements with sense; they make them make sense. In this regard, they do not simply 'have' sense, viz. meaning, they *are* sense, viz. meaning. This, however, does not entail that objects, when seen through the lens of philosophical investigation, prove to be nothing but bundles of theoretical categories. In Lask's own words: "Obviously, existing objects are not hollow logical content, but they are indeed alogical material encompassed by logical validity-content."[50]

Crucial to Lask's characterization of objects qua theoretical meanings is the way in which he articulates the form/matter, viz. category/material, relationship. The word 'relationship' does not fit this context, however, because it suggests the interaction of two elements existing independently of one another, exactly what Lask seeks to counter. Rather, objects are not compounds of material and form; they are more like a chemical emulsion of the two. The two elements form a mixture in which they nonetheless remain separate. In full-blown theoretical meanings, categories do not inform, shape, structure, or organize the material. Such a view entails the kind of logical intellectualism Lask opposes. Instead, categories encompass (*umschließen*), enfold (*umhüllen*), embrace (*umgreifen*), clothe (*umkleiden*), or suffuse with light (*umleuchten*) the material, which, on its part, is 'coated' and not infused with the categorial component. This shift in language conveys the idea that the material-ontological component of objects, namely theoretical meanings, retains an independence of its own vis-à-vis the categorial component. The matter neither precedes nor receives its structure from logical categories; categories are in no way *applied* on the material by an active subjectivity. On the contrary, categories inhabit the same space as materials; they share with them the domain of radical transcendence vis-à-vis subjectivity. Thus, in theoretical activity, the subject capitalizes on the categorial clarity of theoretical meanings because theoretical meanings manifest themselves as already circumfused with the light of categorial intelligibility:[51]

---

[49] LP, 41. For a detailed discussion of this issue and of Lask's notions of meaning and truth see Crowell, *Husserl, Heidegger and the Space of Meaning*, 44–45.

[50] LP, 40.

[51] With this understanding of categoriality as genuinely transcendent, Lask revives a somewhat Aristotelian approach to the problem of categories, the pertinence of which to the tradition of Kantian transcendental philosophy can be legitimately questioned. For an account of this point and an interesting line of interpretation see Crowell, *Husserl, Heidegger and the Space of Meaning*, 51–55.

In theoretical meaning, the logically naked [material] simply renounces its logical untouchedness; it ends up in a new situation, i.e. in the situation of being-affected; however, it remains what it used to be, nothing changes as regards its content and essence, it is not magically transformed into that element which merely surrounds and 'circumvalues' [*umgelten*] it. [...] In the complexion of meaning, the material simply stands there embraced by a category.[52]

The light of categoriality illuminates the "fundamental material [*Urmaterial*]" or "*prote hyle*,"[53] and the two coalesce into an intrinsically dual theoretical meaning – object. Considered as such, however, the fundamental material remains opaque and impenetrable. It maintains its alogical foreignness to intelligibility and only admits of negative characterization as anything other than logical validity. However, the *Urmaterial* should not be considered (as the Aristotelian term *prote hyle* might wrongly suggest) as an undifferentiated mass that progressively undergoes determination as the categorial component sheds its light. This would amount to a slightly modified form of intellectualism, for even if one has moved categories away from the subject all differentiation would still depend upon categoriality at the expense of the material component. On the contrary, Lask considers the *Urmaterial* infinitely multifarious and differentiated, whereas the categorial sphere, *if abstractly considered prior to all contact with its own material*, contains nothing but empty and generic logical form. It is the categorial sphere and not the material sphere that lacks differentiation and, moreover, owes it to the multifariousness of the material it illuminates. Categoriality without material would amount, for Lask, to an endless ocean of intellectual light devoid of anything to illuminate. If we encounter categories *in the plural* and, specifically, as manifold meaning-components (*Bedeutungen*) pertaining to an endless variety of theoretical meanings – that is, objects – we do so because the underlying material is multifarious and it transfers this multifariousness to the, per se, undifferentiated sphere of categoriality. Considered in

[52] LP, 73. I decided to translate Lask's neologism "*von etwas umgolten sein*" with another neologism, as ugly as the German original: "being circumvalued by something" which in the active sounds "to circumvalue something." It is in keeping with Lask's intention who, with his neologism, wants to insist on the idea that validity is in no way "transmitted" to the material which, on its part, remains at bottom logically impenetrable.
[53] LP, 50.

respect of its definitive function of circumfusing with the light of intelligibility, the alogical *prote hyle* categoriality displays itself as a variety of *meanings (Bedeutungen)* that render intellectually accessible the sphere of materials.

Philosophers have sometimes puzzled over the multiplicity of categories and asked questions like "Why are there precisely ten categories considered by Aristotle?" or "Do also mundane things such as 'dirt' or 'hair' have their respective ideas in the intelligible world?" The fact of this multiplicity represents an element of unintelligibility in the midst of the realm of intelligibility; the multiplicity of categories renders possible the intelligibility of per se alogical materials but remains in itself unintelligible. Lask writes that

The multifariousness of the logical forms does not have to be understood in purely logical terms. On the contrary, it reveals a moment of opacity which points towards the meaning-determining power of the alogical material [...] The multiplicity in the sphere of validity, the multiplicity of the forms of validity exists on account of the multifariousness foreign to validity.[54]

For Lask, materials possess an intrinsic differentiation and structure that the categories merely reflect. The multiple categorial forms that we detect in the realm of validity are nothing but "a reflection stemming from"[55] the infinite multiplicity of the materials. In a footnote, Lask characterizes these as "subterranean powers,"[56] thus portraying the upper level of categoriality as some sort of karst topography. The materials shape their respective categories 'from below,' as it were.

Considering this picture, it is quite unmistakable that, despite his announced desire to do away with all "correlation-theories"[57] and affirm the mutual inherence of form and material, for Lask the material component enjoys a primacy over the categorial/logical/conceptual component. This probably arises from his resolute decision to overcome once and for all the intellectualistic strand in the Kantian tradition. Concerning his own philosophical work, he writes:

Everything is transferred to the material sphere in a quite anti-intellectualistic fashion. One should not overrate what lies exclusively in the validity-character, namely, a mere categorial label, a mere logical consecration![58]

---

[54] LP, 61.   [55] LP, 63.   [56] *Ibid.*, n.   [57] LP, 44.   [58] LP, 86.

This emphasis on the material side has an important bearing on Lask's classification of different scientific fields, the core issue that ignited the movement of Southwestern Neo-Kantianism toward ontology in the first place. Note that the issue of ontology became relevant in the eyes of first generation Southwestern Neo-Kantians because of the methodological difference between human and natural science. Contrary to Windelband and Rickert and in keeping with his *Kategorienlehre*'s emphasis on material, in some late notes Lask argues:

Accordingly, a classification of the sciences seems to be possible only with respect to what is investigated, i.e. with respect to the "material", i.e. with respect to the a-theoretical differences of the fundamental region.[59]

Lask goes on to explain that "the difference in terms of generalizing and individualizing method [...] would only be possible if all other factors [*das Übrige*] were of the same kind [*gleich*]. However, the essential difference lies precisely in these other factors."[60] In other words, a distinction in methodological terms works only if the materials to which different methods are applied are fundamentally homogeneous in kind. In this case, all existing differentiation would derive from the different methodological treatments. If one rejects this position for the reasons mentioned above, then the "logical differentiation is per se even misleading, whereas the material differentiation per se is fully correct and decisive."[61]

For Lask, the categorial dimension simply does not have the resources to *produce* differentiations but only to illuminate them. Categories and patterns of concept-formation do not intervene to re-shape our perceptions and *Verstehungen* and to bestow upon them new order, as Rickert would have it. Lask knowingly rejects the core insight of his teacher when he writes, "The whole idea of a re-shaping [*Umformungsgedanke*] falls apart in my philosophy. What remains is solely the selection [*Auslese*]."[62] Rickert's ideas concerning the re-shaping power of categories/concepts and his notion of selection [*Auswahl*] will be considered in further detail in the following chapters. Interestingly, in his 1927 lecture on *Nature and Spirit*, Husserl criticizes Rickert along a line that comes very close to Lask's, albeit without

---

[59] SW, 239.   [60] SW, 242.   [61] *Ibid.*
[62] Emil Lask, *Notizen zur Einteilung der Wissenschaften, Gesammelte Schriften*, vol. 3, 257–293. Here 260. Hereafter NEW.

accepting the latter's radical emphasis on the material component.[63] For Husserl, different kinds of experiential material provide the *motivational ground* to move conceptually in one direction or another. However, this connection need not occupy us any further here. To conclude our inquiry into the ontological trend of Southwestern Neo-Kantianism, it is fitting to consider the work of a rather obscure philosopher in its ranks, Franz Böhm. His short book *Ontologie der Geschichte*[64] brilliantly recapitulates the ontological problems laid out by the previous generations of the school and presents an innovative perspective on the whole issue that, if considered carefully, opens up Neo-Kantian ontology for a phenomenological treatment.

Franz Böhm's *Ontology of History*

As mentioned above, one may dispute, and some have in fact disputed, whether Lask keeps within the framework of Kantianism or more or less intentionally throws out the transcendental-critical method alongside his rejection of intellectualism. In either case, it remains apparent that his emphasis on the meaning-determining (*bedeutungsbestimmende*) power of the material on the sphere of categories comes as a reaction, and perhaps even ends up as an overreaction, to a kind of intellectualism often associated with Kantian philosophy. Stepping back from the legitimate motivations behind his work, two significant problems appear in Lask's treatment of ontology. First, he seems to

[63] See Chapter 5.
[64] F. Böhm, *Ontologie der Geschichte* (Tübingen: Mohr Siebeck, 1933). Hereafter OG. Some biographical facts about Franz Böhm can be found in the monumental work C. Tilitzki, *Die deutsche Universitätsphilosophie in der Weimarer Republik und im Dritten Reich – Teil I.* (Berlin: Akademie Verlag, 2002), 326–328. Franz Böhm had a remarkable academic career. In 1937 he took over Karl Jaspers' chair in Heidelberg, outclassing all other candidates for the position, among them Hans-Georg Gadamer (692–694). Of course, this did not happen without the support of the Nazi party, a necessary condition to work in German academia in those troubled times. However, this does not justify, I believe, the overall dismissive tone with which Tilitzki presents the majority of the philosophers he considers in his book, Böhm included. Whereas the historian seeks primarily to open up the tragic vicissitudes of German academic politics during the Third Reich, nothing prevents the philosopher from retaining what is good in the intellectual efforts of people who eventually fell into the arms of an all-pervasive ideology. In so doing, the philosopher affirms the right to reclaim from history every fragment of meaning and authenticity to be found, even in ages of extraordinary darkness.

have lost sight of the specific theoretical issue that made ontology interesting for Neo-Kantianism in the first place: the demarcation of natural and historical science. He develops his ontological *Kategorienlehre* at a very abstract level and only in a second moment *applies* it to the problems concerning natural and historical science. If, on the contrary, ontological questions keep these problems firmly in grasp, then one need not transform Rickert's ontological dualism (which acknowledges the uniqueness of historical-cultural objects and the asymmetry in the applicability of the generalizing and the individualizing method) into an affirmation of the overflowing multifariousness and differentiation of the materials relative to the merely clarifying function of categories, as Lask does. A more prudent, transcendental-critical approach would acknowledge only as much ontological plurality on the material side as is required by our concrete experiences of thought and scientific investigation. A second problem in Lask's philosophy he actually shares with his teacher Rickert. When Rickert considers the relationship of the categorial component (which he calls concept-formation) to the material component, he presents only one model, a kind of subsumption, whereby a category is *bestowed* on a complexion of experiential data (sensuous or non-sensuous) and restructures them according to a certain conceptual pattern. The bestowal of a category, in this scheme, comes from the cognizing subject who, in so bestowing, carries out an intellectual synthesis. Thus, we find Rickert acknowledging the constitutive-synthetic nature of cognition but interpreting it exclusively in terms of a re-shaping power exerted by our conceptuality upon the inert material of our experience. Lask simply rejects this model and argues for a kind of independent life of the materials surrounded by the light of their respective categorial forms. He does not understand knowledge to be an active synthesis of heterogeneous elements performed by the intellect. Rather, it is just an *attending to* the theoretical meanings that offer themselves to investigation. Lask attributes all formative power to the material and minimizes the 'impact' of cognition, which he interprets as a mere "*Verhalten zum theoretischen Sinn,*"[65] an attending to theoretical meaning. Therefore, both Rickert and Lask conceive of synthesis as either wholly intellectual or not at all.

In light of these problems, in his *Ontology of History* Franz Böhm makes two very interesting moves. First, he re-contextualizes the

---

[65] LP, 82.

discussion of ontology in the nature/history framework and thus goes back to a markedly transcendental-critical line of inquiry after Lask's ontological excesses. Second, he capitalizes on resources in Kant's philosophy that Rickert and Lask seem to ignore. In particular, he makes a case that one does not need to conceive of the material side as thoroughly unsynthesized and per se alien to intelligibility. Böhm points out that, especially in his third Critique, Kant acknowledges forms of synthesis that are not entirely 'guided' by the intellect: for some peculiar objects like works of art, there remains a certain alogical residue that renders their definitive subsumption under a conceptual category impossible. Böhm believes that Kant's transcendental philosophy offers the possibility to conceive of a "gradation of the theoretical,"[66] thus striking a balance between sheer intellectualism and one-sided anti-intellectualism. In other words, for Böhm we can acknowledge different degrees to which the intellect (viz. theory or categorial thought) is active in different ontological domains. Whereas for the domain of sensuous objects (nature) we have to acknowledge with Kant an all-around intellectual constitution, in the domain of historical objects, the intellect works in a somewhat impoverished fashion and in some cases (Böhm mentions aesthetic contemplation) the intellect's activity consists in sheer reflexivity and no genuine constitution.

Notwithstanding some obscurities in the text, two factors make Böhm's *Ontologie der Geschichte* worth reading. First, he presents the problem of ontology from within a Neo-Kantian perspective with remarkable clarity and precision. Second, over the course of his investigation, Böhm admits the necessity of a consideration of subjectivity in the formation of historical objects, whereby one may overcome the strictures of empirical psychology on the one hand and those of merely formal transcendentalism on the other. In this way, he comes very close to acknowledging the necessity of a phenomenological approach in order to tackle the ontological problems left open by Neo-Kantianism in a methodologically appropriate fashion.

Böhm points out the meaning of the ontological problem from a fully Kantian point of view at the very outset of his work:

The possibility of nature itself is secured because it can be shown that the rational constituents of nature in the ontological sense of the term are identical

---

[66] OG, 47.

with the constituents of natural science [. . .] Cognition of nature is possible because the same "ratio" conditions and constitutes *both* knowledge *and* the object [. . .] As for the issue of the possibility of "history itself," this "exchangeability" of the transcendental-logical and the ontological problematic is not to be found.[67]

To give but one of many examples, Kant understands the principle of causality as both an epistemological constituent of natural scientific thought and an ontological constituent of natural phenomena. All epistemological categories of natural scientific thought are convertible into ontological constituents of natural phenomena. If we can attain natural-scientific knowledge, this happens because the intellect recognizes its own categories, as it were, in the objects it sets out to investigate. But the possibility of this recognition arises from the natural object's pretheoretical constitution, in other words, in the work of what Kant calls figurative synthesis (*synthesis speciosa*) and considers a condition of possibility for intellectual synthesis (*synthesis intellectualis*).[68] I will not expand on Kant's notoriously complex notion of figurative synthesis here. It suffices to say that Kant understands figurative synthesis as a form of organization of the spatio-temporal data stemming from the senses, operated by the *Einbildungskraft*, and based on schematic representations rather than categories. He identifies it as a form of pre-theoretical structuring of the data of sensibility that makes such amenable to a subsequent subsumption under a category of the intellect. This "downward movement"[69] from superior forms of synthesis to more rudimentary, pre-theoretical forms of synthesis in Kant's transcendental deduction, Böhm argues, recurs in the context of an ontology of history:

The fact that a material enters into a form presupposes the readiness of the material for the given formation [*Formung*], and the form has to detect such readiness already there in the material. This readiness cannot be produced by the form in the first place.[70]

The Kantian, however, cannot dogmatically presuppose the material content of history. The fact of the readiness of *certain* objects for

[67] OG, 3.
[68] For an excellent discussion of this issue see Y. Senderowicz, "Figurative Synthesis and Synthetic a priori Knowledge," *Review of Metaphysic* 57/4 (2004): 755–785.
[69] OG, 5.   [70] OG, 56.

cognition according to historical forms of conceptualization points back to the necessity of some deeper forms of synthesis occurring at the material level and not impinged *ab ovo* by conceptual thought on a formless substrate. Therefore, a transcendental inquiry into the ontology of historical objects has to lay bare "compositional syntheses,"[71] that is, rules for the organization of the material content of historical objects (Böhm, following Rickert and Lask, calls it "protohyletic matter")[72] prior to its treatment according to the specifically historical pattern of individualizing concept-formation. In a line reminiscent of Kant's doctrine of transcendental schematism, Böhm talks about "extra-theoretical spontaneities"[73] as necessarily responsible for the structuring of materials cognizable according to historical patterns of conceptualization.

An example will clarify what Böhm has in mind with his distinction between historical objects and natural objects and the non-convertibility of epistemological categories into ontological forms in the case of history. Let us consider two objects: the natural phenomenon of electromagnetism and the historical period of the Renaissance. In both cases we can distinguish between an epistemological side (the laws of electromagnetism discovered by natural scientific thought and the body of historical knowledge about the Renaissance) and an ontological side (the phenomenon of electromagnetism itself and the Renaissance itself). In both cases we encounter an object in a robust sense: neither the physicist nor the Renaissance scholar simply plays with her own thoughts. They both work on an object that they had first to isolate and frame against the broader background of nature and history. However, whereas the laws that explain electromagnetism, as well as the basic a priori principles that undergird those laws (causality, substantiality, reciprocal action . . .), fully exhaust the phenomenon of electromagnetism, the historical 'phenomenon' of the Renaissance resists a full exhaustion on the part of the categories employed in historical thought. There remains no undisclosed residue in the phenomenon of electromagnetism after its laws have been figured out, yet something remains intrinsically opaque, unconceptualizeable, and open to further scrutiny about the Renaissance. In Böhm's words: "The concept-formation of historical knowledge does not 'constitute' the object in the same way in which theoretical 'categories' constitute 'nature'."[74] We

---

[71] OG, 24.   [72] OG, 85.   [73] OG, 37.   [74] OG, 46.

apply historical categories to objects the material constitution of which Böhm calls "metalogical,"[75] i.e., their constitution follows patterns of compositional synthesis not entirely 'translatable' into constitutive categories, as is the case with the merely pre-logical constitution of natural objects. In simpler words, we can in principle never have a historical object all figured out in thought in the same way in which we have natural objects figured out, since the pre-theoretical constitution of historical objects follows patterns of synthesis that do not admit of being fully 'lifted up' to constitutive categoriality.

Böhm provides us with some general headings for such spontaneous, pre-theoretical syntheses of historical material: notions such as "organic totality,"[76] "historical temporality,"[77] and ethical "progress."[78] When we talk about the Renaissance, we consider it as an organic totality of mutually illuminating, meaningful components (politics, literature, arts, personalities …) whereby heterogeneous elements present themselves as woven together into a coherent whole. Even if every intellectual synthesis we will perform on the object 'Renaissance' intrinsically pre-supposes this, we can never translate this meta-logical, exclusively ontological 'belonging together' of the parts into the language of intel-lectual, law-like explanation. Furthermore, we experience the objects of history as immersed in an overarching flux of time, which, excluding the time of empirical science, is no homogeneous medium, in which any event could in principle occur at any time.[79] World War I could not have happened at any time in history in the same way in which a certain chemical reaction could. We cannot 'model' historical time in the same way in which we can model natural time. No theoretical category can fully 'recognize itself' in history in the way it can in nature. As Böhm summarizes:

The time of "nature" is *exclusively* the constitutive *condition* of empirical reality. As such, it is an "originary *quantum*," and it can be *measured* with the help of *spatial* relations. The historical time is *not* a constitutive con-dition of the understandable meaning-configurations [*Sinngebilde*] [...] it is an originary *quale* in addition to the understandability of meaning which announces the belonging of this meaning to the world created by humankind.[80]

[75] OG, 8; 21.   [76] OG, 39.   [77] OG, 63.   [78] OG, 133.   [79] OG, 65.
[80] OG, 114.

Finally, if we can talk about history in terms of progress (something that Böhm, in the wake of Kant and the Neo-Kantians, never feels the need to question) this is because the material of history offers itself as somehow pervaded by a pre-theoretical value-content, possibly fixed with concepts such as Rickert's value-relatedness but not entirely comprehended. Basically, a fully conceptual determination of progress in history could exist only in hindsight, 'at the end' of the historical process, as Hegel would have it. Since history continues to unfold, the value-content vaguely intuited and conceptually fixed in different episodes of history admits of a theoretical grasp only in a partial and constantly revisable way. Until history ends, what looks like a huge step forward in the progress of mankind today might prove to be the first step back into the barbarism of tomorrow.

In the context of these instructive considerations Böhm makes some important remarks that help to open up the trajectory of Southwestern Neo-Kantianism towards Husserlian phenomenology. In a further discussion of his theory of historical time, Böhm opposes Dilthey's influential position that identifies understandability [*Verstehbarkeit*] as the fundamental category for historical objectivity,[81] for understandable constellations of meaning as per se a-temporal. The young, ambitious prince who has his one-time right-hand man killed, in order to reassert his own power in the eyes of the populace, for instance, is a timeless character, an understandable configuration of meaning that could occur in different venues of history. Cesare Borgia organizing the murder of his captain Remiro d'Orco, as brilliantly described in Machiavelli's *Prince*, represents this timeless character 'temporalized' in the specific time-venue of Italy in the early sixteenth century.

Understandable meaning-configurations lie beyond history in what Lask would call the realm of validity. They need to be inserted in a temporal scheme and thus rendered dynamic in order to become historical. Thus, Böhm remarks that "the *dynamic* 'material' of the historical is the activity of the subject"[82] and that "in this sense, historical objects are accomplishments of voluntary actions oriented towards values. This dynamic-material function of activity clarifies the meaning of the psychic for the ontic structure of the historical."[83] In other words, only through the psychic life of concrete subjects are intrinsically 'irreal' meaning-configurations realized into concrete historical objectivities.

---

[81] See Chapter 2.   [82] OG, 117.   [83] *Ibid.*

It took the subjective life of a specific person to constitute the historical object "Cesare Borgia" out of the mere ahistorical meaning-configuration "young, ambitious prince." On a broader scale, it took the lives of the several generations of men and women who lived in that historical epoch, their thoughts and desires, their fears and hopes to constitute "the Renaissance" out of the timeless meaning-configuration "period of cultural rebirth."

But what is the "psychic" evoked in Böhm's quote? Is it just the object of empirical psychology? If so, one could not argue for its contribution in the structuring of value-related forms of historical objectivity. Empirical being can in no way claim responsibility for the *transcendental* constitution of further empirical being. Moreover, the Neo-Kantian tradition understands empirical subjectivity as an object of nature, constituted and ontologically exhausted by the categories of natural scientific thought. It belongs in a realm of objectivity that does not pertain to history.

Or is it the transcendental subject as formal unity in multiplicities of representation advocated by Kant? If so, it is unclear why we should give it a special function for the constitution of historical objects as opposed to natural. The Kantian transcendental subject, by definition a formal principle of unity, remains indifferent to all the material differences of the objects of its representations.

Rather, it seems that the material-ontological investigations launched by Windelband, made explicit by Rickert, radicalized by Lask, and finally articulated by Böhm call for a reconsideration of the psychic and its constitutive function beyond the strictures of empirical psychology and of Kantian formalism. After all, the fact that empirical psychology deals with psychic phenomena (a fact so crucial for the Neo-Kantian demarcation of science) does not mean that it deals with psychic phenomena *qua* psychic phenomena, i.e., according to their ontological specificity. This is the point Husserl saw with great clarity after *Logical Investigations*. Consequently, his phenomenological project entails a full-fledged response to the problems left open in the Neo-Kantian treatment of history. However, Husserl is not alone in trying to propose alternative solutions to the problems left open by the Neo-Kantians. A second mainstream current of philosophy in early twentieth-century Germany took on the task of reconsidering the psychic from the perspective of history, as opposed to that of natural science; this was *Lebensphilosophie*. I will examine the work of the two spearheads of *Lebensphilosophie*, Wilhelm Dilthey and Georg Simmel, in the next chapter. This will more thoroughly establish a foundation for understanding, in later chapters, Husserl's own strategy to recast the constitutive role of subjectivity for both history *and* nature.

2 | Life-philosophical accounts of history and psyche: Simmel and Dilthey

"Was ist denn die Wissenschaft?"
Sie ist nur des Lebens Kraft.
Ihr erzeuget nicht das Leben,
Leben erst muss Leben geben.

J. W. von Goethe[1]

Now, in the philosophy of life the whole consciousness,
with all its different phases and faculties,
must inevitably be taken for the foundation [. . .]

F. von Schlegel[2]

Der Grundgedanken meiner Philosophie ist, daß bisher noch niemals
die ganze, volle, unverstümmelte Erfahrung dem Philosophieren zugrunde
gelegt worden ist, mithin noch niemals die ganze und volle Wirklichkeit.

W. Dilthey[3]

Over the long course of history, different phrases have been in vogue to designate the complex kind of reality that we are. After the word 'soul' dominated the philosophical scene for many centuries, the inception of the modern age marked a progressive departure from that language. In a relatively short span of time compared to both antiquity and the Middle

---

[1] J. W. von Goethe, *Zahme Xenien V*, in J. W. von Goethe, *Gedenkausgabe der Werke, Briefe und Gespräche 28. August 1949*, vol. 1 (Zurich: Artemis Verlag, 1949), 647. "What is, then, science? / It is nothing but a force of life / You do not generate life / Life must give life in the first place."

[2] F. von Schlegel, *The Philosophy of Life, and Philosophy of Language, in a Course of Lectures* (London: Henry G. Bohn, 1847), 11.

[3] W. Dilthey, *Weltanschauungslehre. Abhandlungen zur Philosophie der Philosophie, Gesammelte Schriften*, vol. 8 (Göttingen: Vandenhoeck & Ruprecht, 1960), 171. Hereafter GS VIII. "The fundamental thought of my philosophy is that hitherto the whole, full, un-maimed experience, and with it the whole and full reality have never been placed at the foundation of philosophizing."

Ages, a variety of new phrases were introduced: 'thinking being,' 'ego,' 'conscience,' 'consciousness,' 'subject,' *'Geist,'* 'self,' and 'mind,' to name but the most prominent ones. Each phrase is meant to capture at least one specific feature of what we are and, quite often, to pronounce it the most fundamental. The term 'life,' which became a buzzword in late nineteenth-century and early twentieth-century German philosophy, is a further instance of this trend.

Although no unified concept of life can be found among the overwhelming number of self-styled life-philosophers,[4] the term 'life' meets some specific philosophical demands that preoccupy an entire generation of thinkers. First and foremost, all life-philosophers are in some way or other committed to a rejection of traditional forms of metaphysics. Nothing is superior to 'life' itself, be it a divine creator or a universal moral law. Secondly, as briefly anticipated in Chapter 1, the introduction of the notion of life is meant to run counter to a certain brand of Kantianism (notably, the brand of Kantianism offered by thinkers such as Rickert) that was widely perceived as overly intellectualistic and abstract. As this chapter will show, the anti-intellectualistic trait of life-philosophy does not amount to a rejection of Kantianism as such but rather to a different way of being Kantian, at least for the leading figures of life-philosophy. Thirdly, the notion of life points from the very beginning to a supra-individual, trans-subjective dimension of mentality. Contrary to more traditional notions such as subject, soul, mind, and the like, life is not conceivable as a separate substance. The widespread sense attached to the notion of life is that the living individual is what she is only to the extent that she partakes of a broader living reality. In this respect, the notion of life bears a certain similarity to the Hegelian notion of *Geist*. Contrary to *Geist*, however, which in Hegel's view develops according to a precise rhythm and moves teleologically towards culmination in idealistic philosophy, 'life' is more fluid, and none of its configurations can be deemed definitive.

---

[4] On this point see the instructive F. Fellmann, *Gelebte Philosophie in Deutschland* (Freiburg and Munich: Karl Alber, 1983), 7–28. The author suggests that 'life' should be considered a "lived-concept" (20), i.e. a concept that is not primarily characterized in theoretical terms by means of a stringent definition but in terms of the *Stimmung* that it evokes. One could rephrase Fellman's point by reference to J. L. Austin's theory of language and say that life is a primarily performative rather than an informative concept.

This third connotation of the notion of life – according to which life is primarily supra-individual – offers a criterion for an initial broad distinction within the camp of life-philosophy: between those who interpret life's supra-individuality primarily by reference to the biological unity of the human species (Hans Driesch, Oswald Spengler) and those who understand it primarily in historical terms. In this chapter we will focus exclusively on the two leading figures of this second group, Georg Simmel and Wilhelm Dilthey. While both Simmel and Dilthey do make frequent references to biology, it is not *organic* life that they consider paramount to philosophy and the foundation of the human sciences. By 'life' they mean the pre-reflective, pre-conceptualized dimension of lived experience. This dimension forms a coherent whole of meaning that conceptual thought (including natural-scientific concepts) can only grasp in a derivative and imperfect way. Their work is a passionate defense of the primacy of life over conceptual thought and an effort to ground the *sui generis* scientificity of the human sciences in the very dynamic of life. To anticipate a theme to be explored in subsequent chapters, it is important to bear in mind that this is the same connotation of the term 'life' Husserl employs when he refers to transcendental life. 'Life' does not refer here to the dimension of organic existence that we share with cats, trees, and amoebae but rather to that affectively, culturally, and historically connoted dimension of ourselves that is always already at play before we reflect upon it. As Max Scheler aptly emphasizes in a programmatic essay on the philosophy of life, we should understand the phrase 'of life' as a *"genitivus subjectivus."*[5] Life-philosophy aspires to be rather life's philosophy than a philosophy *about* life. It is "a philosophy stemming from the fullness of life, and even – more sharply put – a *philosophy stemming from the fullness of the lived experiencing of life."*[6]

Even though both Dilthey and Simmel, unlike the Southwestern Neo-Kantians, are fairly renowned, the specifically philosophical and ontological dimensions of their thought have for the most part been ignored. Simmel's name appears towards the beginning of most historical handbooks of sociology, and Dilthey's name is similarly evoked here and

[5] M. Scheler, "Versuche einer Philosophie des Lebens: Nietzsche – Dilthey – Bergson," in M. Scheler, *Vom Umsturz der Werte: Abhandlungen und Aufsätze* (Berne and Munich: Francke, 1972), 310–339. Here 311.
[6] *Ibid.*

there as one of the early figures in the movement that Gadamer eventually christened 'philosophical hermeneutics.'

However, both Simmel and Dilthey have very sophisticated views on the theoretical issues of their time, and thus it is unfair to present them as merely anticipatory figures. They both underscore the need to prioritize the material component for a correct demarcation of the different domains of science. They advocate a renewal of Kantianism through a close consideration of the historical world. Although they both stress the continuity between nature and life, they refuse to leave the study of human subjectivity to empirical-experimental psychology, as Rickert would have it. For both Simmel and Dilthey, it is necessary to understand what is at stake in psychology, and to formulate its authentic scientific tasks in closer connection to history than to natural science. Leaving the study of psychology exclusively to the natural sciences in order to preserve the autonomy of the human sciences, as Rickert would have it, is for both Simmel and Dilthey a self-defeating move. Rickert, in their view, severely underappreciates the active, living nature of subjectivity and believes it can be regarded as just another causally determined natural fact. In this respect, as will be discussed in later chapters, Husserl is of one mind with the life-philosophers and disagrees significantly with Rickert and the Southwestern school.

Bringing Kant back to life: Simmel's lectures on Kant

In order to interpret correctly the meaning of historically oriented life-philosophy and to avoid oversimplifying its contrast to transcendental Neo-Kantianism, it is crucial to highlight life-philosophy's indebtedness to Kant. Compared to mainstream academic Neo-Kantianism, life-philosophy recasts the Kantian legacy in a different light. It is known that Wilhelm Dilthey envisioned a *Critique of Historical Reason* that would extend Kant's theoretical treatment of natural science to cover historical science.[7] Dilthey, however, never devoted himself to a fully in-

---

[7] For an excellent reconstruction of Dilthey's project of a critique of historical reason see J. de Mul, *The Tragedy of Finitude: Dilthey's Hermeneutics of Life* (New Haven, CT and London: Yale University Press, 2004), 29–33. A discussion of Dilthey's notion of life will be provided in the second part of this chapter.

depth study and interpretation of Kant.[8] Georg Simmel, by contrast, did
lecture extensively on Kant's philosophy at the University of Berlin, and
in 1904, at the apex of his popularity, published a book comprised of his
lectures on Kant, which he presented as a general introduction to
philosophy. The book is simply entitled *Kant*, and it carries the subtitle
Sixteen Lectures Held at the University of Berlin.[9] The modesty of the
title, however, should not mislead. What Simmel offers is not a didactic
exposition of Kant's philosophy. Even though the presentation of
Kant's thought is remarkably rigorous, as he himself points out at the
very outset, "the purpose of this book is not historical-philosophical but
rather purely philosophical."[10] Simmel sets out to assess and appropriate critically Kant's thought from the stance of life-philosophy. This
leads to a highly interesting reformulation of it, one that sets a philosophical agenda significantly different from that of Southwestern
thinkers, even though it seeks its inspiration in the same authoritative
source.

Simmel presents his program by stating, "It is necessary to measure
up Kant's problems and solutions against what can be referred to as the
life-related questions of philosophy."[11] The book "seeks the significance [*Bedeutung*] of Kant's scientific and, in part, very specialized
theories for the meaning of life [*Sinn des Lebens*] and for the construction of a worldview."[12] At first glance, the most direct way to develop a
'worldview' out of Kant's philosophy would be to read the project of his
criticism as paving the way for a universal voluntarism. On this reading – spearheaded by Fichte – Kant carried out his critique of theoretical
reason in the interest of practical reason; by showing the inherent limits
of the former, he would be making room for the latter. The *Critique of
Pure Reason* would culminate in the *Dialectic*, where it is shown that

---

[8] However, he was responsible for the standard critical edition of Kant's collected
work of the Prussian Academy of the Sciences. For a detailed and informative
description of Dilthey's work as a Kant editor and the significance of this
commitment for his philosophical activity see F. Rodi, "Dilthey und die Kant-
Ausgabe der Preußischen Akademie der Wissenschaften. Einige editions- und
lebensgeschichtliche Aspekte," in F. Rodi, *Das strukturierte Ganze: Studien zum
Werk von Wilhelm Dilthey* (Weilerswist: Velbrück Wissenschaft, 2003), 153–172.
[9] G. Simmel, *Kant. Sechzehn Vorlesungen gehalten an der Berliner Universität*, in
Georg Simmel, *Gesamtausgabe*, vol. 9 (Frankfurt am Main: Suhrkamp, 1997),
8–226. Hereafter K.
[10] K, 9.   [11] *Ibid.*   [12] *Ibid.*

the most urgent questions of life cannot be answered by theoretical reason and therefore demand a transition to practice.

Simmel, on the contrary, shows no hesitation in rejecting the voluntaristic reading of Kant as "completely wrong."[13] On his reading: "Kant and his system are completely intellectualistic; his interest – which shines forth from the content of his philosophy – is to prove that the norms that are valid for thought are valid in *all* domains of life."[14] The label 'intellectualistic,' however, is not meant to be an outright charge against Kant. Contrariwise, for Simmel, Kant's intention to extend the validity of intellectual norms to the whole of life results in a remarkable transformation of his view on rationality, which has no precedent in the tradition of rationalism. In other words, Kant's intellectualism – unlike previous forms of intellectualism – ends up bringing forth a novel understanding of the intellect rather than a one-sided glorification of it. "[In Kant] the power of logical thought shows itself to be all the more dominant, to the extent that it does not repeat the untenable rationalistic attempt to repress the other psychic energies [*Seelenenergien*] from the outset."[15] All the different components of life (sensibility, will, feeling) are unreservedly acknowledged by Kant but only in order to be subsequently placed under a rule issued by the intellect. To give one example, the will as such is independent of the intellect, but *good* will is a willing determined by the intellectual rule expressed by the categorical imperative.

Kant's willingness to extend the sphere of influence of the intellect over the totality of subjective life, however, affects his conception of the intellect itself in a way that becomes most apparent in the treatment of sensibility and its role in objective cognition. Arguing against empiricism, Kant famously defends the necessity of a priori principles that are not taken in from the senses but rather hold valid prior to all experience. However, unlike traditional rationalism, these a priori principles, considered per se, do not grant any kind of *knowledge*. It is not by combining together in thought pure a priori principles that we obtain genuine knowledge. On the contrary, only the synthetic product that results from the joint functioning of intellect and sensibility can be legitimately called 'knowledge.' The pure a priori principles simply organize the impressions arising from our senses, thus constituting the objective world that we call nature. When Kant argues that we cannot have

---

[13] K, 15. [14] *Ibid.* [15] *Ibid.*

knowledge of things as they are in themselves but only of phenomena he is not gesturing towards a hidden promised land of cognition, which regrettably happens to be out of our reach. On the contrary, he is establishing the ambit of validity within which our intellectual categories apply. Phenomenal nature is not an impoverished or subjectively filtered version of nature as it is in itself. Phenomenal nature is the only nature that there is, meaning that phenomenal objects are not pale shadows of alleged noumenal objects; rather, they are the only objects to which we can meaningfully refer. The mistake of both rationalism and empiricism is to have considered the true source of objective knowledge to be what proves, to Kant's critical eye, only a component thereof. This bears important philosophical consequences:

> From this decision between sensualism and rationalism, a fundamental and greatly significant principle arises: the authentic picture of the world [*Weltbild*] only comes about through the joint work of *all* mental energies. The one-sidedness of all doctrines that appoint one of these energies as the carrier of all truth at the expense of the others is thus overcome, while the valuation of the conscious mind in general as the source of the world to which we can refer as knowable is preserved.[16]

In other words, Kant's exaltation of the intellect does not amount to setting it apart from the rest of our mental faculties and appointing it as the exclusive source of true knowledge. Rather, it amounts to showing how the intellect is actively involved in each faculty and how, in this involvement, it displays its all-embracing power. This blending of the intellect into the broader dynamic of life – best exemplified by the inextricable relatedness of intellect and sensibility in theoretical cognition – is for Simmel the initial move that inaugurates the trajectory of life-philosophy and that finds its first full-fledged formulation in Goethe:

> By way of showing that the attainment of truth requires the activity of *all* theoretical powers, Kant opened up a decisive path for <the creation of> a worldview, a path that was of course limited by his intellectualistic exclusivity and that subsequently Goethe thought through for the first time [...] The *whole intellect* cognizes – this was Kant's overcoming of sensualism and rationalism. And now <*scil.* with Goethe> this insight is increased and amplified: *the whole human being* cognizes. In this way, our mental [*geistig*]

[16] K, 27–28.

relation to the world received for the first time its solidest basis. The differ-
ential psychic power that we have to invest in this or that cognitive task is now
viewed as a specifically structured and oriented riverbed in which the *totality*
of our psychic life is canalized.[17]

Simmel would eventually elaborate further on the connection between
Kant and Goethe in a very instructive essay, *Kant und Goethe*.[18]
However, the key point of his interpretation already stands out quite
clearly in this passage. With his idea that knowledge requires the joint
work of two faculties and that intellect alone cannot yield scientific
truth, Kant initiated a movement of integration of all the components
of subjectivity into the superior unity of what Goethe would subsequently call 'life.' Kant's philosophy provides an initial contribution
towards a conception of life that does not construe it as a mere process
'in the world' but rather a process in which what we call 'the world' is
formed, and by which the world is carried. This operation gives rise,
according to Simmel, to a "spiritualization and liquefaction
[*Vergeistigung und Verflüssigung*] of our picture of the world," one in
which "the vital power of the mind [*Geist*] reaches down to the ultimate
and remotest elements of being."[19] In this picture, what philosophy
traditionally called 'reason' is no longer the static mirror of eternal
truths. Its displacement into the ever-changing flux of sensibility reveals
its true nature: a living process forming and transforming the given.
Concomitantly, the traditional 'carrier' of reason, the ego, is no longer
considered a substance that exists beyond the life-process. The ego is not
"*lebensjenseitig*" (beyond life) but it "merges and dissolves into its own
working [*geht in seiner Leistung auf*]."[20] It is nothing over and above its
own functioning; it 'lives' in it.

---

[17] K, 28.
[18] G. Simmel, *Kant und Goethe*, in Georg Simmel, *Gesamtausgabe*, vol. 8
   (Frankfurt am Main: Suhrkamp, 1993), 116–123. In his essay, however, Simmel
   seems to be more cautious than in the above passage. Here he emphasizes the
   divergence existing between the two great German thinkers. Even if both are
   concerned with a restoration of the unity between subjectivity and nature, for
   Kant this unity exists because it is subjectivity that brings nature about in the first
   place, whereas for Goethe the two elements, while remaining distinct and
   independent, share the same essence. (See here, 119.)
[19] G. Simmel, *Was ist uns Kant?* in Georg Simmel, *Gesamtausgabe*, vol. 5 (Frankfurt
   am Main: Suhrkamp, 1997), 145–177. Here, 156. Hereafter WuK.
[20] K, 74.

Thus, the world is a system of factors that mutually carry each other; the ego is the activity that [. . .] brings the sensuous elements to their unity but does not fall out of them – it is the vitality of the world-process [*die Lebendigkeit des Weltprozesses*] which consists in the intelligible connection of those elements, whereby objects are construed and the chaos of sensibility receives a form.[21]

This pathbreaking conception of knowledge, however, is counterbalanced in Kant by a number of strictures whose removal, according to Simmel, goes hand in hand with the development of life-philosophy. First and foremost, there seems to be a tension between the assertion of subjectivity's world-forming power and the conviction that this process of formation can be isolated and attributed to a few unchanging a priori principles. Kant's worldview is guided by the idea that the world, in terms of its fundamental principles, forms a well-rounded system and that, accordingly, the world-forming subjectivity has a wholly "symmetrical," harmonious structure.[22] This conviction is at odds with what Simmel calls "the contemporary feeling of life [*Lebensgefühl*]," which is more inclined to believe in a "never-ending development in the deepest strata of our mind [*Geist*]."[23] The process of subjective world-formation first discovered by Kant seems to unfold in a more erratic fashion than Kant himself would have it.

As Simmel is eager to emphasize, however, Kant's notion of the a priori is not primarily psychological. Rather, it amounts to a fully "a-subjective"[24] set of principles to which our psychic life may or may not conform: "The a priori is in fact only an a priori of cognition. Whenever we fail to apply it, we fail to attain knowledge. Rather, we carry out certain kinds of subjective mental processes which, however, do not qualify as experiences."[25] In this sense, the rigidity in Kant's notion of a priori is connected to the restricted sphere of subjective life that it is supposed to regulate, namely, cognition. But precisely this exclusive interest in the restricted sphere of cognition is what feels unbearably narrow to Simmel and to the movement of life-philosophy. The world-forming power of life extends beyond the scope of intellectual cognition, such that taking up Kant's legacy means moving beyond him and toward a complete integration of all spheres of subjective activity in the overarching unity of life. The more we move in this direction, according to Simmel, the more we see ourselves compelled to abandon the

---

[21] K, 76.   [22] WuK, 157.   [23] K, 38.   [24] K, 40.   [25] K, 46.

systematic notion of the world cherished by Kant and to acknowledge the erratic, inherently opaque nature of the world-forming energy of subjective life.

According to Simmel, another sphere in which Kant's discoveries are at odds with Kant's own doctrines is that of practical philosophy. On the one hand Kant does face the complexity and multifariousness of our practical life. On the other he restricts his inquiry to actions that have *moral* value, virtually ignoring an overwhelming number of actions that either flow from the acknowledgment of different values or spontaneously emerge from the deepest, instinctive strata of our human nature. This is why, to a modern reader, Kant's practical philosophy shows a "peculiar lack of vitality [*Unlebendigkeit*] and a foreignness towards the deepest roots of our essence."[26] The method of generalizing into a maxim an action that has been previously isolated from the totality of life in which it belongs is the most glaring example of Kant's ultimate indifference to life as a whole.[27] Acting morally seems to boil down to acting in a vacuum, whereby the reference to the totality of life – of which the single action is but an isolated manifestation – is suspended and the action in question is held up against an abstract principle of universality.

Simmel suggests that ethics should be more ambitious and "show that the 'ought,' although ideal, nonetheless stands over against life. The fact of life's continuity only makes possible to derive parts from the whole rather than the whole from its parts."[28] In other words, to assess the moral worth of a life on the basis of isolated actions mistakes the holistic nature of life for a mere aggregate of atomized episodes abstractly related to an 'ought' foreign to life. Contrariwise, if practical philosophy made an effort to formulate the 'ought' confronting life in keeping with life's holistic nature, then a number of other values (aesthetic, social, religious, etc.) should be considered on par with moral value, and the overall 'worth' of practical life could not be simply derived from the summation of singular actions abstractly qualifying as moral. In a similar vein, Kant's wholesale dismissal of happiness as a viable criterion to assess a life's moral worth is blind to the fact that different people seek happiness in different ways and that this, far from being an indifferent psychological fact, reveals important features about what kinds of persons they are. Different sources of happiness define different kinds

[26] K, 155. [27] K, 140. [28] K, 142.

of happiness,[29] and not all of them are equal if we set out to assess a life's worth. It would be problematic at best to admit that a person who finds happiness in torturing animals, for example, is in no way different from a person who finds happiness in doing charitable work. The subjective feeling of gratification may be to some extent similar in both cases, but a philosophy concerned with the overall worth of practical life cannot be completely silent, as Kant's philosophy is bound to be, about the difference between these two ways of finding happiness. Simmel speculates that Kant's exclusive consideration of moral value in practical philosophy is due to his overall commitment to the encompassing influence of the intellect: other values, whose cultivation seem nonetheless germane to a worthy life, are definitely more recalcitrant to logical, intellectual treatment.

Life-philosophy thus sets for itself the task to recast the meaning of the transcendental tradition, thereby retaining Kant's fundamental ideas of subjectivity's world-forming power and its sovereignty over nature while discarding Kant's unilateral commitment to the intellect. In order to fully spell out the constitutive action of life in its complexity, it is crucial to consider the sphere of reality in which life most explicitly faces itself and its own products: history. Like nature, history is not an absolute reality but the result of a subjective process of formation. However, unlike nature, history is the place where life encounters itself.

The problems of the philosophy of history

In his book *Die Probleme der Geschichtsphilosophie*,[30] published for the first time in 1892 and republished in 1905 and 1907 in expanded versions, Simmel employs the key ideas of his interpretation of Kant to tackle the highly debated issue of history and its difference from natural science. As we will see in a later chapter, Husserl was quite enthusiastic about Simmel's work and lectured on it in the context of a working seminar in 1922. The book was expanded and revised in close

---

[29] See K, 156.
[30] G. Simmel, *Die Probleme der Geschichtsphilosophie. Eine erkenntnistheoretische Studie*, Gesamtausgabe, vol. 9, 227–419. Abridged English translation by G. Oakes, *The Problems of the Philosophy of History: An Epistemological Essay* (New York: The Free Press, 1977). Hereafter PPH when quoted from Oakes' translation and PGP when quoted from the German for passages not included in the English abridgement.

collaboration with Heinrich Rickert,[31] who apparently read early drafts of the work and gave Simmel helpful feedback. Nonetheless, the centrality of the notion of life marks a significant difference from the approach of the Southwestern thinker. The distinctive trait of history and the human sciences as opposed to the natural sciences for Simmel is the fact that they necessarily, albeit not sufficiently, deal with psychic phenomena:

> If history is not a mere puppet show, then it must be the history of mental processes. So the observable events that history describes are merely bridges that link impulses and volitional acts, on the one hand, and the emotional reactions that these external events produce, on the other.[32]

By way of placing mental life at the core of his understanding of history, Simmel is starting from the opposite theoretical side vis-à-vis Rickert and the Southwestern Neo-Kantians. His demarcation of the two fields of scientific inquiry invokes an initial ontological dichotomy: psychic life as opposed to inert natural matter. The decision to start with ontology rather than logical and methodological considerations sets a different philosophical agenda for Simmel: (1) he has to clarify the relationship between historical science and psychology, provided that the latter also deals with psychic phenomena; (2) on a broader scale, he has to clarify how psychic life relates to nature.

The emphasis on the psychic fabric of historical phenomena and, consequently, on the foundational relation between psychology and history[33] seems to make Simmel's philosophy vulnerable to the Southwestern Neo-Kantians' critique that psychology sets out to discover universal laws of the mind and is therefore indifferent to historical individuality. Psychic phenomena appear to unfold according to universal, natural-scientific causality, and they therefore seem to be irrelevant for scientifically grasping individuality. Simmel's proposal to overcome these difficulties consists in a double move. First, he proposes a metaphysical hypothesis concerning the ontological status of psychic phenomena as embedded in the unitary flux of individual lives. Second, he draws a distinction between the scientific interests of psychology and history that make the two disciplines complementary rather than

---

[31] See the *Editorial Report*, *Gesamtausgabe*, vol. 9, 425.   [32] PPH, 39.

[33] See PPH, 40: "If there were a nomological science [*Gesetzeswissenschaft*] of psychology, then the relationship between history and psychology would be the same as the relationship between astronomy and mathematics."

divergent; on Simmel's account, they enlighten each other mutually in the investigation of the complex reality of life. As for the metaphysical hypothesis, Simmel draws on the same distinction between law and event highlighted by Windelband in his *Rektoratsrede*:[34] laws regulate a certain material whose existence cannot be derived from the validity of the laws. In natural science, for instance, we must conceive of the universe as a fundamentally homogeneous "stuff" whose particular configurations in different spatiotemporal venues depend upon the validity of certain laws. The existence of the stuff that undergoes law-fully regulated differentiation, however, does not in the slightest depend on the validity of the natural laws but is, rather, presupposed by them. If we imagine the same set of laws regulating a different kind of funda-mental stuff, our picture of the universe would be different from the one we know. However, this difference would not depend on the influence of natural laws (which would remain identical in both cases) but on the different fabric of the fundamental stuff. Simmel speculates that some-thing similar could hold for psychic phenomena, so that universally valid psychological laws could nonetheless regulate a variety of funda-mentally heterogeneous individuals:

Consider the fact that matter as such has certain definitive, primary proper-ties. These properties – as we might put it – constitute the material world as a total entity. There is no sense in which this fact contradicts the universality of the laws of matter. On the contrary, it is a condition for their actual, empirical efficacy. In the same way, each mind could possess an original, primary quality. Like the material residue of matter, this quality could not be con-ceived as a nomological modification of some other quality that is even more primary: it would be a presupposition for the possibility of generally valid laws that apply to every mind in the same way. These laws would form the empirical domain of the mental. Clearly, these qualities could vary from one individual to another, but this variation would not affect the universality of the *laws*. Each *individual* mind would simply be an analog of the *entire* material world.[35]

The unfolding flux of mental phenomena would still be regulated by the same set of psychological laws in each individual but the inherence in the peculiar, unrepeatable life of *this* individual would bestow on each of her mental occurrences a radical individuality that no consideration of universal laws could erase. Simmel refers to this "psychological

---

[34] See Chapter 1.   [35] PPH, 41.

facticity" [*psychologische Tatsächlichkeit*] as the "substance of history"[36] [*Substanz der Geschichte*] in the same way in which matter is the substance of nature. Unlike matter, which can be considered homogeneous for the totality of nature, psychological facticity comes infinitely differentiated in individual subjects, whose personalities have an individual, unrepeatable fabric prior to all consideration of causal psychological laws. If this picture is accepted, then the reference to psychic phenomena as the substance of history does not necessarily efface individuality from view. Rather, individuality is built into the ontological fabric of life prior to its differentiation into a variety of causally regulated psychic phenomena.

Simmel, however, does not intend to collapse the distinction between history and psychology outright, in a positivistic fashion. Even though, overall, they deal with the same sphere of phenomena, psychology and history have different foci. They set out to investigate different dimensions or components of psychic phenomena:

The interest in a psychic occurrence is not necessarily a psychological interest. For psychology, an occurrence is essential merely because it is psychic; psychology does not devote any interest to its *content*, which is carried by the psychic energy. Obviously we know about the <psychic> process only by virtue of the contents that are or have been present in consciousness; only, from a psychologist's point of view, the accent falls on the dynamic of this coming and going; the content would be indifferent to him if it were separable from this realization or production through psychic energies... For history, instead, the point is not so much the *unfolding* of the psychological contents but rather the psychological unfolding of the *contents*... In this way history is somehow a medium between the logical, purely objective consideration of the contents of our psyche and psychology, the purely dynamic consideration of the psychic movement of contents.[37]

When a historian examines Napoleon's motivations as he moved with his troops towards Waterloo, she is not so much concerned with the unfolding of motivating representations in Napoleon's individual consciousness but rather in the 'logical' connections obtaining between them that make his historical deeds understandable. Similarly, she considers the growing discontent leading a people to rebel against their sovereign exclusively in its objective connection to the subsequent fact of the revolution, regardless of its undeniable status as a psychic

[36] PGP, 236.   [37] *Ibid.*

fact. Conversely, the psychologist is not interested in the objective concatenation of psychic contents (e.g., discontent brings about frustration, which brings about political unrest, which brings about a revolution) but rather in the lawfully regulated unfolding of psychic states (say, how the increasing intensity of a certain emotion eventually triggers a certain action).[38]

Simmel shows with compelling examples that the historian constantly operates within the framework of countless 'psychological aprioris,' the validity of which she must assume if historical facts are to be clarified and explained. For instance, consider the following argument: the Hebertists, who supported Robespierre during the first phases of the French Revolution, eventually became estranged from him *because* they felt they were in a subordinate position.[39] When we accept such an argument as a sound historical explanation, we assume the validity of a psychological a priori, according to which a group of people who sees a formerly cherished leader gaining too much power and consensus will tend to withdraw their support because they feel subordinate. Every book of history is shot through with 'explanations' of this kind that refer implicitly to some psychological laws the validity of which is assumed a priori. This is true in our everyday interaction with other human beings. If a colleague at work looks unusually absent-minded and despondent and somebody tells us that he is having troubles at home, we accept this as a reasonable explanation of his behavior, thereby assuming as a valid psychological law that troubles affecting a person's private life will have a negative impact on her overall capacity to be focused and productive. The series of observable manifestations of that person's behavior will be woven together and brought to an intelligible unity on the basis of this a priori assumption. Incidentally, we are much more flexible and approximate in our a priori assumptions concerning mental life than in those concerning physical nature. If we

---

[38] The contrast between the contents of life and the process of life occupy predominantly Simmel's late reflections and can be considered the crux of his metaphysics of life. See, for instance, G. Simmel, *The View of Life: Four Metaphysical Essays with Journal Aphorisms* (University of Chicago Press, 2010), hereafter VL. Simmel talks about a "reaching out of the life process beyond each one of its identifiable contents" (VL, 76) and points out how "[n]o single content that has risen to the level of being formulated in consciousness absorbs the psychic process entirely into itself; each one leaves a residue of life behind it that knocks on the door it has shut, as it were" (*ibid.*).

[39] See PPH, 47–48.

observed a sudden increment of productivity and dedication in an otherwise rather laid-back colleague and somebody told us that he is having troubles at home, we would accept the explanation that his change of behavior denotes a different way of coping with his difficult situation. In this case, we would be ready to assume the a priori validity of a completely opposite psychological law: a person who is having troubles in his private life will tend to focus more on his work in order to distract himself or compensate. This is evidence of the complex nature of the a priori that undergirds our experience of psychic phenomena. For Simmel, history as a science borrows this a priori from psychic experience, as it were, and, with this foundation, addresses more intricate phenomena such as groupings, parties, nations, and the like. These entities are treated like personalities in their own right and are understood with the tools of psychological insight. We talk, for instance, of a nation's indignation at the corruption of its leaders or of the joy of a city over the victory of its local football team.

With his analyses, Simmel manages to circumvent successfully the difficulties raised by the Southwestern Neo-Kantians and to offer a convincing argument for the necessity of considering the ontological specificity of life-related phenomena as the criterion for demarcation of different kinds of science. Psychic phenomena are not only the substance of history: they are the paradigm to which we constantly refer in order to make scientific sense of more complex, supra-individual historical objects.

However, it could be replied that unless one is willing to revive traditional forms of substance dualism, psychic life also participates in the encompassing causality of nature. Thus, Simmel owes some explanation of how the ontologically peculiar province of life fits in the natural world. Does life escape natural causality? If so, is there a peculiar set of laws that govern history as the overarching interweaving of psychic lives? Simmel tackles these important questions in the second section of his book devoted to a discussion of the notion of 'historical law.' The possibility of discovering laws of history analogous to those of nature had been the dream of positivistic social thought from Comte onwards. This idea found its most emphatic assertion in Marx and his conviction that the development of history follows strict economical laws, the validity of which transcends the intentions of individual historical subjects. Simmel, however, is extremely skeptical of such claims. He unconditionally defends the continuity between nature and life, but precisely for this reason, refuses to admit a *special* set of laws for psychic life and history; he explains:

> All of human history is nothing more than a piece or part of the total cosmos. Therefore, the development of each phase of history is dependent upon innumerable conditions. The causes or motive forces of these conditions do not lie within the historical phase itself. They are not limited or defined by the concept of history, nor can they be deduced from this concept. The course of human history is not like a self-contained chapter of a book in which only the beginning and the end are implicated within the general forces of the cosmos that influence them; on the contrary, between the course of history and these cosmic forces there is a perpetual relationship of exosmosis and endosmosis. As a result, history acquires properties which have causes that lie beyond history itself. It follows that these causes cannot be deduced from the most exact knowledge of the course of history.[40]

In this sense, observable historical phenomena are infinitely complex bundles of underlying causalities, whereby elements stemming from the most diverse provinces of reality commingle. Simmel warns the enthusiasts of law-based explanation that if we really were to be serious with the notion of causal lawfulness in the sphere of psychic and historical reality, we would have to break down all historical phenomena into all their underlying constituents, including the overwhelming amount of concomitant natural phenomena factoring into them. Something like a historical battle[41] would only be understood if we were able to track down in detail the psychological condition of every single soldier; furthermore, we would have to consider all physiological and climatic components at play. Once this impossible ascertainment of micro-facts had been carried out, we would have to figure out a complex formula to calculate the outcome of the battle. This ideal would render historical understanding utterly impossible.

In more contemporary language, one could say that since there is no closure to the domain of psychic life and history, that is, since both of them are rooted in the causality of nature, no specific kind of law-based explanation can be advocated for them. This does not mean, however, that we have to give up explanations and references to law altogether when we deal with psychological-historical phenomena. Instead, we only have to be aware of the merely hypothetical (meaning, revisable

---

[40] PPH, 125.   [41] See PPH, 135.

in principle) and approximate nature of all our explanations: "Laws of nature are only valid for simple or constitutive elements. For this reason, therefore, laws of history have an approximate or relative significance."[42] Simmel anticipates positions in contemporary philosophy of mind that deny the existence of specifically mental causation, granting that all causal powers reside in the sphere of physical nature.[43] Thus, what appears to us as genuinely psychic or historical causality is nothing but the outward manifestation of an infinitely complex summation of micro-causalities ultimately rooted in nature.

Every individual life (a person) as well as every supra-individual life (e.g., a community), on Simmel's account, can be considered an aggregate of endlessly unfolding mental events centered on an unfathomable point of radical individuality. This fountain (*Quellpunkt*) of life, however, is fully integrated in the natural world and co-determined by its laws and occurrences. It bestows its own peculiar, unrepeatable coloring to what would otherwise be just a series of very complex natural events of the genus 'psyche.' Every living individual represents a point of material dis-homogeneity in the fundamental homogeneity of natural matter.[44] This does not mean a difference in substance but a perturbation in the evenness of nature, as it were, one from which a series of individually colored psychic phenomena wells up and coalesces into the totality of a life. Simmel frequently uses the metaphor of "pulse-beats"[45] (*Pulsschläge*) to characterize the dynamic in which life creates its own contents and unfolds in them. The pulsating center of each individual personality, however, is nothing over and above the natural world. It is a fold of individuality in the midst of nature. Psychic phenomena (and at a higher level, historical phenomena) are natural phenomena bearing a distinctive mark of individuality that refers back to an unfathomable center.

As we will see in the next section, there are important similarities between Simmel's characterization of life and that of the other champion of *Lebensphilosophie*: Wilhelm Dilthey. Although his most crucial writings precede Simmel's chronologically, there is an important sense

---

[42] PPH, 133.

[43] See, for instance, J. Kim, *Physicalism or Something Near Enough* (Princeton University Press, 2005).

[44] Whether or not this is true of both human and non-human individuals would be a very interesting question on this point that, however, I cannot tackle in this book.

[45] PGP, 284.

in which Dilthey's philosophy is a further advancement systematically
for the understanding of the relationship between nature, psyche, and
history. Seeking a strong foothold in the reality of historical life, Dilthey
criticizes the application of theoretical models borrowed from natural
science, such as causality, to life-related phenomena. Following from
this realization of the inadequacy of causal explanations for a satisfying
understanding of life, which he shares with Simmel, Dilthey offers a
number of important insights into the way forward. The set of psychological aprioris operative in our understanding of history, advocated
but not fully articulated by Simmel, becomes for Dilthey the object of a
science yet to be developed – descriptive psychology.

A psychology tailored to the human sciences: Dilthey's *Ideen über eine beschreibende und zergliedernde Psychologie*

When Dilthey's *Ideen über eine beschreibende und zergliedernde
Psychologie*[46] came out in 1894, the research program it presented
shared little to nothing with what had meanwhile become mainstream
psychological investigation. At times, the book reads like a somewhat
odd and belated attempt to invert the already advanced process of
estrangement from the human sciences that characterized the psychology of his time. It is telling that Hermann Ebbinghaus (a former student
of Dilthey and a practicing experimental psychologist), in a vitriolic
review of the book,[47] does not even feel the need to argue against
Dilthey's views and proposals in any detail: he points out that the
elderly philosophy professor simply lacks the technical competence
required to talk about psychology at all. As a matter of fact, Dilthey
and his critic mean two completely different things by 'psychology.' For
Dilthey, the use of quantitative models by practitioners of experimental
psychology like Ebbinghaus is not wrong; rather, such models are

---

[46] W. Dilthey, *Ideen über eine beschreibende und zergliedernde Psychologie*, in
W. Dilthey, *Die geistige Welt. Einleitung in die Philosophie des Lebens. Erste
Hälfte: Abhandlungen zur Grundlegung der Geisteswissenschaften, Gesammelte
Schriften*, vol. 5 (Göttingen: Vandenhoeck & Ruprecht, 1924), 139–240.
Hereafter GS V. English translation by R. Makkreel and D. Moore, "Ideas for a
Descriptive and Analytic Psychology," in W. Dilthey, *Selected Works*, vol. 2,
Understanding the Human World (Princeton University Press, 2010), 115–210.
Hereafter SW 2.

[47] H. Ebbinghaus, "Erklärende und beschreibende Psychologie," *Zeitschrift für
Psychologie und Physiologie der Sinnesorgane* 9 (1896): 161–205.

simply uninteresting and barren. Dilthey arrives at this opinion because he looks at psychology through the eyes of a historian, seeking instruments to understand more deeply the multifarious world of human culture. Ebbinghaus and his peers, on the contrary, look at the discipline through the eyes of naturalists seeking for the missing link toward a total, unified understanding of nature that may include the psychic.

As the title suggests, Dilthey's *Ideen* is not the communication of already achieved scientific results but rather a cornucopia of proposals, critiques, historical surveys, rudimentary analyses, and anthropological remarks, all nested in a distinctively Kantian approach to the foundation of science. This point has, in fact, been downplayed in the existing Dilthey scholarship, for the most part influenced by later hermeneutics and narrative theory: Dilthey's *Ideen* is a Kantian work in which laying the foundation of a certain science means pinning down its constitutive categories while establishing its limits.[48] As I will argue shortly, the notion of *life* as introduced by Dilthey fulfills a double function, both furnishing for humanistic science its objects *and* marking its limits. Moreover, Dilthey's *Ideen* presents us with a decidedly foundational view of scientific inquiry, one in which the descriptive-analytical psychology he envisions "will become the foundation of the human sciences, just as mathematics grounds the natural sciences."[49]

Before we examine his work in some detail, it is appropriate to situate it in the trajectory of the present chapter. Dilthey, like Simmel, is a life-philosopher. With respect to the issue of the foundation of science this means that he gives priority to the ontological fabric of the *objects* of scientific inquiry over methodology. If humanistic-historical science differs from natural science, this is first and foremost because it investigates life-related phenomena as opposed to merely natural phenomena. Unlike Simmel, however, Dilthey does not ground this difference on metaphysical speculation concerning the fundamental individuality of 'psychic facticity.' For him, it is not enough to defend the individual-psychic character of history while conceding that "all of human history is nothing more than a piece or part of the total cosmos"[50] and is therefore governed by the same laws that govern nature. The psychic phenomena that constitute the historical world of culture, he holds,

---

[48] To my knowledge, the only commentator who stresses this point adequately is the above quoted J. de Mul, *The Tragedy of Finitude.*
[49] GS V, 193/ SW 2, 165.   [50] PPH, 125.

present themselves in experience in a way different from that of natural phenomena. Accordingly, the world of psyche is simply misconstrued when viewed in terms of natural causality. Dilthey is thus one step ahead of Simmel in the affirmation of the autonomy of the psychic sphere. Not only does he assert this autonomy but he also lays the groundwork for a novel way of investigating the psyche. As we will see, however, he oscillates between this insight and an anthropological-relativistic bias that stems from his preponderant interest in historical inquiry.

Natural-scientific thought, for Dilthey, works in a distinctive way: in order to explain natural phenomena, it posits a limited number of non-observable elements or constituents of these phenomena and then produces hypotheses concerning the laws that regulate the connection of such elements giving rise to what is phenomenally observable.[51] This is because natural phenomena present themselves as fundamentally disconnected at first. For instance, there is no immediately intelligible connection between the bubbling of the water on the stove and the heat it emanates. No directly observable connection exists between movement and temperature in the water. The fact that increment in temperature is concurrent with increment in bubbling suggests that the two phenomena may be related, but we do not immediately experience how or why. It is only when we posit the existence of molecules and thereupon advance thermodynamic hypotheses that initially disconnected phenomena enter into a meaningful connection we can understand. The connection in what is observed must be created in the first place by constructing hypotheses and positing non-observable elements. With this in mind, Dilthey remarks:

---

[51] This understanding of natural scientific thought is heavily influenced by Helmoltz's so-called theory of signs, which is designed to negotiate the gap between the merely subjective phenomenal world of experience and the purely quantitative world 'as it is in itself.' In a nutshell, Helmoltz operates according to a strong dualism between the world as it appears to the senses and the real world as it is portrayed by physics. Living in the first, we have no direct sensory access to the second. All that we know is that whenever we observe a modification in the phenomenal world of the senses a real modification is occurring in the real world of physics. The phenomenal modification thus stands as a *sign* of the real modification. On the basis of this sign relationship between the two worlds we can then set out to conjecture the nature of the real physical occurrences and the laws that regulate them. The verification of our hypotheses about the physical world, however, is bound to remain indirect.

Now, however, the question arises whether it is legitimate for explanative psychology to transfer the way the natural sciences form hypotheses to the domain of psychic life and supplement what is given with a causal nexus.[52]

The answer, for Dilthey, has to be in the negative. In fact, the reduction to a limited number of non-observable elements and the construction of an underlying causal law, posited hypothetically, are *motivated* in natural-scientific thought by the characteristics of our experience of natural phenomena. The facts of natural science present themselves to consciousness "as phenomena and as given in isolation,"[53] that is, they are experienced as initially disconnected manifestations of a reality that lies behind them. On the contrary, psychic facts "are given *originaliter*, from within, as real, and as a living continuum or nexus";[54] they are not experienced as manifestations of a hidden reality but are themselves reality. Moreover, they are not disconnected but are always part of a broader psychic life in which they are meaningfully integrated with other psychic facts. "Life presents itself everywhere only as a continuum or nexus."[55]

The psychic life-process is originally and everywhere – from its most elementary forms to its highest – a unity. Psychic life does not grow together from parts; it is not composed of elements; it is neither a composite nor a product of cooperative sensory or affective atoms; it is originally and always a comprehensive unity.[56]

This means that we do not need to integrate our experience of the psychic with hypotheses and non-observable elements in order to render it intelligible. The connections and transitions from state to state through which our psychic life unfolds are always directly experienced [*erlebt*] and do not require the intervention of theoretical constructions. This is why Dilthey insists on his famous dictum: "Nature we explain, but psychic life we understand."[57] Rather than expressing two distinct scientific tasks pertaining respectively to the fields of naturalistic and humanistic research, *erklären* and *verstehen* designate for Dilthey two fundamentally different ways of *responding* to natural and psychic facts occurring in our concrete experience. We respond to the facts of nature by trying to figure out their causes and connections with all sorts

[52] GS V, 142/SW 2, 117.   [53] GS V, 143/SW 2, 119.
[54] GS V, 143/SW 2, 119.   [55] GS V, 144/SW 2, 120.
[56] GS V, 211/SW 2, 182, translation modified.   [57] GS V, 143/SW 2, 119.

of hypotheses,[58] whereas we respond to psychic facts occurring in ourselves and other individuals with a mostly successful dynamic of understanding that does not require us to be especially inventive. The upwelling of a feeling of disgust after the perception of the funny smell coming from my fridge does not elicit from me special hypotheses and conjectures in order to be understood: the connection existing between the two psychic facts is immediately given in inner perception. To be precise, the two facts do not simply 'follow' one another: they are non-independent parts of a whole psychic nexus that we might label 'perceiving a disgusting smell.' Moreover, this episode is embedded in a broader nexus of life. This nexus would include, say, my bad habit of procrastinating before performing unpleasant yet necessary activities and my resolution to finally go ahead and clean the fridge. Nothing occurring in my psychic life or in the psychic lives of other human beings escapes this constant integration in an all-encompassing nexus. The decisive fact about psychic life, Dilthey writes, is that "*the transitions from one state to another and the productive influence that links them fall within inner experience. [...] The structural nexus is available in lived experience.*"[59]

If both psychic facts and the principles of their integration into a nexus are *experienced directly*, then the scientific task of psychology is that of a description and analysis of psychic life. Psychology should be conducted along descriptive lines in order to shed light on the *real* psychic life that we experience instead of construing an underlying psychic reality of which our experienced psychic life would be a mere phenomenon.

> By descriptive psychology, I understand a science that explicates constituents and their connection in terms of a single nexus that appears uniformly in all mature human psychic life – a nexus that is not inferred or postulated, but experienced. This psychology is thus the description and analysis of a nexus that is originally and always given as life itself.[60]

The classification and analysis of different classes of psychic occurrences envisioned by Dilthey, however, does not conclude the work of psychology. Considering Dilthey's proposal so far, we are once

---

[58] Incidentally, this kind of response is identical in both scientific and pre-scientific forms of thought.
[59] GS V, 206/SW 2, 177.   [60] GS V, 152/SW 2, 127.

more confronted with the problem of individuality, which is so fundamental in spelling out the difference between the world of nature and the world of *Geist*. The psychological method proposed by Dilthey is, in his words, "description and analysis of a fully developed and mature human type."[61] Accordingly, it grants an understanding of those structures and laws that govern the psychic life of all human beings at all times. However, the historical world is made of individuals, and the humanist is primarily concerned with the *differences* rather than the similarities of his objects of inquiry. As Simmel puts it:

There would be no reason to doubt that the same laws governing the association and reproduction of ideas, differences in sensibility, the development of volition, apperception, and suggestibility would apply with equal validity to Nero and Luther and to Jesus and Bismarck.[62]

However, what is at stake in historical inquiry is not what makes Nero, Luther, Jesus, and Bismarck similar but rather what makes them different, or, better, unique. In light of this point, the descriptive psychology envisioned by Dilthey seems no better in providing a foundation for the human sciences than the much-scorned experimental psychology. Both seem indifferent to individuality and incapable of accounting for its origin. As we saw above, Simmel circumvented this problem by attributing a priori status to individuality. According to his metaphysical hypothesis, the mark of individuality belongs to each individual life prior to all consideration of the laws that regulate its unfolding. Dilthey, on the contrary, cannot adopt a hypothesis at this point; otherwise, he would be working in exactly the same way that he criticized in his experimentalist opponents.

His move is rather to present his descriptive psychology as just the first stage of inquiry into the human psyche. The second stage would be what he labels a "comparative psychology"[63] which would describe and render scientifically intelligible the differences existing between historical individuals. The wish to illuminate and classify individual differences is actually the rationale behind Dilthey's approach to

---

[61] GS V, 213/SW 2, 184.   [62] PPH, 41.

[63] See W. Dilthey, *[Über vergleichende Psychologie.] Beiträge zum Studium der Individualität*, in GS V, 241–316. English translation by E. Waniek, "[On Comparative Psychology.] Contributions to the Study of Individuality," in SW 2, 211–284.

psychology. Since it is guided primarily by an anthropological interest,[64] Dilthey's psychology views the study of uniformities in the human
psyche as a means to an end – a scientific grasp of individuality. This
follows from his understanding of individual differences as *purely
quantitative*, as different *combinations* of the fundamentally homogenous ingredients of a normally developed human psyche. As he argues
towards the end of the *Ideen*:

> The uniformity of human nature manifests itself in the fact that the same
> qualitative determinations and forms of connection appear in all human
> beings (where no abnormal defects exist). But the *quantitative relationships
> in which they manifest themselves differ widely from one another; these
> differences are linked into ever-new combinations, and here we find the initial
> basis for distinguishing individuality. What appears to us in terms of [distinct]
> qualitative characteristics* can be derived from these quantitative differences
> and their relationships.[65]

The task of comparative psychology would be then to identify the "rules
that limit the possible ways in which various quantitative proportions
can co-exist."[66] On this basis, Dilthey views the whole psychic world of
history as endless variation of the same fundamental theme: humanity.
Not only individual human beings but also the more complex supra-
individual entities studied by historians are considered to be combinations of the same set of psychic ingredients: "*Human races, nations,
social classes, professions, historical stages, individualities*: all these
further delineate individual differences within what is uniform in
human nature."[67]

Notions like 'nexus,' 'lived-experience,' 'connection,' 'understanding
vs. explaining,' 'unity,' and the like, which we have so far explored,
constitute the categorial apparatus for the foundation of psychology,

[64] In a manuscript stemming from the same years of the *Ideen* Dilthey is adamant
that "following the old manner of speaking, [descriptive psychology] can be also
designated empirical, as anthropology." W. Dilthey, *Gesamtplan des zweiten
Bandes der Einleitung in die Geisteswissenschaften. Drittes bis sechstes Buch
("Berliner Entwurf") (ca. 1893)* in W. Dilthey, *Grundlegung der Wissenschaften
von Menschen, der Gesellschaft und der Geschichte. Ausarbeitungen und
Entwürfe zum zweiten Band der Einleitung in die Geisteswissenschaften (ca.
1870–1895), Gesammelte Schriften*, vol. 19 (Göttingen: Vandenhoeck &
Ruprecht, 1982), 308. Hereafter GS XIX.
[65] GS V, 229–230/SW 2, 199–200.   [66] GS V, 230/SW 2, 200.
[67] GS V, 236/ SW 2, 205.

which itself provides a foundation for the whole universe of human science. As stated above, however, there is a further Kantian element in Dilthey's conception of psychic life and history: the fact of life itself marks the inner limit of all historical investigation and, in fact, of all intelligibility.

The unfathomableness of life

Dilthey's thought oscillates between two opposites, rendering any definitive statement about his innermost philosophical intention extremely difficult. On the one hand, he is optimistic about the capacity of descriptive psychology to elucidate the basic constituents and dynamics of the human mind. This goes so far as to provide a solid foundation for the vast scientific class of the human sciences. On the other hand, he constantly stresses a sort of duality within the psyche, a duality that renders merely speculative any conjecture about the source of its unity. In other words, if on the one hand 'life' is for Dilthey the encompassing title for all psychic facts observable in the nexus of inner experience, on the other he insistently counterposes this manifest dimension of life (also labeled 'consciousness') with a hidden, obscure life-source that undergirds every psychic process and eludes every attempted grasp in discursive thought.[68] Therefore, psychology is certainly the science of life, but at the same time it is 'only' a science of the surfaces of life. What we can scientifically say about psychic experience only brushes the tip of the iceberg; though we experience the very core of our psychic life, this core escapes our discursive elucidation. As a famous passage of the *Ideen* points out:

We cannot create a nexus that exceeds the one given to us. It is impossible for the science of psychic life to go behind the nexus that inner experience provides us. Consciousness cannot go behind itself. The nexus of inner experience within which thinking functions, and from which it begins, and on which it depends, is for us an ineradicable presupposition. Thinking

---

[68] This claim should not be conflated with later psychoanalytic claims about the existence of a so-called unconscious. Whereas for Freud the unconscious (1) has its own lawfulness, (2) cannot be experienced, and (3) can be studied indirectly, for Dilthey the 'life-source' that underlies our conscious activity can *only* be experienced [*erlebt*], but we cannot advance any meaningful hypothesis about the laws governing it.

cannot go behind its own actuality, behind the actuality from which it emerges.[69]

Discursive thought sprouts up, as it were, on the basis of a continuity of life that it cannot itself represent exhaustively with its own conceptual means. This characterization of the unfathomable 'center' of life keeps with the anti-intellectualistic concern of *Lebensphilosophie*:

A bundle of drives and feelings – that is the core of our psychic structure. The interest of feeling that this core imparts to the play of impressions brings them to our attention as perceptions, relates them to memories, and allows chains of thought to be formed resulting in either the enhancement of existence or suffering, fear, and anger. In this way, all the depths of our being are moved; and from here, as pain goes over into longing, and this then into desire, or into another series of emotional states of mind, there emerge the voluntary acts.[70]

This way of construing the deep-lying source of unity of our manifest psychic life is markedly Kantian. Life as such is presented as a sort of psychic 'thing in itself,' something unknowable beyond its own phenomenal appearance, i.e., its own objectifications in cultural products, expressions, and so forth. However, unlike the Kantian thing in itself for natural scientific thought – that is, the unknowable source of impressions – we do have an experience of life. In fact, an intuitive, non-discursive *experience* of the unfathomable depths of life is all we have. Life does not properly manifest itself: it can be felt, experienced affectively, but not observed and conceptualized after the manner of its own psychic products. So to speak, life does not come to genuine manifestation in its own products; it only shines through them *per spaeculum*. This experience of life [*Lebenserfahrung*] can never be fully translated into concepts but only expressed through metaphors, rites, images, i.e., through the language of art, religion, and metaphysics:

From this unfathomableness of life it follows that life can only be expressed in a metaphorical language [*Bildersprache*]. Acknowledging this fact, clarifying its reasons, and developing its consequences would be the beginning of a philosophy that would really do justice to the great phenomena of poetry, religion, and metaphysics, since it would grasp the ultimate unity at their core. They all speak out the same life, one in images, the other in dogmas, the other in concepts.[71]

---

[69] GS V, 194/SW 2, 166.   [70] GS V, 206/SW 2, 177.   [71] GS XIX, 307.

Furthermore, the idea of a principle that grants unity to our psychic life is clearly an offshoot of the Kantian doctrine of the transcendental ego. Similarly to Kant, Dilthey considers the contrasts between an empirical consciousness (the psychic facts whose connection we experience) and the 'transcendental' source of its unity (the life-source). For Dilthey, too, the ultimate principle is a principle of unification, but it is infinitely more complex than Kant's transcendental ego. It does not stand over and above the process of consciousness but rather underneath. It does not simply grant the belonging of all representations to one and the same stream, but it also governs the succession of these representations with respect to their content and is responsible for their 'affective' coloring. In conclusion, for Dilthey, in a Neo-Kantian fashion, human science has an 'external' border in what is other *than* itself, i.e., naturalistic research based on disconnected outer experiences. On the other hand, however, and in a more traditionally Kantian sense, humanistic research also has a limit in what is other *in* itself, i.e., life as the unknowable source of unity of the psyche.

One final point is left to address: the relationship between the unfathomable depth of life and nature. Incidentally, this is the point where a certain *distance* from the Kantian tradition and a certain proximity to positivism and evolution theory becomes perceptible in Dilthey's thought.[72] The discursively ungraspable life-source is, so to speak, *the point of tangency between psyche and nature*. His characterization of the 'center' of life as consisting of drives and instincts reveals that the more we approach the propulsive center of life, the more (paradoxically) we distance ourselves from what is properly psychic and get closer and closer to nature. As Dilthey writes in his later work, *The Formation of the Historical World in the Human Sciences*: "We ourselves are nature, and nature is at work in us, unconsciously, in dark drives."[73]

The presence of dark drives, instincts, feelings, and other irrational forces at the core of our life (a presence we can only experience and not conceptualize) is, for Dilthey, a symptom of the workings of nature 'within' us. The picture of the relationship between psychic life and nature thus becomes more complex than it is for Simmel, who simply

---

[72] For a convincing discussion of this point see H.-H. Gander, *Positivismus als Metaphysik. Voraussetzungen und Grundstrukturen von Diltheys Grundlegung der Geisteswissenschaften* (Freiburg and Munich: Alber, 1988). Here, 253–254.

[73] GS VII, 80/SW 3, 101.

considered psychic life as an individually colored natural phenomenon. For Dilthey, nature 'gives the input' at the lower strata (instincts, sensations), but, as soon as the input is taken in, it becomes integrated into a system organized according to patterns of meaning and significance, categorically different from natural causality. All that we have is, so to speak, a hunch that the propulsive force steering our conscious life lies in nature. However, we cannot see the transition occurring between merely natural (i.e., physiological) dynamics and basic psychic facts because even the most rudimentary, detectable psychic fact already presupposes this transition. In other words, the point of tangency between mere physiology and genuine psyche recedes the more we try to approach it via psychological observation. The more we analyze the fabric of our psychic life in its most elementary manifestations, the more we leave the province of psychology behind and approach those of physiology and biology. This sheds light upon the revealing and unexpected appreciation of the authoritative experimentalist Wilhelm Wundt in *Ideen*. Even though Wundt espouses the kind of natural-scientific method in psychology that Dilthey rejects, Dilthey praises him for revising the hard-line psychophysical parallelism defended by most experimental psychologists of his time:

He then went on to indicate "that psychophysical parallelism is a principle whose application extends only to the elementary mental processes, to which definite movement-processes run parallel, not to the more complicated products of our mental life, the sensible material of which has been formed and shaped in consciousness, nor to the general intellectual powers which are the necessary presuppositions of these products."[74]

With his characterization of drives, instincts, and impressions as the workings of nature at the core of our psychic life, Dilthey comes very close to Wundt's position that not all of psychic life runs parallel to physiological events. However, at its most basic, psychic life is anchored to nature, even though this anchorage is not discursively thinkable and cannot be considered a sufficient explanation of the complexity of psychic life.

All things considered, there is an equivocal, Janus-faced meaning of 'nature' in Dilthey's thought. On the one hand nature is, in a Kantian

---

[74] GS V, 167/SW 2, 141–142. See W. Wundt, *Human and Animal Psychology*, trans. J. E. Creighton and E. B. Tichener (London: George Allen, 1912), 447.

sense, the phenomenal world that appears in outer perception and stands over against the inner world of our own psychic life. On the other nature is – like Goethe's Mothers – the primordial matrix of this psychic life itself, what gives it impetus and continuity while eluding every attempted conceptual grasp. How these two senses of nature can be reconciled in Dilthey's thought is admittedly hard to see.

Recapitulation and transition

In these first two chapters, I presented and assessed the theoretical problems connected to a demarcation of different groups of sciences as developed in Neo-Kantianism and *Lebensphilosophie*. As I hope became clear over the course of the presentation, both approaches to the problem lead straight to the question of ontology. For the Southwestern Neo-Kantians, ontology is broken down into at least two provinces: empirical being and, in a broad sense, meaning, as adumbrated by Rickert's distinction between *Wahrnehmungen* and *Verstehungen*. However, further developments within the school led to an acknowledgment of the constitutive function of psyche for the institution of meaning and, in particular, for the structuring of abstract meaning-configurations into concrete historical objects. In the conceptual apparatus of the school, however, there are no viable resources to articulate a constitutive notion of psyche. With its picture of the world rigidly split up into *Sein* (being) and *Geltung* (meaning, validity), Southwestern Neo-Kantianism simply has no room for anything psychical outside empirical being.

With life-philosophy, we encountered a different approach to the same issue. Simmel and Dilthey anchor their demarcation of the sciences primarily to their material content: the human sciences investigate psychic and life-related facts, whereas the natural sciences only investigate mechanistic and lifeless phenomena. By placing the notion of life in the center of their inquiry and contrasting it to the notion of nature, Simmel and Dilthey seem to offer a more convincing account of the differences existing between the human and the natural sciences. However, they run into dire difficulties as they try to relate back to nature the life that they carefully distinguished from it at the outset. For both of them, the ontological distinction drawn at first seems to be negated in the end by the assertion of the fundamental continuity of life and nature. For Dilthey, in particular, we saw how this ambiguity results in a problematic duality in the very concept of nature. On the one hand, nature is the phenomenal, 'external' world alien to our inner life. On the other, it is the matrix of life itself. Life, whose autonomy he asserted so emphatically against naturalistic psychology, thus ends up tightly compressed between two dimensions of nature.

The question remains open whether the pluralistic ontology advocated by Rickert and required by the existing plurality of the sciences can be given a foundation that preserves the autonomy of the psychic without thereby reverting to a sort of Cartesian substance dualism. In other words, an understanding of the psychic is required that does not leave it undertheorized between two extremes – of empirical, causally regulated being and unreal, intellectual meaning. In the next chapter, I will move to a more systematic approach and introduce Husserlian phenomenology into the debate. I will attempt a comparison between the notion of standpoint, as articulated by both the Neo-Kantians and Dilthey, and the notion of attitude [*Einstellung*], as introduced by Husserl. While it is generally accepted that this notion is crucial to Husserl's understanding of science, its systematic place in the debate presented thus far has never been explored satisfactorily. As I endeavor to show in the next chapters, the central notion of transcendental subjectivity made available by the phenomenological *epoché* offers a radical way to move beyond the problems left unsolved or unaddressed by the Neo-Kantians and the life-philosophers – a movement towards a truly autonomous ontology of the 'psyche.'

3 | Standpoints and attitudes: scientificity between Neo-Kantianism and Husserlian phenomenology

Natural science does not simply describe and explain nature;
it is a part of the interplay between nature and ourselves;
it describes nature as exposed to our method of questioning.

W. Heisenberg[1]

Without being aware of it and without being rigorously systematic about it, we exclude the Subject of Cognizance from the domain of nature that we endeavor to understand.

We step with our own person back into the part of an onlooker who does not belong to the world, which by this very procedure becomes an objective world.

E. Schrödinger[2]

In this chapter, we shall discuss the Neo-Kantian notion of standpoint (*Standpunkt*) and the Husserlian notion of attitude (*Einstellung*).[3] Within their respective philosophical systems, these two notions underpin a non-dogmatic foundation for science. Both for the Neo-Kantians and for Husserl, a non-dogmatic foundation of science – that is, an account of scientificity according to which scientific knowledge does not consist in mirroring objects of study (i.e., a copy-theory of cognition) – amounts to a philosophical theory according to which objects of knowledge and forms of cognition are thoroughly correlated. Cognition does not grasp readily available objects that exist independently of it. Rather, it contributes by carving out different objective domains and the objects encountered therein.

---

[1] W. Heisenberg, *Physics and Philosophy* (New York: Prometheus Books, 1999), 81.

[2] E. Schrödinger, *What is Life?* (Cambridge University Press, 1992), 118.

[3] I presented an earlier version of this chapter on April 28, 2011 at the Husserl Circle Meeting at Gonzaga University in Florence, Italy. I would like to thank all the participants, in particular Sebastian Luft, for their helpful comments and critiques.

In the first two chapters, we sketched the battle lines of the debate concerning a genuinely philosophical classification of science. Now let us focus more specifically on the theoretical devices employed by the participants in the debate. We shall see that the differences between the different schools are not as clear as they appeared initially. The battle lines begin to blur as these otherwise disparate thinkers strive towards a common goal of removing the naivety of empirical research via a philosophical consideration of the tight link existing between the objects and the subjects of scientific activity.

This context proves a propitious moment to introduce a first, crucial notion in Husserl's phenomenology: the notion of attitude. Attitude is a key to properly understanding both the fundamental differences existing among empirical sciences and the place of phenomenology itself in the universe of scientific activity. As we shall see, Husserl defines his phenomenology first and foremost in terms of a singular attitude. In doing so, he assumes – for good reasons – that the concept of attitude is fundamental, cutting across both phenomenological and non-phenomenological forms of scientific thought. Therefore, one must understand attitude in order to approach phenomenology in a theoretically adequate manner.

The Neo-Kantian 'standpoint' and the Husserlian 'attitude' cannot be reduced to the same *doctrine*. On the contrary, while homologous, the two concepts adumbrate differing accounts of what it means for the objects of cognition to correlate intrinsically with cognitive activity. The Neo-Kantians and Husserl both argue that the object of knowledge is not a dogmatically presupposed reality but a *constituted* entity, shot through with subjectivity, as it were. Neo-Kantian philosophy, however, has no account of what Husserlian phenomenology calls 'change of attitude' (*Einstellungswechsel*), a deficiency which results in insurmountable difficulties for the Neo-Kantian accounts of how *the same* object appears in different guises when we vary our cognitive standpoint towards it.

This gap in the Neo-Kantian concept of standpoint is a product of an exclusively formal understanding of transcendental subjectivity. As we saw in Chapter 1, this exclusivity precludes a fully convincing account of historical objectivity. Extending that discussion, the Neo-Kantians interpret a change in standpoint as a mere psychological fact pertaining to an empirical subject and thus irrelevant to epistemological inquiries. This neglect of changes in standpoint is a mistake. Husserl's discovery of transcendental subjectivity via the phenomenological reduction – a discovery that we shall retrace in greater detail in later chapters, but that must be anticipated here – makes clear that the phenomenon of *Einstellungswechsel* cannot be cast aside. For Husserl, a change of attitude assumes a transcendental-constitutive role that helps to disclose the intrinsically stratified nature of objects of knowledge. Beginning with the Neo-Kantian notion of standpoint, we shall move to Dilthey's proposed distinction between inner and outer experience (*innere und äußere Erfahrung*) and finish with a consideration of Husserl's view.

Kantian synthesis and the plurality of standpoints in Southwestern Neo-Kantianism

The distinctive trait of the Neo-Kantian movement as a whole is arguably its singular attention to the principle of synthetic cognition in Kant's philosophy. Their key philosophical principle is that cognition is never a copy of reality but always a synthesis.[4] Wilhelm Windelband summarizes this view and its consequences with great clarity, stating:

Kant's immortal accomplishment was the discovery of synthetic consciousness. Since the *Critique of Pure Reason* it is forever impossible for a mature philosophical consciousness to conceive of the world as 'given' and mirrored in consciousness as it appears to a naive [spectator]. Everything we hold for given already entails the work of our reason, and our cognitive right on things rests solely on the fact that we create them for ourselves in the first place. The necessity to appropriate in the first place the world that we shall experience depends on the fact that we can only experience a selection [*Auswahl*], and a selection in an ordered connection. The principle for such selection as well as for the order can only be sought within the structure of our consciousness.[5]

Rickert reaffirms his mentor's position in *Kulturwissenschaft und Naturwissenschaft* as follows:

[T]he part of reality that man can include in his concepts, and thus in his knowledge, is almost infinitesimally small when compared to what he must

---

[4] See W. Windelband, *Immanuel Kant. Zur Säkularfeier seiner Philosophie*, in *Präludien*, vol. 1 (Tübingen: Mohr Siebeck, 1914), 112–146. Here 125.
[5] W. Windelband, "Kulturphilosophie und transzendentaler Idealismus," in *Präludien: Aufsätze und Reden zur Philosophie und ihrer Geschichte*, vol. 2, 279–294. Here 282–283.

disregard. Accordingly, if in order to know reality we had to form a conceptual *copy* of it, we should be confronted with a problem that is essentially *insoluble*. Hence, if anything that has thus far been achieved may in any way claim to be considered knowledge, cognition will still have to be regarded [...] not as a *reflective* process by which "phenomena" are faithfully transcribed but as a process of *restructuring* the data of immediate experience; and, we may add, it is always a process involving the *simplification* of the actual multiplicity of reality itself.[6]

In other words, not only would a mirroring duplication of reality be epistemically redundant, it would be intrinsically impossible because consciousness could never conceptualize at once the overwhelming flow of data streaming in from the senses. We are bound to be selective, and selection necessarily implies criteria that cannot simply be extracted from the material undergoing selection. Brute reality has very little to tell a philosopher about the activity of consciousness organizing it into a theoretically understandable whole. Neo-Kantians learned this lesson especially from Kant's transition from the first to the second critique. Unlike the German Idealists, the Neo-Kantians did not feel obliged to overcome the putative fragmentation in Kant's philosophy and integrate its different parts into a continuous system. In fact, they considered the *dualism* between nature and freedom the most compelling insight in Kant's thought.

   Emil Lask expresses adamantly the Neo-Kantian interest in this dualism. Borrowing from the introduction of his early book on Fichte:

The fact that Kant postulated explicitly the *dualism of method*, i.e., the double type of treatment [*Behandlungsart*] of one and the same object also in the investigation of the life of the human race has been heeded too little [...] The same domain of reality is always at the same time nature and "reason", according to the method it is subjected to. However, in order to haul out the reason from the immediate given, one has to approach things already equipped with a measuring rod. In the midst of reality, indifferent towards values, one generates the object of investigation through the standpoint of investigation.[7]

As Lask clarifies in the rest of his introduction, it is only if we consider the human race from the point of view of freedom that we will be able to

---

[6] SH, 32–33, translation modified.
[7] E. Lask, *Fichtes Idealismus und die Geschichte, Gesammelte Schriften*, vol. 1. (Tübingen: Mohr Siebeck), 5–6.

pick out those elements that are relevant to a philosophical narrative about human history from the overwhelming and chaotic mass of events pertaining to human subjectivity.[8] It is worth noting that Lask – along with Husserl, but in opposition to Windelband and Rickert – espoused the idea that natural science does not simply run parallel to human science, but rather grows out of an 'artificial' (albeit fully motivated) abstraction from the world described and investigated by the humanist. In this sense, the world of nature is distilled out of the world of culture, neither prior to it nor simply constructed on its side. We shall expand on this point below.

Kant, however, only identified one deterministic standpoint for the cognition of the phenomenal world and the standpoint of freedom for the cognition of what he calls the noumenal world or the kingdom of ends. Neo-Kantian thinkers accept that there are several different standpoints within each domain. For instance, as Heinrich Rickert pointed out in countless works, we can distinguish between the value-free standpoint of natural science and the value-related standpoint of cultural science as two logically opposed, but equally legitimate, perspectives for a scientific investigation of the phenomenal world.[9] Furthermore, on the basis of this fundamental opposition, we can develop more sophisticated distinctions between subordinate standpoints falling under the two overarching categories of the natural and the historical. As Rickert points out, "the critical principle necessarily leads to pluralism."[10] In other words, once the myth of cognition as mirroring is dispelled, the path is open for a genuinely pluralistic conception of reason. It is only if we believe in an ultimate, residue-less correspondence between cognition and the world that we will pit different scientific methods against one another. Otherwise, we shall welcome any rationally patterned contribution to the investigation of reality.

Moving from this general epistemological framework to a more specific focus, we must ask: how can we define a standpoint? what holds it together? Contrary to what the ordinary meaning of the word 'standpoint' suggests, there is nothing capriciously subjective to standpoints. A standpoint is not a subjective opinion; rather a standpoint is exclusively identified by a definite theoretical goal and the coherent set

---

[8] *Ibid.* [9] See Chapter 1.
[10] Rickert, "Systematische Selbstdarstellung," *Philosophische Aufsätze*, 347–411. Here 356.

of concepts necessary to make that goal attainable. For the Neo-Kantians *a standpoint is an impersonal teleological construction.* Take, for instance, the standpoint of natural science. It can be defined first in terms of a goal, namely, universally valid cognition of natural phenomena. Once the goal is set, it can be proved (at least in a Kantian framework) that from the very notion of this goal a number of correlated principles necessarily follows. For instance, if we are to achieve universally valid cognition of nature, we need notions like causality and law. To adopt the standpoint of natural science means to think and experiment in the theoretical space established by such concepts. But this standpoint's 'logical' validity and coherence holds sway independently of the actual practice of natural science.

A further instance would be the ethical standpoint (today, usually called the standpoint of normativity). The ethical standpoint relies on notions such as 'ultimate ethical standard,' 'freedom,' and 'punishment and reward.' Regardless of whether an empirical subject adopts it or not, the ethical standpoint is teleologically oriented toward the assessment of actions in terms of good and evil, and this orientation entails a number of concepts like the above mentioned.

To cite one last example, the historical standpoint is oriented toward cognition of the individual (be it a historical personality, an institution, or a historical period), therefore necessitating notions such as value, relevance, and context. Again, this standpoint is an ideal construction, the validity of which rests solely on its internal articulation.

Most importantly, every standpoint necessarily includes an object amenable to investigation according to the standpoint in question. This insight is distinctive of transcendental philosophy. The object of knowledge is not dogmatically presupposed, but intrinsic to the process of knowledge itself.

Expanding on an example from Chapter 1, 'Renaissance studies' are the scientific investigations of the object 'Renaissance,' which is itself a construction based on the same kind of conceptuality employed in its scientific investigation. To say that the object 'Renaissance' is a construction does not mean that it is a figment of imagination or that it can be whatever one desires. Historians can make *genuine discoveries* about the Renaissance as much as biologists can make genuine discoveries about stem cells. 'Stem cells' and other such objects are components of the standpoint of natural science, or, more precisely, of the complex subordinate standpoint of natural science known as the biological standpoint. In order to see a cell and, furthermore, a stem cell (a cell that is capable of differentiating into a cell of various tissue types) in the lump of organic matter under our microscope, we need to approach it with very sophisticated conceptual tools. If we are tempted to believe that a stem cell is a more legitimate object than the Renaissance, this is because – a Neo-Kantian would argue – we have cultural and historical reasons for privileging natural scientific thought. After all, the knowledge we actually acquire about a stem cell is not knowledge of this or that particular stem cell, but of the abstract pattern governing the functions of stem cells. Ontologically speaking, such patterns are as 'unreal' as the Renaissance.

In summary, the Neo-Kantians conceive of standpoints as teleological constructions that define different domains of scientific activity. In a transcendental way they include the objects they are 'designed' to investigate. These objects are construed with the same categories that characterize the scientific descriptions and explanations falling under the standpoint in question.

Dilthey's response to Windelband: the distinction between inner and outer experience

In Chapter 2, we highlighted how life-philosophers such as Simmel and Dilthey prioritize a material distinction for a philosophical classification of the sciences. They consider the key distinction to be between physical phenomena and life-related phenomena. In the present context, it is appropriate to examine how they understand the mode of access to phenomena of these two groups. Dilthey gives a remarkably sophisticated account of how the natural world and the human world (*die geistige Welt*) come into view and, in so doing, provide working material to the natural and the human sciences, respectively. He articulates his position in the first part of the essay "Contributions to the Study of Individuality," which appeared in 1896 as a supplement to "Ideas for a Descriptive and Analytic Psychology" (1894).[11] Dilthey outlines here a critical response to Windelband's *Rektoratsrede*,[12] taking particular issue with its central theses that (1) methodology should be the primary

---

[11] For a discussion of Dilthey's "Ideas" see Chapter 2.
[12] For a discussion of Windelband's *Rektoratsrede* see Chapter 1.

criterion to classify the sciences and, therefore, that (2) psychology should be divorced from the humanities.

Dilthey begins by constructing an argument for classification criteria based on the distinction between outer and inner experience – a possibility that Windelband considered but summarily dismissed. Dilthey's reasoning is that if the widespread skepticism surrounding the notion of inner experience could be dispelled by way of a clear definition, then a reliable demarcation of sciences could be elaborated from the contrast between inner and outer experience. In his estimation, inner experience discloses the human world and outer experience discloses the world of nature. These two kinds of experience, however, are not unrelated – they both refer to broadly the same *facts*, although they carve out of these facts different material contents of knowledge. Moreover, inner experience is not an independent source of cognition but, instead, presupposes outer experience as its basis.

Dilthey proposes the following definition: "By *outer* or *sensory* perception I mean the process by which the impressions registered by the senses are combined into a whole that is distinct from the self."[13] In turn, outer perceptions are the building blocks of full-blown outer experience: "By *outer experience* I mean that complex of processes by which discursive thought brings one or several outer perceptions into a nexus of intelligibility that expands our cognition of the external world."[14] According to these definitions, outer perception can be characterized as a process of *externalization*. A certain array of sensory impressions is apprehended as a whole and projected outside of the self as manifesting an external object.[15] The externalizing process of outer perception is thus the doorway into the external world. The combination of multiple outer perceptions in discursive thought gives us outer *experience* properly speaking, that is, increments of knowledge concerning what lies outside ourselves.

Turning our attention from the externalized sensations of outer perception to our inner awareness of them gives rise to *inner perceptions*, which – if combined together by discursive thought – "are brought into a nexus that makes these facts of the human world more

---

[13] GS V, 243/SW 2, 213.   [14] *Ibid.*
[15] It should be noticed that from Dilthey's wording it remains unclear whether the externalized array of sensations should be considered coincident with the external object or a mere appearance of the external object.

intelligible and that expands the conceptual cognition of the inner world."[16] In this mode, inner perception and inner experience are defined by a suspension of the externalizing tendency associated with outer perceptions:

From all these outer perceptions and the resulting outer experiences, I distinguish the *reflexive awareness* that we possess of psychic processes or states mainly by the negative feature that we do not externalize them. Thus the concept of *inner processes* or *states* emerges as distinct from what is *external*.[17]

Dilthey's point is that for everything that we experience as happening (or having happened or about to happen) in the world around us, we can turn our attention inwards and focus on the given thought, emotion, desire, or feeling that the situation arouses in us. In so doing, we are not turning *away from* the external situation but are relating it to ourselves. This is the meaning of Dilthey's famous notion of *Erlebnis*. One could say that we are rather *broadening* the scope of what we experience, but it is critical to notice that this internal turn requires a fundamental reflexive modification of our standpoint. Dilthey insists that this shift of standpoint is not to be considered an entry into a mysterious intra-mental world: "After all, outer perceptions form the ever-present basis for inner perceptions as well, and even when our attention turns to an inner state or process, we remain conscious of its relation to images of objects."[18]

Moreover, inner experience has to constantly "cooperate with"[19] outer experience in order for us to transpose our sense of interiority to foreign subjects and to reconstruct the inner life from which all manner of artifacts in the human world originate.[20] Side remarks in Dilthey's analyses point out that the borders between inner and outer experience

---

[16] GS V, 245/ SW 2, 215. It is interesting to notice how this theory of reflexive awareness and the grasp of inner processes by a shift of attention come close to Brentano's account of self-awareness and the possibility to study psychic occurrences by a shift from the primary to the secondary object of consciousness (the conscious act itself). Brentano and Dilthey both studied under F. A. Trendelenburg (1802–1872), although to my knowledge the influences linking together the three eminent philosophers have never been the objects of scholarly studies.

[17] GS V, 243/ SW 2, 213.   [18] GS V, 244/SW 2, 214.

[19] GS V, 246/ SW 2, 215.

[20] A more thorough discussion of this point is offered in Chapter 6.

are somewhat fluid and, more importantly, that they can overlap in various ways. In philosophy, for example, forms of metaphysical idealism *à la* Berkeley can be seen as willful extensions of the standpoint of inner experience to the external world. Transcendental thinking, in Dilthey's psychological interpretation, is an attempt to "integrate the images of objects given in outer perception into the nexus of our facts of consciousness"[21] – that is, to start from outer perception and interrogate the regularities of inner experience that render outer perception possible in the first place.

Considering the general relations existing between inner and outer perception and their function of disclosing, respectively, the (inner) human and the (outer) natural world, Dilthey draws the following conclusion: "On the basis of the natural sciences, the human sciences study spiritual-cultural facts *as* manifest in objects of sense, the relations of these facts to each other and to physical facts" (emphasis added).[22] The key point of this passage is contained in the *as*. Dilthey maintains that if the inner life of consciousness remained entirely subjective – that is, if we had no notion of other subjects outside of ourselves and of their ability to shape the physical world – we would remain confined forever to the sphere of nature. The human sciences are necessitated by the fact that inner conscious life *manifests itself outside of our own mind*, projecting its plans and demands on the physical world. The notion of *Geist* in Dilthey's *Geisteswissenschaft* does not refer to the internal mental processes of individual subjects. It refers to conscious mental life "as manifest in objects of sense."[23] These objects are not ontologically distinguishable from mere material objects, but they compel us to invest them with an inner perspective. Dilthey writes eloquently:

By contrast to the natural sciences, the human sciences come into being because we are compelled to attribute psychic life to animal and human organisms. On the basis of their life-manifestations, we transfer to them an analogue of what is given to us in our inner perception.[24]

Thus, for Dilthey the difference between inner and outer experience is not absolute and does not entail a strict separation between an outer world of nature and an inner world of sense. Inner experience is an

---

[21] GS V, 246/ SW 2, 216.   [22] GS V, 248/ SW 2, 217.   [23] *Ibid.*
[24] GS V, 249/ SW 2, 218–219.

intensification of the reflexive awareness already present (but generally not attended to) in outer experience. Instead of focusing on situations in the outer world and attempting to gauge their objective content, inner experience focuses on the significance or relevance to life that these situations entail. This 'inward turn' is not a turn away from the external world, but an amplification of the subjective side of every experience of the world. This amplification is the basis for a disclosure of the human world – that is, the interconnected whole of experience and significance in which our human lives unfold.

Drawing on these considerations of the overall connectedness of the human world, the importance of the psychic experience constituting that world, and the extensions of psychic purposiveness into that world, Dilthey forcefully rejects the Windelband-Rickert position that methodological distinctions are the basis for a proper understanding of the human sciences. If this methodological criterion – termed 'idiographic' by Windelband and translated into the jargon of 'individualization' by Rickert – is taken to be the distinctive feature of human science, then it is unclear what to do with those sciences that aim at the discovery of universal regularities but do not treat mere natural facts.

Dilthey calls such sciences "systematic human sciences,"[25] citing linguistics, economics, and certain branches of sociology as exemplars. It seems that, following Windelband and Rickert, such sciences should be assigned to the natural-scientific camp. Ultimately, for them, only history fits the criterion of individualization, thus remaining the only 'human science' proper. But even in history Dilthey notes that the exclusive interest in the individual is far from obvious:

Those histories provided us by Polybius, Machiavelli, Montesquieu, Tocqueville, Taine and among us by Nitzsch, histories that search for uniformities in the way external conditions and historical forces effect individual historical phenomena, serve as disciplinary counter-instances against this abstract separation of the cognition of what is uniform and the description of what is singular.[26]

Rickert, seeing the merit in this criticism, formulates a response in his later book *Kulturwissenschaft und Naturwissenschaft* (1899). First, he points out that descriptions of uniformities and even laws in the human sciences are always a means to an end: they are carried out in order to

---

[25] GS V, 257/ SW 2, 226.   [26] GS V, 257/ SW 2, 226–227.

better understand individuals. This is true of Dilthey's descriptive-
analytic psychology, which is designed to provide the resources for a
better understanding of individual differences in the human world.
Second, Rickert points out that a combination of methodological criteria (nature/history) and material criteria (nature/culture) in the classification of the sciences admits of intermediate disciplines whose
methodological outlook is natural scientific, but whose subject matter
is value-laden. On this account, disciplines like linguistics should be
termed (somewhat awkwardly) 'natural sciences of culture,' as opposed
to 'natural sciences of nature' (such as physics) or 'historical sciences of
culture' (such as art history).

Further details of Rickert's response to Dilthey need not occupy us
here. The critical point is that, for Dilthey, an interest in regularities,
uniformities, and laws can be maintained in the sphere of inner experience. The work of the humanist implies the assumption of a different
standpoint, but this does not necessarily correspond to a change in one's
cognitive tasks and goals. Natural objects and supra-individual uniformities continue to appear in the field of inner experience. However,
they are transfigured by their connection with human agents and their
significance for life. The shift from the outer to the inner world discloses
two materially distinct provinces of reality without fracturing the continuity of our experience.

Lask's defense of a thoroughly material distinction

Emil Lask also makes definite contributions to the question of how we
access different fields of scientific inquiry and how different modes of
access constitute the objects thereby disclosed. While he endorses the
notion of standpoint articulated by Windelband and Rickert in his early
works, in later reflections he departs significantly from their position.
The broad strokes of Lask's later position can be reconstructed from
posthumously published drafts of *Zum System der Wissenschaften*[27]
and *Notizen zur Einteilung der Wissenschaften*[28] (mentioned in
Chapter 1). As will become clear in the final part of this chapter and
in later chapters of this book, Lask largely anticipates Husserl's position. There is no evidence, however, that Husserl ever read these notes,

---

[27] SW.   [28] NEW.

which means that the two thinkers reached virtually the same conclusions by separate paths.

The gist of Lask's position is that, contra Windelband and Rickert, "a purely logical meaning of nature must be absolutely denied."[29] As explained in Chapter 1, for Rickert a purely logical meaning of nature can be found in Kant's dictum that "*nature* is the *existence* of things, insofar as [*sofern*] that existence is determined according to universal laws."[30] According to this principle, the natural-scientific standpoint is applicable to *any kind of material* to the extent that every part of reality is in some aspects determined by universal laws. For Rickert, this is the distinctive feature of natural science *qua* generalizing method. Lask is extremely critical of this argument.[31] He insists: "The character of nature is not a product of the generalizing method but rather of a definite manner of consideration [*Betrachtungsweise*]."[32] Not only does Lask acknowledge, along with Dilthey, that a significant number of human sciences have a generalizing tendency, he also points out that the 'nature' studied by the natural sciences – far from being a merely formal concept – results from a deep alteration of the immediately given material of experience.[33] In this sense, he is not satisfied with an articulation of the relationship between natural and human sciences in which the two scientific disciplines merely run parallel to each other and are cut from the same primary experiential material. Accordingly, for Lask Dilthey's presentation of outer experience as the basis for the natural sciences reveals only half of the truth. The natural sciences are based on an *alteration* of the material delivered by outer experience and not on outer experience *tout court*.

Lask seeks to explain this alteration using the terms "devitalizing" (*ertöten*) and "quantifying tendency" (*quantifizierende Tendenz*). As we know from Chapter 1, he is committed to what he calls a two-elements theory based on the *Urverhältnis* of empirical being and validity. A halo of validity (or value) surrounds the multifarious infinity of 'materials' such that different ways of knowing are merely different

---

[29] NEW, 272.

[30] Kant, *Prolegomena to Any Future Metaphysics that will be able to come forward as a Science*, 89.

[31] He writes polemically in a comment on Rickert: "Always [the] argument [that] since *all* empirical reality can be treated according to the natural-scientific method there can be no difference in the material!" NEW, 269.

[32] SW, 243.　　[33] See SW, 242.

ways of attending to the categorially illuminated material. What appears first and foremost in our transactions with the world is not pure sensuous material ready for natural scientific treatment, but, rather, "sensibility pervaded by value" (*wertdurchdrungene Sinnlichkeit*).[34] Appropriating language from the tradition of life-philosophy, Lask goes on to argue that sensuous material is originally 'enlivened' by its value-pervadedness and thereby correlates with *life* rather than with the intellect alone. Sensuous materials in their original appearance present themselves as substrates for values – for life-related configurations of categorial meaning.[35]

The 'manner of consideration,' or attitude, characteristic of natural science, is not a mere focus on sensuous material but a "ripping out of the sensuous, a rescission of the connections, a revocation of their substrate-character."[36] Sensuous material is not just attended to by natural science. It is first and foremost isolated from the living context of validity in which it originally inheres. This is why "the methodological presupposition for purely empirical natural science is then the artificial ripping out and devitalizing [*Ertötung*] of the sensuous."[37] Although generalization is admittedly a distinctive feature of natural science, "one should not simply take one's point of departure in generalization, rather, only the generalizing *in the devitalized sphere* is natural-scientific."[38] Nature and outer experience figure prominently also in the human sciences, but nature here is "the non-devitalized nature for life."[39]

The process of 'devitalizing' the sensuous sets the basis for another distinctive feature of natural scientific work: the quantifying tendency which guarantees maximal intellectual mastery of the material under scrutiny. Lask makes an important remark regarding mechanics, which Rickert indicates as the fundamental natural science *due to its generality*:

If mechanics really resulted exclusively from the generalizing tendency and if the qualitative invariability and homogeneousness depended merely on this tendency, then, for instance, in physics and chemistry – whose subject matter is not mechanical corporeity in general but has a greater qualitative particularity and concreteness – the qualitative surplus should be investigated (e.g., chemical affinity). On the contrary, also [in these sciences] the qualitative is

[34] SW, 241.   [35] For a clarification of this technical language see Chapter 1.
[36] SW, 241.   [37] SW, 244.   [38] SW, 242.   [39] NEW, 268.

ignored and exclusively the quantitative components are taken into consideration.[40]

For Lask these features of natural science are evidence of its inferiority vis-à-vis philosophical knowledge. In his notes, one finds several instances of Lask's animosity towards natural science, which, unfortunately, was widespread among young German intellectuals in the early twentieth century and subsequently degenerated into Nazi irrationalism.[41] Thankfully, these aspects of his thought are not essential to his most philosophically interesting points. The natural scientific method presupposes a specific treatment of the material delivered by the senses in which these materials are divested of their original inhering values and considered exclusively in their quantitative determinations. Husserl eventually refines these ideas (but, again, he never encountered Lask's notes) and points out how the 'idealizing' process of natural science – far from being a falsification of our original relationship with the world – is necessary in order for thought to overcome the subject-relatedness through which perceptual objects are originally constituted in experience. Husserl's critique is directed at the 'forgetfulness' of this process, namely, taking for real the artificial world legitimately abstracted out of the life-world in which we exist.

Husserl's notion of attitude

We now have a sophisticated enough sense of the debate surrounding 'standpoints' and modes of access to fields of scientific inquiry at the beginning of the twentieth century to appreciate the strength of Husserl's analyses of these issues. The phenomenological notion of *Einstellung*[42] (attitude) is one of the most crucial yet least clarified in Husserl's philosophy. In the context of the present chapter, and for the overall purpose of this book, the concept of attitude is particularly apt for introducing Husserl's perspective on the liveliest philosophical debate of his time. 'Attitude' is also a concept that stands in a genus/species relationship with the very concept of phenomenology. In fact,

---

[40] SW, 249.
[41] In SW, 240, for instance, he deems empirical cognition "castrated" and "blasé."
[42] A first attempt of clarification can be found in my "Systematische Überlegungen zu Husserls Einstellungslehre," *Husserl Studies* 25/3 (2009): 219–233.

phenomenology is first and foremost characterized by its founder as an attitude. Therefore, properly understanding the concept of attitude is requisite to properly understanding phenomenology. The fact that the key *definiens* of transcendental phenomenology – that is, the concept of attitude – fits naturally into the debate about the demarcation of the sciences is one further clue that Husserl's philosophical project is tightly connected to this debate.

The concept of attitude recurs in different venues of Husserl's thought, and it is used in a somewhat non-technical way that makes it hard to pin down. However, one remarkable feature cuts across different usages of the term *Einstellung*: attitudes are paired up in an antagonistic, yet mutually clarifying, fashion.[43] It is possible to identify at least three such pairs: the natural/phenomenological attitude, the naturalistic/personalistic attitude, and the theoretical/evaluative-volitional attitude. Whereas the first pair has been largely explored in Husserl scholarship,[44] the second two pairs remain uncharted. In the context of this chapter, it is apropos to discuss the second two pairs first. A later chapter will address in detail both the ramifications of phenomenological attitude and the role that this attitude plays in the debate between Neo-Kantians and life-philosophers.[45] A general characterization is sufficient for this chapter and will be provided in the concluding remarks.

The pair naturalistic/personalistic attitude is presented extensively for the first time in Ideas II in order to highlight the difference between natural sciences and human sciences.[46] The naturalistic and the personalistic attitude are presented as two different ways of looking at the

---

[43] Interestingly, this way of thinking in terms of mutually illuminating oppositions comes extremely close to the so-called 'heterological' pattern of thought typical of Neo-Kantianism and, in particular, of Heinrich Rickert's philosophy. On the meaning of heterology see Zijderveld, *Rickert's Relevance*, 20–21.

[44] See in particular S. Luft, "Husserl's Phenomenological Discovery of the Natural Attitude," *Continental Philosophy Review* 31/2 (1998): 153–170.

[45] See Chapter 6.

[46] See E. Husserl, *Ideen zu einer reinen Phänomenologie und phänomenologischen Philosophie. Zweites Buch: Untersuchungen zur Konstitution, Husserliana*, vol. 4 (The Hague: Nijhoff, 1954). Hereafter Hua IV. English translation by R. Rojcewicz and A. Schuwer, *Ideas Pertaining to a Pure Phenomenology and to a Phenomenological Philosophy. Second Book: Studies in the Phenomenology of Constitution, Collected Works*, vol. 3 (Dordrecht: Kluwer, 1989), § 49. Hereafter Ideas II.

world, highlighting certain features to the detriment of others. As Husserl puts it:

> While the natural sciences, according to their sense, are characterized by an abstractive filter [*Blende*] through which everything subjective, all mentality is filtered out [*abgeblendet*], the totality of subjectivity would be the *theme* of human science [*Geisteswissenschaft*] overall.[47]

The naturalistic and the personalistic attitude are thus two basic options for interpreting the world: one that filters out subjectivity and another that privileges it. Different forms of scientificity are thus parsed by the role they assign to subjectivity in their overall interpretations of the world.

It should be noted that while Husserl holds fast to the customary distinction between natural sciences (*Naturwissenschaften*) and human sciences (*Geisteswissenschaften*), his distinction between naturalistic and personalistic attitude as the source of the two different classes of science differs from Dilthey's. For Dilthey, the distinction between natural sciences and human sciences depends primarily on their subject matter: natural science deals with physical nature revealed by outer experience whereas human science deals with the world of psychic nexus revealed by inner experience. Husserl's distinction based on different attitudes is perfectly compatible with the idea of a natural science of mentality (e.g., neurophysiology) and of a humanistic science of physical nature (e.g., geography). For Husserl, what matters is not whether a mode of inquiry interrogates subjectivity as its *subject matter*, but whether that mode considers subjectivity a valid factor in its own right (as opposed to filtering it out as an appendage of physical reality).

The paradigmatic example that clarifies the opposition between the two attitudes is the *human body*. The body can be seen merely as a complex instance of physical nature, to which subjectivity is causally annexed as a "second nature."[48] Alternatively, it can be viewed as the organ of the will – as a sort of 'extension' of personal subjectivity in the world. The two attitudes are not compatible, and there is no overarching attitude that could simply mirror what the human body is. The

---

[47] E. Husserl, *Erste Philosophie (1923/24). Zweiter Teil: Theorie der phänomenologischen Reduktion*, Husserliana, vol. 8 (The Hague: Nijhoff, 1959), 286. Hereafter Hua VIII.

[48] E. Husserl, *Einleitung in die Philosophie. Vorlesungen 1922/23*, Husserliana, vol. 35 (Dordrecht: Springer, 2002), 19. Heareafter Hua XXXV.

natural and the personalistic dimensions of the body as disclosed by the two attitudes are layered in a definite way that only a phenomenological description can reveal. That said, a phenomenological description of the two attitudes only discloses the tension between them and is by no means designed to resolve it. We shall revisit this point in the conclusion.

A further important feature of Husserl's phenomenological notion of attitude is that attitudes do not characterize exclusively, or even primarily, scientific activity. We can literally 'look at the world' from a naturalistic or from a personalistic point of view and be more or less aware of it, regardless of whether we thereupon choose *to theorize* in the spirit of the elected attitude. We owe Husserl's fellow phenomenologist Moritz Geiger for a set of illuminating remarks on this issue. In his book *Die Wirklichkeit der Wissenschaften und die Metaphysik*, he points out:

a limitation to science does not belong to the essence of attitude[s]. Rather, attitudes are pre-apprehensions [*Vorgriffe*] vis-à-vis the structure of reality overall – [they are] pre-formations [*Vorformungen*] that are certainly exploited by science but that, however, are at play overall when issues concerning reality are tackled: in ordinary life as well as in dealing with specific metaphysical-philosophical problems or in the construction of entire metaphysical systems.[49]

This is an important difference between the Neo-Kantian notion of standpoint and the phenomenological notion of attitude. Whereas the Neo-Kantians consider pre-scientific experience a fundamentally homogeneous whole, Husserl sees that we are presented with fundamentally different attitudes already at the pre-scientific level. For the Neo-Kantians, divergences in standpoints only arise when we enter the sphere of scientific thought. For Husserl and the phenomenologists, such divergences in science are higher-level manifestations of divergences that originate in pre-scientific experience.

This remark leads us to the third pair in Husserl's doctrine of attitude: the theoretical/evaluative-volitional attitude. This distinction underpins the naturalistic/personalistic distinction and can be viewed as the most basic dichotomy in the sphere of attitude. If it is possible to assume encompassing attitudes toward reality – such as the naturalistic or the

---

[49] M. Geiger, *Die Wirklichkeit der Wissenschaften und die Metaphysik* (Bonn: F. Cohen, 1930), 122.

personalistic attitude – this is because at a more fundamental level it is always possible to assume a theoretical or an evaluative-practical attitude towards single objects or states-of-affairs.[50] Husserl focuses on these basic forms of attitude from Ideas II onwards and offers some illuminating analyses, particularly in the lecture on *Erste Philosophie*. Whereas in early stages of phenomenology his chief concern was to establish the general structure of intentional acts considered in their singularity, the expansion to genetic phenomenology in later phases of his thought implies a broader preoccupation with the dynamics of intentional life as a whole:

> As even a cursory glance reveals, the acts that the ego performing reflection finds as its own (or, better, as those belonging to its own unreflected ego that previously lived in naiveté) are usually, or actually always more or less interwoven, connected, founded upon one another.[51]

Husserl calls a complexion of acts woven together in overarching unity "action" (*Aktion*) and distinguishes between different ways in which an action can be structured. Some actions are "total acts" (*Gesamtakte*) consisting of a number of underlying acts, some of which perform an ancillary function and others of which carry the actual will that holds the complexion together. While I am carrying out a geometrical proof, there is an overarching theoretical action that, if analyzed more closely, turns out to be sustained by a number of 'ancillary' theoretical actions. For instance, I must read the signs on the paper, keep track of the steps I make, and draw lines and figures. In Husserl's terms, I have a dominant action (*Hauptaktion*) (the proof) and a number of acts serving ancillary functions (*dienende Funktionen*), enabling the dominant action. On the other hand, there can be parallel actions that do not 'merge' together into the unity of a total act organized according to the dominant/

---

[50] This is not intended to suggest a direct parallelism according to which the naturalistic attitude would be necessarily theoretical and the personalistic attitude would be evaluative-volitional. We can have forms of theorizing *also* while standing in the personalistic attitude (the most eloquent case is, as we said, human science), on the contrary, we cannot have evaluative-volitional experiences while standing in the naturalistic attitude, which is by definition exclusively theoretical. Although I will not explore this asymmetry in full, it suffices to point out that this is because the naturalistic attitude is a thoroughly 'unnatural' amplification of the theoretical attitude, whereas the personalistic attitude is a 'natural' disposition.

[51] Hua VIII, 100.

ancillary structure. In this case, the meaning of attitudes in the sense of the third pairing becomes manifest. As an example, Husserl writes:

As a botanist, I may be delighted by the beauty of a flower, but this delight is not the dominant action if I am in the attitude of gaining knowledge about the flower by observation and classification. Once I am done with it, instead of this theoretical action, the foregoing aesthetical joy that ran alongside it may become the dominant action. Another example of such a change is the one between the aesthetical observation of a work of art and the observation of the art historian. In this case, we do not say that the two acts function as parts of a total act.[52]

When we are observing an object for theoretical purposes, we are, as Husserl puts it in Ideas II, performing a "seeing in an eminent sense."[53] The act of seeing becomes the dominant action and lets other actions become marginal or un-accomplished (*unvollzogen*). The delight for the beauty of the flower may very well be 'still present' when the botanist starts engaging in his classificatory work, but he does not 'live' in that delight. Nonetheless, the delight runs its course parallel to the new, theoretical dominant action.

From this point of view, attitudes amount to concrete accomplishments of consciousness meant to orchestrate the multifarious fabric of acts characterizing each cross-section of our conscious life. If acts of different classes simply co-existed in consciousness – that is, if they were all 'accomplished' to the same degree and simultaneously – life would be an unmanageable cacophony. The harmony of order and meaning is only achievable because orchestration according to different attitudes is at play. Objects manifesting themselves in experience do not do so 'in one blow'; they reveal different features according to our choice of attitude.

This basic fact about the life of consciousness becomes amplified and generalized when we consider the shift from this level of consideration to that of the naturalistic and personalistic attitudes. Here, not only is the experience of a flower modified, but the overall outlook on reality changes depending on whether or not we admit subjectivity into our broad picture. On the basis of Husserl's analysis of attitudes in the life of consciousness, the naturalistic and the personalistic attitude can be seen as abiding 'habituations' in our way of looking at the world. In this

[52] Hua VIII, 101.   [53] Ideas II, 10.

respect, the personalistic attitude should be considered preeminent because it necessarily becomes habituated for every human being: "We thus have to do here with an entirely natural and not an artificial attitude that would have to be achieved and preserved only by special means."[54] In the personalistic attitude we carry out 'actions' that are generally guided by evaluative and practical concerns. Occasionally, we carry out actions in which the theoretical component is dominant, but the overall preoccupation is still geared towards our welfare as persons.

On the contrary, the naturalistic attitude is a thoroughly *unnatural* focus on the objective 'positings' of our experiences. It has to be learned and practiced, and it can be seen as an abstractive impoverishment of our personalistic experience. While the naturalistic attitude is thoroughly theoretical – that is, it privileges the simple thetic or positional intentional content and its objective determinations as opposed to the intentional content's significance or practical function – it should be emphasized once again that it is the exclusion of subjectivity, not the privilege of theory, which defines the naturalistic attitude as such. There is room for theory in the personalistic attitude, as the existence of the human sciences reveals. Husserl is in line with Dilthey and Simmel in emphasizing that the human sciences are carried out in the same 'intellectual' mode as our pre-scientific life. They emerge from the same kinds of concerns that characterize our everyday transactions in the world, such as understanding other human beings and finding our place in society.

Rather than just living his human life in the best possible way, the human scientist wants to produce theories about human life. In order to do so, subjectivity cannot be excluded. Contrariwise, in the naturalistic attitude subjectivity has to be excluded in order to let objective properties come into relief. Even those natural sciences that have mental occurrences as their subject matter do not treat these mental occurrences as 'active' expressions of living agents who intend, assess, and act on their surrounding world. Mental occurrences are merely natural occurrences whose regularities can be formulated in mathematical terms. Accordingly, we can refine our initial definition by adding that the naturalistic attitude is a wholly theoretical attitude that revolves around the exclusion of subjectivity *qua* subjectivity. The

[54] Ideas II, 192.

personalistic attitude, on the contrary, is a mostly practical-evaluative and occasionally theoretical attitude in which the world is seen as it appears to a human subject: as an open horizon of practical possibilities populated by significant objects and fellow acting subjects.

Phenomenology and the constitutive function of changes of attitudes

The common systematic function of attitudes in phenomenology and standpoints in Neo-Kantianism is now coming into view. In both cases, the objects of our consideration are related in a non-trivial sense to the stance we assume toward them. In the way a human action can be viewed either as a natural fact standing under rigid causal laws or as a moral fact standing under the obligations of practical reason, so too can a flower be experienced according to the evaluative-practical attitude as having certain, scientifically relevant, botanic features or as something beautiful and desirable. On a broader scale, reality can be viewed as a set of complex causal interactions between physical bodies (naturalistic attitude) or as a world of meaning, full of significance for living personal subjects (personalistic attitude).

In spite of this clear similarity, there are important differences that must be spelled out. In order to do so, we must reconsider the way in which the relationship between objects and subjective outlook is articulated in the two philosophical schools. For the Neo-Kantians, as argued above, the object is *produced* by a given standpoint. I can look at a flower as an instance of its class and as the point of intersection of a set of biological laws. On the other hand, the same flower can be viewed historically, say, if it played a role as the emblem of a political party. But are we really dealing with *the same* flower? A lump of gold can be viewed as a sample of metal or as a precious gift. Is it *the same* lump of gold in both cases? Even if our common sense urges us to answer positively, from a strictly Neo-Kantian point of view we would have to reject our common sense inclination. The lump of gold as part of the natural-scientific standpoint is different from the lump of gold given to us in pre-scientific experience and also from the lump of gold that has a certain historical value. Each object is what it is only within the framework in which it is investigated. There is no metaphysically pre-existing object in itself that we subsequently approach according to different standpoints. On the contrary, each standpoint includes the object it is designed to investigate. The standpoints are intrinsically *disjointed* because each of them follows a different logic. Consequently, the objects of different standpoints are necessarily disjointed as well.

Husserlian phenomenology provides the resources to maintain a radical difference between attitudes and, correlatively, differences between the objects manifested therein, while at the same time defend a continuity running through all these differences. As the example of the flower given by Husserl makes clear, attitudes can be *changed*. As he points out in Ideas II, a "characteristic change of attitude belongs, as an ideal possibility, to all acts, and accompanying it is always the corresponding phenomenological modification."[55] We can always switch from a theoretical attitude to an evaluative-practical and then back to a theoretical. In the same way, we can go back and forth between the naturalistic and the personalistic attitude as we walk in and out of the lab. This is more than a psychic fact about humans: it is essential to the very notion of attitude. One and the same subjectivity cuts across all attitudes and is responsible for their orchestration.

We can now broach a provisional characterization of the first dichotomy in Husserl's remarks on attitude: the opposition between the natural attitude and the phenomenological attitude. The natural attitude is the fundamentally unreflective mode in which normally developed human beings conduct their life for the most part. In this attitude, we take for granted the existence of an ontologically self-subsistent world around us, and we apprehend ourselves as human beings existing as entities of that world. Of course, while living immersed in the natural attitude we know nothing about this; the essential features of the natural attitude become visible from the phenomenological standpoint. Part of what it means to assume the standpoint of phenomenology is to be aware of the power of the natural attitude.

To the extent that it admits of human subjectivity, the natural attitude is coextensive with the personalistic attitude. When Husserl uses the phrase 'natural attitude,' however, he wants to emphasize something other than the opposition with the 'unnatural' (i.e., artificial) attitude of the natural scientist. The natural attitude designates the all-encompassing, mostly uncritical, mode of existence of human beings in the world, both when they act as persons (personalistic attitude) *and* when they theorize in the spirit of natural science (naturalistic attitude).

[55] Ideas II, 10.

Even when we assume the naturalistic attitude we do not cease to posit an existing world – which in the naturalistic attitude becomes the subject matter of quantitatively oriented research – and ourselves as the (allegedly) self-effacing human subjects who investigate this world. This is why, in Ideas II, Husserl, after carefully distinguishing between the personalistic and naturalistic attitudes, makes the following remark:

> Upon closer scrutiny, it will even appear that there are not here two attitudes with equal rights and of the same order, or two perfectly equal apperceptions which at once penetrate one another, but that the naturalistic attitude is in fact subordinated to the personalistic, and that the former only acquires by means of an abstraction or, rather, by means of a kind of self-forgetfulness of the personal Ego, a certain autonomy.[56]

From this point of view both the personalistic and the naturalistic attitudes can be viewed as subordinated *modes* of the encompassing natural attitude, one in which the natural attitude plays itself out without any restrictions (personalistic attitude) and the other in which it plays itself out in the mode of the methodologically imposed exclusion of human subjectivity (naturalistic attitude).

In the context of the natural attitude 'the world' is the theme of all themes, one "that has no other theme above itself."[57] Subjectivity is 'read into' this existing world and is considered a segment of nature, be it in the methodologically restricted sense of this term (naturalistic attitude) or in the broader, less determinate sense in which we commonly talk about 'nature' (personalistic attitude). The world is viewed as the totality of what is – both physical and psycho-physical. Our selves – or, in Husserl's terminology, our egos – are apprehended as empirical entities whose defining features and properties stand in a causally regulated continuity with the defining features and properties of other classes of objects in the world. In this framework, the constitutive function that shifts of attitude play with respect to the objects of experience is bound to remain unseen. The world is interpreted as being 'already-there,' endowed with subject-independent properties, and our subjectivity can only be understood as a psychic mirror on which such properties are occasionally reflected.

---

[56] Ideas II, 193.
[57] E. Husserl, *Zur phänomenologischen Reduktion. Texte aus dem Nachlass (1926–35)*, *Husserliana*, vol. 34 (Dordrecht: Springer, 2002), 52. Hereafter Hua XXXIV.

This, however, is not *the only* attitude we can assume toward the world and ourselves. Husserl advocates the necessity of a shift to the *phenomenological* attitude, which alone can do justice to the actual status of subjectivity. In the phenomenological attitude, the naive positing of the world typical of the natural attitude is suspended. In so doing, the self-insertion in the world constantly operating within ourselves is discontinued (Husserl talks about an enworlding self-apprehension that characterizes human subjectivity and that needs to be counteracted methodologically). Through the methodological device which Husserl famously termed '*epoché*' we can cease to take the existence of a world around us for granted and open up the possibility to apprehend our subjectivity in a non-worldly manner; we can learn to see ourselves as *transcendental* egos rather than empirical subjects woven into the causal fabric of the existing world.

The *epoché* sets the basis for the so-called phenomenological reduction – a leading back of everything that presents itself in experience to the constitutive dynamics of transcendental, non-worldly subjectivity. The shift to the phenomenological attitude does not imply depreciation or even rejection of the natural attitude. On the contrary, by interpreting itself as a transcendental ego responsible for the constitution of the world and of itself *qua* human subject in the world, the phenomenologist learns to appreciate the 'depth' of the natural attitude and the hidden subjective workings that make it possible. As Husserl puts it in one of his manuscripts:

Through the phenomenological reduction as 'transcendental reflection,' the ego frees itself from the limits of the naturalness of its existence, the limits of 'naive' humanity; in a sense, the ego frees itself from blinders that prevent it from seeing its absolute, fully concrete existence or, which amounts to the same, prevents it from seeing an infinite wealth of life-possibilities, in which those of natural existence are certainly included but are, so to speak, abstract and imperfect.[58]

As long as the ego interprets itself exclusively as a natural-empirical human subject, the correlations that exist between its attitudes and the 'looks' of the objects disclosed through them are bound to remain partially unintelligible. If the naively posited existence of the empirical world is suspended and seen purely as manifested in subjective

---

[58] Hua XXXIV, 225.

experiences, then a new perspective arises, one in which the multifarious characteristics of experienced objects are seen as 'achievements' – the results of constitutive processes of transcendental subjectivity.[59]

If a flower can be contemplated first in aesthetic rapture and subsequently with scientific rigor, this is because there is a transcendental ego at work, arranging and rearranging the patterns of its own conscious life. The transcendental ego does not merely grant logical unity to representations but is, phenomenologically speaking, a *living agent* free to follow its own paths in the unfolding of experience.[60]

Correlatively, the object has multiple horizons. It is intrinsically stratified, and this makes the assumption of different attitudes toward it necessary in order to reveal progressively all layers of meaning pertaining to it. Going back to the example of the human body, it is *at the same time* a natural body, a biological organism, the bearer of sensations, the organ of the will, and a concrete human person. These are not simply five disconnected objects but five layers of meaning of one and the same object. Some of them come to light only from a naturalistic standpoint; others only if we adopt the personalistic attitude. Nonetheless, we cannot vary these layers as we wish. We can only orchestrate their manifestation depending on the standpoint or attitude we decide to adopt. The unity of the object throughout its layers of meaning is a correlate of the unity of transcendental subjectivity throughout its changes of attitudes.

In this sense, a phenomenological analysis of different attitudes has the capacity to retain the most fundamental insight of Neo-Kantianism about the plurality of standpoints, while giving a more convincing account of why this plurality does not jeopardize the unity of the object and the corresponding unity of our intellectual life.

In Chapter 4 we shall delve deeper into the philosophical exchange between Husserl and the Neo-Kantians. In particular, we will examine the Neo-Kantians' reception of Husserl's first major work after *Logical Investigations, Ideas Pertaining to a Pure Phenomenology and to a Phenomenological Philosophy*, published in 1913.

---

[59] A more thorough description of the shift to the phenomenological attitude will be offered in Chapter 6.

[60] Marcus Brainard coined the felicitous phrase "egoic motility" to talk about the ego's capacity to orchestrate different modalities in the transcendental field of its own experience. See M. Brainard, *Belief and Its Neutralization: Husserl's System of Phenomenology in* Ideas I (Albany, NY: SUNY Press, 2002), 166, *passim*.

4 | *The reception of Husserl's* Ideen *among the Neo-Kantians*

In making its first appearance, phenomenology must
[...] reckon with a fundamental mood of skepticism.

Edmund Husserl[1]

The publication of the first volume of Husserl's *Ideen zu einer reinen Phänomenologie und phänomenologischen Philosophie, Erstes Buch* (1913) (*Ideen I*), provoked a wave of criticism among Husserl's Göttingen students owing to the book's unambiguous commitment to transcendental idealism.[2] Less well known is that the book was also vehemently criticized by those thinkers who represented the mainstream version of transcendental idealism in early twentieth-century Germany, namely, the Neo-Kantians. Interestingly, the sharp criticism of Husserl's transcendental phenomenology as presented in *Ideen* is a point of agreement for the two most prominent schools of Neo-Kantianism, Marburg and Southwestern, which otherwise embodied two significantly different ways of understanding and recasting Kant's transcendental philosophy. This double attack from opposite sides of Neo-Kantianism against *Ideen I* can be considered a clue about the originality of Husserl's work, which could not be easily aligned with existing currents of transcendental philosophy. On the other hand,

---

[1] E. Husserl, *Ideen zu einer reinen Phänomenologie und einer phänomenologischen Philosophie. Erstes Buch: Allgemeine Einführung in die reine Phänomenologie. Erster Halbband: Text der 1.–3. Auflage – Nachrdruck, Husserliana*, vol. 3/1 (The Hague: Nijhoff, 1977), Hereafter Hua III/1. English translation by F. Kersten, *Ideas Pertaining to a Pure Phenomenology and to a Phenomenological Philosophy. First Book: General Introduction to a Pure Phenomenology, Collected Works*, vol. 2 (Dordrecht: Kluwer, 1982), 148. Hereafter Ideas I.
[2] An earlier version of this chapter is published as "The *Ideen* and Neo-Kantianism," in L. Embree and T. Nenon (eds.), *Husserl's* Ideen (Dordrecht: Springer, 2013), 71–90. The present version, however, offers a much refined presentation of Husserl's eidetics, and it has been largely reworked in order to fit in the overall line of inquiry of the book.

Ideen I was written in a rush[3] and is shot through with obscurities, giving rise to all sorts of misinterpretations, especially from uncharitable readers. Husserl is thus partly responsible for not having achieved the desired effect of engaging the Neo-Kantians and convincing them of the necessity to reformulate the task of transcendental philosophy in phenomenological terms.

In this chapter, I intend to present Heinrich Rickert's and Paul Natorp's (Marburg) critiques of *Ideen I* and to offer a response from a Husserlian point of view. I will do so by addressing two fundamental issues in phenomenology: the eidetic and the phenomenological dimension of subjectivity. In a certain sense, Husserl's formulations in *Ideen I* are vulnerable to the critiques raised by these two leading philosophers of the Neo-Kantian movement. However, if we try to spell out more accurately Husserl's position beyond the letter of the *Ideen*, this vulnerability tends to disappear. In particular, Husserl's concept of eidetic knowledge turns out to be less in contrast with Rickert's epistemology than the two thinkers would have it. The much more fundamental disagreement revolves around the notion of subjectivity and Husserl's related claim that phenomenology is the fundamental science for philosophy. Neo-Kantians in general, and Natorp in particular, are skeptical about the possibility of direct descriptions of subjectivity, while Husserl defines phenomenology as an eidetic science of transcendental subjectivity.

The two positions, however, do not amount to just two incomparable visions. Neo-Kantian skepticism towards phenomenology forces the Husserlian phenomenologist to clarify the meaning of fundamental concepts such as essence and intuition. Conversely, Husserlian phenomenology can help rectify some misunderstandings and strictures that characterize Neo-Kantian philosophy while nonetheless preserving the latter's most valuable epistemological insights.

Eidetics, intuition, and conceptual knowledge

In 1911, after reading Husserl's article, "Philosophie als strenge Wissenschaft," in the first issue of *Logos* – the newborn official organ

---

[3] See K. Schuhmann, *Die Dialektik der Phänomenologie II: Reine Phänomenologie und phänomenologische Philosophie. Historisch-analytische Monographie über Husserls "Ideen I"* (The Hague: Nijhoff, 1973), 3.

of Southwestern Neo-Kantianism – Rickert wrote an enthusiastic letter to the founder of phenomenology saying, "I believe that overall our paths will get closer and closer to one another."[4] It was Rickert himself who urged Husserl to participate in the *Logos* project, both as a member of the scientific board and as a contributor. In Rickert's eyes, "Philosophie als strenge Wissenschaft" represented a significant step forward after the *Logical Investigations*: Husserl was now able to locate his project explicitly within the philosophical debate of his time in terms of a scientific philosophy standing in sharp contrast to both naturalism and historicism. In so doing, phenomenology placed itself within the same theoretical space as Neo-Kantianism and articulated its standpoint in opposition to the same rivals.

Considering this thoroughly concordant point of departure, it is initially puzzling to read Rickert's strong attack against phenomenology in his polemical essay, *Die Philosophie des Lebens: Darstellung und Kritik der philosophischen Modeströmungen unserer Zeit* (1920).[5] This short book denounces a trend in early twentieth-century philosophy that Rickert considers frivolous but dangerously widespread: the emphasis on life over rationality and on immediate intuition over conceptual knowledge. Surprisingly, Husserl's phenomenology is listed together with Dilthey's, Bergson's, and Simmel's *Lebensphilosophie* and various forms of biological vitalism as a philosophy "devoid of principles [*prinzipienlos*]" that even "elevate[s] the lack of principles to a philosophical principle"(!)[6] What led Rickert to change his opinion of phenomenology so radically? He explains as follows:

What matters here is obviously not the articulation of the logical in contrast to the psychological: this, in fact, can only lead to a refusal of a philosophy of mere life. Rather, what matters is the doctrine of the "vision of essence [*Wesensschau*]" which Husserl intends to appoint as fundamental science for all philosophy and which granted him followers. Albeit with a conscious one-sidedness and to this extent unfairly, we try to interpret this doctrine, too, as a contemporary trend connected to the tendencies towards lived-experience (*Erlebnis*), considering that phenomenology means the doctrine of a newly discovered kind of intuitive and immediate phenomena [*Erscheinungen*]."[7]

[4] E. Husserl, *Briefwechsel*, vol. 5, *Die Neukantianer* (Dordrecht: Kluwer, 1994), 171. Hereafter BW V.
[5] H. Rickert, *Die Philosophie des Lebens: Darstellung und Kritik der philosophischen Modeströmungen unserer Zeit* (Tübingen: Mohr Siebeck, 1920).
[6] *Ibid.*, 50.   [7] *Ibid.*, 28–29.

In the footnote at the end of this passage, Rickert explicitly cites Husserl's *Ideen I* as the source for his critical understanding of *Wesensschau.*

It is important to underscore that Rickert's critique is not directed against the concept of essence as such. The idea that a scientific philosophy must yield essential, non-empirical knowledge was already prominent in Husserl's "Philosophie als strenge Wissenschaft," the essay about which Rickert was quite enthusiastic.[8] The controversial element, which was not as prominent in Husserl's previous work, but is strongly emphasized in the *Ideen*, is the claim that essential knowledge is a form of *intuitive* knowledge, legitimately comparable to sensory vision. Husserl's statements on this point are famous:

The essence (Eidos) is a new sort of object. Just as the datum of individual or experiencing intuition is an individual object, so the datum of eidetic intuition is pure essence. Not a merely external analogy, but a radical community is present here. *Seeing an essence is also precisely an intuition,* just as an eidetic object is precisely an object.[9]

Later in the book Husserl even reinforces his view by suggesting not only that essences are objects given intuitively just like perceptual objects, but also that everyone is good at intuiting essences: "The truth is that all human beings see '*Ideen*,' 'essences,' and see them, so to speak, continuously."[10] Indeed, there is something utterly plain and non-emphatic to Husserl's presentation of *Wesensschau*:

Thus, for example, any tone in and of itself has an essence and, highest of all, the universal essence tone as such, or rather sound as such – taken purely as the moment that can be singled out intuitively in the individual tone (alone, or else by comparing one tone with others as 'something common').[11]

On Husserl's account, to encounter a tone is to encounter a datum of experience already structured according to some essence before we reflect phenomenologically upon it. This is why I can wonder, for instance, whether the whistle I just heard was the whistle of the train or the whistle of someone calling her dog but not whether what I just sensed was a tone or a smell. I may be in doubt as to what kind of object my birthday present is supposed to be, but not as to whether I am

---

[8] See E. Husserl, *Philosophy as a Rigorous Science*, in E. Husserl, *Shorter Works* (University of Notre Dame Press, 1981), 173. Hereafter PRS.
[9] Ideas I, 9.   [10] Ideas I, 41.   [11] Ideas I, 8.

contemplating a physical thing or a mental act. The fundamental differences *in genera* that are here at play do not seem to stem from our intellectual activity; rather, they simply present themselves in experience in concomitance with the experience of individual data. Accordingly, there is a sense in which to experience something *as a tone* means to experience more than a mere individual datum. For Husserl, this basic fact has little to do with intellectual concept-formation, and it would be wrong to understand a situation like the one just mentioned in terms of the intellect or some hidden faculty being at work, enhancing raw sensations with non-sensible categories.

Rickert, however, contends that such a fact cannot be produced as an example of genuine *knowledge*. Genuine knowledge, for him, is always the result of conceptual mediation and thus implies a departure from a merely receptive-intuitive dimension. Knowledge is necessarily discursive, so the claim of some sort of non- or pre-discursive *knowledge* is for Rickert a *contradictio in adjecto*. We attain scientific knowledge *only* to the extent that we "re-structure [*Umformen*]" our immediate intuitions by means of concepts and, in so doing, bestow upon them order and articulation. For Rickert, Husserl's emphasis on essential knowledge being a form of intuition can be viewed as a particularly clear instance of what he calls *intuitionism*, a widespread theoretical "short cut" that demeans the toil of conceptualization in philosophy by overemphasizing and misinterpreting the merely receptive role of intuition.[12]

Vehement critiques against every form of intuitionism are present in several essays and book chapters and represent the backbone of Rickert's philosophical work from the 1920s onwards. In his last journal article, "Kennen und Erkennen" (published in 1934, more than twenty years after the publication of Husserl's *Ideen*),[13] he launches a further attack against phenomenology by analyzing the very same example given by Husserl at the outset of the *Ideen* and offering a

---

[12] In a recent paper Helmut Holzey offers a convincing sketch of the Neo-Kantian critique of the concept of intuition: H. Holzey, "Neo-Kantianism and Phenomenology: The Problem of Intuition," in Luft and Makkreel, *Neo-Kantianism in Contemporary Philosophy*, 25–40. However, in spite of the rather broad formulation in the title, he considers exclusively Natorp's thought and ignores Rickert's contribution on this issue. It seems to me, however, that Rickert's critique of phenomenological intuition is actually much more reflective and sophisticated than Natorp's.

[13] H. Rickert, "Kennen und Erkennen. Kritische Bemerkungen zum theoretischen Intuitionismus," *Kant Studien* 39 (1934): 139–155. Hereafter KE.

different account of the way we grasp the "essence" of a tone. That the addressee of Rickert's polemic is still Husserl, and in particular the Husserl of the *Ideen*, is unmistakable considering the example and the language Rickert uses. As the title of his paper suggests, there is a sharp difference between sheer *acquaintance* [*Kenntnis*] with the intuitively given individual tone and scientific *knowledge* [*Erkenntnis*] of the essence of a tone as such. A process of knowledge begins when we start to analyze the intuited tone and differentiate between several elements pertaining to it:

The sheer intuition of the tone gives "everything at one fell swoop." Knowledge does not and cannot do so. Rather, knowledge dissects through a number of assertions the single tone – which we perceive intuitively "as a whole" – into a series of "moments." Such moments are fused together immediately and intuitively only in perception. Within knowledge, these moments must be separated from each other and become the objects of predications each one for itself.[14]

It is only *after* the intuitively given tone undergoes such a dissection into a variety of moments (intensity, duration, pitch, etc.) that we can discern the essential moments for *any tone whatsoever*. Rickert insists, in open polemic against Husserl's *Wesensschau*:

Therein and *only* therein [in the process of cognitive dissection] do we find the general "essence" of the tone that we previously intuited in perception. In other words, only in this way do we attain knowledge of the tone as tone; of that tone which beforehand we only made acquaintance of intuitively. But then we moved with our knowledge way beyond intuitive acquaintance. Such process, which discloses for us the essence of something, can by no means be understood as a form of ... intuition. Rather, through our act of knowledge, we necessarily restructure [*umbilden*] the cognitional material given to us in intuition ... Such restructuring is unavoidable for every knowledge which endeavors to delve into the general "essence" of something.[15]

From a phenomenological point of view it would be all too simple, to dismiss these critiques by rejecting the notion of intuition Rickert operates with as too narrow. Indeed, Husserl works with a broad concept of *Anschauung* which shares little with Kant's. Whereas, for Kant, intuition amounts to the blind intake of sense data (at least as far as a finite

---

[14] KE, 149.   [15] KE, 150.

intellect is concerned),[16] for the Husserl of the *Logical Investigations*, intuitions come to fulfill previously empty intentions. This fulfilling function is exerted by sensuous intuitions when the previously empty intention is a simple perceptual intention and by a combination of sensuous and non-sensuous intuitions when the previously empty intention is a higher-order intention presenting a whole state of affairs, e.g., a judgment or an aesthetic evaluation.

However, it should be emphasized that Rickert's point in his critique of intuitionism is not orthodox Kantian. From Kant's perspective, intuition would provide exclusively *sensuous* material, and therefore, all non-sensuous components of experience must derive somehow from the intellect. In another essay, written a few years before "Kennen und Erkennen", Rickert was adamant that not only sensuous material but also *"non-sensuous* [material] is immediately given in intuition"[17] and that *"the non-sensuous* [material] *lies in our immediate lived-experiences or intuitions beside the sensuous* [material] *as a wholly autonomous 'Quality'."*[18] To speak the language of phenomenology, not only things but also meanings are in a robust sense *given* and not imposed on or applied to sensuous content. In the example of a tone, not only sensuous acoustic data are given in intuition but also elements of generality that we subsequently express with concepts such as pitch and intensity. Rickert would be of one mind with Husserl in emphasizing the necessity to broaden the concept of intuition and extend it to elements of generality and meaning within experience.

However, Rickert wants to underscore that the intuitive *givenness* of elements of generality cannot yet be considered *knowledge*, let alone essential, scientific knowledge. Essential knowledge is, for Rickert, a process of *transformation* of the given according to demands and criteria that are not extracted from the given but rather flow from the cognizing agent. Of course, we do not have intuition only of the sensible but also, in Rickert's language, of the "intelligible."[19] *But intuition only provides the material, be it sensible or intelligible.* It is our task as rational agents thereupon to carve our concepts so that we can create a systematic theoretical *kosmos* out of the scattered fragments of

---

[16] I am obviously referring to empirical intuition and not to the pure intuition of space and time in Kant's transcendental aesthetics, a doctrine that both Husserl and the Neo-Kantians rejected as untenable for reasons that need not occupy us here.
[17] MPU, 128.   [18] MPU, 136.   [19] MPU, 140.

intelligibility given to us in sheer intuition and thereby bring about essential knowledge. We need to reorganize conceptually also the non-sensuous elements of intelligibility given in intuition in order to transform a fragmented "chaos of manifestations [*Gewühl von Erscheinungen*]" into a proper *mundus intelligibilis*.[20] Husserl's emphasis on intuition is, for Rickert, only a rhetorical expedient to downplay the role of conceptual constructions in *his own* thought and in so doing create a result which is appealing to younger generations. This is why he charges Husserl of practicing an "ostrich philosophy. Due to fear of constructions he sticks his head in the sand of intuitions, in order not to have to see the constructions he cannot do without."[21]

The same line of criticism is expressed in Paul Natorp's review of Husserl's *Ideen*, published in the 1917/18 issue of *Logos*. After declaring his interest in Husserl's project of a pure phenomenology, one that he perceives as close to his own project of a critical psychology, Natorp focuses on Husserl's concept of intuition and essence. He expresses his concerns by questioning Husserl's talk of an "originarily *giving act* or *consciousness*" that presents us intuitively with essences.[22] The word *Anschauung* suggests a "passive receiving"[23] of the corresponding object. However, Husserl's insistence on *Wesensschau* being a *giving act (ein gebender Akt)* seems to suggest that, in this connection, we cannot understand intuition in terms of mere receptivity. Natorp suggests, paraphrasing Kant, that with a priori knowledge "there is an *originary appropriation* of something that was by no means already there beforehand."[24] In other words, we still can use metaphors such as grasping, seeing, and intuiting to underscore how we do not arbitrarily create a priori knowledge but rather follow a necessity that belongs to the 'things themselves.' On the other hand, we have to be aware of the fact that a priori knowledge pertains to a more fundamental "continuity of thought"[25] that connects, disconnects, distinguishes, and articulates. Every isolated positing of an essence conceals the underlying "process of thought, which is the authentic 'giver' of essences."[26] The emphasis on the processual trait of eidetic knowledge is thus manifestly a point on which Rickert and Natorp are in agreement against Husserl.

[20] See MPU, 139. For a more thorough discussion of this point see Chapter 1.
[21] MPU, 117.
[22] P. Natorp, "Husserls 'Ideen zu einer reinen Phänomenologie'," in H. Noack (ed.), *Husserl* (Darmstadt: WBG, 1973), 40. Hereafter HIP.
[23] HIP, 40.   [24] HIP, 41.   [25] HIP, 42.   [26] HIP, 43.

Natorp reinforces this idea by referring explicitly to Plato's thought, considering that Husserl always hinted at Plato as a major source of inspiration concerning eidetics.[27] Natorp, an esteemed interpreter of Plato, decrees that Husserl "did reach Plato's *eidos*, however, he stood still at the *first level* of Platonism, i.e., the level of rigid *eidē* 'standing there in being' motionlessly. He did not follow Plato's last step, which was actually Plato's greatest and most characteristic step: bringing the *eidē* into *motion* and fluidifying them into the ultimate continuity of the process of thought."[28] Natorp refers here to Plato's dialectical method as the way to grasp the essence of things.[29]

To summarize, we can identify two closely related critiques of Husserl's account of eidetic knowledge in *Ideen I* from the Neo-Kantian camp. (1) Eidetic knowledge cannot be intuitive because intuition only provides the material of knowledge, be it sensible or intelligible. Knowledge is necessarily conceptual-discursive, and conceptuality involves a departure from the immediacy of intuition. (2) Eidetic knowledge is *processual*. It is the result of a thought-process that needs to be taken into account if we want to be able to justify the validity of our eidetic insights.

Husserl's reaction to this criticism is documented in some of his lecture courses and manuscripts. Overall, he is rather dismissive of it and does not seem willing to take it too seriously. In his 1922 lecture "Introduction to Philosophy," for example, he offers a brief retort to those who criticize intuition as a valid method, in which he simply insists that philosophers should only talk about things whose evidence they are able to *see* in the first place. Knowing from one of his letters that Husserl received and read *Die Philosophie des Lebens*,[30] it is reasonable to assume that the addressee of his retort is precisely Rickert, although Rickert's name is not mentioned explicitly. This is Husserl's defense of phenomenological intuitionism in "Introduction to Philosophy":

---

[27] Karl-Heinz Lembeck points out correctly that Natorp's intention in his review can be viewed as the attempt to give a new interpretation to Husserl's concept of intuition based on a 'dynamic' understanding of Plato's theory of Ideen. K.-H. Lembeck, "Begründungsphilosophische Perspektiven: Husserl und Natorp über Anschauung," *Phänomenologische Forschungen* (2003): 97–108.

[28] HIP, 44.

[29] This is not the place to expand further on Natorp's idiosyncratic reading of Plato. See P. Natorp, *Plato's Theory of Ideas: An Introduction to Idealism* (Sankt Augustin: Academia, 2004).

[30] See Husserl's letter to Rickert of August 9, 1920, BW V, 182–183.

Being radical means delving down to the ultimate roots, seeing these very roots, and, as a matter of principle, drawing all thought (both its details and its principles) exclusively from such self-givenness. Unfortunately, the much-abused word "intuition" permits one to categorize phenomenology under the heading of "intuitionist philosophy," and thus place it under the same umbrella with all sorts of mythical enthusiasm and unscientific extravagancies.

Phenomenology, as the expression of a will to absolutely honest and justified science, neither appeals to nor builds upon supernatural illuminations. Phenomenology ignores all kinds of mysterious "intellectual intuitions" and it offers no technique through which devotees would be enhanced with unheard-of spiritual powers. Phenomenology is a field for the conceivably most prosaic kind of work conducted in a spirit of highest and most radical conscientiousness. In phenomenology, the "method of intuition" has a simple and prosaic meaning. It means that I only judge reliably when besides meaning something, I am also in a position to present [ausweisen] and exhibit [aufweisen] what I mean. The most radical kind of exhibiting is seeing or something analogous to ordinary seeing, and even this principle must be exhibited through an act of exhibition via pure seeing.[31]

It is perfectly understandable that Husserl was frustrated about Rickert's mischaracterization of phenomenology as irrationalistic intuitionism. However, precisely the fact that 'intuition' is a much-abused term in philosophy seems to call for a more thorough explanation of what intuition means in phenomenology.

Both remarks by Rickert and Natorp are strong. To reiterate, they claim that (1) eidetic knowledge is conceptual-discursive rather than intuitive and (2) eidetic knowledge is processual rather than a momentary insight. The benevolent interpreter of Husserl is compelled to go beyond the letter of *Ideen I* in order to provide a satisfying answer to them. In answering the first critique, it is safe to concede to Rickert that intuition cannot *per se* already qualify as knowledge. Husserl, however, does not seem to claim otherwise in *Ideen I*. Instead he wants to emphasize the fact that the scope of intuition is not restricted to sensibility but includes ideal objects and, among them, essences to which all a priori valid predications pertaining to a certain sector of reality (in Husserl's terms: ontological region) can be referred. He does not dwell extensively on how the intuitive givenness of essences can function as the basis for a *science of essences*, although he makes clear that

---

[31] Hua XXXV, 288.

precisely this is the project he envisions under the heading "phenomenology." Accordingly, and in order to do justice to Husserl's project, we have to draw a distinction between intuitive *vision of essence* and conceptual *knowledge of essence*, i.e., between *Wesensschau* and *Wesenserkenntnis*.[32] Having an intuitive vision of essence does not yet amount to having a fully articulated knowledge of that essence.

Husserl's awareness of this distinction can be exemplified with a brief anticipation of his studies on nature and spirit, which shall be detailed in later chapters. In the second book of *Ideas*, which was only published posthumously, Husserl endeavors to articulate both an ontology of nature and an ontology of spirit, and in so doing to clarify the distinction between the natural and human sciences. On the one hand he points out that we have to interrogate our pre-predicative experience and gain an insight into the intuitively given essence of each domain. On the other hand he underscores the necessity thereupon to select the correct conceptuality to build up an eidetic *science* of nature and an

---

[32] The distinction between *Wesensschau* and *Wesenserkenntnis* has been recently addressed and framed in terms of an intuition of essence "upriver" and "downriver" of an eidetic judgment in C. Majolino, "La Partition du réel: remarques sur l'eidos, la phantasia, l'effondrement du monde et l'être absolu de la conscience," in C. Ierna, H. Jacobs, and F. Mattens (eds.), *Philosophy, Phenomenology, Sciences – Essays in Commemoration of Edmund Husserl* (Dordrecht: Springer, 2010), 573–660. Here, 593. Whereas the intuition of essence 'upriver' of an eidetic judgment simply consists in the possibility of viewing an individual as an example of its class (*this* tone is also *a* tone), through a corresponding shift of attitude, the transition to a pure *eidos* and thereby the intuitive vision of an essence as fulfilling intuitively an eidetic judgment requires a specific method of disengagement of reality and fantasy-variation. I cannot expand further on this point here but I wish to refer to Majolino's excellent work for an extended and convincing treatment. It should be noticed, however, that in Husserl there are at least two different problems regarding the status of eidetics, which he does not always keep distinct as they should be. One problem is how we bring *already formulated* judgments entailing eidetic claims to phenomenological fulfillment. This requires going through a number of methodologically regimented steps, which should help us discern whether what we judge to be essential actually is essential. A different problem is how we form eidetic judgments in the first place. This requires that we are somehow already aware, prior to all judging, that the things we encounter and the experiences we have are structured according to stable regularities, of which we can meaningfully ask whether they are merely empirical or essential. It is in the process of testing the eidetic necessity of recurring properties of experienced individuals and individual experiences that we set the basis for the constitution of objects of a new kind (essences), which subsequently can become the subject matter of discursive predication.

eidetic *science* of spirit. There is a kind of conceptuality that faithfully brings to expression what has been *seen* through *Wesensschau* and a kind of conceptuality that is at odds with the corresponding *Wesensschau*.

The conceptuality of mechanistic causality, for instance, is at odds with the kind of eidetic insight that characterizes our experience of mentality, revealing it as a domain of experiences linked in terms of interrelated motivation. In order to express this eidetic insight and to grant truly phenomenological scientificity to our ontology of mentality, we need to replace mechanistic conceptuality with the conceptuality of motivation. This is why Husserl, for example, characterizes natural causality as "extra-essential [*außerwesentlich*]"[33] when we consider the unfolding of psychic life. We can, of course, employ the conceptuality of mechanistic causality in order to explain the connection between two mental events, say: (A) "reading in the newspaper about the economic crisis" and (B) "deciding to run to the bank to withdraw all my money." We could, for instance, observe the configurations of neuronal activity in the brain in A and B and, by way of repeatedly observing and hypothesizing, finally discover the causal law regulating the transition from A-like states to B-like states.[34] The kind of knowledge attained in this case is by no means false or trivial for a phenomenologist.

Rather, as far as the mental is concerned, this kind of knowledge would be deemed extra-essential, because the conceptuality at work does not match with the eidetic intuition of the purely motivational connection linking A and B, the essential features of which should be brought to conceptual expression in a significantly different way. *Essential knowledge is concept-formation in accord with an underlying vision of essence. Extra-essential knowledge is concept-formation following theoretical demands other than those suggested by an underlying vision of essence.*[35] In this sense, and in keeping with the spirit of

---

[33] E. Husserl, MS A VI 16/25a, edited by U. Melle, published in T. Nenon and L. Embree (eds.), *Issues in Husserl's* Ideen II (Dordrecht: Kluwer, 1996), 1–8. Here 2.

[34] Whether there really are such things – i.e., causal laws formulable in mathematical terms that regulate the transition from a state belonging to a certain psychic class and states of a different class – is a complex question with no obvious answer, in spite of all recent enthusiasm for so-called reductive theories of the mental.

[35] Interestingly, this position comes close to that of Rickert's student Emil Lask. In his insightful reflections on Lask's philosophy, Steven G. Crowell writes: "Thus

Rickert's critique, essential knowledge is not some sort of mystical intensification of the vision of essence but an essentially different kind of accomplishment. The first is concept-formation *on the basis* of the latter. Troubles and crises arise when extra-essential knowledge supplants essential knowledge and thereby blurs the underlying vision of essence.

After establishing the distinction between *Wesensschau* and *Wesenserkenntnis*, we can also argue for a certain superiority of Husserl's position over Rickert's: Rickert has no robust account of the boundaries imposed upon concept-formation by experience.[36] We cannot form concepts of any sort if we intend to produce *essential* knowledge about a given sector of reality. We have to hold fast to an underlying eidetic intuition and orient our conceptualization to a faithful articulation of the essence as it is given intuitively. In a certain sense, it holds true that intuitions are reorganized in cognition, as Rickert would have it. This is true for both empirical and eidetic intuitions. But not every form of conceptual reorganization is equally legitimate for every kind of intuition. If we want to attain *essential knowledge*, we rather have to mold our concepts according to an underlying essential intuition; in Husserlian language, we have to make sure that the connections of concepts that we use to describe an essence can really receive intuitive fulfillment.

the problem of knowledge appears as the problem of choosing (or discovering) the proper category for given material ... Error, on this view, consists in predicating of some material a category in which it does not stand." Crowell, *Husserl, Heidegger and the Space of Meaning*, 63–64. However, Husserl is less exclusive than Lask. Extra-essential knowledge, although not in accord with an underlying vision of essence (in Lask's language: category), is not to be deemed erroneous outright. It is regrettable that Lask passed away before having the opportunity to read Husserl's *Ideen* which would have offered precious insights to carry forward his own philosophical project had he been able to develop it further. Crowell, however, wrongly attributes to Rickert, too, the position that "the sciences are rooted in pretheoretical experience, and their governing categories will differ according to the way their objects present themselves in such experience" (Crowell, *Husserl, Heidegger and the Space of Meaning*, 275). While Rickert does acknowledge a kind of proto-conceptualization happening through natural language in pre-scientific experience, he couldn't be further from the view shared by both Husserl and Lask that pre-scientific experience somehow dictates the categorial boundaries in which the sciences can legitimately operate.

[36] On the contrary, the idea of *experiential* boundaries imposed on concept-formation, if this latter is to attain essential knowledge, represents the crucial novelty that stems from Husserl's eidetics.

The above considerations give us resources to answer the second critical remark, according to which eidetic knowledge is necessarily a processual and not a momentary insight. Natorp is right to quote Plato and highlight the difference between Husserl's and Plato's conceptions of essence. Famously, Plato maintains that we can never "see" essences directly in our earthly life. For Plato, the act of 'seeing an essence' (on earth) is a metaphor for a *dialectical* and thus mediated act of discovering true relations in the intelligible realm. We only "see" an essence, albeit imperfectly, to the extent that we are able to produce a definition and justify it within a system of logically connected definitions by means of dialectical reasoning. This is why "seeing an essence" and "producing a definition" are fundamentally synonymous in Plato's thought. By recasting Plato's conception, Natorp thus fails to distinguish between *Wesensschau* and *Wesenserkenntnis* and seems to suggest that on closer inspection *Wesensschau* is actually nothing but *Wesenserkenntnis* and, to be precise, *Wesenserkenntnis* before logical and conceptual justification is undertaken.[37] Natorp represents here a longstanding tradition in philosophy according to which essences manifest themselves only in cognition. On this account, 'seeing an essence' amounts, by necessity, to 'having a successful intellective grasp of a general truth.' The kind of subjective act in which essences manifest themselves in the first place would be, accordingly, a judgment articulating a true definition. Definitions are necessarily relational and involve a thought-process of comparison and distinction in order to be articulated. Therefore, no essence can be posited in isolation from the continuity of thought that makes definition possible.

Husserl, however, does not follow Plato and the tradition stemming from his philosophy on this point. By simply seeing an essence we do not necessarily acquire knowledge of some sort. For Husserl, a vision of essence is *not* the culmination of a cognitive process of abstraction from the objects in the visible world. Essences are not entities, the viewing of which coincides with or is a metaphor for successful cognitive achievement. Rather, essences are for Husserl *objects* in a robust formal-logical sense, i.e., substrates for true or *false* predications. We thus have to

---

[37] For a brief but illuminating characterization of the Neo-Kantian idea of justification in transcendental philosophy and its difference from Husserl's phenomenology see Crowell, *Husserl, Heidegger and the Space of Meaning*, 173–174.

distinguish between experiential *access* to essences and discursive-conceptual *articulation* of essences. These two moments are distinct although we generally consider essences for theoretical purposes and are, therefore, interested from the very beginning in carrying out conceptual articulations of them. This, on Husserl's account, might be the reason why the Platonic tradition conflated predicative articulation of essences via dialectics with the simple seeing of an essence on the basis of the individual data of experience.

Husserl's following remarks are eloquent enough:

[An essence is] something that can be thought of vaguely or distinctly, which can be made the subject of true and false predications;[38] essences can be an intuitive consciousness of essences, in a certain manner they can also be seized upon, without becoming 'objects about which';[39] like other objects [essences] can at times be intended correctly, at times falsely, as, e.g., in false geometrical thinking.[40] The consciousness of an essence's givenness is often not adequate ideation, i.e., it is not ideation, in which the essence comes to a full and authentic givenness.[41]

Considering these quotations, the last one in particular, we can see why Husserl does not see a contradiction in the intuitive *and at the same time* actively "giving" aspect of *Wesensschau*. The process of eidetic cognition starts with the mostly vague and unthematic awareness that a given datum of experience belongs to a certain class. This is because its manifest properties display associative similarities and overlap with those of previously experienced objects of the same class. In this kind of consciousness, our apprehending regard is guided by what Husserl calls empirical types. Empirical types could be characterized as bundles of anticipations formed over the course of past experiences. Thereby, the merely contingent features of the apprehended object are fused together with its specific, essential features. What is *essential* to that particular kind of object does not stand out in a way that allows for further theoretical determination. Nonetheless, already at the level of

---

[38] Ideas I, 10.   [39] Ideas I, 33.

[40] Ideas I, 44. Neither Plato nor Natorp would be willing to accept false geometrical thinking as a case in which a vision of essence is nonetheless operative. For Husserl, on the contrary, this would be a case of vision of essence followed by an unsuccessful attempt to gain knowledge of the corresponding geometrical essence.

[41] E. Husserl, *Vorlesungen über Bedeutungslehre. Sommersemester 1908, Husserliana*, vol. 26 (Dordrecht: Kluwer, 1987), 108.

simple perception and type-based apprehension, the objects encountered in experience implicitly harbor essences 'in' them. That this is
Husserl's view is confirmed by the following passage stemming from a
1918 manuscript commenting on the *Ideen*:

If one moves behind logical consciousness, back into sensuous consciousness,
it is possible that a red sensuous object appears without being apprehended as
red, thereby maintaining its sensuous unity, within which, then, the implied
red maintains its unity. *The essence individuates itself in this object and in a
certain sense it is entailed in it: however the essence is entailed in the object
implicitly.* For the essence itself it is indifferent whether it is grasped here or
there on the basis of examples, whether this or that object is given as one of its
individuations, whether it is categorially grasped in this or that way.[42]

The first step toward the full vision of an essence consists in thematizing
the vague awareness of an object's belonging to a given class and
subsequently testing the 'essentiality' of its salient properties with the
aid of a methodological procedure that Husserl later dubbed 'eidetic
variation'.[43] When we perform an eidetic variation, we actively move
from the awareness of a certain property as belonging to a given
instance, through a generalization of that property for all instances of
its class, and finally to the redirection of our focus from the infinite
variety of possible instances to an object of a new kind: the essence of
the class at issue, to which the property is attributed.

With the example of a tone, we start by hearing a tone and being
aware of it *as a tone*. Subsequently, after focusing on its salient properties while holding the whole given tone firmly in grasp, we can see with
evidence that some of these properties must be present a priori in "any
tone whatever." Varying the given tone and producing in our imagination further examples of tones will let the essential properties of a tone in

---

[42] E. Husserl, *Ideen zu einer reinen Phänomenologie und phänomenologischen
      Philosophie. Erstes Buch: Allgemeine Einführung in die reine Phänomenologie.
      Zweiter Halbband: Ergänzende Texte (1912–1929)*, Husserliana, vol. 3/2
      (The Hague: Nijhoff, 1976), 581. Hereafter Hua III/2. My italics.
[43] It should be remarked that the procedure of eidetic variation is not explicitly
      present in the *Ideen* and is introduced by Husserl only later, especially in his
      lectures of transcendental logic in the 1920s. However, it has been convincingly
      shown that the method of eidetic variation is nothing but a refinement of the
      procedure employed by Husserl from the start in his phenomenological analyses.
      See D. Lohmar, "Die phänomenologische Methode der Wesensschau und ihre
      Präzisierung als eidetische Variation," *Phänomenologische Forschungen* (2005),
      65–91.

general separate from the purely contingent properties. At this point, we can shift our attention from the infinite variety of possible examples to a new object that is intuited as the *ideal carrier* of all the features pertaining to any tone whatsoever. The "originarily giving act" of *Wesensschau* is thus not, as Natorp would have it, a hidden construction or, as Plato would have it, the result of dialectical reasoning but a move from the unthematic to the thematic, from the implicit to the explicit in order to pick out what is essential to given kinds of objects. At this point, and only at this point, are we ready to articulate conceptual knowledge of essence and, for instance, write down the sentence 'to the essence tone belong pitch and intensity.' Note that at the beginning of this process, when we just heard a tone, we already heard something having pitch and intensity. However, we most likely did not seize on pitch and intensity as discrete properties, and we certainly did not spend time sieving through the tone to isolate pitch and intensity as essential properties from other merely contingent properties. The initial experience of a tone is characterized by a set of properties 'fused together,' as it were, and it is guided by the empirical type 'tone,' which we formed over the course of our foregoing experience. Moving in a further step to consider the tone's salient properties should be considered a shift of focus in the overarching experience of the tone, rather than an achievement of our discursive-conceptual capacities. Moreover, it is not enough to discriminate between properties that are in some way always recurring, such as pitch and intensity, and properties that are merely accidental, such as, say, the length of the tone's duration. It is only when we engage in a process of variation, in which we disengage all the empirical, contingent experiences of tones we had, and range over an indefinite manifold of possible tones, that the *essentiality* of certain properties will stand out. Pitch and intensity, to stay with our example, are then recognized as being essential properties of any tone whatsoever, rather than empirically recurring features of all tones that we hitherto happened to hear and of those we will happen to hear in the future. Redirecting the ascription of properties identified as essential from the indefinite manifold of possible tones to an object of a new kind (the essence 'tone') is a theoretically relevant move to the extent that it inaugurates a new sphere of inquiry, in which we do not operate with variants and instances of empirical items but with a stable and indefinitely accessible class of ideal objects. There is no need to have further experiences of tones in order to hold fast to the truth of the judgment "to the essence 'tone' belong pitch and intensity" because this judgment now intends an ideal object of a new kind that is distinct from the variety of instances on the basis of which it was initially constituted.

To recapitulate, the essence is 'given' to us in three guises: (1) *per speculum*, as it were, i.e., through the lens of the individual that we choose to view as an example of its class; (2) through the process of imaginative variation, as a new ideal object that carries its own determinations and can at any time be referred back to an infinite variety of possible individuals; (3) as the fulfilling factor of a potentially infinite number of eidetic judgments, that is, as the correlate of indefinitely articulable *Wesenserkenntnis*. However, a synthesis of coincidence runs through all these forms of consciousness of an essence. One and the same essence is implicitly, unthematically, present at first, then it is made the object of explicit consideration and finally it is cognized via connections of concepts, of which it provides the intuitive fulfillment.

To sum up and conclude this section: I argue that the problems raised by Rickert and Natorp about Husserl's theory of essence can be overcome if we hold fast to (1) a robust distinction between *Wesensschau* and *Wesenserkenntnis* and (2) an understanding of the *giving act of Wesensschau* as a movement from the unthematic to the thematic and not as a hidden, unexplicated process of conceptual thought.[44]

Difficulties with an eidetic science of consciousness

After the distinction between unthematic, vague awareness of an essence, vision of essence, and knowledge of essence has been established we are equipped with the appropriate theoretical tools to face the next challenge posed to *Ideen I* by the Neo-Kantians. This second challenge hits upon another crucial point of Husserlian phenomenology: its self-understanding as "a *descriptive* eidetic doctrine of transcendentally pure lived experiences [*Erlebnisse*]"[45] and the connected claim to be, as such, the most fundamental of all sciences. The underlying issue is manifestly one and the same, since the fundamentality Husserl claims for phenomenology rests on its investigating the domain

---

[44] In this sense, as Nicolas De Warren aptly emphasizes, "an 'intuition of essence' requires a complex form of activity and passivity." N. De Warren, "On Husserl's Essentialism," *International Journal of Philosophical Studies* 14/2 (2006): 255–270. Here 262.

[45] Ideas I, 167, translation modified.

of being presupposed by all further domains of being, namely, lived-experience. However, for the sake of clarity, it can be fruitfully articulated in two sub-points, addressed respectively by Natorp and by Rickert. The first sub-point is whether the eidetic method presented above is really adequate for a philosophical study of subjectivity and experience. The second sub-point is whether the concept of *phenomenon*, on which phenomenology rests, is really as fundamental as Husserl would have it, and therefore whether a phenomenology *per se* is fit to carry the burden of being the most fundamental of all sciences. Let us start with the first sub-point and turn once more to Natorp's review, in order to then conclude with a consideration of the second sub-point.

After a paraphrase of the chapters of *Ideen I* devoted to the phenomenological reduction and the disclosure of pure consciousness, Natorp focuses on Husserl's claim that every positing of being and value must refer back to a positing consciousness that is not in turn posited on the basis of something else, but rather is immediately given. This positing consciousness is pure consciousness conceived of as "*phenomenological residuum*"[46] after all further positings of being have been suspended via *epoché*. Its purity consists in its independency from empirical being and, in particular, from an empirical body. Its 'conscious' aspect depends on the fact that after the performance of the phenomenological *epoché* we are still dwelling in the realm of accessible experiences, which we can thematize and study in a direct, intuition-based fashion.

According to Husserl, the kind of task connected to this discovery of pure consciousness is a description of its general structure (intentionality) and of the different classes of experience (perception, recollection, fantasy) from an eidetic point of view. But, Natorp asks, is the kind of knowledge that we thus acquire really *essential knowledge* of pure consciousness?[47] In other passages of his work Husserl characterizes the nexus of *Erlebnisse* as a whole, not as a patchwork of juxtaposed experiences but as an endless and continuous *stream*. But then Natorp argues that, on closer inspection, "the stream in its streaming is something other than what can be grasped and fixed in reflection."[48] Certainly, to a reflective gaze, pure consciousness *appears* as a self-contained nexus of lived experiences of different kinds. However – Natorp stands here very close to Rickert's remarks discussed

---

[46] Ideas I, 65. [47] HIP, 49. [48] HIP, 50.

above – "the 'immediateness' of pure consciousness [i.e., pure consciousness as it appears to a reflective gaze] is not already as such also immediately known [*erkannt*] or knowable."[49]

One could rephrase Natorp's concern employing the Husserlian conceptuality worked out at the end of the previous section. According to that framework, pure consciousness manifests itself in a certain way under our reflective regard. However, the sheer thematization of pure consciousness in reflection is not yet knowledge of pure consciousness. We should ask ourselves, according to the above distinctions, whether the eidetic knowledge of consciousness envisioned by Husserl really catches what is essential to consciousness! If our eidetic insight tells us that consciousness is essentially a *stream*, then we will have to work out concepts and methods of investigation that do justice to its streaming nature, provided we want to achieve essential and not extra-essential knowledge. But if we then set out to analyze *Erlebnisse* (lived experiences), treating them as isolated objective units, and, furthermore, if we try to 'extract' from them static essential structures, such as "the *eidos* of perception," "the *eidos* of recollection," and "the *eidos* of imagination," are we not missing precisely what Husserl himself acknowledged as the essential trait of consciousness, namely, its being a stream? In fact, Natorp reads Husserl as making precisely this mistake:

But in this way [i.e., via an eidetic analysis], is the *overflowing stream* of consciousness not *brought to a halt* against its own nature and is its *concreteness* not resolved into a sum of *abstractions*, in particular if thereby (following Husserl) the singular experience is immediately grasped in '*eidetic generality*'?[50]

Natorp's counterproposal, presented in his *Allgemeine Psychologie*, for dealing philosophically with the stream-like nature of consciousness can be left aside here.[51] Rather, we should try to answer Natorp's challenge using Husserlian resources. A first, somewhat obvious but in no way trivial remark is that Natorp's statement that "consciousness is essentially a stream" is not itself a stream but rather a piece of eidetic

---

[49] *Ibid.*   [50] HIP, 53.
[51] This is what he called "reconstructive method." For a full-fledged account of Natorp's reconstructive method see Sebastian Luft, "Reconstruction and Reduction: Natorp and Husserl on Method and the Question of Subjectivity," in Luft and Makkreel, *Neo-Kantianism in Contemporary Philosophy*, 59–91.

knowledge, based on eidetic intuition and conceptually expressed. Accordingly, we cannot escape eidetic knowledge or, at least, eidetic claims about consciousness if what we want is a descriptive *science* of consciousness. Furthermore, correctly executed *Wesensschau* reveals that consciousness is not just a stream but rather a stream that assumes very specific forms. I do not know *what* perceptions, recollections, expectations, and fantasies I will have in the future, but I know a priori *that* I will have all of them or, in other words, *that* the forms which my conscious life assumes will be necessarily and exclusively perceptions, recollections, expectations, fantasies, and the like. Again, this insight is just as essential as the one revealing that consciousness is essentially a stream. Metaphorically, there is a difference between a formless torrential stream and a stream that flows obediently between well-formed banks. Consciousness resembles much more the second kind of stream than the first. In this sense, the different classes of lived-experience and their eidetic investigation are not abstract falsifications of consciousness's streaming nature. Rather, within the Husserlian project of a science of essences, such a classification goes hand in hand with it.

Phenomenologically speaking, we need both an eidetic study of *Erlebnisse* and their basic intentional structure *as well as* an eidetic study of the stream in which all these *Erlebnisse* are constituted. Corresponding respectively to these two tasks are what Husserl calls static phenomenology and genetic phenomenology. Static phenomenology distinguishes and describes different classes of experiences, whereas genetic phenomenology studies how experiences come about on the basis of more rudimentary elements, such as sensations or instincts, and how they are connected together through temporality and association. The influence of Natorp's thought on Husserl's development of a "genetic method" has been rightly emphasized by several scholars.[52] However, in a way that some scholarly work does not seem

---

[52] The first to underscore this influence was Iso Kern in his monumental work *Husserl und Kant: Eine Untersuchung über Husserls Verhältnis zu Kant und zum Neukantianismus* (The Hague: Nijhoff, 1964), 366–367. Recently, Natorp's influence on Husserl has been the object of renewed attention: D. Welton, "The Systematicity of Husserl's Transcendental Philosophy," in D. Welton (ed.), *The New Husserl: A Critical Reader* (Bloomington: Indiana University Press, 2003), 255–288; S. Luft, "Natorp, Husserl und das Problem der Kontinuität von Leben, Wissenschaft und Philosophie," *Phänomenologische Forschungen* (2006): 99–134.

to adequately appreciate, Husserl's move *towards* genetic phenomenology does not mean a move *away from* static phenomenology or a
change of mind about fundamental phenomenological concepts such as
essence and intuition.

Husserl was well aware of the dynamic nature of consciousness
much earlier than his publication of *Ideen I*[53] as indicated in his famous
1904/05 lectures on time-consciousness.[54] While it is true that the
investigations carried out in these lectures are not yet termed genetic
phenomenology they foreshadow the subsequent articulation of genetic
phenomenology: even in the investigation of the dynamic structures of
consciousness, the phenomenologist is not concerned with facts but
with essences. In this connection, such essences are the underpinning
structures of a dynamic process. However, they are not themselves
dynamic but, rather, as Husserl puts it in a later manuscript, *"rigid
lawfulnesses"*[55] [*starre Gesetzlichkeiten*], where "rigid" means invariable, selfsame validities.[56] For these, too, the ultimate source of legitimacy must be intuition and not mere logical consistency or speculative

---

[53] This is the substance of Husserl's response to Natorp's critical review of *Ideen*
when in a letter to the Neo-Kantian philosopher he writes: "I overcame the stage
of static Platonism already more than one decade ago" (letter to Natorp, June 29,
1918, BW V, 135–136. Quoted in Luft, "Natorp, Husserl und das Problem der
Kontinuität von Leben, Wissenschaft und Philosophie," 106 n. 18).

[54] Interestingly, in spite of all his emphasis on the dynamic nature of consciousness,
Natorp does not have a theory of time-consciousness. I cannot expand here on
Husserl's investigations into time-consciousness and its import in genetic
phenomenology. An illuminating study of these issues is offered in N. De Warren,
Husserl and the Promise of Time: Subjectivity in Transcendental Phenomenology
(Cambridge University Press, 2009).

[55] E. Husserl, *Die Lebenswelt. Auslegungen der vorgegebenen Welt und ihrer
Konstitution. Texte aus dem Nachlass (1916–1937), Husserliana*, vol. 39
(Dordrecht: Springer, 2008), 11. My italics. Hereafter Hua XXXIX.

[56] Sebastian Luft seems to downplay this important point when he writes:
"Obviously, with a modification of phenomenology's *theme* the characterizing
trait of eidetic science undergoes a transformation too. Accordingly, an eidetic
science of transcendental subjectivity deals with 'laws of genesis', such as the laws
of motivation and association" (Luft, "Natorp, Husserl und das Problem der
Kontinuität von Leben, Wissenschaft und Philosophie," 124–125). This
statement can be read as suggesting that static phenomenology deals with
essences, whereas genetic phenomenology deals with eidetic laws. This is
misleading for two interconnected reasons. (1) The concept of eidetic law is not
peculiar to genetic phenomenology. Rather, *every* essence – also 'static' essences
such as the essence of a tone or the essence of perception – can be converted into
eidetic laws of the form "for every conceivable *x*: if *x* is an F then *x* is a G"
(R. Sowa, "Husserls Idee einer nicht-empirischen Wissenschaft von der

construction. Husserl's preoccupation with intuition and intuitive legitimatizing even in the difficult field of genetic phenomena is witnessed, for instance, by his untiring work on the so-called time-diagrams, which are meant to contribute precisely an intuitive legitimatizing for the complicated genetic structure that characterizes time-consciousness.[57]

Natorp's critical remarks on Husserl's alleged static Platonism are thus only acceptable insofar as they gesture towards the necessity of a genetic phenomenology of pure consciousness, a chapter missing in *Ideen I*. However, Natorp notwithstanding, both static *and* genetic phenomenology are and must be eidetic sciences of consciousness whose aim is to achieve universal, rigid, and unchangeable validities and not just to defend the allegedly unobjectifiable fluency of the stream of consciousness. If the talk of genesis is to be justified, one has to include in this very notion that 'something' which the genesis at issue is supposed to generate. Husserl's most important discovery is not simply that there is a genetic and dynamic trait to consciousness. Rather, for him, the stream of consciousness moves *teleologically* towards its self-realization in lived-experiences, the structure of which can be grasped in eidetic universality and does not depend on mere physiological underpinnings. Thus, out of raw (unapprehended) *hyle*, full-blown *Erlebnisse* are generated on the basis of which objects of all kinds and, ultimately, an existing world are posited. This dynamic, which Husserl calls 'constitution', is describable through and through in eidetic terms.

Phenomenology's foundational claim

In light of these last remarks, which are meant both to reinforce phenomenology's eidetic project and to highlight the necessity to extend it

---

Lebenswelt," *Husserl Studies* 26/1 (2010): 59), for example, "if x is a tone then x is an object with an intensity and a pitch." (2) The "laws of genesis" too *qua* eidetic laws can be in turn converted into "static essences," or, better, re-articulated in terms of a vision of essence, such as "to the essence of time-consciousness belongs the threefold structure retention/primary impression/ protention." (The law-like formulation would be: "if x is a time-consciousness then x is an entity the structure of which is retention/primary impression/ protention.")

[57] To learn about Husserl's work on the diagrams see the instructive paper: J. Dodd, "Reading Husserl's Time-Diagrams from 1917/18," *Husserl Studies* 21/2 (2005): 111–137.

beyond the scope of static analyses, we can turn to the aforementioned second aspect of this wave of criticism concerning phenomenology's claim "to be the science fundamental to philosophy."[58] Although Natorp also expresses some serious doubts about this claim in his review,[59] it is Rickert who voices the Neo-Kantian concerns vis-à-vis phenomenology's self-understanding in the sharpest fashion. In *Ideen I* Husserl famously insists on the fact that while all empirical being depends on phenomena of consciousness for its manifestation (and its cognition is thus mediated) phenomena of consciousness do not depend on further phenomena and are thus immediately and absolutely given.[60] However, Rickert points out that, on closer inspection, the very notion of 'phenomenon' in construed in a threefold way. A phenomenon is necessarily a phenomenon *of* something *for* a subject. Even if we carry out a phenomenological reduction, as Husserl intends to do, and consider the object of the phenomenon purely as intended, Rickert argues:

If the word phenomenon – on this condition – is not to become entirely meaningless, isn't a subject to whom the phenomenal [*das Erscheinende*] appears or who intends via the phenomena the unknown object that appears therein, even more necessary? How can one claim, however, to bring such an ego into the "phenomenological" sphere just like the phenomena that appear to it? Does one not thereby have to leave the realm of the immediate in the first place?[61]

In other words, Rickert's line of argument could run thus: phenomenology is a science of phenomena that claims to be the fundamental science for philosophy. Fundamentality must go hand in hand with immediacy of the investigated object. Should phenomena turn out to refer necessarily to something other than phenomena, and thus not immediately cognized, then it will be knowledge of this further element that deserves to be deemed fundamental. However, on closer inspection, the concept of phenomenon refers *per definitionem* to something other than itself. Therefore, phenomenology cannot be the fundamental science.

---

[58] Ideas I, XVII.   [59] HIP, 50.
[60] See Ideas I, 95–96. It is appropriate to recall that 'phenomenon' for Husserl amounts to 'lived-experience', i.e., perception, recollection, expectation, and so forth.
[61] MPU, 115.

Rickert indicates with remarkable clarity the following problem:

In a "phenomenology" deserving this name, one has to call immediate either the phenomena or the subject and, accordingly, denominate mediate [*vermittelt*] either the phenomena or that subject for which they are phenomena. In this respect, already the concept of phenomenon – should this word maintain its significant meaning – introduces an element in the observation, through which the permanence within the immediate of unbroken lived-experience [*Erlebnis*] and its intuition is rendered a priori impossible.[62]

Leaving aside the vaguely Hegelian reminiscence of these remarks, whose line of thought is *prima facie* very distant from Husserlian preoccupations, Rickert's position could be pinned down to one rather direct question: does phenomenology, *qua* science of phenomena, have the resources to defend the claim of being the fundamental science for philosophy? And, furthermore: is the concept of phenomenon self-sufficient when it comes to a genuinely philosophical assessment of the import of phenomenology?

Here a very important point has to be emphasized. Husserl's 'phenomenology,' *pace* Rickert, is not strictly speaking a science of conscious phenomena but a science of the *essences* of conscious phenomena. Husserl is certainly committed to a view that considers the essential structures of consciousness to be fundamental vis-à-vis the essential structures of other spheres of reality. This is because the discoverability of other essences (recall the example of the tone given above) presupposes the workings of consciousness according to its essential structures. However, Husserl does not believe that the phenomena themselves, that is, the actual *Erlebnisse* of an actual conscious subject, have a foundational function vis-à-vis other objects, such as the objects of external perception. Unlike Descartes and Brentano, Husserl does not argue for the primacy of immediate knowledge of inner objects over mediate knowledge of external objects. Phenomena are immediately *experienced* manifestations; they do not enjoy a kind of epistemic priority. Moreover, strictly speaking they are not the subject matter of phenomenology but rather what delivers to phenomenology, as to all other sciences, its specific subject matter, namely, essences. To the extent that phenomenology studies *the essence* of this process of 'delivery,' viz. manifestation of all kinds of subject matters through conscious

---

[62] MPU, 116.

experiences, it claims to be fundamental vis-à-vis all other empirical and a priori sciences. However, 'fundamental' here does not mean first in an ideal chain of epistemic justification beginning with immediate cognition of mental events. Phenomenology is foundational because it provides descriptions of what is essential in order for whatever chain of epistemic justifications to begin in the first place, namely, the manifestation of something in experience prior to all cognitive-judicative activity. If we were to express phenomenology's most basic principle in the shortest formulation possible, the following statement would be a good candidate: *no cognition without previous manifestation.* Applying this principle, we should simply make sure that we do not operate with too narrow a notion of manifestation. It is phenomenologically unwarranted to restrict the sphere of acceptable intuitions yielded by direct manifestations to sensory experience.

For instance, when we talk about a pure ego, do we abandon *entirely* the sphere of manifestation and intuition, as Rickert would have it? The answer to this question has to be negative. We would have to abandon intuition, if by intuition we meant exclusively 'direct vision in reflection' or something along these lines. But this has never been Husserl's only concept of intuition. Although the transcendental ego cannot be located directly among its own phenomena, there are plenty of ways to make the transcendental ego intuitive and its corresponding concept clear. For instance, we can describe the phenomena of attention, a kind of experience that remains mysterious if we refuse to see an ego at work who chooses to focus on what would otherwise remain merely in the perceptual "background."[63] Furthermore, we can describe voluntary acts, characterize them as acts springing from an inner ego-center, and finally contrast them to acts sourced from the external world.[64] The list could go on. In all these cases we have possible lines of analysis for the clarification of the concept of ego. Pursuing these lines of analysis, we render the ego intuitive by reference to directly describable experiences without thereby pretending to "see" the ego in the same way in which we see a desk or the perception of a desk in reflection. Similar

---

[63] See Ideas I, §37.

[64] On this point and on Husserl's indebtedness to Pfänder see M. Ubiali, "Die Willensakte und der Umfang der Motivation: Eine Gegenüberstellung von Pfänder und Husserl," in P. Merz, A. Staiti, and F. Steffen (eds.), *Geist–Person–Gemeinschaft: Freiburger Beiträge zur Aktualität Husserls* (Würzburg: Ergon, 2010), 241–267.

clarifications could be given about all fundamental insights of phenomenology, a task that would require much work and more space than this chapter can reasonably accommodate.

To summarize and conclude, the Neo-Kantian critiques are precious because they compel the phenomenologist to shed clarifying light on crucial elements of her endeavor. When Rickert and Natorp cast doubt on the notion of *Wesensschau*, they offer the opportunity to distinguish between vision of essence and knowledge of essence and, thus, the opportunity to clarify the kind of cognition phenomenology yields. When Natorp suggests that consciousness is dynamic and that, therefore, the eidetic method might be intrinsically inadequate to capture what is essential to it, he necessitates a more accurate understanding of the relationship between static and genetic phenomenology like the one sketched above. Finally, Rickert's remarks on the concept of phenomenon help clarify the status of phenomenology as a foundational philosophical discipline.

In Chapter 5, we will turn to Husserl's direct criticism of Rickert, which occurred over ten years after the publication of *Ideas I* and dealt specifically with the problem of the natural and the human sciences.

5 | Husserl's critique of Rickert's secretly naturalistic transcendentalism: the Natur und Geist lectures (1919–1927)

Authentic science tolerates no naivety.

Edmund Husserl[1]

Autonomous thinkers are not exactly the best readers. . .

Edmund Husserl[2]

As a glance at the rubric of his lectures and seminars reveals, Husserl worked intensively on the topic of nature and *Geist* from the 1910s until the end of his life. Various reasons can be identified as to why Husserl increasingly channeled his intellectual energies into this avenue of research. Briefly put, it can be argued that the bundle of problems pertaining to a philosophical demarcation of nature and *Geist* and, correlatively, of natural and human science provides the ideal context for phenomenology to clarify its status and display its fullest philosophical potential. Drawing a line of demarcation of this kind entails (1) some general notion of what "science" means, a topic on which Husserl worked intensively for decades starting with his *Prolegomena to a Pure Logic* back in 1899. Moreover, it presupposes (2) a theory about the relationship between epistemology and ontology that addresses the mutual dependencies and the blurring asymmetries linking nature/*Geist* on one hand and natural/human science on the other. Husserl's understanding of phenomenology as 'correlative research' focusing on the relation between meaning-bestowing acts and their objective correlates (the constituted noemata) offers precisely such a theory. Demarcating different scientific fields also requires (3) a capacity to see beyond the contingency of already existing disciplines and articulate distinctions that hold valid despite the vagaries of the history of

---

[1] Hua XXXII, 16.
[2] Husserl in a letter to Rickert, August 9, 1920 after reading *Die Philosophie des Lebens*. BW V, 183.

science. Phenomenology alone, as opposed to all sciences of facts (*Tatsachenwissenschaften*), is capable of articulating these universally valid distinctions through its eidetic orientation. Talking philosophically about different fields of scientific inquiry entails (4) being sensitive about the far-reaching implications connected with these topics, which have a direct impact on worldview. Husserl explicitly acknowledges that the "dire problems of a worldview are connected"[3] with the philosophical understanding of nature and *Geist* and, in particular, that the absolutization of nature characteristic of the naturalism of his time "propagated a worldview that rendered impossible a truly great and free spiritual life [*Geistesleben*], directed towards the eternal ends of mankind."[4]

In this chapter I will examine Husserl's critique of Rickert as a particularly significant context for correctly understanding the specificity of Husserl's phenomenological approach to this issue. Husserl must have been well aware of the importance of this critique, considering that he devoted to it a vast portion of his last lecture course held at the University of Freiburg in 1927, entitled *Natur und Geist*. To be precise, there is no other of his contemporaries whom Husserl criticized in such detail and to such an extent in any of his published or unpublished writings. Whereas references to other contemporary philosophers in Husserl's work are generally cursory or limited to a few short quotes, the critique of Rickert covers about fifty pages in the main text of the lecture and is supplemented by another twenty pages of appendixes. In fact, the disagreement between the two brings to light important elements that remained underdeveloped in Husserl's earlier treatments of the difference between nature and spirit (e.g., the second book of *Ideen*), such as the difference between pre-scientific experience and its conceptual articulation.

It is important to underscore from the beginning that for Husserl the demarcation at issue cannot be carried out by means of simple conceptual oppositions such as the one between the individualizing and the generalizing method laid forth by Rickert, the one between inner and outer experience proposed by Dilthey or the more customary one between psychic and physical phenomena defended, for instance, by Brentano. In a sense, all these distinctions are taken into consideration and their value is preserved in Husserl's thought, although they are

---

[3] Mat IV, 8.   [4] Mat IV, 9.

recast in a different framework. Let us begin by examining the first of Husserl's lecture courses on *Natur und Geist* (1919) and then move to the second, where the extensive critique of Rickert is to be found. As we will see, the polemic against the Neo-Kantians in general and Rickert in particular is already present in the earlier course, even though no name is mentioned explicitly. It is only in the later course that Husserl identifies the exact target of his critique.

Natur und Geist (1919): the movement back to experiencing consciousness

Husserl's first lecture course on *Natur und Geist* was delivered in Freiburg in 1919, two years after he officially occupied the prestigious First Chair of Philosophy left vacant by Rickert, who accepted an offer from the University of Heidelberg as the designated successor of his teacher Windelband. Considering the hardships of wartime, and the reduced academic activity in the years 1916 to 1918,[5] it can be argued that *Natur und Geist* is the first lecture course that Husserl taught in fully normal working conditions at the University of Freiburg. The decision to focus on nature and *Geist* is perhaps motivated by a willingness to link his own work, albeit critically, to that of his predecessor, whose monumental study, *Die Grenzen der naturwissenschaftlichen Begriffsbildung*, counted as a cornerstone in this area of philosophical inquiry. However, the lecture follows very closely the systematic line of inquiry outlined by Husserl in his three-book project, *Ideas Pertaining to a Pure Phenomenology and a Phenomenological Philosophy*, of which the first volume appeared in 1913, arguably winning him the full professorship at Freiburg. Further, the lecture adumbrates for the first time topics that will occupy Husserl in *Crisis* fifteen years later.

Husserl introduces his lecture emphasizing how the existence of a scientific culture is "the distinctive fundamental trait of Greek-European culture"[6] and how the progressive realization of the ideal of scientific knowledge permeated the history of the West from its inception. However, the historical development of science did not follow a

---

[5] It should be noted that the majority of the students were involved in the military. Moreover, the catastrophe of World War I affected the Husserl family dramatically with the death of their second son Wolfgang in 1916.

[6] Mat IV, 3.

logical pattern, and it failed to do so due to the very essence of science itself. The major breakthrough in the study of nature was rendered possible by the creative genius of Renaissance men such as Descartes and Galileo, whose application of mathematical models to natural phenomena inaugurated a new era of discoveries and practical possibilities, leading to the birth of a vast array of disciplines. Similarly, although a few centuries later, the humanistic-historical sciences came to fruition, thereby achieving an admirable degree of precision and differentiation. Considering this situation, Husserl writes:

one would expect that fundamental clarity concerning the radical distinctions which separate in principle the main regions of scientific disciplines, concerning the essential characteristic of the domains and the characteristic of methodology – which depends on the domains – [already] held sway. Oddly enough, however, this is not the case at all. *Naivety* and *Reflection* characterize the development towards all superior accomplishments of reason.[7]

What should have been first from a logical point of view, i.e., a precise delimitation of the areas of competence of different disciplines as well as the methodologies apt to fulfill their different theoretical tasks, only comes to light as a desideratum in hindsight, when scientific inquiry already reached a certain degree of maturity. As Husserl points out parenthetically, this fact exemplifies a universal law of all rational activity, a law that unveils rationality's 'unextinguished debt,' so to speak, to its opaque native soil of sensibility. He says:

Apperceptions that grew at the level of passive sensibility and passively grown drives lead up to a manner of acting characteristic of a naive stage. Success and failure and their modification ignite a reflection on the whys and wherefores of this success or failure. This happens in various stages and with an increasing degree of clarity and insight.[8]

All beginnings are naive or "crude,"[9] as Vico would have it, and this is true also of scientific research. "But the level of authentic science only breaks through via a *radical philosophical reflection* about meaning, cognitive value and achieved goals of such intellectual work."[10] The

---

[7] Mat IV, 5. [8] *Ibid.*

[9] G. B. Vico, *The New Science: Revised Translation of the Third Edition 1744* (Ithaca, NY: Cornell University Press, 1968), 109: "the nature of everything born or made betrays the crudeness of its origin."

[10] Mat IV, 6.

rather paradoxical task of philosophical inquiry vis-à-vis specialized research is thus established: it has to take care of the foundations after the building has been already raised, injecting intelligibility into the practice of science and, in so doing, counteracting its foremost risk, "the mechanization of method."[11] The iterated success of scientific practices and their crystallization into a well-defined set of teachable operations, in fact, leads to an increasingly mindless appropriation and application of the scientific method, whose inner rationality is thus in constant jeopardy:

The sciences flourish on the basis of a technicized methodology that can be successfully appropriated without being innerly and truly understood. In this way several specialized disciplines shoot in the air beside one another, without being accompanied by a clear awareness of their research goals – determined by the specificity of their radically different regions – and of their contrasts with the research goals of other scientific regions. This, however, ends up hindering the progress of scientific culture, it relegates the sciences to a lower stage, which, for sure, renders possible an infinite wealth of results but also blinds the sense for the ultimate goals of knowledge and for a work in depth rather than in breadth.[12]

Considering this danger, it is clear that the philosophical classification of sciences is not merely geared towards bringing some conceptual order in the multifarious and unpredictable world of specialized research. Rather, it aims at a theoretical enhancement of the work of specialized research, in order to bring to genuine fulfillment the ideal of knowledge naively embraced but never fully attended to by specialized researchers. Thus, for Husserl, philosophical work is not meant to preach reforms but to illuminate and lift up to a higher level of intelligibility the already existing scientific work. At the same time, a fundamental clarification of the regions and tasks pertaining to different areas of scientific inquiry is meant to have a bearing on the future development of science itself, prevent intellectual energies from being wasted along inevitably barren paths of research, and overcome the one-sided picture of the world that emanates from the yet underdeveloped natural sciences.

These initial remarks outlining the work to be accomplished by a philosophical classification of the sciences already entail an important

---

[11] *Ibid.*   [12] Mat IV, 6–7.

idea: the genuine theoretical tasks of a certain branch of science are dictated by the *ontological* specificity of its region of inquiry. What makes for the ontological specificity of a certain region is not imposed by theory but rather *presupposed* in every theoretical operation. Whereas for regions of being standing far apart from one another, such as, say, the region of numbers and the region of physical objects, it is relatively easy to draw distinctions and avoid misleading overlaps, things are significantly different when it comes to a philosophical distinction of the regions of nature and psyche, "which seem to encompass one another and yet to be radically distinct."[13] In order to counteract this problem, in his lectures Husserl puts into play an operation that will characterize the bulk of his philosophy from the early 1920s onwards, namely, the regression to pre-theoretical consciousness as the sphere in which regional distinctions are originally constituted. The question connected to this regressive move could be formulated as follows: what is available to a subject in general prior to all scientific theorizing?

First and foremost, Husserl points out that we are constantly aware of our life as an ongoing process of perception: *"The life of the I is a constant perceiving."*[14] This basic fact entails a number of further elements that must be considered equally fundamental: perceptual awareness necessarily entails temporal awareness, and thus the distinction between first-hand experiences (impressional perceptions of present objects) and memories (reproductive perceptions of past objects), as well as the distinction between a subjective (*'immanent'*) and an objective (*'transcendent'*) side of all conceivable perceptions. In other words, we can always distinguish between two attitudes – a reflective attitude in which we seize on the momentarily given profile of a certain object and a straightforward attitude in which we simply attend to the object as such. Whereas profiles are experienced as constantly changing appearances in the 'immanent' stream of our consciousness, the object as such is a 'transcendent' unity that stays the same through all variation of immanent profiles. If we then move to examine the realm of such pre-theoretically given transcendent objects, a basic distinction is immediately available: "Objects and subjects, i.e., alien subjects."[15] Some objects are experienced as lifeless physical things, some other objects are experienced as animated bodies, i.e., physical things in which a superadded psychic stratum inheres.

[13] Mat IV, 8.   [14] Mat IV, 22.   [15] Mat IV, 25. Reprised in Mat IV, 118.

Physical things, whose unitary transcendent reality is intuited as non-coincident with the multiplicity of their immanent appearances, are thus the fundamental type of pre-theoretically available objects. Using Husserl's famous terminology in *Ideas II*, which he recasts in this lecture, these objects are experienced as *res temporalis* (they endure in time), *res extensa* (they are extended in space), and *res materialis* (they are the abiding substrates of real properties, which are causally dependent from the surrounding circumstances).[16] Even animated bodies are experienced, at a fundamental level, according to these three lines of apprehension. Accordingly, if we focus purely on these fundamental characteristics, we can begin to circumscribe the domain of nature: "Nature in its specific sense, the subject matter of natural science, are the mere things, the things as mere nature."[17] However, the suspension of the psychic component in the apprehension of animated bodies does not yet suffice to isolate the fundamental layer of nature. In fact, not all properties that inhere in natural things are natural properties:

The objects that are consciously pre-given to an I assume new predicates to the extent that this I turns towards them and makes them into the themes of ever-new acts, e.g., evaluative and practical acts. [They assume,] for instance, predicates of value, abiding determinations that accrue to the objects and with which objects are then pre-given to consciousness in the future.[18]

Husserl proposes to call these predicates, for lack of a better name, "predicates of significance."[19] Such predicates have a hybrid nature. Like purely physical predicates, they are experienced as belonging to the object as abiding properties. However, unlike physical predicates, they cannot be conceived in abstraction from the subjective activities that brought them about in the first place. That a piece of timber is experienced as "sturdy" and not simply as, say, brown or heavy, depends on its having been prepared according to certain techniques that render it particularly apt to support, say, the weight of a human body. The overwhelming bulk of the objects that we encounter in our human world are endowed with predicates of significance, and it is only by way of a willful abstractive impoverishment of the total content of our experience that we can isolate a sphere of pure nature, which comprises exclusively ultimate substrates and their "real predicates,"[20] such as

---

[16] See Ideas II, §§12–17; Mat IV, 121–124.   [17] Mat IV, 121.
[18] Mat IV, 122.   [19] *Ibid.*   [20] Mat IV, 150.

extension, size, etc. However, such purely natural objects are entailed as an underpinning core in every conceivable culturally formed object. At any time, we can abstractively divest full-blown physical objects of their predicates of significance and isolate in them the 'purely natural' core. To call this methodological procedure[21] 'abstraction,' however, does not imply that it is somehow illegitimate. On the contrary, if we abstract from all predicates of significance, "there remains for us as an intuitive core the *pure real*, i.e., what is ultimately presupposed in all meaning-bestowals through subjective acts as the object *prior to all acts*, prior to all subjective operations."[22] The core of pure nature is thus a fundamental layer that can be isolated in the broader concept of "reality,"[23] which, as Husserl points out, also includes other subjects and predicates of significance.

These fundamental distinctions allow Husserl to articulate a distinctive concept of *culture*, which he then proceeds to set up against Rickert and the Southwest Neo-Kantians. "Culture" Husserl says, "would then be in general the *correlate of active [leistende] subjectivity*."[24] It includes all objects and activities endowed with significance by the meaning-bestowing operations of a subject or a community of subjects.[25] In this respect, as Husserl points out, the term *Geisteswissenschaft* and the expression *Kulturwissenschaft* are equivalent and simply emphasize two different sides of the same coin. Like 'morning star' and 'evening star,' they are just two ways to refer to the same phenomenon. As the following passage emphasizes:

In the contrast [articulated] up to this point, we have on the one hand nature as the world of mere realities, as the world considered without significance, as the world considered unconcerned with all significance. On the other hand,

---

[21] Husserl often refers to this impoverishing procedure that allows us to isolate the stratum of pure nature as *Abbau* (dismantlement). For an extended discussion of *Abbau* see my entry in H.-H. Gander (ed.), *Husserl-Lexikon* (Darmstadt: WBG, 2010), 17–18 as well as my article "Different Worlds and Tendency to Concordance: Towards a New Perspective on Husserl's Phenomenology of Culture," *The New Yearbook for Phenomenology and Phenomenological Philosophy* 10 (2010): 127–143.

[22] Mat IV, 125.　　[23] *Ibid.*　　[24] Mat IV, 139.

[25] Husserl's further distinction of "social cultural objects" (those endowed with intersubjective significance for a plurality of communalized subjects) and "a-social cultural objects" (those whose significance is available exclusively for an isolated subject) (Mat IV, 139) does not need occupy us further here and is however internal to the broader notion of culture.

[we have] the world full of significance, the world in its significance, bestowed by individual or communal subjectivity [...] The juxtaposition of nature and spirit means nothing but this, in particular when we think about the "*Geisteswissenschaften*" in their ultimate sense and about the meaning that the word "*Geist*" may have (and in fact has) in this expression. If we talk about *culture*, we have in mind the *products* of meaning-bestowing subjectivity, which endows things with spiritual meaning [*vergeistigen*] through operations of significance [*Bedeutungsleistungen*] and also brings about 'spiritual' connections.[26]

In this sense, the *Geist* explored by the *Geisteswissenschaften* is the author of culture, and, therefore, it cannot be expunged when it comes to a material definition of cultural science, as Rickert would have it. *Wertbeziehung* (relatedness to value) can be definitely distinguished from *Wertung* (active valuation), but it cannot be correctly understood without reference to *Wertstiftung* (value-institution), which is an eminently subjective activity. Husserl's reference to Rickert is evident in the continuation of this thought:

From this point of view, it is a *merely verbal dispute* [*Wortstreit*] whether the true distinction should be the one between nature and culture or the one between nature and spirit. The real issue, i.e., the working out of the radical ontological and phenomenological distinctions, to which the terminology must refer back and to which we have to constantly appeal in science, was missing completely.[27]

Given Husserl's statement in the last sentence, this matter regarding the dispute with Rickert and the Neo-Kantians might seem settled. We cannot conceive of culture without taking into account an active subjectivity responsible for its formation, so *Geist* and *Kultur* are correlative terms that have to be contrasted *as a pair* to nature. Nature designates the most fundamental sphere of reality upon which the sphere of significance (reality in the broader sense) is founded. In this way, objects endowed with significance encompass the sphere of natural objects, which are not ontologically different from but rather inhabit the core of cultural objects. This picture of the relationship between nature and *Geist/Kultur* remains a constant in Husserl's thought. However, a defense of active subjectivity as involved in cultural creation and, therefore, as integral to a definition of cultural science does not

[26] Mat IV, 139–140.   [27] Mat IV, 140.

suffice, in Husserl's view, to offer a valid alternative to Rickert. In later years, Husserl realizes the necessity to address and criticize directly the epistemological framework behind Rickert's expulsion of subjective processes from the realm of *Geist*. Furthermore, and starting from this critique, Husserl sets out to clarify why it is illegitimate to consider culture-forming subjective activity simply as an illusion to be explained away from a naturalistic point of view. These two aspects are most likely at the origin of Husserl's reconsideration of Rickert's philosophy almost ten years after his first foray into the intricate problems of nature and spirit in 1919.

Natur und Geist (1927): the plan of the lecture and the formal distinctions

In his last lecture course before retirement, Husserl tackles once more the problem of a philosophical demarcation of natural and human sciences. His decision to give renewed attention to this problem deserves some questioning: why retrieve the issue of *Natur und Geist*? Unlike other areas of phenomenological research, where the fundamental lines of clarification seem to be more or less settled, the problematic of nature and spirit remains thoroughly open until the latest stages of Husserl's philosophical itinerary. Neither the static studies in the phenomenology of constitution in the second book of *Ideen* nor the distinction between real predicates and predicates of significance in the first lecture course on *Natur und Geist* in 1919 seems to have fully satisfied Husserl's avidity for philosophical clarification in this field. So we find him grappling with this issue anew in 1927 and launching his analysis in an entirely new fashion. Most importantly, this late foray into ontology and theory of science is conducted with a largely Kantian and Neo-Kantian vocabulary. The recourse to specifically phenomenological jargon is minimized, and priority is given to a direct engagement with contemporary discussions in the philosophy of science. As a careful look at the table of contents reveals, the structure and concept of these lectures repeat – in outline, but unmistakably – the order of exposition and even the systematic approach of Rickert's seminal works *Kulturwissenschaft und Naturwissenschaft* (1910) and *Die Grenzen der naturwissenschaftlichen Begriffsbildung* (1896–1902). For once, Husserl seems to resist his tendency to suspend customary ways of posing philosophical problems in order to bestow new meaning upon them and sticks instead to the terms in which the issue of nature and spirit was discussed among his contemporaries. He accepts, so to speak, to play the game according to the Neo-Kantian rules and sets out to show that his many years of phenomenological training allow him to be a better Kantian than his contemporaries who follow the letter but not the spirit of the old master from Königsberg.

The opening lecture presents ideas that can be found almost verbatim in Rickert's works and to a certain extent constitute a common ground of agreement for all the early twentieth-century philosophers reacting against positivism and irrationalism. After setting aside the idea that philosophy should be understood as a mere individual *Weltanschauung*, i.e., "a supreme goal for the personal striving towards cultural education [*Bildungsstreben*],"[28] rather than a science, Husserl proceeds to contrast the distinctive scientificity of philosophy to that of specialized empirical research: "Philosophy has its characteristic sphere of interest and knowledge in what is universal, as opposed to the singular sciences, whose sphere lies in what is specific."[29] The 'universal' at stake, however, is not understood here in the Aristotelian sense of the conceptual as opposed to the perceptual but as the concrete totality of what is, i.e., the world as a whole. Husserl goes on to underscore that

although every particular science has its particular thematic sphere, it is manifest that all thematic spheres of all the sciences are at the same time inextricably united. They constitute a total sphere, a universe in the specific sense of the uniqueness of a totality, and this is what philosophy deals with.[30]

Philosophy is characterized by an "interest for the totality,"[31] a totality that is not a mere concept but the world itself, in which all sectors of reality isolated and explored by the specialized sciences are embedded. The very same idea that 'the totality of the world' (*das Weltganze*) is the specific object of philosophy can be found ubiquitously in Rickert's work. In the polemical essay titled "Scientific Philosophy and *Weltanschauung*," for instance, he writes: "The particular sciences limit themselves essentially to [investigate] this or that part of what we call the totality of the world [*das Weltganze*]. Philosophy, on the contrary, endeavors to grasp the world as the totality of all its parts."[32] For

---

[28] Hua XXXII, 3–4.   [29] Hua XXXII, 5.   [30] *Ibid.*   [31] Hua XXXII, 7.
[32] H. Rickert, *Wissenschaftliche Philosophie und Weltanschauung*, *Philosophische Aufsätze*, 325–346. Here 326. Hereafter WPW. Rickert also goes on to

both Rickert and Husserl, however, interest in the totality of the world is not a merely cumulative interest, since the world as a whole is not simply the sum total of its parts. These parts, in fact, are not juxtaposed like the detachable pieces of an assemblage, they are interwoven into complex relations with one another. In Husserl's words:

In truth, the various sciences do not stand beside one another as juxtaposed parts. On the contrary, and in spite of all relative differentiation, they are innerly related to one another and they penetrate one another in a variety of ways: partly after the manner of generality and particularity, and partly after the manner of indivisible correlation.[33]

The incapacity to shed light on the world as a whole and, consequently, the incapacity to rationally justify the partitions of the world-whole underlying the division of labor in the sciences constitutes a defect of scientificity intrinsic to specialized research. Thus, philosophy, as the science of the world-whole, does not articulate its work merely parallel to that of the positive sciences. Its goal is to restore the unity of all science originally envisioned at the dawn of Greek philosophy by way of infusing into the existing sciences ultimate clarity concerning their legitimate areas of research in light of the world as a whole. The kind of research apt to achieve this goal is termed by Husserl *Grundlagenforschung*, i.e., an inquiry into the foundations. The basic point of departure of this investigation is the insight that prior to all scientific activity we have an experience *of the world*.[34] Although the idea of a regression to pre-theoretical experience was already present in his earlier lectures, the specification that pre-theoretical experience is an experience *of the world* marks an important advance in Husserl's treatment of the *Natur und Geist* problematic. As he states:

This world is pre-given through the universal experience that runs through the lives of us all. For the individual living in the modern scientific culture and even more so for people who are oblivious to such culture, "the" world is there prior to all science and even prior to all discussing, naming and judging of everyday life.[35]

emphasize that the very idea of partitioning reality into different fields of inquiry logically implies a concept of the whole, which, however, remains undertheorized in the context of empirical and specialized research. For an extensive treatment of this issue see Chapter 7.

[33] Hua XXXII, 6.

[34] A more focused investigation of these points will be offered in Chapter 7.

[35] Hua XXXII, 14.

However, this pre-given world is constantly targeted by our practical, aesthetic and theoretical intentions. It thereby receives new meaning and differentiation, while undergoing different forms of conceptualization as it is reorganized in terms of more specific spheres of reality. This dynamic of targeting, apprehending, reorganizing, and conceptualizing our experiences against the background of the world as a whole is not entirely erratic. It has a logic that can and must be laid bare. Accordingly, Husserl assigns to his phenomenological *Grundlagenforschung* the task of "measuring out [*durchmessen*] the path which leads from mute, unconceptualized [*begriffslos*] experience and its universal interweavings first of all to the typical, vague and primitive generalities which suffice in everyday life and then from there to the authentic and true concepts that must be presupposed by authentic science."[36] As will become clear in what follows, the first important point of contention between Rickert and Husserl revolves around the very concept of 'world-whole.' Whereas for Rickert the notion of world-whole functions merely as a regulative ideal for scientific philosophy, Husserl points out that we have an *experience* of the world as a whole and that this experience has an identifiable structure. Of course, the experience of the world is not a straightforward consciousness comparable to that of a perceptual object. Nonetheless, we have an anticipatory experience of the *horizons* surrounding everything that there is, and the concrete explorations of these horizons – both in science and in everyday life – are guided by some a priori principles that are not merely formal-logical but material-ontological.

Before these differences are addressed, however, the details of Husserl's analysis must be taken into view. Following one further step of Rickert's strategy in *Kulturwissenschaft und Naturwissenschaft*,[37] Husserl begins by pointing out the existence of two evidently distinct groups of sciences. To begin with, natural and human sciences constitute at least two distinct *types* in our cultural world. In more contemporary talk, it could be argued that natural and human sciences present themselves at first as two groups bearing internal family resemblances. The existence of a *real* distinction between the two groups, however, has been variously disputed; as Husserl argues: "The differentiation in terms of types may be apparent and therefore [remain] unanimously undisputed. However, it can be seriously attempted to interpret it away and dismiss the essential distinction through considerations which can

---

[36] *Ibid.*, 16.   [37] SH.

perhaps be extremely dubitable but which are, subjectively speaking, very convincing."[38] The human sciences have been viewed as yet under-developed natural sciences; they are still stuck at the stage of morphological descriptions and classifications of their objects, but they are nonetheless aimed at producing explanations based on quantitative data and causal laws. This view evidently rests on two interconnected assumptions: (1) that there is one overall meaning to the word "science," i.e., law-based explanation, and (2) that the relationship between morphological descriptions and law-based explanations is an a priori relationship – that of a means (description) to an end (explanation). Our will to know would remain, in all cases, unsatisfied until a law is achieved.

The question of the epistemological relationship existing between description and explanation and the function of both procedures is, for the more mature Husserl of 1927, "the core issue in the controversy between natural and human sciences."[39] For the naturalistically minded scientist, all morphological description is a "mere transitional stage [*bloße Durchgangsstufe*] towards an objective, broadly speaking naturalistic consideration of the world."[40] Classificatory descriptions are necessary but only as provisional stepping-stones towards the achievement of a law. For the humanist, on the contrary, a morphological description is "an end in itself"[41] (*Selbstzweck*): it does not require transition to an 'objective truth' based on quantitative parameters and standing under a causal law. Moreover, for humanists like Husserl, the question arises as to

whether this idea of objective sciences directed towards what exists as it is in itself can exhaust all scientific tasks, and whether these sciences and all their positions of tasks do not perhaps themselves harbor some kind of subjectivity or relativity, which leads to necessarily correlated sciences, sciences of a subjectivity and its subjective surrounding world with subjective formations, i.e., all those merely subjective components put out of play by objective

---

[38] Hua XXXII, 23. [39] *Ibid.*, 194.

[40] *Ibid.* See also E. Husserl, *Phänomenologische Psychologie. Vorlesungen Sommersemester 1925, Husserliana*, vol. 9 (The Hague: Nijhoff, 1962), 350. Hereafter Hua IX. "In natural science, description is a mere transitional component [*Durchgangsstück*] of the objective method. What description actually grasps is not what is objective itself, which only announces itself indirectly therein."

[41] Hua XXXII, 194.

science. These sciences would study subjectivity *qua* subjectivity, [and thereby constitute] a science functional to the living human being and as such directed towards the human being itself in its fullness of life, as experiencing and variously acting, as constantly related to its own intuitive surrounding world and shaping this world from within its own life.[42]

In light of these important remarks, it is not hard to see why Husserl disagrees with both Dilthey's and Rickert's respective characterizations of the difference between the two groups of sciences. As for Dilthey, his distinction between descriptive *Verstehen* as the exclusive prerogative of human science and explanation as pertaining exclusively to natural science fails to acknowledge the existence of a descriptive stage also in the natural sciences (the gathering and classification of observational data) as well as its merely transitional status. A naturalist would not dispute the necessity of *beginning* with understanding and morphological description both in the investigation of nature and in the human sciences. He would reject the necessity of *ending* with such descriptions, so that Dilthey's distinction would still hold valid but apply solely to the contingent stage of development of the human sciences.

As regards Rickert, his insistence on Kant's definition of nature[43] being purely formal, and therefore applicable to any kind of object, disregards the fact that the very project of seeking universal laws already entails a tacit decision about the highest epistemic aim (law as opposed to mere morphological description) and therein an assumption about the ontology of the object under scrutiny. When he advocates the right of a natural-scientific psychology to seek universal laws of the mind Rickert assumes that mental phenomena and physical phenomena are ontologically homogeneous, so that the task of seeking universal laws is equally legitimate in both fields of inquiry (i.e., it constitutes in both cases the highest epistemic aim). Moreover, Rickert fails to acknowledge the true ambition behind the project of the *Geisteswissenschaften*. The human sciences do not simply aspire to achieve autonomy from the natural sciences. If their claim is taken seriously, then it must be acknowledged that they set out to encompass the natural sciences and subsume them and their truths under the rubric of "cultural formations." Thus, Rickert's

---

[42] *Ibid.*, 193.
[43] "[T]he existence of things, insofar as [sofern] that existence is determined according to universal laws." Kant, *Prolegomena to Any Future Metaphysics that will be able to come forward as a Science*, 50–169. Here 89.

attempt to justify the relative right of the individualizing method of the human sciences beside the generalizing method of the natural sciences fails to capture the full scope and task of humanistic inquiry.

In consideration of these elements, the problem that Husserl sets out to resolve is how to make a rationally informed decision about the point of contention between the naturalist and the humanist presented above. Unless one is willing to reduce the crucial issue of the relationship between morphological description and law-based explanation to a matter of personal taste and worldview, some criteria must be found to assess the legitimacy of the epistemic claims put forth by the humanist and the naturalist. These criteria, for Husserl, can only be achieved by a rigorous consideration of our pre-theoretical experience of the world. It is impossible to come to a decision based on the exclusive consideration of the existing sciences. The analytical gaze must go back to the experience which gives us the objects subsequently investigated by the sciences and carry out "a demarcation of the possible domains as the self-enclosed and infinite structures of the experiential world as such."[44] Every possible domain of experience has to be characterized in terms of its "fundamental concept,"[45] which expresses the essence of the domain at issue. For instance, we can see intuitively that the fundamental concept 'space' expresses the essence of the self-enclosed domain of inquiry of geometry. This essence must be rendered the object of explicit consideration in order to spell out all its further determinations. This operation, in Husserl's terminology, advances the science at issue from the stage of a factually existing discipline to the stage of a "science in the pregnant sense" *(im prägnanten Sinne)*,[46] i.e., a science that is fully aware of its legitimate sphere of competence, of the authentic tasks connected to it and of its position in the overarching whole of scientific research. As Husserl points out: "Therefore, the domain of a science in the pregnant sense is not something pre-given without further ado; on the contrary, it indicates an important task and a fundamental component of the task of an authentic philosophical classification and, at the same time, of an investigation of the foundations [*Grundlagenforschung*]."[47] In this context, Husserl chooses the term *region* to designate a domain that is essentially unitary and self-enclosed. A domain of this kind will have a number of "axiomatic concepts"[48] (a more technical phrase for 'fundamental concepts'), which express what belongs essentially to it. "*The idea*

---

[44] Hua XXXII, 26.   [45] *Ibid.*, 27.   [46] *Ibid.*, 28.   [47] *Ibid.*   [48] *Ibid.*, 29.

of region as an essentially enclosed sphere of being *is in itself prior to the idea of the corresponding science.*"[49]

However, as Aristotle realized early on, what is first in itself is not always first for us, and so the phenomenologist finds herself in the problematic situation of having to unearth the axiomatic concepts of all possible regions of being and, thereby, departs from the already existing sciences, moving retrogressively to their hidden, intuitive sources. This is why Husserl, instead of addressing directly the essences of different regions of being, devotes a long portion of his lecture to a clarification of the different sciences, following Rickert's strategy of analyzing the sciences primarily in view of their formal structure and subsequently in terms of their material content.

First and foremost, Husserl characterizes science in general as a specific "kind of intellectual operation"[50] that results in true assertions and theories. These latter do not simply stand disconnected beside each other but, rather, belong together in a web of theoretical truths. Husserl asserts that a science in general must be a coherent unity of theoretical truths held together by reference to the same nexus of thematic objects,[51] and he goes on to draw three distinctions for a purely formal classification of the sciences. The first distinction is the one between a priori and a posteriori sciences. While a posteriori sciences consist of empirical judgments about really existing beings, a priori sciences are exclusively concerned with essential possibilities.[52] They do not posit

[49] *Ibid.*   [50] *Ibid.*, 31.
[51] It is interesting to remark, in passing, that Husserl's characterization of a science in general in his 1927 lecture course does not fundamentally differ from the one he gave more than two decades earlier in his *Prolegomena to a Pure Logic*. In his earlier book Husserl characterized the unity of a single science in these terms: "The truths of a science are essentially one if their connection rests on what above all makes a science a science. A science is, as we know, grounded knowledge, i.e., explanation or proof [...] Essential unity among the truths of a single science is unity of explanation [...] Unity of explanation means [...] homogeneous unity of explanatory principles." E. Husserl, *Logische Untersuchungen. Erster Band: Prolegomena zur reinen Logik, Husserliana*, vol. 18 (The Hague: Nijhoff, 1957). English translation by J. N. Findlay, in *Logical Investigations*, vol. 1 (London: Routledge, 1970), 229. Similarly, in this text Husserl characterizes the "theoretical unity" of a science in terms of the "systematic unity of a nexus of proofs" [*Begründungszusammenhang*] (Hua XXXII, 32), in which an infinite multiplicity of objects to be investigated are posited as belonging together in the same thematic sphere. For a helpful discussion of Husserl's notion of science see Majolino, "La Partition du réel," 588.
[52] Hua XXXII, 33–34.

any particular fact but only general, essential rules to which facts must necessarily conform. One has to think here about geometry and its theorems, which do not entail judgments about really existing figures in the empirical space, but rather about pure spatial configurations and relations whose properties logically precede those of objects in the empirical space. Second, it is possible to distinguish between purely formal and content-related *(sachhaltig)* sciences.[53] The purely formal sciences comprise formal logic and pure mathematics. Their judgments and laws are valid for 'anything whatsoever' *(Etwas überhaupt)*, that is, they do not necessitate any specification concerning the content about which they judge. On the contrary, content-related sciences relate specifically to a determinate class of objects. For instance, geometry deals with objects that are extended in space, physics deals with material objects, psychology deals with psychic objects, and so forth.

It might be tempting to assume that this second distinction is a mere restatement of the first. However, Husserl points out that we can assume an a priori attitude also when we are investigating a region determined by content. Geometry would be, also in this case, a good example; something similar is what Kant envisioned with his 'transcendental logic' and the groundbreaking idea of a *natura formaliter spectata*. In this sense, for Husserl, the second distinction is at the same time a general distinction in its own right and a subdivision internal to the first distinction: a priori sciences can be further broken down into formal and content-related. On the other hand, *a posteriori* sciences can only be content-related, since there is no such thing as a *purely empirical* set of formal conditions of objectivity.

The third distinction is the one between *concrete* and *abstract sciences*, and it brings into view an important relational element that was missing in the previous distinctions. The concepts 'concreteness' and 'abstractness' can be clarified by reference to the fundamental distinction of substrate and determination in a given object. Every conceivable object *has* some determinations ('this apple is red,' 'the number 7 is uneven,' etc.) that all refer back to a substrate *of which* they are determinations. Some of these determinations are 'absolute determinations', i.e., they can be originally experienced only as determinations, although they can be eventually treated as relative substrates in more sophisticated intellectual operations. Coloration and extension are good examples of

---

[53] *Ibid.*, 34–35.

absolute determinations. We can only experience color or extension attached to a colored or extended object, although we can eventually discover determinations pertaining to color as such (e.g., 'red is a primary color'). Moreover, most determinations only manifest themselves in a necessary connection with other determinations, as the example of color and extension proves: we can only experience color spread over a certain spatial extension and, conversely, we can only experience spatial extension as filled with some color. Husserl points out:

> Every individual being, then, exists only as a totality of moments belonging together, to which corresponds the idea of a *total concept* related to all the moments of the object as the concept's individuation [*Vereinzelung*], i.e., the concept encompasses [*begreift*] the object according to all its moments. In this way we obtain the first ideas of *concretum* and concrete concepts. Every individual being must be called *concretum* to the extent that it entails a manifold of inextricably 'intergrown' moments and exists in their overall intergrownness (*concrescere*).[54]

In a broader sense, however, we can also understand a 'total concept' as a concept expressing the entire *"concrete essence"*[55] of a given object, that is, a general notion (*Allgemeinheit*) that expresses the species to which the object in question belongs. For instance, when we say of something that it is a 'thing,' we definitely do not rehearse conceptually the entire wealth of its specific, individual determinations, but nonetheless 'thing' is a total concept that embraces in a very broad way what that individual being essentially is. In this sense, 'thing' is a concrete concept since it entails in a single brushstroke all essentials pertaining to a potentially infinite number of individuals. For example, the concept 'thing' entails a priori also extendedness, temporal duration, sensuous qualities, and so forth.

In a more ordinary use of the terms 'concrete' and 'abstract' we might be inclined to deem the concept 'thing' abstract compared to more 'concrete' concepts such as 'tree' or 'rock.' 'Concrete' would thus designate concepts that express more specific kinds as opposed to the increasing 'abstraction' we encounter as we ascend the scale of *genera*. Husserl recognizes this way of understanding 'concrete' and 'abstract,' but he insists that a distinction centered around the notions of individual (concrete) and determination (abstract) is "inevitable"[56] and more

[54] *Ibid.*, 38. The allusion to the etymology of the word "concrete" by adding in parenthesis the Latin word *concrescere* (literally "to grow together") is Husserl's.
[55] *Ibid.*, 38.   [56] *Ibid.*, 40.

fruitful for the sake of classifying the sciences. According to Husserl's proposal, we can have "concrete concepts with very different degrees of generality";[57] for instance, both the concepts 'thing' and 'artifact' are concrete to the extent that they express the concrete essence of a wide range of individuals, even though the former is more general than the latter. Consequently, 'abstract' are first and foremost those concepts that refer to non-independent moments of a given kind of object, i.e., to absolute determinations that cannot be experienced apart from the objects in which they inhere and whose theoretical treatment requires previous *abstraction* from these objects. In the wake of this distinction, we can proceed to discriminate between *abstract and concrete sciences.* Concrete sciences are those studying concrete individuals or classes of individuals, whereas abstract sciences are those focusing exclusively on abstract moments of these individuals. For instance, natural science as a whole is a concrete science that studies material bodies as wholes in a manner dissimilar to mechanics, which, compared to natural science, is an abstract science that considers "bodies purely as the substrates of movements and moving forces."[58] The concepts of abstractness and concreteness, however, can be easily functionalized and proven relative: for instance, geometry is an abstract science to the extent that it isolates extension from the full concreteness of material bodies given in experience. However, plane geometry is abstract if considered in comparison with geometry as a whole, to the extent that it further isolates two-dimensional figures from the totality of extended figures in general.

In light of this distinction, it turns out that all formal sciences are abstract, since they isolate from the full concreteness of objects determined by their content the formal-ontological determinations common to anything whatsoever and deal exclusively with them. The operation of progressive abstraction from material determinations that leads to the field of formal ontology Husserl calls *formalization.*[59] However, and this is the important result of Husserl's analysis, not all a priori

---

[57] *Ibid.*

[58] *Ibid.* Interestingly, Husserl points out in passing that "perhaps even universal physics is abstract, if it were possible to prove that mere material nature is nothing but a non-independent structure of the fully concrete world" (*ibid.*, 40).

[59] For an illuminating discussion on these issues see D. Lohmar, "How are Formal Sciences Possible? On the Sources of Intuitivity of Mathematical Knowledge according to Husserl and Kant," *The New Yearbook for Phenomenology and Phenomenological Philosophy* 6 (2006): 109–126.

sciences are abstract, in the same way in which not all of them are devoid of content: "orientation towards concreteness is possible also in *a priori* research."[60] If we characterize a priori research as the inquiry into mere possibilities, then we have to distinguish between mere formal possibilities and real, i.e., content-related, possibilities. Accordingly:

Every possible world has [...] a double *a priori.* A formal-mathematical *a priori,* to the extent that the world with its infinities can be contemplated in emptily formal generality (in our sense: analytically) as a mathematical manifold under abstraction from all its material determinations [*von allem sachhaltig Bestimmenden*]. However, <every possible world> also possesses its universal and concrete material *a priori,* which, together with the analytical *a priori,* can precede all experiential research and, if it is grasped scientifically, can serve experiential science as a methodological instrument.[61]

In contrast to the operation of formalization, which results in a purely formal a priori, Husserl calls *rationalization*[62] the intellectual operation that moves from the contemplation of facts in the world to the contemplation of their material a priori, which constitutes specifically their concrete essence.

As stated above, unlike the first two distinctions, the distinction between concrete and abstract sciences is relational. Abstract sciences deal with non-independent parts of concrete objects, which, in turn, are the subject matter of concrete sciences. Accordingly, every abstract science is a priori embedded in or encompassed by one or more concrete sciences. In this respect, it is possible to introduce a further distinction (capitalizing on the concrete/abstract distinction) that will prove important to clarify the relationship between natural and human sciences and, indeed, phenomenology. The fourth distinction introduced by Husserl is that between independent and non-independent sciences. The independence or non-independence of a science depends on the complex configurations of *concreta* and *abstracta* in its field of inquiry and in those encompassing it. Husserl gives a clear definition, stating:

The field of a science will have to be called independent when its theoretical exploration [*Verfolgung*] never has to lead beyond this field; no matter how far we penetrate its infinite horizons, it is a self-enclosed horizon that never has to be overstepped. In the opposite case the field is non-independent and then the theoretical interest will necessarily have to stretch out until it reaches

---

[60] Hua XXXII, 42.   [61] *Ibid.,* 44.   [62] *Ibid.,* 48.

the thematic totality; this means, however, that for complete satisfaction of the theoretical interest we need a science directed to this totality, to this fully independent field of being. Such science would be the basis on which the foregoing initial science [*Ausgangswissenschaft*] depends and in which it is, at the same time, incorporated.[63]

Husserl suggests the example of geography as a non-independent science, whose consistent exploration necessarily leads to overstep the thematic field 'earth' and take into consideration the solar system, the universe, and ultimately the totality of nature, in which the earth is embedded as a concrete but non-independent object. Although the earth is definitely not an abstract object such as a surface or a color its reality and its physical structure are manifestly unthinkable outside the solar system and, on a broader scale, outside the overarching totality 'nature.' In this broader respect, the earth is only a relative *concretum* and it is abstract vis-à-vis the totality of nature, which constitutes the field of inquiry of an independent science, i.e., natural science. In a way similar to natural science, the theoretical exploration of purely formal objects in the mathematical sciences (*mathesis universalis*) does not require us to overstep the borders of mere contentless ideality. The formal sciences are thus independent. Therefore, it becomes manifest that *there can be independent or dependent sciences of both concrete and abstract objects.*

Introducing the notion of independence and non-independence of a science with respect to the closure of its field of inquiry, Husserl enhances his analysis with a fruitful perspective that sets the stage for his critique of Rickert. All sciences deal with infinities. These can be the intensive infinities of a concrete object (such as the earth in geography) or the extensive infinities of an indefinite number of objects, concrete or abstract (such as the totality of physical objects in natural science, mental objects in psychology, or formal-logical objects, such as sets in the formal sciences). However, and this is the crucial point, not all infinities are *worlds*, i.e., systematically structured fields of concrete singularities.[64] If we consider the fields of inquiry of formal sciences such as, for instance, set theory, we quickly realize that the a priori laws governing those fields (e.g., the basic properties of all the binary operations to be possibly carried out on sets) allow for instantiation in an

---

[63] *Ibid.*, 52–53.   [64] See *ibid.*, 57.

infinite number of 'objects' that are disconnected from one another. There is no such thing as a 'world' of sets that is progressively explored by set theory. Based on the laws of set theory, we can assemble in our perceptual field or generate in our thought an infinite number of completely disconnected sets, without in so doing violating any a priori principle pertaining to this formal field. No set generated in thought according to the laws of set theory entails conditions for the generation of the next set. The situation is completely different if we take into consideration content-related sciences, such as natural science. In this case

[t]he totality that characterizes the field's concept [*Gebietsbegriff*] means much more. It must be thought, and therefore also be thinkable, as a connected unity of co-existence: the manifold objects falling under the field's concept as all being *at one* [*in eins*] and then furthermore as being connected with one another in this co-existence so that an orderly progress of knowledge is prefigured, through which ideally all truths relative to these objects can be considered *a priori* attainable in a systematic progression.[65]

Whereas the extension of the concept 'set' as the thematic field of set theory embraces a disconnected infinity of individual sets without entailing any condition about their possible co-existence, the concept 'nature' as the thematic field of natural science embraces a totality of necessarily *co-existing* physical objects. Although the conditions for this co-existence can be variable (we can generate in thought an indefinite number of possible natures), the notion of *some* lawfully regulated co-existence of the singularities entailed in the extension of the concept 'nature' belongs to it a priori. The notion of a priori conditions of co-existence thus marks the distinction between a mere conceptual extension and a world. The objects of a possible *world* (as opposed to an empty mathematical manifold) must stand in some a priori relation to one another, that is, they must have a definite 'position' in that world, and this position must be in principle *accessible* from any point of departure internal to that world following the appropriate path. This is the only scenario in which the ideal of factual knowledge is not completely overwhelmed and rendered impracticable by the infinity of the object to be known. Even if the infinity, say, of the natural world is not accessible in one flash, we know that everything that exists in nature

---

[65] *Ibid.*

is *in principle* accessible, that causally regulated paths exist which lead from any given object or state to any other. To stay with the example of nature, this is precisely the meaning of spatiality and temporality for natural objects. There is a spatio-temporal order that governs in advance the accessibility of natural objects in experience, so that, for instance, past objects can be only accessed in memory, future objects can be expected, present objects that are removed from the most proximate perceptual field can be rendered accessible through appropriate changes in spatial position. Moreover, the contingent state of any given object in any given spatio-temporal position delineates a whole set of empirical laws that determine causally both the object at issue and the infinite manifold of objects surrounding it. Husserl summarizes his understanding of a world amenable to empirical knowledge, as opposed to a mere indeterminate manifold of instances of a certain concept:

Cognitive mastery of an individual totality presupposes (in order to be able to become a practical goal in the first place and then a theme for a science) that each of its concrete objects in its individuality be knowable, and this in turn presupposes that the totality has the universal form of a system, as an orderly and *construable system of positions*, in which the *quale* of the single objects individuates itself. The construability, however, means that [the totality in question], as a system of forms of accessibility, must be navigated stepwise and that these steps must be repeated and summed after the manner of the 'again-and-again' [*Immer-wieder*] in constantly the same way. In other words, it must be possible to generate the system in a constructive way starting from any position; it has to be homogeneous; each constructive element, each generative step must allow for iteration and the sameness of each step must be always recognizable.[66]

Content-related distinctions: the weakness in Rickert's theory and phenomenology as *Lebensphilosophie*

At this point, it is appropriate to recall that all the distinctions examined so far were purely formal. They did not advance any claim based on the specific content of different sciences. Even when content-related sciences were considered in contrast to empty formal sciences, this distinction was not itself based on contents but purely on the formal 'style' of investigation. Content-related sciences are those sciences that have a

[66] *Ibid.*, 64.

materially determined content as their subject matter, as opposed to formal sciences that deal with the pure forms of 'something in general' (*Etwas überhaupt*). The criterion for this distinction is, again, formal. However, a completely new standpoint has to be introduced in order to engage more directly the customary distinction between *Natur* and *Geist*. This distinction is drawn according to a material criterion. The discussion of material criteria for the demarcation of science at this point in his analysis is critical to Husserl's subsequent critique of Rickert and his teacher Windelband. In fact, Husserl will be able to prove that the fundamental methodological distinction between individualizing and generalizing sciences invoked by the two Southwestern thinkers only appears to be purely logical, while being in fact a spurious mixture of material and formal principles.

Sciences can be distinguished on the basis of the object that they investigate – physical objects in the case of natural science and the human psyche in the case of *Geisteswissenschaft*. If we attempt to delineate a genealogy of this distinction, it is not difficult to identify its original source in Descartes's metaphysical separation of *res extensa* and *res cogitans*. The assumption that guides scientists who adopt this distinction (or the less metaphysically committed one between physical and psychic phenomena) is described by Husserl in the following terms: in the same way in which physical phenomena delivered by our senses can be viewed as changing, subjective manifestations of natural objects in themselves, psychic phenomena can be viewed as changing, subjective manifestations of 'souls,' 'minds,' or 'psychic subjects' in themselves. In both cases, thus, scientific theorizing should aim at determining what is true in itself with the aid of mathematical concepts and laws since, by definition, truth lies behind the sphere of what is immediately experienced and requires a peculiar process of 'idealization' in order to be achieved.[67] In the same way in which natural science sets out to determine the inner workings and structures of nature by peeling off the subjectivity from its manifested phenomena, so psychological science should determine the mind as it is 'in itself.' To the extent that it combines an ontological dualism *and* a methodological monism, the customary distinction of *Natur* and *Geist* stemming from both Descartes's philosophy and a number of naturalistic thinkers is deficient in Husserl's eyes. Whereas the method of excluding

---

[67] See *ibid.*, 70–71.

subjectivity and determining (with the aid of mathematical concepts) the 'thing in itself' of nature *is fully motivated* by the stratified experience of the physical thing given in perception, mental phenomena seem to call for a completely different treatment. If we follow purely the way in which they offer themselves to our theoretical regard in experience, we quickly realize that with psychic phenomena there is no such thing as a series of changing manifestations offering mere profiles of an alleged thing in itself. Rather, it is clear that, while they are critical for the manifestation of an existing nature, psychic phenomena do not themselves manifest something like an existing mind. They completely coincide with their function of manifesting non-mental, transcendent being. There is no mental 'residue' to be determined that would become available once the merely subjective appearance of psychic phenomena was peeled off with the aid of mathematics.

These remarks are crucial to understanding why Husserl considered Windelband's and Rickert's attempts to move away from the Cartesian distinction via a purely methodological distinction ill-suited. In a sense, their proposal ends up tacitly accepting precisely the key idea of the Cartesian distinction. The fact that empirical psychology seems to have no bearing on the concrete development of the humanities is sufficient for Rickert to expel psychology as such from the human scientific field. This fact motivates him to revert to a purely methodological criterion as the proper point of departure and underscores that psychology employs a generalizing method aimed at the discovery of general laws like all other natural sciences. Husserl instead, similarly to Dilthey, would draw a different conclusion from psychology's uselessness for humanistic research and ask whether we have sufficient reason to hold fast to the natural-scientific ideal in psychology. His answer is that we do not, since our experience of psychic phenomena does not offer any motivation to move in the direction of a mathematically formulated determination of a psychological *an sich*. This is not because we immediately 'understand them', as Dilthey would have it, but because their objective structure does not present the same stratification that characterizes natural phenomena and renders their natural-scientific treatment legitimate and, at points, necessary. If we follow our experience, rather than our historically conditioned theoretical habits, we should lay forth a completely different set of tasks for the sciences of psyche.

Without anticipating too much about Husserl's indebtedness to and critique of Wilhelm Dilthey, a topic for Chapter 6, it is now important to highlight the reason why, according to Husserl, Rickert simply did not have the theoretical resources to reformulate the meaning of psychology. Briefly put, Rickert failed to address the above distinction between a merely empty mathematical manifold and a world. His fundamental idea, which "goes through his entire work and gives it systematic coherence," is, as explained in Chapter 1, "*the 'overcoming' of the infinite multiplicity of the world that has to be known via the two correlative paths of generalization and historical individualization.*"[68] The fundamental line of his inquiry is the following: an infinite world is there and has to be mastered. How is this possible? By simplifying the overwhelming abundance of data streaming in from the senses via theoretical "incisions"[69] (or 'cuts') in the unbroken flow of our experience. Such incisions are guided by two different patterns of conceptualization. One is the generalizing method geared towards the universality of laws, which effaces what is individual from view but allows for useful predictions and calculations. The other is the individualizing method, which focuses on individual occurrences in their singularity, thus allowing a great degree of sophistication but no law-based explanation. In both cases, the "heterogeneous *continuum*"[70] of our unconceptualized experience is turned into something discrete and thus rendered amenable to our theoretical understanding.

Husserl highlights that Rickert's line of argument is a somewhat trivialized version of Kant's transcendental deduction, in which the applicability of the categories to the manifold of sensibility has to be justified. Rickert simplifies this difficult Kantian task through a vaguely "pragmatic"[71] demand, namely, that we *need* conceptual simplification and reorganization of the given in order to navigate our way through the world's infinity. Husserl's remark on this pragmatic element is almost mocking:

The activity of generalizing, the creation of concepts and laws and finally of completely non-intuitive exact concepts as well as natural laws should be the means to make the infinity knowable. However, at this point one could say: does the infinity have to do us the favor of yielding to our

---

[68] *Ibid.*, 87.   [69] See SH, 34.   [70] *Ibid.*   [71] Hua XXXII, 91.

thought-productions [*Denkerzeugnisse*], of being knowable via concepts and laws? Why should the endless world have to care about our cognitive interests and demands?[72]

Rickert construes the world prior to our conceptualization as "entirely uniform" or "monistic."[73] But, Husserl asks, in front of a completely chaotic and unstructured world, how could we ever come up with the idea of a law-based conceptual mastery of it? How could the vision of a theoretical understanding via concepts and laws appear as a practically attainable goal? How could *total* chaos *motivate* a rational agent to bring about order? Interestingly, Hermann Lotze – one of the first exponents of Neo-Kantianism and a major source of inspiration for the Southwest German school – brought to light one of the weakest spots in a critical theory of knowledge when he stated that the suitability of sense-data for subsumption under our intellectual categories should be considered a "fortunate fact" (*eine glückliche Tatsache*)[74] and thus remains inexplicable within a critical framework. If the sphere of sensory intuition (or, more generally, experience) is considered *per se* entirely inchoate and unstructured and thus thoroughly alien to conceptuality, then the fact that it is nonetheless amenable to conceptual organization is indeed a piece of good luck. But, from Husserl's perspective, this simply shows the intrinsic weakness of theories of knowledge that begin with an impoverished and generic notion of unconceptualized experience, such as Rickert's. Husserl points out:

If knowledge grasps, conceptually and authentically, what exists and how it exists [*Seiendes und Soseiendes*], then precisely what exists is itself conceptual. Concepts are not our private thing, which only pertains to us cognitive agents. What exists is, in turn, not in itself alien to concepts.[75]

---

[72] *Ibid.*

[73] SH, 13. It should be remembered that this kind of 'monism' does mean that for Rickert the entire world is made of one single kind of ontological 'stuff.' His ontology is, as discussed in Chapter 1, pluralistic. The 'world' comprises empirical objects (physical or psychical) as well as meanings. This dual ontology, however, goes hand in hand with a 'structural' monism and affirmation of the world's uniform lack of *order* and organization prior to the conceptual operations of generalization and individualization.

[74] Quoted in W. Windelband, "Kritische oder genetische Methode?," *Präludien*, vol. 2, 99–135. Here 104.

[75] Hua XXXII, 92.

According to Husserl, Rickert's account treats the unconceptualized experience of the world as a merely formal mathematical manifold[76] in which no laws governing the conditions of real co-existence for the manifold's members are to be discerned. Rickert skips a serious inquiry into the material a priori of world-experience. He moves from a merely formal contemplation of unconceptualized experience as "immeasurable manifold"[77] to its simplifying reorganization under universally valid *empirical* laws, whereby the immeasurability is overcome and the manifold is theoretically mastered. But, in this way, precisely the possibility of this transition, the very idea of reorganizing the manifold according to empirical laws, remains unaccounted for. In contrast to Rickert's characterization of unconceptualized experience as a heterogeneous *continuum*, Husserl emphasizes forcefully that

the world must have a *structure of homogeneity*. If I ask about the conditions for possibility of knowledge of the world as infinite manifold, this question is guided by the empty representation of a manifold, i.e., [I am moving from] the analytical *a priori* towards the synthetic. But the observation of experience itself (which bestows sense upon the world) shows through free variation of this experience and the experienced world that what is far must be similar to what is near. This presumption is induction, and each induction is a pre-figuring of sense and being based on analogy. Therefore it is evident that if this world and a world in general are to exist, they must exist as homogeneous worlds.[78]

Put simply, it is because we recognize patterns of order and stability already at the level of unconceptualized experience that we are motivated to cognize nature in scientific terms. In order to spell out the essential, a priori laws underlying these patterns of order and stability we have to delve into the multifarious manifestations of the world in its material richness and orient ourselves in the mode of a priori research, as outlined above. This does not mean that we cannot ask formal

[76] On Rickert's account, however, a mathematical manifold would be already a reorganization of our inchoate intuitive experience, only, one where the heterogeneous *continuum* is not turned into a heterogeneous *discretum* via conceptual incisions but rather into a *homogenous continuum*. In mathematics, all heterogeneity and differentiation in the experiential world is renounced in favor of a pure contemplation of homogenous continuity (see SH, 34–35). For our present concerns, however, the details of Rickert's philosophy of mathematics can be left aside.
[77] SH, 32.   [78] Hua XXXII, 249.

questions. The problem with Rickert's take on the transcendental deduction is that his analyses are "of a formal style but, as we can see, they are not pure."[79] A really pure transcendental deduction starting from the analytical a priori and then moving 'downwards', as it were, to a consideration of the material a priori should begin with the merely empty representation of a manifold of 'somethings in general' and spell out those minimal formal-ontological requirements that allow for non-contradictory judgments. Once this important part of the deduction were accomplished, it should be asked what further conditions must be added in order for the merely empty manifold to be a manifold of really existing beings, that is, co-existing entities in a real world. This would open up an overwhelmingly wide field for a priori research that could not, however, be derived from further elaboration on the formal onto-logical conditions but would instead require materially oriented inves-tigations of a completely different kind. "World-experience remains [for Rickert] an empty word."[80]

Rickert's failure to address the material a priori structures of the world that undergird different regions of being leads him to a tacit acceptance of naturalism, which is clearly proved by his unqualified embrace of empirical psychology:

The traditional biases become visible in Rickert not only in that he deduces the antediluvian ideal of mechanism as ideal for the physical sciences, but he even advocates the same ideal also for *psychology* and thereby also for the whole world as valid, as something obviously entailed deductively [*mitdeduziert*] by the formal generality of his deduction.[81]

Husserl, as a trained natural scientist and mathematician, is well aware of the progressive move away from mechanism and classical physics occurring in his time[82] and cannot help but mock Rickert's old-fashioned appeal to mechanistic causality in physics while at the same time denouncing its even more pernicious effects in psychology. The naturalistic bias in Rickert's thought, which makes him accept the same (outdated) method in both natural science and psychology, leads to another absurdity in Husserl's eyes, which is the divorce of subjec-tivity and value carried out in Rickert's classification of the human sciences. Commenting on the excerpts from Rickert's writings collected in preparation for his lectures, Husserl writes:

[79] *Ibid.*, 237.   [80] *Ibid.*, 100.   [81] *Ibid.*, 243   [82] See *ibid.*, 241–242.

I realize in hindsight that I presented Rickert's theory of reference-to-value [*Wertbeziehung*] too limpidly. His own presentation is actually pretty unclear and convoluted. The simple idea that the historian can empathize with the people who carry out valuations and study the way in which they are determined by their subjectively intended values without installing himself on the ground of their evaluations does not become clear.[83]

Husserl seems not to realize that Rickert's failure to take into consideration psychic subjects carrying out evaluations and the possibility to empathize with them is deliberate! It is part of his strategy of divorcing the human sciences from psychology in order to preserve their autonomous method. However, as a matter of fact, while it is true that little or nothing can be contributed to the human sciences by a strictly naturalistic psychology, it is hard to see how their progress could depend on complete disregard for the psychic processes of acting subjects who create culture on the basis of acknowledged values.[84]

To sum up, for Husserl, Rickert's formalistic theory of knowledge (1) fails to provide genuine justification for the ideal of scientific knowledge and (2) falls prey to the naturalism inherited from the Cartesian tradition. His abstract understanding of experience not only fails to grant true autonomy to the human sciences but also offers an outdated and deficient account of the possibility of natural science. In the wake of Rickert's failure, Husserl points out:

---

[83] *Ibid.*, 232.

[84] Incidentally, Husserl's charge that Rickert completely disregards valuing subjectivity is not entirely fair. Rickert's point is that valuing subjectivity is not the *fundamental concept* of the domain of culture, and therefore it should not be considered as the starting point in a philosophical investigation of the human sciences. Once the genuinely fundamental concept of *value* has been established, a consideration of historically living subjectivity is certainly helpful and even necessary. This line of thought, however, becomes more explicit in later editions of Rickert's *magnum opus*, *The Limits of Concept Formation in Natural Science*, and it is not fully articulated until the fifth edition, which came out in 1929 two years after Husserl's lectures on *Natur und Geist*. Here he states clearly that "[T]here must be human beings in every reality that is a possible object of a historical representation. By virtue of the individuality of their volition and action, they constitute individuals with respect to social values. It also follows that the mental life of a human community, which is significant because of its singularity, stands at the center of every historical representation" (LCF, 132). For Rickert, however, the recognition of living subjectivity as the center of historical representation entirely presupposes the validity of the values that this subjectivity intends and cultivates. For a discussion of Rickert's notion of value see Chapter 1.

All thought in aprioristic abstraction (including content-related thought such as geometry) offers a guarantee, offers real evidence for ultimate foundation only if it is drawn from the whole fullness of concreteness. Thought becomes groundless if it does not take its departure precisely in that 'ground,' which is the whole actuality of life with every single element that constitutes its fullness, and if it fails to constantly look back towards this ground, being aware in full clarity how all abstractions spring from this life-source.[85]

In this context, Husserl drops the crucial remark that his transcendental phenomenology actually sides with life-philosophy against the abstractions of Southwestern Neo-Kantianism. He emphasizes that "the reaction of the various good, but, in part, also mistaken life-philosophies against rationalistic science"[86] depends on the incapacity of abstractly rationalistic accounts of scientific cognition to provide genuine clarity about the material conditions for the possibility of knowledge, thus opening an unbridgeable chasm between science and experiential life. Even if the general tendency of life-philosophy to relativize and historicize all knowledge is absolutely alien to Husserl, he acknowledges without reservation that cognition in general and science in particular must be integrated into a larger dynamic of experiential life, which provides the motivational basis for scientific activity and whose aprioristically oriented scrutiny yields essential truths that undergird all higher-level cognitive activities. The task thus outlined coincides with philosophy's innermost vocation and clarifies its function in the broader edifice of science. A longer passage from an appendix to the lecture offers an illuminating recapitulation of Husserl's point as well as an extremely significant clue to understanding Husserl's position in the context of the *Naturwissenschaft/Geisteswissenschaft* dispute. It sounds almost like a short manifesto:

It is the *fundamental characteristic of the new phenomenology*, which does not call itself life-philosophy but, preserving the authentic ancient meaning of philosophy as the universal science, *is* a life-philosophy, that it is everything but inclined to renounce science, the great heritage of millennia, and rather advocates science anew, but then universal science springing from the conceivably most radical foundation or rather self-responsibility of the cognizing agent. Phenomenology wants to make such science possible through its method. Obviously, in this way, phenomenology also wants to enable a conservative preservation, but also a reconfiguration of the sciences handed

---

[85] Hua XXXII, 239.   [86] *Ibid.*

down historically and currently at work. [Phenomenology wants] to enable a radical, critical appraisal and a new foundation [*Neufundamentierung*] of these sciences, that relieves them of all paradoxes and controversies about their fundamental principles [*Grundlagenstreitigkeiten*] and overcomes all absurd tension between science and life. Therefore, the fundamental character of phenomenology is *scientific* life-philosophy, i.e., a science that does not presuppose and is not based on the already existing sciences, but is rather *radical* science, having as its fundamental scientific theme the concrete universal life and its life-world, the real concrete surrounding world. Taking its departure from here and drawing purely on the most concrete intuition it has to bring the type-pattern [*Typik*] of this surrounding world into rigorous concepts that can be verified at any time. From there, phenomenology has to work out systematically the fundamental conceptuality that has to serve all possible sciences, thereby showing that, on the other hand, all possible sciences can only have meaning in relationship to the fundamental structures of the reality of life [*Lebenswirklichkeit*].[87]

Aside from the somewhat rhetorical tone, Husserl's point in this illuminating passage is clear enough. He intends to distance himself from all forms of transcendentalism, such as Rickert's own brand, that begin with a misrepresentation of experiential life, whereby this latter is construed as an inchoate and structureless continuum, in order to then force on this caricature of experiential life the allegedly world-forming power of conceptuality. However, concepts that are alienated from experience from the outset cannot be reconciled with it deductively in a second moment. In this respect, Husserl feels entirely consonant with the tradition of life-philosophy, which emphasizes the continuity between life and cognition as well as the origin of all concepts in life-dynamics. However, unlike most life-philosophies, Husserl's phenomenology wants to remain scientific and even 'hyper-scientific,' so to speak. The immersion in the multifarious plenitude of the life-world and its forms does not displace thought into a realm of absolute relativity and contingency. Contrariwise, it is precisely the orientation towards material a priori structures in the midst of the intricacies of experiential life that grants phenomenology its own peculiar and radical kind of scientificity. In a sense, mainstream life-philosophy implicitly accepts the misrepresentation of experiential life offered by transcendental thinkers *à la* Rickert and simply refuses the universal validity of the

---

[87] *Ibid.*, 240–241.

concepts forced on it. It celebrates the allegedly erratic and unfathom-able dynamics of life and its surrounding world instead of working to overcome them in conceptual thought. But this unconvincing picture of experiential life as a fundamentally malleable, erratic, and heterogene-ous whole is common to both currents.

Husserl is more radical and rigorous than most life-philosophers in that he devotes his efforts to offer a different, more reliable picture of how experience is structured and how, in the case of physical nature, it motivates empirical investigation geared towards the discovery of causal laws. However, his defense of the demands of life-philosophy is a precious clue to make sense of his project. In this respect, a closer consideration of Husserl's intellectual exchange with philosophers like Simmel and Dilthey is of paramount importance for an adequate assess-ment of his phenomenology. This will be the theme of Chapter 6.

6 | Historia formaliter spectata: *Husserl and the life-philosophers*

Life as operative comes first.

Edmund Husserl[1]

The final remarks of Chapter 5 indicated that Husserl understood his phenomenology to be deeply consonant with life-philosophy. This consonance, however, has nothing to do with an alleged prioritization of intuition over conceptual thought, as Rickert maintained in his essay *Die Philosophie des Lebens*.[2] What mattered to Husserl was rather the acknowledgement of living subjectivity as opposed to inert nature and the defense of the human sciences as rooted in an autonomous science of psyche. This chapter will examine some systematic points connecting Husserlian phenomenology and life-philosophy. Husserl did not produce a critique of life-philosophy as extensive and articulate as his critique of Rickert. However, from the beginning of the 1920s onwards, he read carefully both Dilthey and Simmel and realized that they stood much closer to his own project than he had initially thought.

Instead of focusing on a single lecture course or set of manuscripts, we shall follow some helpful cues provided by Husserl in various notes on the life-philosophers scattered throughout his work and try to develop systematically the indications entailed therein. In most cases, Husserl valorizes the intuitions and the demands expressed by the life-philosophers while criticizing their actual doctrines and the unquestioned presuppositions upon which they are built.

Husserl's personal contact with the main exponents of life-philosophy was sparse during his life. His academic relationship with Dilthey, nonetheless, went through highs and lows, though the two always remained on friendly terms. In *Philosophy as a Rigorous Science* (1911) Husserl harshly criticized Dilthey's writings on philosophy and worldview. The critique argues that Dilthey's insistence on the

---

[1] Hua VIII, 475. [2] See Chapter 4.

historicity of philosophy, i.e., its relativity to ever-changing historical conditions, amounts to an unacceptable concession to relativism and skepticism. In his essay, Husserl equates Dilthey's conception of philosophy as *Weltanschauung* to unscientific "wisdom"[3] and advocates for the necessity of preventing philosophy as a scientific endeavor from being conflated with or even replaced by such wisdom.[4] Dilthey, who had been an enthusiastic reader of the *Logical Investigations*, was rather shocked to receive such a harsh rebuke by Husserl. In the ensuing correspondence between the two, Dilthey lamented what he considered Husserl's complete misunderstanding of his true intention, and Husserl replied insisting on the necessity of rigorous eidetic analyses geared towards the establishment of absolutely valid a priori norms in the sphere of culture, which – one is tempted to add – is obviously easier said than done.[5] What could have been the beginning of a fruitful exchange was soon truncated by Dilthey's death in the fall of 1911. As a matter of fact, in *Philosophy as a Rigorous Science*, Husserl presents Dilthey's position in an exceedingly simplified fashion, and the profoundest elements of his thought are not even addressed. One gets the impression that Husserl is using Dilthey just as a straw man to attack historicism more generally and, in so doing, keep with the theoretical standards of the journal *Logos*, which the Southwestern Neo-Kantians used to express their aversion towards both naturalism and historicism.

It is worth noticing, however, that in *Philosophy as a Rigorous Science* Husserl does not even mention the concept of life. As outlined in Chapter 4, the standard Neo-Kantian attack on historicism generally revolved around the inadequacy of mere life as a fundamental principle for philosophy. It set up the erratic and ultimately opaque dynamics of historical life against the atemporal validity of concepts, counterposing valid conceptualization against mere intuitive contemplation of the vagaries of history. Husserl criticizes the reduction of philosophy to a

---

[3] PRS, 52.

[4] We shall dwell more extensively on Husserl's complex understanding and progressive appropriation of the notion of *Weltanschauung* in Chapter 7.

[5] The exchange between Husserl and Dilthey was originally edited and published alongside an instructive introduction by Walter Biemel in *Man and World* 1/3 (1968), 428–446. It was subsequently included in the critical edition of Husserl's *Briefwechsel*. See E. Husserl, *Briefwechsel*, vol. 6, *Philosophenbriefe* (Dordrecht: Kluwer, 1994), 41–51. Hereafter BW VI.

multiplicity of contingent historical opinions, but he does not seem to share with Rickert and the other editors of *Logos* the idea that this unpalatable reduction is a direct consequence of a philosophical prioritization of life. It would be illegitimate to make too much of this omission, but it can be taken as an interesting hint that, at this early stage of his *Auseinandersetzung* with the life-philosophers, Husserl was already less dismissive of them than were the Neo-Kantians.

Fifteen years later, after actually reading *Ideen über eine beschreibende und zergliedernde Psychologie* (1893) and *Der Aufbau der geschichtlichen Welt in den Geisteswissenschaften* (1910), Husserl changed his mind about Dilthey's philosophical value. In his lecture course *Phänomenologische Psychologie* (1925)[6] he praises Dilthey's *Ideen* as a work "characterized by genius"[7] and goes on to remember its author with the following laudatory remarks:

[H]e had an incomparable capacity for surveying everywhere the concrete life of the mind, individual and socio-historical, in its living concretions, for grasping intuitively its typical shapes, its forms of change, its motivational connections, and for carrying out with respect to them great surveying explications which make intelligible to us the characteristic being and genesis of historical mentality in its concrete necessity.[8]

Of course, this does not mean that Husserl suddenly became a Diltheyan. In spite of his late reappraisal, he still maintains some serious reservations about Dilthey's method – which he considers extremely unsystematic[9] – and most importantly about Dilthey's understanding of the philosophic status of his own analyses. His lack of a rigorous concept of *eidos* gave the impression that his descriptions of the basic types of psychic and cultural facts did not have any general validity and simply applied to average, normally developed human beings.[10] However, as we shall see shortly, in spite of his unsystematic style and his misleading self-understanding, Dilthey was a trail-blazer for a genuine phenomenological foundation of the historical world.

---

[6] Hua IX, 3–236. English translation by J. Scanlon, *Phenomenological Psychology: Lectures Summer Semester 1925* (The Hague: Nijhoff, 1977). Hereafter Phen. P.
[7] Phen. P., 3.   [8] *Ibid.*, 4.
[9] With a slightly condescending tone, Husserl states that Dilthey "was much more a man of brilliant intuitions of the whole than of analyses and abstract theorizings" (*ibid.*, 3).
[10] *Ibid.*, 11.

Things are different as far as Simmel is concerned. We have little information about the actual historical contact between him and Husserl. The few letters that the two thinkers exchanged are of no philosophical value, but they testify to the friendly relationship between them.[11] A more interesting fact is that Husserl read some of Simmel's theoretical works on history very carefully and in 1924 even adopted Simmel's *Die Probleme der Geschichtsphilosophie* for his philosophical exercises or *Übungen*.[12] Husserl would generally select classics in the history of philosophy such as Kant's *Critique of Pure Reason* or Locke's *Essay* for his *Übungen*, and Simmel is one of the few among his contemporaries who had the privilege of being read and discussed in Husserl's seminar. It is hard to overestimate this fact. Husserl's marginal notes on his personal copies of *Die Probleme der Geschichtsphilosophie* and of two other essays by Simmel, *Das Problem der historischen Zeit* (1916) and *Vom Wesen des historischen Verstehens* (1918), show that despite all specific differences he considered Simmel a major source of inspiration, directing Husserl's own efforts towards a phenomenological elucidation of the essence of the historical world.

Moreover, from the 1920s onwards Husserl integrates more and more into the language of phenomenology terms and phrases that he borrowed from the tradition of *Lebensphilosophie*. For instance, Husserl uses Simmel's metaphor of *Pulsschläge* (pulse-beats), to designate the generation of single acts of consciousness issuing from the transcendental ego,[13]

---

[11] See BW VI, 401–411.

[12] See K. Schuhmann, *Husserl-Chronik: Denk- und Lebensweg Edmund Husserls, Husserliana Dokumente*, vol. 1 (The Hague: Nijhoff, 1977), 281. The *Übungen* were small seminars in which the professor would read and comment on a philosophical book of his choice. Attendants in Husserl's *Übungen* reported that he would very often go off on tangents and actually present his own ideas rather than commenting on the selected book. On a side note, it is an interesting coincidence that Husserl's very last doctoral student, a certain Hellmuth Bohner, devoted his dissertation to "A Study of the Development of Georg Simmel's Philosophy." Bohner defended his dissertation in the spring of 1928. See Schuhmann, *Husserl-Chronik*, 327.

[13] See, for instance, Hua VIII, 81, where Husserl explains to his students the meaning of the phenomenological reduction as a consideration of one's experience under suspension of its naively accepted validity, so that this experience is taken purely "as a pulse of my own egological life." The expression *Puls* is repeatedly used in the continuation of the text (see Hua VIII, 83; Hua VIII, 99), in later lectures (Hua IX, 8) and in manuscripts stemming from the same period (e.g., Hua VIII, 472). The *Erste Philosophie* lecture from which the above passage is taken was given during the same semester in which Husserl held his

as well as *Lebensganze* and *Lebenszusammenhang* – two terms clearly stemming from Dilthey – to talk about the overarching unity in the temporally unfolding stream of subjective experiences. Considering all these elements, it is fair to say that the tradition of *Lebensphilosophie* and in particular Simmel, whose works Husserl read intensively and even adopted for his own teaching, had a very significant yet subterranean impact on the development of Husserl's thought.

The historical world

Briefly put, the theoretical problem framing Husserl's confrontation with the life-philosophers is: what does it mean that history can be construed as a *world*, as the phrase 'historical world' as opposed to the 'natural world' seems to suggest? Are we using the word 'world' metaphorically when we talk about history as a world, or is there any substantial analogy between the subject matter of the natural sciences and the subject matter of the human sciences? And if there is any robust sense in which we can talk about the historical (or 'human') world, upon what phenomenologically detectable conditions does our experience of this world rest?

Let us recall the analysis of the last chapter: a world, in Husserl's view, must be distinguished from a mere mathematical manifold as construable in terms of a system of positions governed by a set of material a priori principles of co-existence. The two fundamental principles governing the world of nature are spatio-temporality – which provides the two basic forms of co-existence of *simultaneity* and *succession* – and causality – which provides the framework for all possible interactions between spatio-temporally co-existing realities. Husserl considers these two principles first and foremost in their intuitive dimension, that is, as they are experienced prior to their formulation in mathematical terms by natural science.

seminar on Simmel's *Probleme der Geschichtsphilosophie*. In other manuscripts he uses expressions such as "*Lebenspulse*," literally "life-pulses." E. Husserl, *Zur Phänomenologie der Intersubjektivität. Texte aus dem Nachlaß. Dritter Teil: 1929–1935, Husserliana*, vol. 15 (The Hague: Nijhoff, 1973), 28, hereafter Hua XV; *Zur Phänomenologie der Intersubjektivität. Texte aus dem Nachlaß, Zweiter Teil: 1921–1928, Husserliana*, vol. 14 (The Hague: Nijhoff, 1973), 160, hereafter Hua XIV; Hua XIV, 202; Hua XIV, 409. Elsewhere he uses the expression "*lebende Pulsschläge*," "living pulse-beats" (Hua XIV, 359).

Obviously, we cannot construe the historical world as a causally regulated system of realities appearing in space and time. Nonetheless, according to Husserl, there are similar a priori principles of regulation in the world of history. Dilthey and Simmel pointed in the right direction when they indicated the notion of 'psychic facticity' or 'psychic nexus' as the fundamental concept for making scientific sense of the historical world. However, they both found themselves entangled in insurmountable difficulties when they had to clarify the structure and status of such nexus.

First, Simmel's insistence that "psychological facticity" should be considered the "substance of history"[14] as well as Dilthey's character- ization of *inner* experience as the doorway into the human world[15] can be potentially misleading. They might be interpreted as meaning that the historical world exists only in the interiority of historical individu- als. Simmel's important discovery that the a priori principles presup- posed by historians fundamentally coincide with those operative in psychology and in everyday human interaction could degenerate into a reduction of history to mere interiority. In this connection, Simmel's and Dilthey's lack of a rigorous notion of intentionality becomes partic- ularly troublesome. Their rightful emphasis on the preeminent meaning of psyche for history tends to blur the distinction between subjects and objects in history and to undermine the transcendent nature of the historical world. While Husserl agrees with the spearheads of life- philosophy that cultural manifestations and ultimately history itself can only be understood by reference to living subjects, he underscores the necessity of retaining a distinction between the historical world as a *subjective achievement* and the (transcendental) subjectivity whose workings give rise to the constitution of such a world. The following passage from one of Husserl's research manuscripts seems to rectify Simmel's and Dilthey's confusion and provide a basis for a correct formulation of the *problem* of the historical world:

Man is a historical creature, he lives in a 'humanity' [*Menschheit*] that exists in historical becoming, which creates history. Humanity is *subjectivity as carrier of the historical world*, a phrase that does not mean "the life that lives historically and constitutes history" but rather indicates its worldly [*umwelt- lich*] correlate as human surrounding world [*Umwelt*], which carries in itself

---

[14] PGP, 236. See Chapter 2.   [15] See Chapter 3.

spiritual-cultural [*geistig*] meaning received from man, from humanity as a whole; as a title for ontic qualities of realities and of their ontic historicity; as having this meaning from human activity, from human interests, goals and systems of goals.[16]

The full recognition of the transcendence of the historical world as *product* of historically active subjectivity has the advantage of indicating a rigorous method for phenomenological analyses: from the identification and description of essential features of the historical world they will have to inquire *back* into the essential features of the subjectivity responsible for its constitution.

Second, if psychology deals exclusively with isolated individuals, how can it be fundamental for the human sciences? Husserl recognizes that Dilthey's brand of descriptive psychology has a certain superiority compared to his teacher Brentano's: from the very start Dilthey is interested in psychology as a possible foundation for the human sciences. He states:

From this goal, the following requirement resulted immediately and obviously: to go back to inner experience in which mentality [*Geistigkeit*] offers itself in its own essential content. However, through the theme of the humanities as sciences of the socio-historical world from the very beginning, the gaze was stretched beyond the individual subjects of historical life and it was directed towards historical life itself, which is interiorly unitary in each human being and still supraindividual.[17]

Dilthey, however, does not have sufficient conceptual resources to clarify this apparently mysterious link between the psychic life of individuals and the supra-individual being of historical life as a whole. He remains firmly anchored in the mainstream tradition of *Individualpsychologie*, which considers exclusively the psychic life of isolated subjects. Dilthey feels the need for an extension of psychic life into a unitary *field* exceeding single individuals but does not have anything philosophically significant to offer to this purpose. In Husserl's words:

Dilthey talks about nexuses of spiritual life [*Zusammenhänge des Geisteslebens*]. – He has in view the intersubjective unity of historical life. But how does a human being reach out of his own psychic nexus and the motivations entailed therein – how can my life be motivated by alien life? To

[16] Hua XV, 180.   [17] Hua IX, 355.

begin with, Dilthey did not see clearly the problems of personality in community, towards which he is nonetheless directed, and remained stuck in the stream of experiences [*Erlebnisssstrom,*][18]

Individually oriented psychology from Locke onwards operates under a strong naturalistic assumption that prevents it from seeing the purely 'spiritual' unity of the human world. The assumption is that since human bodies are spatially separated and interact with one another only occasionally and exteriorly, then the 'souls' attached to these bodies, too, must be originally separated and interact with one another only occasionally and exteriorly. Husserl labels the result of this assumption a "naturalistic fragmenting [*Zersplitterung*] of spirit [*Geist*],"[19] which, of course, bears fateful consequences for the desired psychological foundation of the human sciences.

This last remark leads us straight into the third and final major shortcoming in the life-philosophical accounts of psyche and history: the relationship between nature, psyche, and history remains fundamentally ambiguous and ultimately obscure.[20] When Simmel states that "all of human history is nothing more than a piece or part of the total cosmos,"[21] and when Dilthey remarks that "we ourselves are nature, and nature is at work in us, unconsciously, in dark drives,"[22] they both make implicit concessions to a naturalistic view of subjectivity. If history is a psychic nexus, but human psyche is fundamentally continuous with inert nature, which is taken to be 'at work' in it at the most fundamental level, then both psyche and history are ultimately mere appearances, that is, they are the way in which inextricably complex tangles of natural events appear at the macro level. The insistence on the different nature of historical and psychic events, on their understandability and on their occurrence in motivated connections is ultimately arbitrary. Husserl seems to point out rightfully that the life-philosophers cannot have both a secure and autonomous domain for the human sciences grounded in descriptive psychology *and* an implicitly naturalistic understanding of psyche. Either there is only *one* field of inquiry, namely, universal nature – but then all methodological distinctions and claims of autonomy for the human sciences are ultimately unwarranted – or there has to be a sense in which the field of psyche is a *closed* field of inquiry in its own right. Only as a closed field of inquiry

---

[18] *Ibid.*, 356. [19] *Ibid.*, 357. [20] See Chapter 2. [21] PPH, 125.
[22] GS VII, 80/SW 3, 101, translation modified.

strictly distinct from nature can psyche offer a robust foundation for the correlative field of history. Otherwise, both psychology and history will have to be considered, to use contemporary language, merely epiphenomenal disciplines, or, in Husserl's terms, merely transitional disciplines, whose legitimacy only lasts until the actual scientific work of causal explanation is carried out.

Based on the distinctions presented in Chapter 5, it should be clear that the closure of a scientific field does not mean that this field is *really* (metaphysically) separate or separable from other fields. Accordingly, to 'close' the field of psychology does not necessarily amount to defending Cartesian substance dualism. For Husserl, the phenomenological *epoché* and reduction are the methodological tools necessary to close the field of psychology and in so doing raise it and the human sciences founded upon it to the rank of truly autonomous sciences. However, as we shall see in the next section, to close the field of psychology necessarily results in a significant modification of the meaning of subjectivity.

Closing the field of psyche – opening up the field of history: on the meaning of the phenomenological *epoché* and reduction for the project of a purely descriptive psychology

To begin articulating the problem of the closure of the psychic field, it is helpful to recall the following passage from the *Natur und Geist* lecture (1927):

The field of a science will have to be called independent when its theoretical exploration [*Verfolgung*] never has to lead beyond this field; no matter how far we penetrate its infinite horizons, it is a self-enclosed horizon that never has to be overstepped. In the opposite case, the field is non-independent, and then the theoretical interest will necessarily have to stretch out until it reaches the thematic totality. This means, however, that for a complete satisfaction of the theoretical interest, a science directed to this totality, to this fully independent field of being is necessary, i.e., a science on which the above initial science [*Ausgangswissenschaft*] is dependent and in which it is at the same time incorporated.[23]

How does psychology fit this description? Do the infinite horizons of its field of inquiry never overstep the domain of the purely psychic?

---

[23] Hua XXXII, 52–53.

Psychology seems not to be an independent science. This is because a satisfactory exploration of its field of inquiry manifestly requires a consideration of *sensations* and basic *sensuous feelings* (such as pleasure and pain) whose occurrence depends causally on stimuli at the neural and hence physiological level. If this is the case, then the field of what is purely psychic verges on nature; therefore, the 'thematic totality' pertaining to psychology must be considered nature *qua* encompassing the causes of psychic events. Strictly speaking, psychology should be considered a non-independent branch of the natural sciences.

The status of sensations has always been a vexing question for theorists of psychology. A good document to illustrate the controversies surrounding this question is the first chapter of Brentano's *Psychology from an Empirical Standpoint* (1874). Brentano reports the opinions of various eminent psychologists of his time, all dealing in some way with the problem of sensations. John Stuart Mill – in many respects the father of modern psychological theories – recommended simply excluding them from consideration in psychology, leaving them entirely to physiology. Fechner advocated for a sharp distinction between a descriptive psychology dealing with classes of mental states, and a separate discipline, which he labeled psychophysics, investigating those mental phenomena that necessarily require consideration of underlying physiological occurrences.[24] Brentano himself draws a distinction between genetic and descriptive questions in psychology, and, while he agrees on the necessity of keeping the two apart, he recognizes an "inevitable encroachment of physiology upon psychology and vice versa."[25] In this context, however, "it will be the task of the physiologist to investigate the ultimate and immediate physical causes of sensation, even though in so doing he must obviously also look at the mental phenomenon."[26]

In spite of this distinction, however, neither Mill nor Fechner nor Brentano manages to entirely disregard sensations and their physiological causes in their 'purely psychological' inquiries.[27] Moreover, mere

---

[24] See F. Brentano, *Psychology from an Empirical Standpoint* (New York: Routledge, 1995), 6.

[25] *Ibid.*, 7.   [26] *Ibid.*

[27] Brentano concedes: "It will definitely be the task of the psychologist to ascertain the first mental phenomena which are aroused by a physical stimulus, even if he cannot dispense with looking at physiological facts in so doing" (*ibid.*).

exclusion or relegation of sensations to a separate discipline does not amount to closing the field of psychology. Such proposals concede that, strictly speaking, the field of psychology is not closed. The most fundamental building blocks of psychic life are brought about by causes that lie outside the purely psychic domain. On this basis, theorists of psychology propose partitions within the sphere of psychic events according to which 'higher-level' events such as perceptions or volitions can be 'abstractly' isolated from their sensory basis, which is considered a 'lower-level' stratum whose scientific treatment *necessarily* leads to a quest for non-psychic, physiological causes.

This is, in very brief compass, the same picture of mental life accepted and assumed methodologically by the pioneer of experimental psychology, Wilhelm Wundt, and endorsed by Dilthey.[28] One advantage of this two-layered model of mental life is that it squares nicely with a broadly Kantian conception of experience. It allows for a distinction between a purely *passive-receptive* source – the natural phenomenon of sensibility, which only provides the 'material' content of experience – and an *active-forming* power of psyche, which processes the materials received from the senses and molds them into experiences and any other kind of higher-level conscious act built upon experiences.

Husserl was familiar with this position, and it is evident from his analyses of corporeity and psyche that he was influenced by Wundt's model of psychic life. On the one hand Husserl recognizes a certain plausibility to this model, and for his entire life he never ceases to describe subjectivity in terms of two layers, first '*Seele*', which roughly corresponds to the lower level in the Wundtean scheme, and second '*Geist*', which indicates the active-forming power characterizing the higher level. On the other hand his progressive deepening of the meaning of the phenomenological reduction makes him aware of a danger inherent in this model. By 'naturalizing' the lower part of subjectivity – the *Seele* directly caused by physiological processes – the higher part is itself made entirely continuous with the world of nature. Husserl becomes increasingly aware that a complete shift of attitude is possible, one in which the dual model is retained but is no longer interpreted as consisting of two separate parts – one natural, the other genuinely psychic. Let us consider a few exemplary passages where the evolution in Husserl's approach becomes tangible.

---

[28] See Chapter 2.

In the long and illuminating supplement to the third part of *Ideas II* (which can be considered a small treatise in its own right),[29] Husserl fleshes out the idea that "the spirit [*Geist*] has a psychic [*seelisch*] basis."[30] He then goes on to define sensibility as this "psychic [*seelisch*] basis of the spirit, and of the spirit on all conceivable levels."[31] Within the sphere of sensibility Husserl further distinguishes between "sensuous data,"[32] such as color data presenting themselves in the visual field, "sensuous feelings"[33] founded upon these data, such as instincts, drives, and the like, and finally "secondary sensibility," corresponding to all the sedimented products of past experiences that resurface passively in present experience and influence the way in which we apprehend new objects and situations.

Husserl contrasts this fundamentally passive sphere of subjectivity with the active life of the *Ego*, which consists of conscious acts that radiate freely from the *Ego*-center and apprehend the rudimentary unities in the passive sphere as manifestations of full-blown objects. In this context, Husserl sketches some of his first genetic analyses and attempts to describe the main characteristic of the psychic (*seelisch*) field of passivity underlying the egological life of the spirit (*Geist*). He points out that the apprehending regard of the active *Ego* never turns towards an entirely inchoate mass of sense data. Prior to all active 'turning-towards' (*Zuwendung*) of the *Ego*, sense data organize themselves associatively according to laws of similarity and contrast. Such passive, pre-egological organization constitutes what Husserl in later texts calls "sensuous saliences" (*sinnliche Abgehobenheiten*), which stand out as structured wholes from the environing perceptual background and knock at the door of the active *Ego*, as it were, demanding its attention. Husserl terms this phenomenon *affection* and repeatedly underscores that affective unities within the sphere of passivity should

---

[29] Ideas II, 344–381. A valuable examination of this supplement is offered in T. Sakakibara, "The Relationship between Nature and Spirit in Husserl's Phenomenology Revisited", *Continental Philosophy Review* 31 (1998): 255–272. Here 258–262. The author, however, fails to acknowledge the development of Husserl's position on this matter and reads back into this early document Husserl's later position. To be sure, pre-egological passivity "is never to be understood in the natural-scientific sense" (Sakakibara, "The Relationship," 259). However, in his first attempts to shed some light on these difficult issues, Husserl did try to understand the underlying psychic basis of spirit as continuous with the inductive causality of the natural world.

[30] Ideas II, 345.   [31] *Ibid.*, 346.   [32] *Ibid.*   [33] *Ibid.*

not be understood as products of some unconscious apprehending activity but purely as self-organized sensuous coalescences that the *Ego* finds available as being 'already there' in all its active accomplishments. Commenting on the phenomenon of affection, Husserl makes the following crucial statements:

No active Ego-motivations arise through "association" or through "psychophysical lawfulness"; thus, they do not arise the way all formations of sensibility do. To be sure, the whole natural machinery is presupposed, the "natural mechanism." Can it now be said that what proceeds from the Ego and occurs in the Ego as "affecting," in penetrating into the Ego as motivating, drawing it to itself ever tighter – still prior to any yielding – is no longer nature? No, the affection belongs quite certainly in the sphere of nature and is the means of the bond between Ego and nature. Moreover, the Ego also has its natural side. All Ego-actions, just like the Ego-affections, come under the law of association, are arranged in time, work afterwards as affecting, etc. But at best it is the Ego thought of as purely passive that is mere nature and belongs within the nexus of nature. But not the Ego of freedom.[34]

Husserl is thus attempting to draw the distinction between nature and *Geist* within the sphere of consciousness in terms of a distinction between a passive-natural side of the ego and an active-spiritual side. Although in the above passage he distinguishes between 'association,' as a set of specifically psychic laws regulating sensuous data, and 'psychophysical lawfulness,' as a separate set of concomitant regularities in the organization of sensuous data deriving from underlying physiological causes, both sets of laws are considered 'natural.' According to this description: "Ego and nature stand in contrast, and every act also has its natural side, namely its underlying basis in nature: what is pre-given as affecting is a formation of nature."[35] This picture of psychic life does not fundamentally depart from Wundt's, except perhaps for Husserl's

---

[34] *Ibid.*, 349, translation modified. In the English edition, the German term *Naturgetriebe* is wrongly translated as "natural drives," thus mistaking the singular word *Getriebe*, which means "machinery," for the plural word *Triebe*, which means "drives." This mistake is particularly pernicious in this context, where Husserl is drawing subtle distinctions between feelings, drives, and instincts as belonging to nature and free actions as belonging to *Geist*. Unfortunately, the entire English edition of Ideas II is shot through with such basic translation mistakes, which a serious copy editor could have easily detected, thus sparing the reader the necessity of constantly double-checking the original German text in order to make sense of Husserl's descriptions.

[35] *Ibid.*, 350.

distinction of associative laws and specifically psychophysical laws. This adumbrates the idea that association may not be itself a psychophysical phenomenon. Husserl, however, does not develop it in this context.

Indeed, just a few years after penning the above statements, in his first lecture course on *Natur und Geist* in 1919, Husserl starts raising some doubts about the tenability of the Wundtean model, which, however, he still considers a valuable stepping stone for a correctly executed phenomenology of consciousness. He concludes his analysis of psyche and the body with the following remarks:

A certain parallel ordering of the psychological [. . .] is certainly legitimate. It is possible, then, to follow the idea that in animal psychic life we must distinguish between an underlying stratum [*Unterstufe*], which runs immediately parallel to the physical-corporeal dimension, and a higher layer, which has no such immediate relationship to the physical but is physically conditioned in a mediated fashion via its connection with the underlying layer. Accordingly, we would have (1) the direct parallelistic regulation of the underlying layer; (2) the rules of dependency of the upper layer from the lower layer; (3) possibly, specific rules pertaining to the upper layer. After this surely valuable distinction [is drawn], a question arises: what kind of rules are to be considered particularly for the psychic [*das Psychische*] of the higher layer? As for the underlying layer, we obviously have to think about sensations [*sinnliche Empfindungen*] and phantoms, sensuous feelings and drives. The higher layer consists of the manifold shapes of consciousness qua intentionality, although obviously whether this distinction should be understood as a real separation has to be seriously pondered.[36]

In this lecture Husserl leaves the question open, but it is clear that the picture of subjective life as split so that the natural 'psyche' stands in contrast to the free activity of the 'spiritual' ego is no longer fully convincing. In the very last lines of this lecture, he reiterates his standard critique of naturalism in psychology and points out the different perspective on subjectivity opened up by phenomenology using language that clearly echoes Dilthey:

Phenomenology opened up for us endless fields for knowledge of the I and consciousness in which *completely different regulations, regulations of inner motivation* come to light. [We discover] nexuses that, already in singular

---

[36] Mat IV, 218.

cases, have a completely different characteristic: that of *understandability*, the only authentic understandability.[37]

Most importantly, however, one should add that the 'different' perspective on the ego and consciousness opened up by phenomenology regards *all dimensions of subjectivity* and not just the upper stratum. A few years later, in his 1920s lectures on ethics, Husserl summarizes in the following terms what he considers to be the fundamental mistake of naturalistic psychology and, in a certain sense, also of his earlier articulation of the *Seele/Geist* distinction:

[The main mistake of naturalistic psychology is] that it posited the passivity of association and of the whole psychic life unfolding without the activity of the I at the same level with the passivity of the physical natural process [...] However, passive motivation is, like all spiritual causality [...] a sphere of understandability standing under pure essential laws and, therefore, having a completely different meaning than natural causality and natural lawfulness.[38]

Husserl continues pointing out that this wrong-headed equation of physical passivity and passivity in the sphere of psyche led to "the naturalistic tendency to reinterpret all ego-activity, including the freedom of spiritual [*geistig*] agency in the sphere of purely rational motivation as an illusory formation [*Scheingebilde*] springing from merely passive sources."[39] He now reasserts the distinction between the higher and lower levels of subjectivity but interprets them in significantly different terms:

Within subjectivity [*Geistigkeit*] we have two levels. They are indivisible because they are essentially related to one another: the lower level – that of the mere psychic [*seelisch*] – and the higher level, that of *subjectivity* [*Geistigkeit*] in an eminent sense. The lower level is that of pure passivity [...][40] [and] the higher level is the whole personal life and, from there, all socio-historical living and acting [*Leben und Leisten*] reaching beyond individual persons.[41]

How did Husserl recalibrate his description of subjective life? And why did he come to consider it a thoroughly coherent nexus of

---

[37] *Ibid.*, 220.
[38] E. Husserl, *Einleitung in die Ethik. Vorlesungen Sommersemester 1920 und 1924, Husserliana*, vol. 37 (Dordrecht: Springer, 2004), 333. Hereafter Hua XXXVII.
[39] *Ibid.*   [40] *Ibid.*, 110.   [41] Phen. P., 99.

understandability? The answer to these questions has to be sought in Husserl's other works on the meaning of the phenomenological *epoché* and reduction. While there is no single, univocal rationale behind the performance of the phenomenological *epoché* and reduction, and while strictly speaking one should talk about phenomenological *epochés* and reduction*s* in the plural form, in the context of our discussion one fundamental meaning of these theoretical devices stands out as central: *they are geared towards the closure of the field of psychology.*

Let us try to describe in just a few brushstrokes the trajectory leading to the problem of how to close the field of psychology from within a phenomenological perspective. As we saw in Chapter 5, for Husserl, a first and fundamental distinction in the world of pre-theoretical experience is that between things and living bodies, whereby living bodies are things endowed with a subjective dimension. Accordingly, *"[e]very-thing subjective*, including concrete subjectivity itself, figures in the world of experience as *naturalized*, that is, as enhancing something natural with subjective meaning or content."[42] In the development of a scientific culture, it is possible, and even inevitable, that a motivation to study this subjective component in its specificity will arise. This is, in very brief compass, the scientific motivation behind psychology. Psychology, properly understood, aspires to be a discipline capable of isolating and studying the psychic side of psychophysical entities called animals and, more specifically, of human animals. In order to focus on its desired subject matter, psychology necessitates an abstractive *epoché*, which Husserl characterizes in the following terms:

As a psychologist I must behave with respect to myself and my own psychic dimension, too, in the way I behave with respect to others: as if I observed, as if I were an 'unparticipating' observer of my self and my worldly life, and as such an observer I have to put out of play the validity I constantly effectuate as I live forth naturally. In so doing, I modify my naive experiencing so that it becomes my real psychological theme, and a truly pure theme.[43]

A correctly executed psychological *epoché* necessarily modifies subjective experience in comparison to natural, non-scientific self-reflection. While the occasional consideration of our subjective experience in everyday life does not affect the positings of existence entailed in

---

[42] Hua XXXIX, 278.   [43] Hua XXXIV, 129.

the experience under scrutiny, a purely psychological consideration has
to target and suspend all extra-mental being and focus exclusively on
experiences qua experiences. For instance, if I find myself contemplating
my own perception of a stick in the water, marveling at the optical
illusion that makes the stick appear bent, I am in so doing implicitly
'endorsing' the position of an existing stick appearing bent in the water.
This 'positing' (*Setzen*) is essentially entailed in the first-order perception I am now focusing on. However, if my contemplation of this
perception is motivated by a purely psychological interest, then,
according to Husserl, I will have to bracket the existence of the stick
as belonging in the mind-independent nexus of physical nature and
concentrate purely on the subjective content of my experience. In so
doing, I will be entitled to consider the stick and its pretension to
existence only insofar as they are manifested in the purely subjective
nexus of my own experiencing. I will not judge and make scientific
claims regarding my experience *based on* the assumption of the stick's
extra-mental existence.

As long as this psychological *epoché* is carried out on single experiences it does not seem to pose any problem. I can, in fact, at any time
sort out one of my experiences, bracket the extramental existence
posited in it and carry out psychological observations. On the contrary,
serious problems arise if the psychologist starts wondering about the
broader scope of her work. Experiences and their objects do not exist in
isolation. A stick I am perceiving at a given moment is what it is and
possesses its validity as a real 'existent' only insofar as it belongs in an
overarching nexus of further real existents. Similarly, my perception of
the stick only occurs as a momentary eddy in the endless flow of my
subjective life. It is inextricably connected with other experiences I had
(or may have), which in turn posit (or would posit) other existents, and
so on *ad infinitum*. To continue with our example, while I may successfully suspend the validity of the stick the moment I decide to contemplate psychologically my experience of it, I would nonetheless continue
to posit, albeit implicitly, the existence of the whole world in which the
stick is taken to exist. Among other things, this world contains the
psychologist's own body, which, according to psychology's self-
understanding, is the other 'half' of that psychophysical entity whose
subjective life psychology is determined to study scientifically. The
existence of this body is the necessary condition in order for subjective
life to exist in the first place. In fact, the body is the source of all

causalities inaccessible to a purely psychological gaze whose workings give rise to basic psychic facts, such as sensations.

The unaffected validity of the world, and of all experiences of worldly existents surrounding every single experience under psychological scrutiny, thus jeopardizes the consistency of the psychologist's scientific endeavor. If she intends to achieve real purity in her subject matter, and if her scientific aims exceed the occasional investigation of isolated experiences, then there has to be a way to extend the psychological *epoché* from single experiences to the entire nexus of subjective life and, correlatively, to the entire world therein intended and posited as existing. In other words, a genuinely *phenomenological*, universal *epoché* is needed, one which from the very beginning brackets and modifies the world into a world-phenomenon and considers it only to the extent that it manifests itself in the subjective nexus of a world-experiencing subject. This approach purifies focused investigations of single experiences or series of experiences of their extra-mental positings from the start and allows these investigations to cohere in a nexus that is no longer entangled with nature.

Following these considerations and finally carrying out the phenomenological, universal *epoché* brings to light something extremely relevant to our theme: I can posit and study subjective life in a scientific manner "without having to posit my own corporeity beforehand."[44] In other words, if I execute the phenomenological *epoché*, and thus decide to bracket the validity of the world in its entirety from the start, my own body itself as a component of the world undergoes the bracketing. It, as much as any other existent in the world, is 'phenomenalized,' considered only to the extent that it lays claim to existence within nexuses of subjective experiences. Along with my body, my entire existence as a human being, as a psychophysical entity, is bracketed and taken purely as a datum of experience. Once inside the phenomenological brackets, I can no longer take my body as the source of physiological causalities that are inaccessible to the psychological gaze and that bring about psychic life in the first place. Metaphorically speaking, the body no longer stands 'behind' consciousness, engineering its existence in the natural world. It is an appearing worldly item with its characteristic index of validity that the phenomenologist is ready to consider precisely qua index of validity.[45]

---

[44] Hua XXXIX, 42.

[45] This, however, does not mean that the body is *just* another worldly item like any other physical thing one may or may not happen to perceive. Husserl devotes long

Recalling the problem we started with – the status of sensations as immediately caused by extra-psychic factors – we can now see what the phenomenological *epoché* accomplishes. It *blocks*, as it were, the natural tendency of psychological inquiry to overstep its disciplinary borders when it comes to consider the most elementary components of psychic life.[46] By phenomenalizing the body, it impedes the leading back of sensibility (in the broad sense described above) to proximate physical causes and in so doing it *closes* the field of psychology.[47] Briefly put, the phenomenological *epoché* and reduction result in a *de-naturalization of sensibility* (meaning by 'sensibility' the entire sphere of *Seele* defined above). The picture of subjective life after this de-naturalization is that of an entirely closed or "self-contained"[48] sphere, which Husserl increasingly characterizes with his borrowing the Leibnizean concept of "monad."[49] Each monad is a "unity of thoroughly connected understandability, in which only the fact of sensations remains as a non-understandable residue."[50] Obviously, in the phenomenological register, sensations, or, better, the sphere of primary sensibility, cannot be further explained because they are the ultimate, most basic manifestation of subjective life. They have to be taken as an element of irreducible facticity within consciousness. The essential laws governing the inner development of a monad's life and the purely spiritual connections

---

and detailed analyses to the body's way of appearing and its constitutive function with respect to other worldly things due, for instance, to the role of kinaesthesia. Moreover, in every conceivable phase of my waking life, my own body necessarily appears in my perceptual field, unlike all other things that come and go.

[46] In a manuscript dated 1932, Husserl definitively confirms that he now considers the *totality* of subjective life, including both the higher and the lower levels, as an enclosed system of understandability distinct from nature in the following terms: "[But] all these 'sensations,' the kinaestheses and the sensuous intuitions [*sinnliche Anschauungen*] are nothing natural; natural science knows no kinaestheses, no perspectival modes of appearing, etc., let alone subjective perspectival appearances, subjective orientations, etc." (Hua XXXIX, 616–617). The phrase '*sinnliche Anschauungen*' is presumably intended in the Kantian sense.

[47] The de-naturalization of sensations does not imply a denial that sensations relate to the body *tout court*. Sensations are experienced as localized in the body, be it in the immediate sense in which tactual sensations occur in identifiable spots of the body or in the indirect sense in which, for instance, acoustic sensations are localized in the ear. This, however, is a line of analysis that differs significantly from the psycho-physiological quest for unexperienced physical *causes* of sensation.

[48] Phen. P., 165.   [49] *Ibid.*   [50] Mat IV, 218.

linking together an open community of monads thus become the psychic foundation of the historical world.[51]

We have two implications of the *epoché* to highlight before we conclude this discussion. First, the shift from the psychological to the phenomenological attitude is not without "the corresponding phenomenological modification"[52] on the objective side. The bracketing of the body and the corresponding bracketing of the 'human being' as psychophysical subject necessarily brings about a modification in the meaning of subjectivity studied by phenomenology. Psychologists are determined to study the psychic side of human beings, but, in Husserl's ideal narrative, they realize that in order to capture their field of inquiry in its purity the naively embraced validity of the world has to be bracketed *tout court*. Accordingly, the purity of the subjective field necessarily implies giving up the human being as the horizon of interest of the discipline initially understanding itself as pure psychology, but whose consistent pursuit leads to its reformulation as purely *transcendental* phenomenology. The *closed* subjectivity sought after by psychology cannot be human, and its actual attainment implies a redefinition of the status of psychology, which has to reinterpret itself as transcendental phenomenology. In a certain sense, then, if psychology decides to remain true to the initial *formulation* of its task, then its field of inquiry is bound to remain open because the psychic side of a human being can only be separated from its physiological basis abstractly. If, on the contrary, psychology follows the demand for a closed and autonomous field of inquiry consistently, this leads to a phenomenological 'revolution,' which discloses a new dimension of subjectivity, one which can be studied with an entirely autonomous method but 'loses' its specifically human connotation. This does not mean, as one might be tempted to think, that the subject matter of phenomenology is some kind of over-human incorporeal entity, as is sometimes alleged by caricatured presentations of Husserl's thought. Husserl believes that he has discovered a previously unseen dimension of subjectivity, which for each subject carrying out the reduction numerically coincides with his or her human psyche. There is absolutely no sense in which we would

---

[51] Ludwig Landgrebe correctly points out that "The inner historicity of each individual is the *a priori* presupposition of the historical world." *Faktizität und Individuation. Studien zu den Grundfragen der Phänomenologie* (Hamburg: Meiner, 1982), 47.

[52] Ideas II, 10. See Chapter 3.

somehow possess two 'subjectivities.' Our psychic life is one and one only. Transcendental subjectivity is not ontologically *separated* from the human psyche. It is human psyche seen in a new light, one in which its specifically human connotation is suspended and in which what had been previously understood simply as the psychic side of a psychophysical entity is now seen purely as subjectivity, prior to all ascriptions to psychophysically existing entities in the real world.

Second, the closure of psychology's field does not amount to a retreat into the ethereal spaces of a purely mental world purged of any reference to the 'real' world in which we live our natural life. The phenomenological bracketing does not remove the index of 'reality' or 'genuine transcendence' attaching to the objects around us. Upon closer scrutiny, it turns out that the closure of psychology's field and its consequent redefinition as transcendental phenomenology implies a dramatic *opening* of the sphere of interest of this newborn science of subjective life. As Husserl realizes early on:

Thanks to the intentionality of the *cogitatio* or of 'consciousness,' as we also said, phenomenology, which we could also designate the 'science of pure consciousness,' encompasses in a certain way all that it has excluded so carefully; it encompasses all cognitions, all sciences and, on the objective side, all objects, including the entirety of nature.[53]

In other words, it is only when subjectivity is considered a segment of the world, namely, as the psychic side of a psychophysical entity called 'human being,' that its exclusive consideration seems to imply a withdrawal from the rest of the world. Subjectivity grasped in its transcendental dimension, on the contrary, encompasses the world itself. The world's validity is retained in its suspended form within the phenomenological brackets. 'World' now becomes the title of an endless system of interconnected realities manifesting themselves as such within the self-contained nexus of transcendental-subjective experiences. Husserl mints the efficacious term *Ichall* to indicate the shift of theme enacted by the phenomenological attitude: it redirects the phenomenologist's gaze from the *Weltall* (literally world-all), which is the ordinary German word for 'universe,' to the transcendental *Ichall*, literally ego-all. The

---

[53] E. Husserl, *Einführung in die Phänomenologie der Erkenntnis. Vorlesung 1909, Husserliana, Husserliana Materialien*, vol. 7 (Dordrecht: Springer, 2005), 64. Hereafter Mat VII.

gaze is still firmly directed to all things of experience but in a new key. Whereas the key to the whole in the natural attitude is 'world,' in which everything is experienced as worldly, the key to the whole in the phenomenological attitude is 'I,' and everything is experienced as manifested to my experiencing ego. As early as 1917, in his essay on phenomenology and theory of knowledge, Husserl gives a clarifying account of the 'shift of key' produced by phenomenology:

Instead of the world encompassing me, I encompass the world. The world encompassed me, the human being. I, however, the I who carries out this radical reflection, do not have a space, a world 'outside' of myself, encompassing me. I do not have a world of things that could hold valid beside this I as having equally legitimate and equally absolute being, things interwoven causally with this I and mirrored by it, as if the I were a mirror.[54]

In the next section, we shall consider a further shift of attitude, this time occurring within the scope of phenomenology, namely, the shift from the *Ichall* as phenomenological theme to what Husserl calls *Monadenall*, i.e., the intersubjective 'whole of monads,' which becomes accessible via a consideration of the constitutive function of empathy. It is important however, to retain the meaning of *Welt, Ich,* and *Monaden* as modifiers of *All,* the totality of what is. Like three different musical keys, they determine three different 'tones' of the world that we experience. They are not three competing theories but three perspectives on being, disclosing three different and yet interrelated 'universes.' If it is possible to experience and cognize the worldly universe (*Weltall*) at the natural level, however, this is because the egological universe (*Ichall*) and even deeper the intermonadic universe (*Monadenall*) are latently operative.

Monads with windows: the constitutive function of empathy for the historical world

Let us now move to consider the second point of contention between Husserl and the life-philosophers mentioned at the beginning. How is a purely spiritual connection among experiencing subjects to be understood? Is it possible to overcome the dogmas of individual psychology? How does this contribute to a foundation of the historical world?

---

[54] E. Husserl, *Aufsätze und Vorträge (1911–1921), Husserliana,* vol.25 (Dordrecht: Kluwer, 1986), 176. Hereafter Hua XXV.

Husserl is well aware that talk of a 'purely spiritual' unity among experiencing subjects sounds extremely odd and even irrational. Moreover, the meaning of this expression cannot be gauged simply by turning one's regard to what is left out of the sphere of pure nature.[55] Husserl addresses these problems explicitly in one of his research manuscripts:

> In contrast to the whole of nature [*Allnatur*] stands now the whole of spirit [*Allgeist*]. Why do we balk at using this word? Why does it not figure in ordinary language or life, or does it do so only in a sense that cannot be possibly in question here? Actually, for a good reason. The thematic abstraction of the whole of nature [*Allnatur*] gives as a result the self-contained structure of the fully concrete world of experience, a structure that has to be investigated as a separate theme [...] But what is left out, what is extra-thematic in this context, is *not a unity of the subjective* which would be a similarly self-contained unity of experience as a 'world' of experience, as a whole of spirit [*Allgeist*], as a spiritual universe to be treated thematically in the same way in which natural science treats nature.[56]

By closing off the subjective sphere, the phenomenological *epoché* and reduction set the necessary conditions for understanding the universal nexus of subjectivity in a scientifically rigorous fashion. However, the specific kind of unity holding together this nexus still requires clarification. The key class of experience to consider here is *empathy*.

As is well known, *Einfühlung* was a buzzword in early twentieth-century German philosophy and psychology. Its specific meaning varied for different thinkers, but at bottom it was used to designate a subject's experience of subjectivity other than his own. However, the spectrum of meanings attached to this phrase was overwhelmingly wide. Philosophers and psychologists often used *Einfühlung* indiscriminately to indicate both (1) our experience of other human beings as subjects and (2) our experience of cultural artifacts serving specific social or artistic purposes. Even in those rare cases in which the usage of *Einfühlung* was limited to the first type of experience, its meaning oscillated between at least three connotations, which a genuinely phenomenological analysis must keep strictly distinct: (1a) *Einfühlung* as the conscious act in which a living, experiencing subjectivity is ascribed

---

[55] For the obtainment of nature through an impoverishing abstraction from the world of experience see Chapter 5.

[56] Hua XXXIX, 272–273.

to certain bodies; (1b) *Einfühlung* as the capacity to 'empathize' with other subjects and understand their motivations, feelings, etc.; (1c) *Einfühlung* as the active 'turning towards' other subjects recognized as such in order to establish social bonds.

The merit of Husserl's work is to discriminate both conceptually and terminologically between these three meanings. He generally employs the term *Einfühlung* (which, for lack of a better translation, we will render, as is customary, with 'empathy')[57] only to indicate the meaning (1a), which he considers foundational in respect to the other two. For (1b) he often employs the Diltheyan term *Nachverstehen*[58] or variants of it such as *Hineinverstehen*[59] (literally "understanding-into") or *Sich Hineinversetzen*[60] (somewhat freely: "putting oneself in someone else's shoes"). Obviously, in order to be able to understand someone else's intentions, motivations, and feelings, it is necessary first to acknowledge the other as an embodied self. Therefore (1b) thoroughly presupposes (1a). For (1c) Husserl uses the phrase 'social acts' or 'I-Thou acts,' and he repeatedly stresses the necessity of distinguishing them from simple acts of *Einfühlung* (1a). In specifically social acts, other subjects are recognized as subjects of will: they are given orders, they are listened to, and so forth. Such acts require a subject's taking the initiative with another subject and not merely the recognition that the other is a subject and not a mere thing. This brings to light a further, important difference obtaining between acts of the class (1a) vis-à-vis (1b) and (1c). While *Nachverstehen* and social acts require a certain amount of effort and interpretation and are open to failure (I can fail to understand the

---

[57] Unfortunately, the meaning of the word "empathy" in English is much closer to (1b) than to (1a). Sometimes translators tried to obviate this problem rendering Husserlian *Einfühlung* with the neologism "intropathy"; see, for instance, A. Steinbock, *Home and Beyond: Generative Phenomenology after Husserl* (Evanston, IL: Northwestern University Press, 1995). "Intropathy," however, sounds too esoteric a translation for a term that in German was actually rather ordinary. After all, considering that Husserl deemed the German word *Einfühlung* problematic to render the phenomenon (1a), it does not seem too inappropriate to render it with the likewise problematic word "empathy" in English.
[58] See Hua XXXIX, 57; 162; 167; 171; 340; 393; *passim*. Hua XV, 133; 166; 224; 233; 472; *passim*.
[59] Hua IV, 194/Ideen II, 204.
[60] See, for instance, Hua XIV, 149, where Husserl indicates the equivalence of *Nachverstehen* and *Sich-Hineinversetzen*. Other occurrences are Hua XV, 427; Hua XXXIX, 303; 340; 393; Hua IV, 275.

other's true intentions or fail to establish a social bond), *Einfühlung* in the Husserlian sense only requires our perceptual attending to a certain class of objects in our experience – those presenting themselves as human bodies – and, upon fulfillment of this simple requirement, it cannot fail.[61]

For the purpose of the present chapter we shall first focus on empathy in the Husserlian sense (1a) and then examine its constitutive function for the historical world. In so doing, we will deliberately skip a thorough description of other functions of empathy revealed by phenomenology, such as the constitution of a fully objective sense of nature as the infinite sphere of realities accessible by anyone. Incidentally, the possibility of describing conscious acts in different ways depending on the dimension of experience to be clarified is a fundamental characteristic of the phenomenological method. There is no 'standard' line of description of conscious acts that would be simply dictated by the acts themselves

---

[61] Two remarks are important to strengthen this point. (1) To say that *Einfühlung* in the sense of (1a) cannot fail does not mean that we cannot be wrong about what we take to be a subject. I can experience a mannequin as a human subject from afar and then discover that it was just a mannequin. However, as long as the illusion lasts I have a genuine, and in this sense successful, *Einfühlung*. The same goes for the possibility of experiencing a perfectly designed robot as a human being. If the robot is perfectly designed, this means precisely that it succeeds in giving rise to genuine *Einfühlungen* in subjects experiencing it. For a helpful discussion of this issue see V. Costa, *L'esperienza dell'altro: per una fenomenologia della separazione*, in A. Ferrarin (ed.), *Passive Synthesis and Life-world – Sintesi passiva e mondo della vita* (Pisa: ETS, 2006), 109–125. (2) Sometimes it has been alleged that the very recognition of a subject as different from a mere thing depends on social conditions and is not as "automatic" as Husserl takes it to be. The notorious example of slaves in the ancient world being considered as mere tools is invoked as evidence. This position seems to be geared towards the assertion of a certain primacy of (1c) over (1a). However, it is extremely unconvincing. The master considering his slave as a tool presumably did not fail to tell him or her apart from his hammer or chair. He would not attempt to pick up his slaves and do things with them as he would do with artifacts. The master would in fact issue orders and expect his slaves to obey. This means that the word "tool," when it designates a human slave, is used metaphorically in order to express his or her being entirely subdued to the master's will. The master, therefore, was not lacking *Einfühlungen* in the presence of his slaves. On the basis of a fully successful *Einfühlung* (1a) he would have been establishing or perpetuating a social bond (1c), in which no mutual exchange of orders and services was contemplated. The moral meaning of such a situation cannot be assessed here; however, this brief description should suffice to show that *Einfühlung* (1a) is, in a sense, morally neutral. It takes more than mere recognition of the other as a living human subject to treat him or her in a morally respectful way.

regardless of the context of phenomenological clarification in which the description at issue is carried out.

A glance at the life-philosophers' treatment of empathy reveals a weakness that, in Husserl's eyes, prevented them from grasping its constitutive function for history. For both Simmel and Dilthey our experience of others is not strictly speaking *experience* but rather an *inference* based on the observation of the other's behavior. As we saw in previous chapters, Dilthey emphasizes the importance of *expression* (*Ausdruck*) as the original manifestation of subjective meaning. On the basis of observed expressions, we are able to *relive* (*Nacherleben*) the original life-sources from which such expressions sprung and then move to understand (*Verstehen*) their constituent motivational factors. In other words, observed expressions ignite a dynamic of re-experiencing *within* the observing subject. In this sense, the process of understanding relates not so much to foreign life actually expressing itself (which for Dilthey remains ultimately unfathomable) but rather to the inner re-production (*innere Nachbildung*) of this life operated by the observing subject. In short, what I try to understand is the inner picture that I created for myself based on the empathetic re-living or re-experiencing of foreign life ignited by the observation of some external expression. Given this framework, it is no surprise that Dilthey does not feel obliged to distinguish between our experience of other people and our experience of cultural products, as mentioned above. In both cases, we are faced with expressions (be they bodily gestures and utterances or patches of color on canvas and the like), and we attempt to reconstruct and understand *within ourselves* the life at their origin. Moreover, Dilthey does not at all distinguish between our capacity to attribute subjectivity to bodies other than our own (empathy in the Husserlian sense: (1a)) and our attempts to interpret expressions of foreign subjectivity (*Nachverstehen*: (1b)). On Dilthey's account, what we labeled (1a) is nothing but an extremely thin kind of (1b). Attribution of subjectivity to another body always goes along with attempts to understand concrete expressions and it is itself, in a sense, a very basic attempt to understand.

Simmel is even more explicit than Dilthey. In one of his very last essays, "On the Nature of Historical Understanding" (1918), he describes our awareness of foreign subjects in the following terms:

On the basis of initial appearances, another person is a collection of observable impressions. We see, hear and touch him. But consider the following propositions. An animate mind lies "behind" all these appearances. They all have a mental status, an inner aspect that is not exhausted by their observable properties. In short, the other individual is not a marionette, bur rather a person who can be understood from within. These propositions presumably do not have the status of given facts, at least not in the same sense that the observable impressions of the individual constitute given data. On the contrary, they inevitably retain the character of presumptions [*Vermutungen*] which can never be conclusively verified [...] We do not experience [that the other person is animated or has a mind] as a fact which has the compelling vivacity of a sense impression.[62]

His personal copy of Simmel's essay shows that Husserl studied this text intensively. Beside the passage just quoted Husserl annotates: "Completely wrong interpretation of empathy."[63]

What is wrong about Simmel's interpretation of empathy is that it degrades our experience of other subjects to a *Vermutung*, which would perhaps be better translated as 'conjecture' based on a hypothetical inference.[64] On this account, there would be no fundamental difference between forming the conjecture that my wife went to the gym based on the observation that she is not at home and her sneakers are missing and forming the conjecture that my wife is a minded being like me based on the observation that she moves around, talks, laughs, cries, and so forth. In both cases, we would form our conjecture based on incomplete information. Moreover, following Simmel, there is a sense in which, while the conjecture that my wife went to the gym is verifiable (I can go to the gym and see if she is there), the conjecture that she is a minded being is not. This is because I will never have direct access to her 'mind,' and all conceivable reassurances I could possibly receive from her on this matter can only be understood and given credit *assuming that* they are manifestations of a minded being.

---

[62] G. Simmel, *Vom Wesen des historischen Verstehens*, in Georg Simmel, *Gesamtausgabe*, vol. 16 (Frankfurt am Main: Suhrkamp, 1999), 151–179. Translated by G. Oakes, "On the Nature of Historical Understanding," in G. Simmel, *Essays on Interpretation in Social Science* (Totowa, NJ: Rowman & Littlefield, 1980), 97–126. Here 99.

[63] E. Husserl, BQ 445; Georg Simmel, *Vom Wesen des historischen Verstehens* (Berlin: Ernst Siegfried Mittler und Sohn, 1915), 4, from Husserl's private library preserved at the Husserl Archives Leuven.

[64] In his earlier work, *Die Probleme der Geschichtsphilosophie*, Simmel suggests that our mostly unaware attribution of a mind to other human beings is based on a "hypothesis" (PGP, 240). For an excellent discussion of these issues see T. Karlsruhen, "Simmels Evolution der Kantischen Voraussetzungen des Denkens," *Simmel Studies* 11 (2001): 21–52. Here, 28–40.

It is not hard to see that Simmel's theory leads to absurd conclusions. It seems to undermine one of our most elementary experiences, namely, that the world is populated by other minded beings like us. This experience is rendered entirely hypothetical and thus unfit to do any further philosophical work towards a clarification of the status of the historical world. The rationale behind Simmel's conception of empathy is clear: He wants to point out that the historical world is not a ready-made reality outside of ourselves that determines us from without but, rather, in a Kantian fashion, is the product of constructive intellectual processes that begin already in everyday interaction. However, this seems to be too strong a reaction against 'realistic' tendencies in historical theory, one that completely obliterates elementary data of our experience. In a later manuscript, Husserl aptly remarks that when it comes to describing our awareness of other subjects: "Regardless of how one may prefer to call it: 'empathy' or 'experience through understanding' [*verstehendes Erfahren*] or what have you, it is in any case *experience.*"[65]

Husserl's insistence on empathy being a robust kind of perceptual experience and not an unverifiable conjecture is consistent throughout his career. This is part of the reason why he is not particularly fond of the term *Einfühlung*,[66] which vaguely suggests an emotional rather than perceptual awareness of other subjects. Before we move to present in outline Husserl's positive account of empathy, we should pause to reflect on the problem that prevented Simmel from attributing empathy the status of a genuine experience. In a nutshell, Simmel points out that unlike the perception of other subjects' bodies, our "experience" of their mind lacks entirely the vivacity supplied by a specific sensory basis. In other words, what we can see, touch, smell, etc. is just another body. On the contrary, there are no sense data manifesting to us directly the other's subjective life. At first blush, this seems to be a strong reason to deny empathy the status of a genuine perceptual experience.

However, there is a phenomenological problem with Simmel's analysis already present in his understanding of perceptual experience of a simple thing. Every perceptual experience, properly described, is a mixture of authentic presentation and a surrounding horizon of further possible presentations that are not impressionally present but are

---

[65] Hua XXXIX, 617.
[66] See, for instance, Hua VIII, 63 n. 1, where Husserl remarks in passing that he considers the term *Einfühlung* unfit to designate our experience of other.

nonetheless *experienced*. For instance, while I am perceiving my laptop, what I have authentically present in my impressional consciousness is only one profile at a time. In this moment I am seeing – in the eminent sense of 'having sensuously present in consciousness' – only one profile, presenting me with the screen and the keyboard. However, the concrete content of my experience of the laptop includes the awareness that I could change my position and that currently unseen sides would appear and replace the profile I am momentarily experiencing. These unseen sides, although they are not sensuously present in consciousness, are part of my current experience of the laptop. Without being somehow aware of the unseen sides of my laptop while they do not appear, my experience would not qualify as perception. In Husserl's terminology, the currently unseen sides of my laptop are nonetheless *co-present* and are necessarily *apperceived* or *appresented* on the basis of what is momentarily presented.[67] At the same time, what is momentarily present in consciousness would be absolutely nothing if it were not embedded in an apperceptive horizon. It would be just a fleeting sensory impression and not the manifestation of an existing thing.

In our exploration of perceptual things, we are constantly aware of turning merely apperceived sides into properly perceived sides, while what was just perceived falls back into the apperceptive horizon of co-presence. In light of this analysis of perception, which is far more accurate than Simmel's, there is nothing anomalous or deficient about empathy being a genuine experience of something unseen. Seeing beyond the momentary content of our consciousness is not an anomaly of empathetic experience but rather an essential trait of any genuine perceptual experience whatsoever. In this sense, what renders empathy possible is just the same apperceptive transcending of what is momentarily given that is already operative in the perception of simple things.

Let us follow briefly Husserl's felicitous description of empathy offered in the *Erste Philosophie* lecture (1923/24), delivered the same years he was deepening his study of Simmel.

Husserl points out that we have an original experience of subjectivity's inherence in a physical body: the experience of ourselves. We constantly see our body, we 'hold sway' in it, we use it to move in space and we are tactually aware of its material existence in the world of natural things. He asserts:

---

[67] "All appresentation is founded in presentation." (Hua XXXIX, 410.)

Only to the extent that things in my bodily surroundings equal my own living body and that element in it which bestows on its physical behavior the rank of animating expression, can and even must such things be apprehended and experienced as living bodies. I do not say this on the basis of some objective-psychological theories [...] but rather by observing my perception and its characteristic structure as perception of my own living body and of alien living bodies.[68]

In the more famous *Cartesian Meditations* a few years later (1929) Husserl will refer to "analogizing apprehension"[69] of the other's body based on the "associative pairing"[70] linking it with my own body, whereby the experienced similitude between our two bodies allows for the transference (*Übertragung*) of the sense 'embodied subjectivity' – originally experienced in my own body – into the other body. In the *Erste Philosophie* lecture, the terminology is less technical, and Husserl's main concern is to stress that in empathetic experiences other subjects are *genuinely experienced*. This experience has a kind of immediacy to it that comes to expression when in ordinary language we say 'I see the other person' and not just 'I see his or her body.' Perhaps having in mind Simmel's "completely wrong" characterization of empathy Husserl insists that this experience is "no inference" and "not a kind of mediated thinking" because the other is "*really* experienced."[71] In order to explain how this real experience can occur despite the impossibility of the other's mind presenting itself through sense impressions, Husserl articulates the explanation outlined above. He holds that the experience of others in empathy is an immediate perception, restating:

[A]nd still this perception entails a certain mediatedness, which distinguishes it essentially from the perception of my own body. In my own body, as we saw, both the thingly [*dinglich*] living body and the psychic component that embodies itself in it, as well as the way in which this embodiment occurs, are originally perceived. The psychic component is namely my own. On the contrary, while the other's living body is originally perceived in my spatial surrounding world as much as my own body, the psychic component embodied in it is not likewise originally perceived. It is not really and authentically

---

[68] Hua VIII, 62.
[69] E. Husserl, *Cartesianische Meditationen und Pariser Vorträge (1931)*, *Husserliana*, vol. 1 (The Hague: Nijhoff, 1963), 140. Hereafter Hua I.
[70] Hua I, 147.   [71] Hua VIII, 62.

self-given, it is only co-intended after the manner of appresentation. In this regard, there is a similarity with that anticipation through which in every outer perception something co-perceived, something intended as being there concomitantly, is included, such as, for instance, the unseen rear side of a seen thing. But the analogy is not perfect [...] This indicating intention does not demand and does not contemplate a resolving perception, as is the case with all pre-figuring moments in the perception of a thing in space. *The perception of an alien living body* is rather [...] essentially *perception through originary interpretation* [*Wahrnehmung durch ursprüngliche Interpretation*].[72]

Like the rear side of a perceptual thing, the psychic life of an alien subject is not seen but is nonetheless experienced alongside what is authentically perceived, the alien human body. However, unlike the rear side of a perceptual thing, the psychic life of an alien subject cannot be brought to direct manifestation by further perceptual exploration of his body. It is an appresented component that is bound to remain appresented. This appresentation *is* its way of being originally given.

It would be wrong-headed at this point to interpret the impossibility of self-givenness in direct presentation as a lamentable deficit in our experience of alien subjectivity. This is because it would be illegitimate to impose the requirement of impressional self-givenness characterizing simple perceptual experience on our experience of alien subjectivity. Empathy, as Husserl points out, is just a "specific, fundamental form of experience," which still "has to be designated as perception" in virtue of its originally giving trait but which has its own "ways of confirmation"[73] and legitimatization vis-à-vis simple perception. Following Nicolas De Warren's apt characterization, in empathetic experience the demand of intuitive fulfillment that belongs to every form of intentionality, and in particular to simple perception, is in a certain sense *withheld*, and thereby consciousness becomes open to the experience of something other-than-itself.[74] To put it in simpler words, seeing the other's mind just like we see our own mind is a wrong ideal if applied to our experience of alien subjectivity. A first-personal seeing of the other's mind would not be the optimal version of what in our empirical world, unfortunately, only happens in the mode of appresenting indication.

[72] *Ibid.*, 63.   [73] *Ibid.*
[74] N. De Warren, *Husserl and the Promise of Time: Subjectivity in Transcendental Phenomenology* (Cambridge University Press, 2009), 239. De Warren does not mention directly the *Erste Philosophie* lecture, but the longer passage quoted above (see n. 68) directly confirms his reading.

Appresenting indication is *precisely* the way in which subjects are genuinely present for each other through empathy, and the demand of intuitive fulfillment after the manner of simple perception is just out of place for this type of experience.

After the acknowledgment of the genuine experiential status of empathy, the stage is set for an analysis of its constitutive function with regard to the historical world. In short, Husserl shows that empathy does not yield merely occasional experiences of isolated subjects. On the contrary, a complete analysis of empathy and its essential characteristics reveals that empathetic experience discloses for every subject an *open horizon of other subjects* extending indefinitely into the past and into the future. Let us recall the talk of 'monads,' which was adopted to stress the self-contained nature of transcendental subjectivity. Commenting on this self-containedness of empathy, Husserl makes the following remark, which is of crucial importance for the continuation of our analysis:

Every ego is a "monad." But monads have windows. They have no windows or doors to the extent that no other subject can really enter. However, through such windows (the windows are empathetic experiences) the other subject can be experienced in the same way in which one's own past experiences are experienced through recollection.[75]

The suggested analogy between empathy and recollection brings to light a feature of empathy that deserves close scrutiny. Empathy can be described as a kind of *presentification (Vergegenwärtigung)*. Presentifications are those experiences through which something absent is experienced. This occurs, for instance, when we remember our childhood bedroom, when we imagine a crocodile, or when we expect the train to arrive soon at the platform. All these objects cannot present themselves to us perceptually the moment we want to experience them. While I am standing on the platform waiting for the train, there are a limited number of things that present themselves to me 'by themselves' in perception: the tracks, the wires, the timetable, the benches, and so forth. My childhood bedroom does not. If I decide to remember it, I am the 'operator' of its presence. In Husserl's language, I presentify it for myself. Similarly, if I decide to picture for myself the imminent arrival of the train, the expected train is made present by me. In a different sense, if I decide to kill time playing with my thoughts and start to imagine a crocodile, a crocodile now appears before 'my

---

[75] Hua XIV, 260.

mind's eye' *as if* it were present. However, when I imagine, I do not posit the imagined objects as being present somewhere else, having been present or being about to be present. I am just not concerned with their reality or irreality. Husserl, therefore, distinguishes two fundamental classes of pre-sentifications: *positional* (those in which the presentified object is posited as being, having been, or being about to be) and *non-positional* (those in which a mere semblance of presence is evoked and no position of being takes place, including picture-consciousness[76] and free-floating imagination).

In light of the above remarks, it may seem odd that Husserl would describe empathy, too, as a kind of presentification. Is not empathy a genuine experience of self-givenness? Actually, *all presentifications are genuine experiences*; they are genuine experiences happening in a different experiential 'mode.'[77] Remembering my childhood bedroom means having a genuine experience of my childhood bedroom in the mode 'recollection.' Imagining a crocodile means having a genuine experience of a crocodile *as if* I were perceiving it, or in the mode 'fantasy.' Similarly, experiencing another subject means experiencing his or her presence through a specific kind of presentification, empathy, thanks to which the perceptual presence of the other's body receives the enhancement 'living subjectivity' simply by following the compelling

---

[76] Here, of course, more specific distinctions would be needed. There is clearly a difference between a photograph and a painting, in that the object depicted in the photograph 'must' have existed at some point, while the subject of a painting can be entirely imaginary. Similarly, there is a difference between a portrait and an abstract painting. However, Husserl distinguishes between the actually appearing object of an image and the '*sujet*' that was originally depicted or photographed. Even in the case of photographs or portraits, the actually appearing image seen in the canvas or the photographic paper is not posited as being (Napoleon is not actually hanging on the wall or failing to do so; he is merely appearing in the painting), and the reference to the *sujet* once depicted is extrinsic to the actual experience of the image. For an illuminating discussion of these important issues see N. De Warren, "Pamina's Eyes, Tamino's Gaze: Husserl's Phenomenology of Image-Consciousness Refashioned," in Ierna, Jacobs, and Mattens, *Philosophy, Phenomenology, Sciences*, 303–332.

[77] It should be mentioned that Husserl changed his mind on this point. In the *Logical Investigations* he still described non-perceptual experiences as inauthentic presentations, following his teacher Brentano. Later, he realized that presentifications lack nothing in terms of the content that they present and are therefore authentic. The phenomenological difference between presentifications and simple presentations (perceptions) has to be entirely ascribed to the *mode* in which such content presents itself.

experiential motivation entailed in the experience of that body's similarity with my own.

At this stage of our analysis we must turn to consider two essential features of all presentifications: *intentional implication* and *iterability*. Intentional implication is the key phenomenon that 'holds' together monadic life, first at the individual level and then, via empathy, at the communal level. It is the hinge of the historical world. To characterize it briefly, intentional implication is the *inherence of a latent ego in every act of presentification*. In fact, whenever I remember something, the full content of my recollection includes my past *ego* perceiving the object I am remembering. Whenever I expect something to happen, such as the thunder after a flash of lightning, the full content of my expectation includes the future *ego* perceiving the object I am expecting. Most importantly, as soon as we unearth the *latent ego* intentionally implicated in our own reproductive presentifications, such as recollections and expectations, we experience this *ego* as fundamentally coinciding with our present *ego*. My own recollections qualify as my own precisely because at any time I can unearth the latent *egos* implicated in them and experience these *egos* as coincident with my present *ego*. The same goes for expectations and future *egos*. A good way to catch hold of the distinction between the latent *ego* of presentifications and the *ego* carrying out a presentifying act in the present is to consider all those experiences in which I can no longer 'endorse' the validity of my past perceptions. For instance, I can remember seeing a round tower before I approached it and realized that it was, in fact, square. It is not my present *ego* who sees the round tower, because to see a round tower is to endorse the validity of a round tower as an actual existent. Rather, my present *ego* sees itself seeing a round tower in the past, although the focus of its attention while remembering is generally on the tower and not on the recollection. In this experience, the present *ego* can still 'identify with' the past *ego*, but it is the identification, or coincidence, of two elements originally experienced as distinct.

The experienced coincidence between the latent, presentified *egos* and the *ego* carrying out a presentifying act in the present grants the unity of one's own life-nexus, which Dilthey recognized but never accounted for. Moreover, the experience of *intentional implication* within one's own subjective life supplies the *model* for a further clarification of empathy. In the lecture on *Erste Philosophie* – which is the most important source available for a description of intentional implication and iteration – Husserl describes empathy as feeding on the experienced similarity of my body and the other's body:

In this connection, this similarity motivates originally a presentifying function, an indication of a similar psychic life. This life, however, is not indicated in a kind of recollection or expectation, which would allow for an identification of the co-presentified *ego*-subject with myself; it is an *ego*, but an other. The characteristic intentional structure of this kind of perception, which owes a main portion of its accomplishment to a presentification, reveals an *ego* and yet not myself as implicated subject; it makes me aware that another *ego* is in front of me, and without this the words 'other *ego*' or 'neighbor' would be meaningless for me.[78]

Obviously, no synthesis of coincidence occurs between the implicated *ego* and my own present *ego* having an empathetic experience. However, the other *ego's* life is connected intentionally to my own life, and we now live as subjects whose lives never *really* intersect but are nonetheless inextricably linked to one another. Empathizing with other subjects opens up for me an entirely *new* horizon, one that extends my own life-possibilities beyond my self. Husserl describes this phenomenon in a manuscript written some ten years after the *Erste Philosophie* lecture:

Let us consider that the perceptual present in its concreteness implicates actual and potential empathy, too. By virtue of the characteristic structure of such presentifications – which are of a new kind vis-à-vis the presentifications that make me aware of my own past and future life – alien life (present, past, and future) manifests itself as implicate. Now I possess not only the synthesis of my 'own' immanent time, in which the unity of my own stream of life in its own life-temporality [*Lebenszeitlichkeit*] is constantly aware for me as the horizon of my present life, which can be disclosed through recollections. Now the *horizon of empathy* [*Einfühlungshorizont*], through which being and conscious life of alien subjects is there for me, is co-aware, too, in my present life and as belonging to each previous life-present, as a horizon that, like my own, can be disclosed.[79]

As we can easily ascertain, the disclosure (or exploration) of another subject's life does not occur via direct presentifications of his or her conscious acts. However, it can occur through communication and interpretation in which I adopt the other's validities as my own and

---

[78] Hua VIII, 135.   [79] Hua XXXIX, 89.

progressively come to share the infinite horizon of his or her world. To conclude this description of intentional implication, it is important to notice that empathy does not grant just a fleeting experience of some other mind. The recognition of the other as a subject, i.e., as an *ego* not coinciding with but implicated by my own *ego*, establishes a permanent horizon of life that I experience as connected with my own in the specific sense of intentional implication.

The second decisive feature of presentifications relevant here is *iterability*. Let us consider the following experiences: I can expect to remember something; I can remember that I often used to recall a certain episode of my life; I can expect another subject to remember a certain episode of their life, in which they expected something to happen. Presentifications can nest inside one another like Russian dolls. The intentional implication characterizing presentifications considered singly can be iterated indefinitely, thus giving rise to increasingly complicated layerings of latent *egos*.

Considering this phenomenological fact, we can formulate the following essential insight: *every field of present experience of any conceivable* ego *whatsoever harbors an infinity of actual and possible implicated* egos, *which in turn have fields of experiences harboring an infinity of actual and possible* egos, *including the ego initially considered, and so on.*

Thereby an *intersubjective present* as synthetic intersubjective simultaneity of streams of life qua streams of presence is constantly constituted. Each stream is implicated horizonally in every other, and each stream implicates its own past in a way that this past is a past of the simultaneously implicated past of that stream's co-subjects, in an open infinity, through empathy. The same holds for the future. The community as community of reciprocity [*Wechselgemeinschaft*] entails that in my present my simultaneous "us-all" [*Wir-All*] is implicated and that this totality is one and the same for each subject of my *us*, in a way that can be disclosed.[80]

This universal, intersubjective implication building the unity of a total horizon begins with a very elementary kind of iteration: I can empathize with someone empathizing with me. In empathy, I can experience myself *simultaneously* as subject and object of empathetic experience. I experience myself as the other's other. The reciprocity of empathy

---

[80] *Ibid.*, 90.

establishes the most fundamental kind of mutual recognition, which can then be indefinitely iterated to include an infinite community of (actually or potentially) empathizing subjects being one another's others.

> On the basis of this most fundamental form of being-there-*for-one-another*-reciprocally the most disparate *I-Thou-acts* and *Us-acts* become possible [...] In this way, highly multiform communal life becomes possible. Its remarkable characteristic consists in this: not only many subjects live in general, but they live in a way that through the intentionality of empathetic experience each of them has all others given as their others; as being co-existents, partly in the form of an original experience and partly in the form of a definite or open and indefinite knowledge, they are present in the subjects' existential field.[81]

These last lines provide an important clue regarding the foundation of the historical world that we are pursuing in this chapter. The universal reciprocity rendered possible by empathetic experience establishes the first, fundamental a priori governing the historical world. In the same way in which *space* is the a priori form of co-existence in the sphere of nature, the reciprocal *being-there-for-one-another* established by empathy provides the a priori form of co-existence in the sphere of history. From every conceivable *ego*, it is a priori possible to construct a system of definite 'spiritual' positions encompassing all actual and possible *egos* (past, present, and future) following the lines of intentional implications and iteration entailed in every actual or possible empathetic experience.

In the next section, we shall examine another fundamental constituent of the historical world, namely, historical time. We have established the principle of simultaneity (co-existence) of all conceivable transcendental monads, so we now move to considering the principle of their succession which is also responsible for the intelligibility of all cultural products and historical situations.

Simmel and Husserl on the rigidity and plasticity of historical time

Another important source for assessing Husserl's critical appropriation of life-philosophical themes is Simmel's essay *Das Problem der*

---

[81] Hua VIII, 137.

historischen Zeit (1916).[82] Together with the above-mentioned *Vom Wesen des historischen Verstehens*, it was part of a series of studies Simmel undertook in order to start a thorough revision of his major work *Die Probleme der Geschichtsphilosophie*.[83] Husserl's abundant marks on his personal copy of Simmel's essay and his positive marginal comments prove that he considered this work extremely valuable. Simmel endeavors here to characterize in just a few brushstrokes the specific meaning of time for the historical world. In particular, he is interested in the ontological difference between time in the sphere of history and time in the sphere of nature. While natural time is nothing but a quantitative variable in processes that can occur and recur in any venue of the universe, time in the sphere of history binds facts to absolutely unique positions. Moreover, it configures itself in ways that differ significantly from the linear, mono-directional pattern of natural time. As we shall see in what follows, Husserl will eventually recast some of Simmel's analyses in his own language.

One preliminary remark before we move to analyze Simmel's text: Husserl's phenomenological investigations of time cover many different phenomena and span his entire life. The bulk of his work on time revolves around a phenomenological clarification of the constitution of primal time in immanent consciousness. In other words, Husserl's time-analyses set out to reconstruct how the immanent flow of primordial data (*Urhyle*) organizes itself synthetically and, in so doing, constitutes the most fundamental meanings of 'past,' 'present', and 'future' as dimensions of experiences. The doctrine of original impression, retention, and protention, designed to describe this fundamental self-organization of inner consciousness, is one of Husserl's profoundest achievements, and it has been the object of detailed analyses and interpretations in the past decades. Reconstructing or even summarizing this remarkably complex area of Husserl's thought would require a significant amount of space and a digression from the line of inquiry we are pursuing in this book. However, like everything else in the life of subjectivity, the constitution of historical time presupposes the synthetic

---

[82] G. Simmel, *Das Problem der historischen Zeit*, in Georg Simmel, *Gesamtausgabe*, vol. 15 (Frankfurt am Main: Suhrkamp, 2003), 287–304. Translated by G. Oakes, "The Problem of Historical Time," in Simmel, *Essays on Interpretation in Social Science*, 127–144. Hereafter PHT.

[83] See G. Oakes, Introduction, in Simmel, *Essays on Interpretation in Social Science*, 7–8.

work of primordial time-consciousness. Therefore, I have elected to assume some basic familiarity with Husserl's analyses of inner time-consciousness. What we are about to analyze with the aid of Simmel is not so much the constitut*ing* consciousness of time but rather a constitut*ed* dimension of time, which in turn functions as a constitutive a priori condition for the possibility of a historical world.

Simmel begins his essay asking the following questions: "What is the relationship between time and the other components of history? And what is the special import of the concept of time that is germane to history?"[84] First of all, Simmel points out that time is the fundamental principle of individuation for historical realities: "A given aspect of reality qualifies as historical when we know how to fix it at a certain position within our temporal system."[85] This means that the simple fact that an event happened does not suffice to qualify it as historical. We must be able to locate this event in a more or less precisely determined moment in the whole of history. This is because mere understanding, which Dilthey deemed the organ of historical knowledge, does not supply any meaningful information about the historical reality of the fact at issue:

Understanding – that is, the ability to empathize or to project oneself into a structure of elements – is exclusively concerned with ideal contents. Understanding is a consequence of the coherence and the association of these ideal contents. From the perspective of understanding, therefore, the question of whether these contents fall under the categories of reality or fantasy, the present or the past, is of no consequence.[86]

In other words, there is no real difference between understanding the fictional character of a novel and understanding a historical figure of the past. What we understand is a series of ideal 'contents' whose connection is indifferent to reality or fantasy. The mere fact that we can understand some meaningful connections does not prove anything about the actual historical occurrence of the objects to which these connections pertain.[87] Understandability and temporal situatedness are thus two completely independent 'sources' for the constitution of an object as 'historical.'

---

[84] PHT, 127.   [85] *Ibid.*   [86] *Ibid.*, 128–129.

[87] This issue was touched upon already towards the end of Chapter 1, where we examined Franz Böhm's OG. Böhm, in fact, makes reference to Simmel's essay on historical time.

Let us imagine, following Simmel's suggestion, isolating a certain historical phenomenon and understanding thoroughly its immanent constituent factors. This phenomenon could be "ideally located at any position within a temporal sequence without producing any change in its character."[88] For instance, let us imagine understanding thoroughly the immanent reasons behind the transition from the republican age to the imperial age in ancient Rome. There is a sense in which, abstractly speaking, this "interpretive complex" (*Verstehenskomplex*)[89] is indifferent to the specific time-venue in which it occurred. We could imagine it moving an entire century backward or forward and still retaining all its immanent meaning-constituents. This would not alter our understanding. However, if we consider the totality of history, in which this phenomenon occurred, things change significantly:

Suppose, on the other hand, that the interpretive complex embraces the totality of all known contents. Then this relationship between temporal location and interpretation is no longer possible. From our perspective, what exists both before and after this totality is only empty time, a vacuum in which no change of position is possible. This is because, within such a temporal vacuum, no position can be differentiated from any other position, just as no body can have a "location" in the vacuum of absolute space. The spatial location of bodies is only reciprocally determined as a consequence of their spatial interrelationships. The totality of the corporeal world, therefore, is non-spatial, for there is nothing which exists outside of this totality that could serve as a point of reference to "define" its location. For the same reason, time is only a reciprocal relationship between the contents of history. History as a whole, on the contrary, is atemporal.[90]

Simmel is suggesting that the apparent isolability and movability of historical facts (or groups of facts) is only due to our necessary disregard for the broader totality of history in which they occurred. We can isolate and treat the transition from the republican to the imperial age in ancient Rome as an abstract historical fact *per se*. However, true understanding of its meaning would require the extension of our sphere of interest to what happened immediately before and immediately after this transition. In turn, true understanding of this now expanded time-period would require further extension to an earlier past and a later future, and so forth. If we followed this procedure indefinitely we would come to embrace the totality of human history up to the present moment

---

[88] PHT, 131.   [89] *Ibid.*   [90] *Ibid.*

and realize that every single event in it has an irreplaceable time-venue
that cannot be exchanged with any other event. Simmel continues:

It is only at this point that we can understand both the significance as well as
the paradoxical character of this heuristic construct. As the foregoing account
demonstrated, the reciprocal process of interpretation which forms this complex into a coherent whole is only preliminary and fragmentary. Such a
process of interpretation qualifies as complete only if the complex is extended
in both temporal directions – for our understanding of an event is complete
only if we can identify its *consequences* – until the limits of the complex
approximate the limits of our knowledge. Within this *total* sequence, the
location of each content is definitively and, in principle, unambiguously
determined.[91]

Husserl finds these analyses extremely helpful but he complains that
they are "too formal."[92] He means that Simmel does not explicitly
address the fact that, ultimately, the reason why history only admits
of absolutely determined and non-interchangeable temporal positions is
that history is the development of *spiritual* (*geistig*) realities as opposed
to mere natural things. In the lower part of the page from which the
above quotes are taken Husserl comments:

The historical is individual: by that we mean that this content can only occur
once. In this sense, the natural is in principle not individual. This depends on
the following fact: spirit [*Geist*] and spiritual facts [*geistige Tatsachen*] and
thus the whole spiritual world [*Geisteswelt*] (which has a unity as spiritual)
<can> develop (life); things on the contrary are dead and have no
development.[93]

In other words, we cannot move historical facts around the axis of
historical time because in the very conception of a totality of history,
"we are guided by the idea of a total development [*Entwicklung*] in the
Aristotelian sense. Within this total development individual developments have their function, which demands to be understood."[94] Husserl
is suggesting that it is only in a purposive (teleological) system that the
constituent parts have absolutely determined and non-interchangeable
positions. Therefore, Simmel's correct insight into the characteristic

---

[91] *Ibid.*, 131–132.
[92] E. Husserl, BQ 442; Georg Simmel, *Das Problem der historischen Zeit* (Berlin:
Verlag von Reuther u. Reichard, 1916), 12–13, from Husserl's private library
preserved at the Husserl Archives Leuven.
[93] E. Husserl, BQ 442, 9.   [94] *Ibid.*, 10.

rigidity of historical time should be supplemented by a consideration of the specific purposiveness of historically developing spiritual facts. If we consider this spiritual purposiveness, then the absolute temporal position of historical events and the characteristic 'uniqueness' of their contents reveal two sides of the same coin: historical events are stages in the development of a teleological system. The failure to recognize this teleological character of the historical whole leads Simmel to separate 'form' (historical time) and 'content' (complexions of events) of history and to prioritize form over content:

A historical status can be ascribed to events even though they may be repeated thousands of times with exactly the same qualitative properties. The thesis that the historicity of an event is defined by reference to the uniqueness of its content seems to be based on an illegitimate inference or extrapolation from the uniqueness of the cosmic process as a whole. This total process, of course, cannot be repeated. This is because every repetition – including the repetition of eternal recurrence – is already included in the cosmic process itself. Any such repetition would be identifiable as some aspect of the cosmic process. In principle, the occurrence of an unlimited number of events with exactly the same content is possible. Therefore, I fail to understand the import of the uniqueness of the individuality of these events if the expressions 'uniqueness' and 'individuality' are meant to refer to the content of the events in question. The concept of the uniqueness or individuality of an event makes sense only if it refers to the time-*frame* in which a given content is located. The concept of time entails that such a time-frame is non-repeatable.[95]

Husserl remarks on the side that this idea of indefinite repeatability for historical events is "definitely wrong,"[96] and he utterly debunks the Nietzschean thought of eternal recurrence evoked by Simmel in this passage: "I consider <eternal recurrence> nonsense. It contradicts everything historical."[97] This abstract consideration of the 'content' as strictly distinct from the form of historical events is "wrong specifically for spiritual facts,"[98] and it is precisely Simmel's disregard for the ontological specificity of the type of facts he is considering that prevents him from seeing the material impossibility in the thought of history as an endless repetition of identical yet univocally temporalized facts.

Let us leave aside, for the moment, the question concerning the kind of teleology Husserl has is mind. The idea that history is a purposive system, in any case, is common to a number of thinkers of his time,

---

[95] PHT, 134.   [96] E. Husserl, BQ 442, 14.   [97] *Ibid.*   [98] *Ibid.*

including Dilthey. It can be understood in the minimal sense that historical individuals act upon goals, so history as a whole is oriented towards a system of goals that may or may not coalesce into one single overarching goal for mankind. We shall consider this issue more specifically in Chapter 7.

For now, and to conclude this section, it is important to dwell on another feature of historical time: its plasticity. In the framework of a rigidly established sequence of temporal positions 'filled' with non-repeatable historical contents, we can detect a certain *rhythm* characterized by typical patterns. Historical events are absolutely non-repeatable with respect to their content, but a distinctive typicality characterizes historical time. Husserl introduces the notion, otherwise uncommon for him, of *Tempo* (rhythm) when commenting on a passage in which Simmel examines the concept of duration in history.[99] Historical duration (*Dauer*) differs significantly from the mere persistence in time (*Beharrung*) of natural things. If we imagine the paradoxical situation of an absolute historical stasis, say, ten years of government in which absolutely nothing happened that would allow us to distinguish those ten years from what happened before and after them, these ten years would count as a "historical atom"[100] and in a sense they would have no genuine 'duration' at all.

Hussel comments:

> Rhythm [*Tempo*]! In the sphere of life, and then also in the sphere of history, duration is a concept that measures through a quantitative determination [*Größenbestimmung*] the rhythm of what happens, and this is an essential component of the intuitive spheres of life.[101]

The idea that a definite rhythmic movement characterizes historical time illuminates a feature that Simmel only mentions in passing but that Husserl develops in a more detailed way in some of his manuscripts. There is an essential *periodicity* (*Periodizität*) to historical time, which, in turn, has its roots in essential features of historically living human persons.[102] Husserl identifies various types of periodicity. The most fundamental is the alternation of sleep and wakefulness, which originally correlates with the alternation of day and night. Furthermore, we can think of the periodical recurrence of certain instincts such as hunger.

---

[99] PHT, 137.   [100] *Ibid.*   [101] E. Husserl, BQ 442, 19.
[102] See Hua XXXIX, 591.

This gives rise to typical, recurring *qualia* of time, such as the distinctive feelings of preprandial and postprandial time. At a higher level, the day, the week, and the year consist of the rhythmic alternation of work and leisure,[103] and these two encompassing forms of life set the tone for various arrays of interests and goals. Moreover, the passing of time occurs in the form of 'ages' and 'aging,' both at the individual and the supra-individual level:

Historical time has "ages" [*Zeitalter*]. In a broad sense, this statement indicates a thoroughly oriented articulation, so that all differences of historical hour, historical year, historical decade, etc., would be "age"-forms [*Zeitalter-Formen*]. In a precisely analogous sense, personal time – the time of personal life – too, has the form, the apriori of its form of "change" [*Wechsel*], as type-pattern [*Typik*] describable in terms of ages. All periods [*Abschnitte*], also in the subjective measurement, are measures of ages [*Altersgrössen*]. How old [*alt*]? One year, five months, etc.; day, hour, etc. Measures of ages, measures of an oriented subjective time. What grows old in it is the subject of life. Life, on its part, is not called old or young, so that the age, too, would not be age with respect to life but with respect to the living subject.[104]

Besides displaying the overall feature of periodicity at various levels, the plasticity of historical time allows for contractions and expansions in the sphere of what we consider present in the specific sense of historical contemporaneousness. In Husserl's description:

An individual subject lives his intentional life in correlation with his intentional surrounding world. Experiencing, representing, thinking, suffering, and acting, a subject is constantly related to this conscious surrounding world. What does "present" mean for such a subject? The form of the tense *praesens*? Every occurrence in the surrounding world, which is still becoming; every enduring that is still enduring now is present happening and being, and this present stretches as far as the past (the past accessible to recollection) that, as past-horizon, is intentionally connected to the now. The present war and peace, the present emperor, the present crisis, my present trip, etc. The same goes for my life as present.[105]

---

[103] *Ibid.*, 308.   [104] Hua XIV, 217.

[105] *Ibid.*, 221. These descriptions allude to the notion of 'living present,' which is paramount in Husserl's later work on time, especially in the so-called C-manuscripts. It should be mentioned that the first occurrence of the phrase 'living present' to describe the temporal fabric characterizing living subjectivity can be found in Simmel's essay *Life as Transcendence*, the overture to his metaphysical work *Lebensanchauung* (1918). After describing the time of life as consisting of

These descriptions are, of course, quite rough, and they merely indicate directions for further phenomenological research. Husserl himself never developed them beyond the preliminaries. However, they suffice to establish a further a priori condition for the possibility of history as a *world*. Historical time is the form of succession and contemporaneousness of historical events. It is characterized by *rigidity* with respect to the temporal positions pertaining to each historical event and *plasticity* regarding the typical patterns according to which such rigidly determined events assume their place in specific nexuses of significance. Every conceivable historical event occurs in a definite context of periodicity (at night, during the day, in the past decade, etc.) and is thus caught up in the specific rhythm of personal life.

Natural causality and motivational causality

After considering empathetic being-there-for-one-another and historical time as two ontological a prioris of the historical world, we have to consider briefly the third a priori, i.e., motivation. Husserl describes motivation as "psychic causality" and "specifically personal causality."[106] This means that motivation in the sphere of history plays the same role played by inductive causality in the sphere of nature: it is the explanatory principle for all observable manifestations and changes. Prior to all natural-scientific experimenting and theorizing, in the observation of nature we are aware that the physical circumstances in which a given thing is immersed determine the way in which it appears to us – the circumstances *cause* (in the natural sense) the thing's observable behavior. A red apple in a poorly illuminated room will appear grey; an ice cube taken out of the freezer will start to melt. If we ask *why* such phenomena occur, we are asking for a plausible account of the circumstances surrounding the apple or the ice-cube and the way in which these two objects 'respond' to these circumstances, according to their intrinsic properties. A red apple 'responds' to the circumstance of poor illumination by appearing grey. An ice cube 'responds' to the circumstance of

'thick' phases comprising a quantum of past and future within every span of present, Simmel states: "The living present consists in the fact that it transcends the present" (VL, 7). Given the tenor of Simmel's description, it would not be unwarranted to speculate that this essay may have been a major source of inspiration for Husserl's later formulation of his notion of living present, which is largely coincident with Simmel's.

[106] Phen. P., 108.

higher temperature by starting to melt. In these cases, we are able to distinguish, albeit implicitly, between the intrinsic properties of a thing (redness, coldness), the momentary appearance of that thing (grayness, melting-ness), and the circumstances *causing* this momentary appearance. Repeated and refined observation can lead to very precise predictions of a thing's possible ways of appearing in varying circumstances. Such predictions can be eventually formulated in mathematical terms, increasing significantly their precision and comprehensiveness.

In a similar way, we are aware that spiritual facts (including both mental events in single individuals and cultural events in communities) always happen in a given context of significance. The circumstance of hunger gives rise to the desire to eat, which in turn triggers certain actions geared towards the acquisition of food. Seeking food is the way in which a psychic subject 'responds' to the circumstance of being hungry. In this case, too, we are implicitly distinguishing between a subject with its intrinsic properties (e.g., the ability to move around, identify certain things as edible, etc.), its momentary way of appearing (the actual activity of seeking food in the given moment considered), and the circumstances *causing* this way of appearing (hunger).

Here the meaning of *cause* is different from that of natural causality. If we ask *why* in this context, we want to hear about the *motivation* that drives a certain subject to act in a certain way.[107] As Simmel recognized,[108] in this context we can have very different outcomes and accept as valid opposite sets of motivations under similar circumstances. However, this does not mean that motivational causality is a 'softer' kind of lawfulness compared to natural causality. In the sphere of history it is possible to contemplate concatenations of motivations having a strict *necessity* to them. However, this motivational necessity does not amount to natural *inevitability*, but rather to compelling force or psychic *irresistibility*. To stay with our previous example, we can explain the behavior of someone stealing food by reference to the *irresistible* urge to eat and a circumstance of indigence. This course of action can be contemplated in its typicality; it is characterized by a

---

[107] The same goes for cultural artifacts. To understand a cultural artifact means to understand the circumstances in which it was produced and the motivations behind its production.

[108] See Chapter 2.

certain intuitable necessity. However, other constellations of motivational irresistibility could obtain in similar circumstances. We can explain the behavior of someone who chooses to starve to death rather than stealing food, for instance, by reference to the irresistible force of moral ideals. The 'irresistibility' of morality, in this case, supersedes the irresistibility of hunger. This is also a course of action that can be contemplated in its ideal typicality, which is more or less perfectly reflected in concretely occurring courses of action.

Dilthey and Simmel first introduced a robust notion of motivation as the key concept in understanding the historical world. Dilthey, in particular, contrasted natural causality and psychic motivation and, as we saw, insisted on the illegitimacy of natural-scientific methods in the sphere of psyche and history. Husserl's own contribution to their achievement is twofold. First, he extends the notion of motivation to the entirety of psychic life. Second, thanks to his different understanding of empathy, he acknowledges a distinctive kind of intersubjective motivation reaching beyond the inner subjective life of an isolated individual.

In keeping with his above-mentioned critique of naturalistic psychology and its reduction of the passive sphere of subjectivity to mere nature, Husserl considers thoroughly motivational all those associative and instinctive phenomena that occur without the active participation of the ego. Deliberate actions based on the active recognition of reasons or on the conscious pursuit of a goal are not the only things that qualify as motivational. In Husserl's words:

Everywhere in the spiritual [*geistig*] sphere two kinds of motivations interweave: the rational and the irrational, i.e., the motivation of higher, active subjectivity [*Geistigkeit*] and the motivation of lower, passive or affective subjectivity [*Geistigkeit*].[109]

We can view rational motivation in two ways: (1) as the law objectively linking together conscious acts and (2) as the 'force' compelling the *ego* to act and judge in a rationally justifiable way. Husserl explains this twofold meaning of rational motivation in the following terms:

Motivation can exist here in the most authentic sense whereby it is *the Ego that is motivated*: I confer my thesis onto the conclusion because I judged such

---

[109] Hua XXXVII, 108.

and such in the premises, because I have given my thesis to the premises [. . .] In each case here I am accomplishing a cogito and am determined in doing so by the fact that I have accomplished another cogito. Obviously, the thesis of the conclusion is related thereby to the thesis of the premises. These are Ego-theses, yet on the other hand they are not themselves the Ego, and so we also have as motivation a particular relationship among the theses. But the theses as theses have their "material," and that produces lines of dependencies as well: the full assertions and, correlatively, the full lived-experiences have a "connection of motivation."[110]

In all such cases the Ego can take responsibility for its acts and, if necessary, justify its positions. Even mistaken judgment or incorrect reasoning belongs in the sphere of rational motivation. I could explain the mistaken reasons that led me to judge in a certain way and eventually come to recognize the correct reasons I previously overlooked.

In contrast to this level of rational motivation, which plays itself out entirely in the sphere of position-takings (*Stellungnahmen*), stands irrational, or, better, "a-rational"[111] motivation. This kind of motivation is rooted in sensibility and in the constant interaction between present and past experiential life. This second dimension is the most familiar:

A thought "reminds" me of other thoughts and calls back into memory a past lived experience, etc. In some cases it can be perceived. In most cases, however, the motivation is indeed actually present in consciousness, but it does not stand out; it is unnoticed or unnoticeable ("unconscious").[112]

I can suddenly remember that I am late for my dental appointment after running into an acquaintance on the street. At first, I see no connection between these two events, but upon further inspection I realize that the last time I saw this person was in my dentist's waiting room. Seeing that acquaintance *motivated* remembering my dental appointment. In this case, I am not taking any rationally justifiable position, and I cannot be held responsible for the welling up of this recollection in connection with the foregoing perceptual act. The thought of my dental appointment 'popped up' into my mind without my active participation. However, the two events are linked in a way that we can clarify and has little to do with inductive, natural causality.

Experiences like this one reveal in a particularly evident fashion a motivational connectedness that encompasses the entirety of our

---

[110] Ideas II, 232.   [111] *Ibid.*, 234.   [112] *Ibid.*

experiential life, including the sphere of simple perceptions. To a phenomenological analysis, the simple perceptual experience of my acquaintance walking on the street possesses already in itself a motivational structure. While I followed my acquaintance walking on the street, I 'unconsciously' carried out an ongoing synthesis of all the perceptual phases in which his walking body appeared to me. Every new profile of my acquaintance's body was integrated into an overall perception and apprehended as manifesting one and the same 'thing,' thereby motivating my expectation of being presented with ever-new profiles as long as my acquaintance abided in my perceptual field. Husserl describes this state of affairs:

Apprehensions of things and of thingly nexuses are "webs of motivation": they are built through and through from intentional rays, which [...] refer back and forth, and they let themselves be explicated in that the accomplishing subject can enter into these nexuses. I have the unitary intentionality in which a thing is given to me in one stroke. Then from every way of running through it, there results a series of continuous acts unfolding in the first-posited sense and in a harmonious sense conforming to every further givenness. That is to say, everything here is "motivated," including every new positing and every phase of the unitary total positing as well as every new partial positing.[113]

In this case, too, we are not motivated in the sense of being rationally compelled to think or act in a justifiable way. The 'webs of motivation' characterizing the unfolding of single perceptual experiences as well as the totality of our subjective life run their course without the active engagement of our *egos*. However, it is crucial to notice that whatever our *ego* actively engages with must have been previously 'arranged' (technically: constituted) in the sphere of passive, irrational motivation. If I am able to link the perceptual experience of my acquaintance with my impending dental appointment, and if I am able to make the rational judgment that I should better change my plans and run to the dentist, this is because, prior to my active engagement, unnoticed 'webs of motivation' constituted meaningful nexuses that I am now in a position to consider and act upon. This means that irrational motivation does not stand over and against rational motivation but rather prepares the terrain for it. Husserl summarizes this point with a quite effective

[113] *Ibid.*, 236.

metaphor: *"Passive motivation is the native soil of reason [der Mutterboden der Vernunft]."*[114]

Given this distinction between passive and active motivation, we have now to address a last decisive feature of motivation: motivation is, so to speak, contagious. Through the channels of empathy, not only can I understand alien motivations, but they can be appropriated and become my own. Motivation is the way in which monads bring about effects (*wirken*) in one another and through one another. In this context, too, we can distinguish between motivations that occur passively in our intersubjective life, such as the involuntary attraction or repulsion we might feel towards another subject, and active, deliberate attempts to motivate others by communicating our will to them. This second type of intersubjective motivation characterizes social acts and can be realized in various ways, such as by asking favors or by imparting orders.

Through active communication, both linguistic and non-linguistic, one subject can realize, or bring about, another's will. In Husserl's characterization, it is the master's will that realizes itself in the slave's action, it is the general's intentions that find their fulfillment in the soldiers' battling and so forth. This, of course, does not mean real 'possession' of someone's mind but communication of one's will, the corresponding adoption of the other's motives and subsequent action.

The above considerations establish the third a priori of the historical world besides empathetic being-there-for-one-another and historical time: motivation as the specifically historical-personal type of causality. A correct interpretation of motivation based on its extension to the totality of subjective life (thanks to the phenomenological reduction) and to the sphere of intersubjective interaction (thanks to the theory of empathy) thus completes Husserl's phenomenological-ontological analysis of the historical world and sheds further light on his indebtedness to and critique of the tradition of *Lebensphilosophie*.

Conclusion: the philosophical meaning of the *Geisteswissenschaften*

To conclude this chapter and to introduce the themes of the final two chapters of this book, let us consider what Husserl takes to be the philosophical meaning of the nineteenth-century turn towards the

---

[114] Hua XXXVII, 331.

Geisteswissenschaften. For Husserl, this new group of sciences is not simply another area of human knowledge besides natural science. There is a systematic, philosophically relevant meaning to the 'discovery' of the world of *Geist* after the long centuries of Renaissance and French Enlightenment naturalism.[115] Thus, as we briefly suggested in Chapter 5, a philosophically informed consideration of the human sciences must recognize that the 'subjectivity' that they set out to understand and investigate scientifically encompasses both the natural sciences and nature itself as their subject matter. The natural sciences are themselves cultural achievements, and 'nature' in the specific sense of a theme for quantitatively oriented research only became accessible through intellectual operations that occurred at a certain point in history, notably, in the work of Renaissance men such as Galileo and Descartes. Serious consideration of this fact thus leads the philosophically reflecting theorist of science to two options. The first option is a thoroughgoing historical relativism that would dissolve the very notions of science and reality into merely contingent cultural products. This is the position Husserl (and Rickert) attributed to Dilthey. The other option would be to engage in deeper analyses of the subjectivity investigated by the human sciences and to face the paradox of subjectivity being both a fact in the world *and* the field of manifestation in which every fact in the world (including the fact of subjectivity) receives its meaning. This line of consideration would inevitably lead to the discovery of transcendental, as distinct from empirical, subjectivity and thus to a rationale for the performance of the phenomenological reduction.

In other words, for Husserl there is a systematic path leading from the natural sciences to the human sciences (including pure psychology) to transcendental phenomenology. In an important sense, the human sciences stand 'closer' to phenomenology than the natural sciences: while the transition from the natural sciences to the human sciences implies a complete switch of theme, the transition from the human sciences to transcendental phenomenology occurs by means of a switch of attitude within the same thematic sphere: subjectivity. This switch of attitude, as we described above, determines a redefinition of the theme (from human to transcendental subjectivity) and an expansion of the field of

---

[115] Incidentally, Husserl considers this discovery to be the specific contribution of German idealism to Western culture. See Mat IV, 140.

inquiry (from the psychic 'segment' of the existing world to the endless egological universe in which the existing world as such is constituted).

Husserl offers a synthetic sketch of the systematic progression he has in mind in a footnote to a manuscript stemming from the same period as the *Erste Philosophie* lecture:

The consistent progression from natural science to human science leads to the intentional encompassing of nature in spirit [*Geist*] to the encompassing of spirit through spirit itself. Natural science and nature itself, worldly science and the scientifically cognized world itself as such, turn into a formation [*Gebilde*] within universal spirit. This motivates the thought of an absolute science of spirit [*Geisteswissenschaft*] as the way into an absolute, universal science.[116]

In other words, transcendental phenomenology as the universal science encompassing both physical nature and human, historical subjectivity overcomes the apparent opposition between the image of the world delivered by the human sciences and the natural sciences. Phenomenology has the resources to elucidate their status as constituted formations brought about by the intentional workings of transcendental subjectivity. Another passage from a manuscript summarizes Husserl's understanding of phenomenology in the framework of the *Natur-Geist* opposition as well as the philosophical contribution this discipline is supposed to make towards overcoming such opposition:

Phenomenology is the science of transcendentally pure, universal spirit and, moving to a consideration of the world, it is the universal spiritual science that recognizes in everything worldly formations [*Gebilde*] of universal subjectivity [*universale Geistigkeit*]. Phenomenology overcomes [*aufheben*] the separation of natural and human sciences to the extent that, as universal science, it turns all sciences in general into branches of the one spiritual science: the science of transcendental universal spirit.[117]

Based on these considerations, we are now in a position to assess the meaning of Husserl's late analyses of the life-world and the specifically philosophical project Husserl envisioned for his phenomenology within the intellectual debates of his time. This will be the theme of Chapter 7.

---

[116] Hua VIII, 276 n.   [117] *Ibid.*, 361.

7 | The life-world as the source of nature and culture: towards a transcendental-phenomenological worldview

Die Welt, die wir erleben ist unsere Tat.

Wilhelm Windelband[1]

Die Frage, was bin ich, was ist der Mensch, die Menschheit, beantwortet die Transzendentalphilosophie durch ihre tiefste Auslegung der Subjektivität als sich selbst und Welt konstituierender.

Edmund Husserl[2]

In this chapter, I will attempt to position Husserl's late work on the life-world within the debate between the Neo-Kantians and the life-philosophers that I have endeavored to reconstruct thus far. I will suggest that we look at Husserl's transcendental-phenomenological ontology of the life-world through the prism of what I will call the *Kantian liberation narrative*. In this light, it should become clear that Husserl increasingly joined forces with the best philosophical minds of his time in order to combat naturalism and articulate a humanistic worldview: one characterized, in Simmel's words, by a "spiritualization and fluidification [*Vergeistigung und Verflüssigung*] of our picture of the world."[3] This, however, should not be taken to mean that Husserl's transcendental phenomenology is ultimately *all about* articulating a humanistic worldview. Transcendental phenomenology remains for Husserl a discipline in its own right, one that has a foundational function for all philosophical problems and all empirical sciences. The

---

[1] "The world that we experience is our deed." W. Windelband, "Kulturphilosophie und transzendentaler Idealismus," in W. Windelband, *Präludien: Aufsätze und Reden zur Philosophie und ihrer Geschichte*, vol. 2, 279–294. Here 283.
[2] "Transcendental philosophy answers the questions 'who am I?' 'what is man, what is mankind?' through its deepest interpretation of subjectivity as constituting itself and the world." Hua XV, 153.
[3] WuK, 156.

articulation of a humanistic worldview should be understood as the way in which transcendental phenomenology plays itself out in the philosophical debate of Husserl's time and as a consequence of its commitment to a non-naturalistic view of subjectivity. With the aid of a notion stemming from the Aristotelian tradition, we could argue that phenomenology's commitment to a humanistic worldview is not *essential* to it but counts among its *per se* accidents, that is, those accidents that *flow from* a thing's essence but are not themselves part of that thing's essential content. To the extent that phenomenology sets out to articulate essential features of consciousness in general, it is in a sense indifferent to specifically human concerns regarding the factual existence of conscious beings in a cultural world. However, to the extent that phenomenology is committed to a non-naturalistic view of subjectivity, that is to say, to the extent that phenomenology unearths the transcendental dimension inherent in any conceivable consciousness, when phenomenology plays itself out in the culturally formed world of humans, it assumes the shape of a humanistically oriented philosophy. Admittedly, there is a certain degree of contingency to this connotation of transcendental phenomenology. However, this is the inevitable degree of contingency that every theoretical enterprise primarily concerned with pure possibilities must take in when it sets out to articulate its standpoint in the sphere of factually existing culture.[4] I will expand on this important issue in Chapter 8. First, a detailed discussion of Husserl's notion of life-world in the context of his late phenomenology and of the Kantian liberation narrative is necessary.

The Kantian liberation narrative

In the predominantly Neo-Kantian atmosphere of early twentieth-century Germany, the philosophical giant from Königsberg was interpreted primarily as an epistemologist; however, the most ambitious thinkers were well aware that Kant's lifework had much deeper implications that reached far beyond the establishment of norms for empirical knowledge. In particular, as we mentioned in Chapter 2, Kant was considered a mandatory point of reference towards the establishment of a *worldview* or *Weltanschauung* – a comprehensive stance on the world as a whole beyond the restricted perspectives of the specialized sciences.

---

[4] For a discussion of Husserl's notion of *eidos* see Chapter 4.

In this sense, Kant was celebrated as the thinker who liberated Western thought from the mental shackles of naturalism and cleared the way for a novel understanding of our position in the world. This is the substance of what I will refer to as the 'Kantian liberation narrative.' In this narrative, Kant set the basis for a philosophical overcoming of naturalism qua worldview and opened up a new perspective for a philosophical consideration of the historical world. Needless to say, the Kantian liberation narrative is truly a Neo-Kantian narrative, that is, it is an idiosyncratic interpretation of Kant from the point of view of the nineteenth-century problem of naturalism. Kant's own main preoccupation is clearly not the rejection of naturalism (a category that he did not possess) but rather the rejection of metaphysics as a science. The Neo-Kantians, however, articulate their own narrative about the importance of Kant by drawing on resources that are indeed present in Kant's work. Therefore, the Kantian liberation narrative is not so much a misreading as it is a *highly selective* reading of Kant, developing some elements in transcendental philosophy that deliberately depart from its letter but self-avowedly further its spirit.

In his 1924 book *Die Probleme der Geschichtsphilosophie. Eine Einführung* Rickert offers an illuminating presentation of the Kantian liberation narrative, stating:

> Kant famously compared his theory of knowledge with Copernicus' deed [*Tat*], and we can follow his comparison in yet one further direction. Precisely because of the "Copernican standpoint," transcendental idealism means a reversal [*Umkehr*] in the direction that philosophy saw itself necessitated to follow on the basis of the new picture of the world delivered by astronomy. However – and this is decisive – such reversal leaves wholly intact the natural-scientific picture of the world and nonetheless enables philosophy to revive the problems of a philosophy of history. Thus, the dependency of the philosophy of history from cosmology is overcome.[5]

The heliocentric revolution in Renaissance astronomy crushed the medieval belief that man stood at the center of the universe. The spatial displacement of the earth as the seat of mankind was almost immediately interpreted as a dethronement of man. The door was open to the appointment of nature as the true 'center' of all things and to a demeaning self-understanding of man as just one among many manifestations

---

[5] Rickert, *Die Probleme der Geschichtsphilosophie*, 138.

of nature. In this situation, Kant's philosophy almost worked like a counterrevolution. Rickert continues:

Through Kant the subject is repositioned back in the "center" [*Mittelpunkt*] of the world under full recognition of modern teachings about nature. Obviously, this is no longer a spatial center. However, the way in which this repositioning happens is much more significant for the problems of the philosophy of history. Now, once again, everything "revolves around" the subject. "Nature" is not the absolute reality. Rather, according to its general essence, nature is determined by "subjective" forms of apprehension. Precisely the "infinite" universe is nothing but an idea of the subject, the thought of a *task* [*Aufgabe*] that is necessarily assigned to the subject while being insolvable. Through this Kantian "subjectivism" – which has nothing to do with psychologism and anthropologism, and therefore can only be understood as subjectivism with a grain of salt – the foundations of the empirical natural sciences are in no way altered. On the contrary, they are even reinforced. However, the foundations of naturalism as worldview, which denies every "objective" sense to historical life and therefore renders a philosophy of history impossible, are completely undermined.[6]

The profusion of inverted commas in Rickert's text indicates that through the Kantian revolution terms such as "nature," "center," "subject" undergo a significant redefinition. The picture of the world in the pre-modern age featured *man* as standing in the *spatial center* of an *ontologically self-subsistent universe* created by God. The Kantian picture of the world features *subjectivity* understood exclusively qua rationality standing in the *transcendental center* of *nature* qua product of the shaping activity of the categories applied on sensory data. In a sense, this novel picture of the world dispels the potential sense of self-entitlement flowing from the foregoing view, according to which man's dignity over the rest of creation is automatically granted by his God-given position in the physical universe. After Kant, rationality is deemed the only authentic source of a subject's dignity, and it is through the exertion of rationality that subjects get to actively occupy their legitimate place at the center of that universe which is now understood as their own achievement. Once the productive meaning of rationality is recognized and the apparent absoluteness of nature is overcome, the stage is set to acknowledge other spheres in which subjects may exert

---

[6] *Ibid.*, 138–139.

their innermost shaping powers or fail to do so: in particular, the sphere of human history. In Rickert's words:

Now, not only man stands, as a subject with his theoretical reason, at the center of that "nature" which he understands scientifically. He also understands himself immediately with his practical reason as the agent who can bestow upon cultural life a positive meaning. [He understands himself], namely, as autonomous, "free" personality aware of his duty, and practical reason has primacy. With respect to this primacy, what meaning can the fact that the stage of history is a spatially and temporally fleeting speck in a random point of the natural whole still claim for itself? Nature is no longer "the world," but rather an apprehension of sensory being carried out by the scientific man. In both the theoretical and the practical sphere, for the autonomous, law-giving subject, the spatial and temporal conditions of nature have become indifferent with respect to matters of value. The autonomous man leaves to science, which has destroyed the old and dogmatic picture of the world, all conceivable freedom regarding the investigation of nature, including psychic life. However, the autonomous man will never concede that the science dealing with the sensory-real being of things would have to decide anything about value or disvalue, about meaning or meaninglessness of the world in its entirety.[7]

Interestingly, a version of the Kantian liberation narrative can be found in philosophers as distant from Rickert as Simmel and Dilthey. In the preface to the second edition of his *Die Probleme der Geschichtsphilosophie* (1905), Simmel states programmatically that "it is necessary to emancipate the self from historicism in the same way that Kant freed it from naturalism."[8] His description of Kant's achievement regarding the liberation from naturalism is remarkably similar to the one Rickert offers some fifteen years later. Simmel states:

Consider Kant's question: how is nature possible? As a contribution to our *Weltanschauung*, the value of Kant's answer to this question lies in the freedom which the self or ego achieves in its relationship to everything that falls within the domain of mere nature. The self produces nature as its own idea. The general, constitutive laws of nature are simply the forms of our mind. Nature is thereby subjected to the sovereign self.[9]

However, Simmel continues, Kant did not complete his empowering project of liberation. The discovery of history in the nineteenth century

---

[7] *Ibid.*   [8] PPH, VIII–IX.   [9] PPH, VIII.

poses a new threat to the sovereignty of the mind and seems to degrade the self to what Gadamer would eventually characterize as "a flickering in the closed circuits of historical life."[10] Simmel describes the problem in the following terms:

Consider the two forces which threaten modern man: nature and history. In Kant's work, the first of these forces is destroyed. Both seem to suffocate the free, autonomous personality. Nature has this property because mechanism subjects the psyche – like the falling stone and the budding plant – to blind necessity. History has this property because it reduces the psyche to a mere point where the social threads woven throughout history interlace. The entire productivity of the psyche is analyzed as a product of evolution. In the work of Kant, the autonomous mind escapes the imprisonment of our empirical existence by nature [...] The mind frees itself from enslavement by nature. But this enslavement is now transformed into another: the mind enslaves itself [...] [H]istory as a brute fact, a reality, and a superpersonal force threatens the integrity of the self quite as much as nature.[11]

It is particularly remarkable to find traces of the Kantian liberation narrative even in the work of Dilthey, who is generally charged with historicism and cultural relativism. At the very end of his essay *The Essence of Philosophy* (1907), which provoked the ire of Rickert and Husserl alike for its apparent debasement of philosophy to historically contingent wisdom, Dilthey reveals his true philosophical intentions and in so doing he disproves, to a certain degree, the uncharitable interpretations of his theory of *Weltanschauung*:

The last word of the mind which has surveyed all these *Weltanschauungen* is not the relativity of each but the sovereignty of the mind over against every single one of them, and also the positive consciousness of how in the various attitudes of the mind the one reality of the world exists for us.[12]

Dilthey sees a potential threat to the 'sovereignty' of the self in philosophy's illusion to be able to restitute the fullness and complexity of historical life in a system of concepts claiming to understand and thus 'exhaust' the actually inexhaustible meaning of this life. His project of a comparative study of historical worldviews seeking regularities and

[10] H.-G. Gadamer, *Truth and Method* (New York: Crossroad, 1989), 276.
[11] PPH, VIII.
[12] W. Dilthey, *Das Wesen der Philosophie*, GS V, 339–416. English translation by S. A. Emery and W. T. Emery, *The Essence of Philosophy* (Chapel Hill: North Carolina University Press, 1969), 66.

recurring patterns is undertaken in order to affirm the superiority of the living subject over all cultural formations.

The problem of worldview

While both Neo-Kantian thinkers such as Rickert and life-philosophers such as Simmel and Dilthey subscribe to some version of the Kantian liberation narrative, they disagree on the meaning of 'worldview' and on the significance of this term for philosophical inquiry. Adequate understanding of the dispute surrounding the notion of *Weltanschauung* is therefore necessary in order to understand Husserl's critical appropriation of this term and his distinctive take on the Kantian liberation narrative.

The term *Weltanschauung* can be traced back to Kant's *Critique of Judgment* (1790),[13] but it only gained prominence in the German philosophical debate during the second half of the nineteenth century. It was probably Dilthey who began to employ it consistently in order to designate philosophy's distinctive function in the broader system of human culture. In short, unlike specialized research, which only provides knowledge about parts of reality, philosophy's vocation is to provide knowledge about the world as a whole prior to its partition into separate fields of inquiry.

The necessity of a comprehensive worldview over and above the fragmented pieces of knowledge accumulated by empirical research was heartfelt both inside and outside late nineteenth-century academia. In a time of rapid evolutions and sudden revolutions in virtually all fields of science, the younger generations of educated Europeans longed for existential grounding in a more stable kind of knowledge. They expected philosophy to accomplish what specialized research had to set aside programmatically for the sake of actual progress. Philosophy had to offer knowledge about the meaning of human life and the world.

Dilthey expressed this understanding of philosophy in various writings throughout his career. As he states in some early notes on the notion of worldview:

---

[13] For an informative discussion of the historical roots of this term see D. Naugle, *Worldview: The History of a Concept* (Grand Rapids, MI and Cambridge: Eerdmans, 2002) and B. Kreiter, "Philosophy as *Weltanschauung* in Trendelenburg, Dilthey, and Windelband," unpub. Ph.D. thesis, Vrije Universiteit Amsterdam.

I want to prove that philosophical systems, too, as much as religions and artworks, entail a view of life and the world, which is not grounded in conceptual thought, but rather in the vitality of the people who create these systems.[14]

On this account, a *worldview* has to be understood as the *terminus a quo* of all philosophical thinking. Unlike the specialized sciences, philosophies are not just impersonal connections of concepts. They are cultural productions in which the unique *life* of an individual seeks to express itself conceptually, and in so doing articulates its stance towards the world as a whole. Given the fundamental connectedness of individuals to the overarching whole of historical life, a great philosopher is an individual in whom resonates the feeling of life (*Lebensgefühl*) of an entire historical epoch and who is able to bring this feeling to conceptual expression. This, in turn, enables other individuals to better understand themselves.

As we anticipated above, for Dilthey, worldviews display a recurring set of features that can be spelled out:

To the extent that they attempt to provide a complete solution to the riddle of life, all worldviews entail regularly the same structure. This structure is in each case a nexus in which the questions concerning meaning and significance of the world are decided on the basis of a picture of the world [*Weltbild*]. Ideal, highest good and supreme principles for the regulation of life are derived from this decision.[15]

Dilthey believes that the available worldviews fundamentally amount to three recurring types: naturalism, idealism of freedom, and objective idealism.[16] What matters to our characterization of Dilthey's position in this chapter, however, is that the sources of such worldviews are not considered to be conceptual. This is because concepts necessarily analyze reality and in so doing fail to grasp the whole. The human position before life and the world in their totality precedes and grounds all subsequent philosophical and cultural achievements. Only a human being as a whole is receptive to the world as a whole and feels the pressing need to fathom its meaning. The theoretically oriented human being engaging in philosophical inquiry can only achieve partial glimpses of the world, and in order to do so he has to leave out of consideration all those components of the world that do not correlate with the

---

[14] GS VIII, 30.   [15] *Ibid.*, 82.   [16] See *ibid.*, 100–120.

intellect. True philosophy, on the contrary, should shake off its exclusively theoretical perspective, recognize its origin in the same mysterious awareness of the world as a whole that gives rise to religion and art, and strive to delve deeper and deeper into the riddle of life. In so doing, philosophy would dispense with the illusion of being able to solve the riddle of life through a definitive connection of concepts.

A similar version of worldview as the *terminus a quo* of all philosophical thinking is present in Simmel's work. His emphasis on the metaphysical meaning of individuality as the ontological fabric of psychic being[17] provides an extremely pertinent framework for his understanding of philosophy as the product of a *Weltanschauung*. In a short essay, *On the History of Philosophy*, he suggests that each philosophy should be regarded as a worldview, as "an expression of the existential relationship between a mind and the cosmos as a whole."[18] In his previous work *Hauptprobleme der Philosophie* (1910) he explains:

Precisely what people call *Weltanschauung* depends mostly on the different being of personalities. Precisely the picture of the whole – which appears to entail the maximum and most pure degree of objectivity – reflects the specificity of its carrier [*Träger*] much more than the objective picture of some detail generally does.[19]

In this light, unlike the history of specialized disciplines, the history of philosophy is not a history of progressive discoveries that become part of an impersonal corpus of objective truths while previous theories are discarded as outdated. "The history of philosophy gradually realizes the timeless domain of possible philosophical positions,"[20] and such positions correspond to different types of human personality seeking to express their characteristic response to the mystery of the world as a whole.

Unsurprisingly, Windelband and Rickert were extremely critical of this understanding of *Weltanschauung*. If philosophies emanate from an unfathomable existential relationship between individuals and the world as a whole, then they turn out to be ultimately contingent

---

[17] See Chapter 2.

[18] G. Simmel, "On the History of Philosophy," in Simmel, *Essays on Interpretation in Social Science*, 198–204. Here, 199.

[19] G. Simmel, *Hauptprobleme der Philosophie*, in Georg Simmel, *Gesamtausgabe*, vol. 14 (Frankfurt am Main: Suhrkamp, 1996), 7–157. Here 26.

[20] Simmel, "On the History of Philosophy," 199.

constructions whose truth-claims cannot be objectively adjudicated. They can only be assessed in terms of their success or failure in expressing a certain personality or human type. In this sense, philosophies would not be much different from works of art.[21] This, however, seems to contradict the scientific spirit of most great philosophers and to completely disregard the fact that, generally speaking, serious philosophical theories lay claim to truths that any human type can ideally assess and appropriate.

Rickert, in particular, agrees emphatically with most philosophers of his time that philosophy should be concerned with the world as a whole. As he states in his programmatic essay *Vom Begriff der Philosophie*: "It shouldn't be disputed that philosophy has to investigate the whole and finally achieve what we call a *Weltanschauung*, which is not a very apt term but it can hardly be given up."[22] However, a worldview for Rickert is not so much the *terminus a quo*, but rather the *terminus ad quem* of philosophical thinking. Philosophy should *yield* a worldview after completing as satisfactorily as possible a systematic survey of the fundamental constituents of reality and their mutual relationships. Rickert does not deny that we generally turn to philosophy motivated by questions about the meaning of life and the world. However, he believes that philosophers should make an effort to provide plausible answers to these questions in a scientific spirit by committing themselves primarily to rational scrutiny rather than existential pathos. A *Weltanschauung* should thus be a task for the philosopher who has first learned to contemplate the world as a whole and to relate it back to its constituent parts. In particular, adequate comprehension of the world as a whole must include an inquiry into the problem of value, which is the most relevant for the formation of a worldview. Only if we learn to look at reality as relating to objectively valid values and appreciate the meaning of subjectivity as the medium in which reality receives its relation to value can we hope to overcome the strictures of naturalism and subjectivism and find our legitimate place in the world.[23]

---

[21] The suggestion to consider philosophical systems almost like works of art is Simmel's.

[22] H. Rickert, "Vom Begriff der Philosophie," *Philosophische Aufsätze*, 3–36. Here 3.

[23] On these issues see Rickert's seminal paper "Vom System der Werte," *ibid.*, 73–105.

While Rickert continues to use the term *Weltanschauung* to designate philosophy's ultimate goal in his writings until roughly 1920, his later work marks a terminological shift. Especially in his essay *Wissenschaftliche Philosophie und Weltanschauung* (1933)[24] and in his last book *Grundprobleme der Philosophie* (1934)[25] Rickert renounces the language of worldview and prefers to talk about philosophy as "scientific knowledge of the world as a whole."[26] With this terminological shift, Rickert seems to implicitly acknowledge that *Weltanschauung* is now a trite buzzword irreversibly associated with the anti-rationalistic tendencies of the life-philosophers and is thus lost for scientific philosophy. Rickert contends that what he now calls pejoratively "*Weltanschauung*-philosophy" is unfit to investigate the world as a whole. As a matter of fact, in Rickert's eyes, the unduly scorned 'theoretically oriented man' proves to be the only type of subject fit for philosophy. If we philosophize 'as whole human beings,' as Dilthey would have it, and not as 'purely theoretically oriented human beings,' our stance will be co-determined by the particularity of our emotions and desires, and we will not be able to elevate ourselves to a contemplation of the world as a whole. Rickert contends:

Only when man detaches himself from all a-theoretical interests of life and existence and tries to think exclusively in theoretical or scientific terms does he reach the freedom and autonomy required to take into view all that there is in the world, i.e., the world as a whole. Beforehand there is no occasion for man to raise questions that go beyond the 'small' world that he has built for himself and to which alone his pre-scientific *Weltanschauung* refers.[27]

For Dilthey, by contrast, only if the totality of our human energies is at play does the world as a whole disclose itself to us. Rickert views the practical and emotional sides of our life as restrictive rather than disclosive. The will and the heart bind us to particulars of the world that are significant for us. The intellect alone, precisely *because* of its one-sidedness, allows us to leave these particulars behind as particulars and view them as part of a bigger world that transcends our plans and expectations. On Rickert's account, Dilthey conflates the necessity of

[24] H. Rickert, "Wissenschaftliche Philosophie und Weltanschauung," *ibid.*, 325–346. Hereafter WPW.
[25] H. Rickert, *Grundprobleme der Philosophie. Methodologie, Ontologie, Anthropologie* (Tübingen: Mohr Siebeck, 1934).
[26] WPW, 333.   [27] WPW, 338.

a reflection on the totality of the human being with a reflection of the totality of the human being, that is, a reflection carried out *by* man as a whole. Of course, a philosophy that aims at comprehensiveness as opposed to specialized empirical research must by definition consider everything in its systematic account of the world, including the emotional and practical dimensions of existence. However, this does not necessarily mean that when we do philosophy we should let our prejudices, personal emotions, and practical goals co-determine and even provide justification for our philosophical claims. This is a conflation that undermines not simply one way of doing philosophy as opposed to another but philosophy as a discipline overall. Rickert is willing to recognize some value to inspirational teachings based on existentially grounded intuitions of the whole, but he maintains that philosophy conducted in a scientific spirit is superior to such teachings and should be kept strictly separate from them.

Husserl and *Weltanschauung*

Rickert's emphatic statement of the necessity to distinguish *Weltanschauung* philosophy and scientific philosophy reiterates almost literally the proposal Husserl put forward over twenty years earlier in *Philosophy as a Rigorous Science*. Here Husserl writes: "*Weltanschauung* philosophy and scientific philosophy are sharply distinguished as two ideas, related in a certain manner to each other but not to be confused."[28] At that time, Rickert still cherished the term worldview and believed that it could be used in a scientifically and theoretically oriented sense to designate the ultimate goal of philosophical thinking. Husserl, on the contrary, had already expressed his reservations about the dominant trend of *Weltanschauung* philosophy from the lectern two years before penning his contribution to the first issue of Rickert's journal *Logos*. In an introductory course on the phenomenology of knowledge in 1909 he began his lectures with the following statements:

Why do people turn to philosophy? First and foremost not, as is the case in all other disciplines, in order to be 'productive' and to finally become a professor. The urgency of life and the riddle of existence, which cause so much suffering

[28] PRS, 191.

to the *dóskolos*, lead to philosophy, and life demands an answer. For the intellectually educated person, however, this answer must have something like a scientific form, which is called 'system.' The Greeks felt the need for salvation and thus craved salvation-granting metaphysics, or, better, religion; they wanted religion. However, the person educated in the spirit of Greek science could only accept such religion in the shapes of philosophy, also called 'dogmatics.' Most philosophies are of precisely this kind. Each of them is actually the 'dogmatics' of a faith, of a thoroughly personal faith, of the philosopher's so-called worldview. All this should be recognized in its beauty and right, in its life-inspiring and life-ennobling power. But couldn't we and shouldn't we recognize validity to philosophy as science, too? Couldn't we legitimately hope great things from its development and growth? If not for the fulfillment of our personal life, for our personal salvation, for us living here and now in our time, so at least for mankind in the future? People call for philosophy as deed, as life-power [*Lebensmacht*]. Couldn't philosophy as science open up for future mankind higher and nobler life-possibilities, which may reward our sacrifices, efforts and renouncements in the present?[29]

Husserl's tone is remarkable, considering his otherwise rather dry style. In spite of Husserl's dismissal of philosophy as some kind of life-empowering wisdom, this quote already adumbrates an important idea critical to his subsequent appropriation of the notion of worldview: a human being educated in a scientifically minded culture will be ready to *genuinely* embrace a worldview only if this presents itself in a scientific form. In this lecture, however, he is much more interested in marking his own position against all forms of *Weltanschauung*-philosophy. He continues his preliminary remarks as follows:

You are perhaps surprised. I defend philosophy as science. Those among you who have been able to examine the cultural life of our time shall definitely know that reasons to embark on such defense are not missing. Consider the major transformation that occurred this past decade: the new and ever-growing yearning for worldview, religion, for a life in spirit, for a thoroughly autonomous personal life in freedom, beauty, and moral deed. This great transformation makes itself known also in the resurgence of interest in philosophy. And philosophy should be our guide. However, people argue: how could and how would this miserable academic philosophy, this philosophy as science, help us? We need a philosophy that gives concrete expression to the deepest will to life of our time, to its ideals, its hopes, and its endeavors. We need a philosophy that has grown out of the richest personal life, so that it manages to awaken, strengthen, and

[29] Mat. VII, 8.

nurture further life of the same breed. Such philosophy is the creative achievement of a genius who concentrates in himself all the dominant tendencies of our
time, finds in them his own most personal will to life, and objectifies them in a
perfect literary creation: the philosophical artwork. Very good, I say. Let us
welcome such philosophers and their philosophy. Once it is there, it should
quicken us, too. We are, too, children of our time. However, should we, who
are not original geniuses but rather simple working people, just twiddle our
thumbs? Shouldn't we continue to serve the goals of mankind in our unpreten-
tious way, through the forms of science, which is not directed towards what is
temporal, but rather towards what is eternal? Science obviously does not procure
to the yearnings of our life fulsome satisfaction. On the contrary, it lifts us above
our own *ego*, above our time and all its miseries to a region of eternal values.[30]

The affirmation of science as a domain of timeless values as opposed
to the vagaries of historically conditioned worldviews is characteristic
of Husserl's position in this period. While most Neo-Kantians would
support wholeheartedly Husserl's affirmation of the timeless validity
of the ideal of science, they would highlight a potential danger in his
sharp distinction between *Weltanschauung* and scientific philosophy.
Emil Lask raises his concerns in his notes after reading Husserl's
Philosophy as a Rigorous Science:

The more powerful and fundamental the material under scrutiny, the greater
the mission of knowing. This, however, is only possible in philosophy,
where precisely the *whole* is the material. Therefore, it is wrong-headed to
counterpose philosophy as worldview and philosophy as rigorous science.
Obviously, the term *Weltanschauung* is ambiguous: a worldview can be wholly
a-contemplative; it can be contemplatively oriented and stand in the service of
life; finally, it can be theory building upon the dynamics of life [*Lebensverhalten*],
and in this sense philosophy is a theoretical doctrine of *Weltanschauung*. Husserl
contends in *Logos* (*"Philosophy as a Rigorous Science"*) that science is entirely
"impersonal." Now, obviously, philosophy is all about contemplative objectivity
[*Sachlichkeit*]; however, *everything* is included in it! Husserl contends that
philosophy does not need wisdom but theoretical ability. This is a false opposition! It needs both [. . .] Likewise, profundity [*Tiefsinn*] and "scientific clarity" do
not stand in opposition. On the contrary, profundity is assumed as material by
theoretical clarity, and thereby it is systematized, ordered, and illuminated. All
this is precisely the specific achievement of theory: the intellect approaches the
'depths,' delves into them, and raises them to clarity. What is chaotic is thereby
destroyed, but the content is indestructible.[31]

[30] Mat. VII, 8–9.   [31] SW, 252.

In other words, for Lask, the point is not so much to purge philosophy of unscientific wisdom but also to illuminate and reorganize theoretically those intuitions about the meaning of life and the world that play such an important role in people's 'will to philosophy.' After all, if philosophy has to be a theoretical exploration of the world as a whole it cannot programmatically exclude from its purview any of the world's parts, including those existential and emotional responses to life's mystery that often drive people to philosophy.

It can be shown, however, that Husserl progressively changed his mind regarding the problem of worldview and that he eventually came to appreciate the meaning of this notion for philosophy. His later work can be read as a deliberate effort to set the basis for a phenomenologically inspired worldview, which is designed to provide a viable alternative to the dominance of naturalism. In this way, Husserl appropriates Rickert's initial position, according to which philosophy should *yield* a worldview, while Rickert, as we showed above, moves to embrace Husserl's earlier position in *Philosophy as a Rigorous Science* and advocate for a sharp distinction of philosophy as a science and philosophy as worldview.

What factors let Husserl revisit his position on *Weltanschauung*? As is often the case with the development of philosophical ideas, we can indicate both external and internal factors. The most important external factor was the outbreak of World War I in 1914. There is no doubt that this event had a profound impact on Husserl.[32] At the personal level, tragedy struck when Husserl's youngest son Wolfgang, then twenty-two years old, died in 1916 in the battle of Verdun. Besides, as an intellectual, Husserl had to face the spiritual bankruptcy of his time, and he slowly came to realize that the sources of such misery were rooted deeply in the lack of authentic self-understanding characterizing Western civilization. The best minds of the West were increasingly put to work on specialized problems using the quantitative and statistical methods of empirical research without being enlightened about the dignity of their own 'subjectivity,' as the source of both scientific methods and (in a transcendental

---

[32] For example, scholars have convincingly shown that World War I marks a radical turning point in Husserl's conception of ethics, so that it is now customary, following Ullrich Melle, to distinguish between Husserl's 'pre-war' ethics, revolving around the project of a formal axiology, and his 'postwar' personalistic ethics. See U. Melle, "The Development of Husserl's Ethics," *Études phénoménologiques* 7/13–14 (1991): 115–135.

sense) of the natural world that such methods are designed to investigate. In a word, Western civilization had been overtaken by naturalism. This was not just a set of doctrines explicitly endorsed by some philosophers, such as those Husserl masterfully refuted in the *Prolegomena to a Pure Logic* (1899) and in the first part of the aforementioned *Logos* essay.[33] Naturalism was rather a worldview widely spread at all levels in European societies. It certainly flew from the specialized sciences of nature, but its influence reached far beyond the community of specialists. It became almost a 'fundamental mood,' to borrow an expression from Heidegger, which was common to practicing scientists and ordinary people alike. In order to combat naturalism, targeted refutation of specific philosophical theories – such as psychologism in epistemology and Cartesian substantialism in the philosophy of mind – proved insufficient. A *Weltanschauung* presenting itself in a scientific guise, such as naturalism, could only be overcome by way of setting the basis for a novel *Weltanschauung*, which, in Husserl's hopes, would have eventually extended its influence on Western civilization as a whole and dispelled naturalism. Phenomenology, from the years of World War I onwards, can be read as an attempt to work towards this *Weltanschauung*, which Husserl recognized that he shared with his Neo-Kantian colleagues and with classical German philosophers, such as Fichte. In this way, he appropriates what I referred to as the 'Kantian liberation narrative' and employs the powerful conceptual and methodological arsenal of his phenomenology to articulate a humanistic worldview with the highest possible scientific rigor.

The first traces of this development can be found in Husserl's correspondence with Rickert during the first years of World War I. In 1915, after congratulating Rickert for his recent appointment as the successor of his teacher Windelband in Heidelberg, Husserl confesses that he owes to Windelband's great works in the history of philosophy his fascination with Kant and classical German philosophy, which, however, under Brentano's influence, lay dormant for quite a while.[34] He writes:

---

[33] For a full account of Husserl's refutation of epistemological and psychological naturalism see my "Unforgivable Sinners? Epistemological and Psychological Naturalism in Husserl's *Philosophy as a Rigorous Science*," *Rivista Internazionale di Filosofia e Psicologia* 3/2 (2012): 147–160.

[34] Actually it is fair to say that Husserl initially shared with the Brentano school utter contempt for Kant and, especially, for the German idealist. Helmuth

Thanks to [Windelband's works,] my soul, already in my naturalistic beginnings, was filled with a secret yearning for the old romantic territory of German Idealism. However, German Idealism did not gain its full contours for me through Windelband. Going my own hardscrabble path, building up from below, I was in a position to recognize the greatness and the eternal meaning of German Idealism (setting aside all romantic conceptuality) only when, without noticing at first, I found myself in the idealistic camp. (As you can imagine, Fichte now attracts me more and more.) Thus, in this last decade I feel tightly connected with the leaders of the German idealistic schools. We fight as comrades against the naturalism of our time as our common enemy. We serve, each of us in their own way, the same gods, and since this is something serious and holy to us, something to which we committed our entire life, each of these ways harbors in itself its own necessities and is bound to be indispensable for the advancement of philosophy.[35]

Just two years later, in 1917, an editorial event added further momentum to Husserl's revision of his position on *Weltanschauung*. Dietrich Mahnke, who had been Husserl's student in Göttingen, published a short book entitled *The Will to Eternity: Thoughts of a German Warrior on the Meaning of Spiritual Life*.[36] The book is the perfect example of a very popular genre at the time, the so-called *Kriegsbuch*. War-books were mostly rhetorically inflated pamphlets exalting the putative spiritual significance of the war and self-righteously defending the German cause. Needless to say, they were generally of little philosophical value. War-books proliferated in Germany in the 1910s and even first-rate intellectuals such as Thomas Mann and Max Scheler fell prey to the fascination of such an immensely popular genre and gave their own contributions to it.

The only philosophically interesting aspect of Mahnke's book is his deliberate attempt to develop a *Weltanschauung* based on phenomenology, which Husserl, by his own admission, found both intriguing and

Plessner recounts a rather amusing anecdote on this matter. Once, in Göttingen, as Plessner was accompanying Professor Husserl home while attempting to explain to him the outlines of his dissertation project on Fichte's *Wissenschaftslehre*, Husserl suddenly blurted out the following statement: "In my opinion the whole of German Idealism has always been shit. All my life I have always sought [and at this moment he lifted up his walking stick and pushed its top, bending the stick, against the doorpost] reality." Reported in R. Boehm, *Vom Gesichtspunkt der Phänomenologie* (The Hague: Nijhoff, 1968), 28–29.

[35] Husserl in a letter to Rickert, December 20, 1905, BW V, 178.

[36] D. Mahnke, *Der Wille zur Ewigkeit: Gedanken eines Deutschen Kriegers über den Sinn des Geisteslebens* (Halle: Niemeyer, 1917).

eye opening. Mahnke was well aware of Husserl's outspoken aversion to *Weltanschauung* philosophy. Therefore, he begins his dedication to Husserl asking rhetorically whether he should dare associate his name with a series of thoughts "which correspond so little to his ideal of 'philosophy as a rigorous science'."[37] However, he continues addressing Husserl directly:

> You too, the master of eidetic intuition [*Wesensschau*], do not fail to realize that the needs of life require a "*Weltanschauung* philosophy" besides "rigorous science." The highest goal of such *Weltanschauung* philosophy is not the purity and depth of truth, but rather the purity and depth of human existence. For the spiritualization of everyday life we do not need a definitively secured metaphysics, but rather a practical life-wisdom, albeit only provisionally concluded.[38]

The bulk of Mahnke's work is geared towards the illustration of his own *Weltanschauung*, which can be summarized in the rather blunt idea that "the meaning of all spiritual-cultural life [*Geistesleben*] is the will to eternity."[39] Mahnke sees in Husserl's method of *Wesensschau* a source of glimpses into eternity – the eternity of objectively valid eidetic laws – and considers the contemplation of essences to be especially beneficial to the soldier meditating on the meaning of his life in the trenches. *Wesensschau* is thus not just a method to obtain scientific truths: it has an existential meaning which can be brought to light in order to quench people's thirst for life-sustaining wisdom.

Husserl was enthralled by Mahnke's work, writing an enthusiastic review recommending the book wholeheartedly to "all friends of philosophy."[40] In 1931, over ten years later, he refers to the book in a letter to Mahnke and recounts that he randomly picked it up from the shelf and could not stop rereading it.[41] However, as one would expect, Husserl's appropriation of *Weltanschauung* resulted in a project of a completely different tenor than the bellicose nationalism of his student Mahnke's. This is the project commonly known as phenomenological life-world ontology. Life-world ontology, which will be the theme of the next sections, goes hand in hand with what we could provisionally call a *deconstructive genealogy of naturalism as worldview*. This remark is particularly important in order to characterize Husserl's take on the

---

[37] *Ibid.*, VII. [38] *Ibid.*, VIII–IX. [39] *Ibid.*, 4. [40] Hua XXV, 295.
[41] E. Husserl, *Briefwechsel*, vol. 3, *Die Göttinger Schule* (Dordrecht: Kluwer, 1994), 477. Hereafter BW III.

idea of "worldview" as the obscure *terminus a quo* of philosophy proposed by Simmel and Dilthey. As we mentioned above, Husserl progressively appropriates Rickert's earlier notion that philosophy should yield a scientific *Weltanschauung* alternative to naturalism, and in this respect he opposes views that construe *Weltanschauungen* as the unfathomable existential sources of philosophical thinking. However, a new phenomenological *Weltanschauung* cannot be developed without first acknowledging the power of naturalism and inquiring into its sources. There is a sense in which, *pace* Rickert, these sources are indeed hidden and obscure. Husserl's bold claim, however, is that the method of phenomenology can illuminate the obscure, thereby exposing the true nature of these sources, which do not lie deep in the subconscious of human character-types, but rather in the forgotten vicissitudes of Western history and the intricate intentional shifts that inaugurated the long course of modern science. Such shifts, as we will see, are not merely accidental. They are motivated by the way in which we experience nature. However, they tend to be forgotten the more modern science becomes a habituated mind-set. This leads to a fundamental distortion of the relationship between the concrete world of experience and the idealized world of natural-scientific inquiry, whereby the latter supplants the former. Naturalism is nothing but the 'cultural' climate ensuing from this distortion. To the extent that the original distortion has been forgotten, naturalism is indeed experienced *as if* it flew from unfathomable depths. However, these are nothing but the depths of history, and they can be probed with the aid of intentional analysis and the recognition of the inherent tradition linking together the present and the past transcendental subjects. To proceed systematically, however, the first step is to become familiar with Husserl's descriptions of the life-world as such.

Life-world ontology as intuitively and contemplatively oriented inquiry into the structure of the world-whole

As we saw in Chapter 5, Husserl argues that philosophy is characterized by an "interest for the totality"[42] of what is, namely, the world as a whole. There we noted in passing that he shares this view with Rickert, and at this point we are in a position to fully grasp its philosophical

---

[42] Hua XXXII, 7.

centrality in context. We deferred a full assessment of Husserl's take on the world as a whole and his differences from Rickert, and it is now time to address this important issue.

Let us start this section with what might strike the reader as a minor philological remark, but which should assume philosophical significance in light of the foregoing analyses. The editor of the voluminous collection of Husserl's manuscripts on the life-world, *Husserliana XXXIX*, reports that Husserl gathered the overwhelming bulk of these manuscripts (several hundreds of pages spanning over three decades) in a bundle marked with the title *Zur Weltanschauung*, i.e., "towards worldview."[43] There can be no doubt, then, that Husserl saw his laborious work on the life-world as responding to the heated debate surrounding the notion of *Weltanschauung*, and we can certainly assume that he was well aware of the philosophical ladenness of this term. The world as a whole that needs philosophical elucidation, however, is not a limit-idea that merely serves to orient our inquiries. Husserl upholds his unwavering commitment to intuitiveness and takes the expression *Weltanschauung* quite literally. If what philosophy is supposed to achieve is insight about the world as a whole, phenomenology sets out to actually get down to eidetic descriptions of the world as it is intuitively (*anschaulich*) given in our experience. Thus, phenomenology in its mature form pursues a *Weltanschauung* in two senses. (1) In the *ordinary* sense of the word *Weltanschauung*, phenomenology aspires to contribute to the Kantian liberation narrative and breathe new life into its anti-naturalistic understanding of the world. (2) In the *literal* sense of the word *Weltanschauung*, phenomenology yields *Anschauung* (intuition) of the *Welt* (world); it aims at a descriptive elucidation of our concrete awareness of the world as a whole prior to the thematization of its parts in the specialized sciences.[44]

These two pursuits are interrelated. For Husserl, it is only by carrying out the program in (2) that the aspiration expressed in (1) can find its actual fulfillment. This is because the correct execution of the program in (2) goes to show that there is no meaningful sense of the phrase 'world as a whole' independently of the nexuses of experience of living subjects and their intentionality. Transcendental subjectivity thus proves to be

---

[43] Hua XXXIX, 737.
[44] The use of *Weltanschauung* in this second, literal, sense is documented for instance in Hua XXXIX, 127.

not at all a subordinated thematic sphere in the overarching thematic whole called "world," as Rickert would have it, but the very source of meaning and validity of the world-whole itself. In a nutshell, Husserl's phenomenological execution of an eidetically oriented *Weltanschauung* is geared towards the establishment of the following version of the Kantian liberation narrative qua worldview: "In our 'relating-ourselves-to', in our multifarious intentionality, we are [. . .] the carriers of the world's 'being'."[45]

Husserl's notion of the life-world does not amount to just the *idea* that the world as a whole is broader than the world investigated by any of the positive empirical sciences. For Husserl, there is a concrete sense that in every experience of something in the world we are implicitly experiencing *the world as a whole*, which is available for us as a constant horizon. The aforementioned manuscripts entail a wealth of detailed descriptions of this eidetic state of affairs. Husserl admits that "the world as world of experience" is "definitely a ticklish theme."[46] This is because, strictly speaking, our experience is always directed towards some worldly object and not towards the world itself. In this sense, "the experience of singularity precedes the experience of the world and 'knowledge' of the singular precedes 'knowledge' of a universe, or, better, of 'the' universe of singularities."[47] Nonetheless, no experience of a singular perceptual object is conceivable as standing in complete isolation. Every concretely experienced perceptual object has both an internal horizon of further manifestation (new profiles presenting us with previously unseen sides and properties of the given object) and an external horizon of further surrounding objects that at any time can be turned into objects of our primary attention. Another way of describing this is to say that every single object of experience *emerges from* a surrounding horizon of objects of possible experience, which is constantly co-given alongside the actual focus of our present experience. The external horizon does not suddenly come into view only when we turn our attention away from the object we are experiencing. It is an implicitly co-aware background constantly accompanying our experience of individual beings and all of our practical transactions. Most importantly, this external horizon is not merely the empty awareness that we could put an end to this particular perceptual experience and switch to consider another object. Moving from a given perceptual

---

[45] *Ibid.*, 603.   [46] *Ibid.*, 130.   [47] *Ibid.*, 126.

object to the exploration of its external horizon is not a leap into the unknown. The external horizon of any conceivable object is entirely *structured* and can be described as a horizon of previously acquired validity. It is always already present, albeit implicitly, as a horizon of further existents that will appear according to my kinaesthetic orientation and motion, that will exhibit certain typical patterns encountered in previous experiences, that will in some way enrich or reconfigure the web of my anticipations, and so forth.

Based on these descriptions, it is possible to clarify the sense in which we can talk about the world *as experienced* from a phenomenological perspective: the world is the total synthesis of the external horizons of all real and possible things, and to the extent that these horizons are structured according to common essential regularities they merge into one all-encompassing horizon. The world-horizon is constantly pre-supposed (literally: pre-posited, or *voraus-gesetzt*) in every particular positing of existing being, and it is *pre-given* as a ground of already established validity into which the establishment of new validities nec-essarily flows. Husserl deems this pre-givenness of the world "the fundamental *a priori*,"[48] meaning the a priori structure on the basis of which all further a priori structures are detectable and articulable. Correlatively, our awareness of the world qua horizon can be described as follows:

World-consciousness is consciousness in the mode 'certainty of being' [*Seinsgewissheit*]. This certainty did not arise through a single being-positing act occurring in the life-nexus, through an act of grasping something as existent or even through a predicative judgment of existence. All that already presupposes world-consciousness in the mode 'certainty of being.'[49]

How can we account for this certainty of being? Did we reach the "bedrock where our spade is turned,"[50] to borrow an effective meta-phor from Wittgenstein, and all further analysis is utterly impossible? Husserl's strategy to solve this dilemma is to move from a merely static description, in which the world figures as the horizon surrounding every singular existent, to a genetic-dynamic description in which both the total horizon 'world' and existents considered singly are 'set in motion,'

---

[48] *Ibid.*, 125.   [49] *Ibid.*, 61.
[50] See L. Wittgenstein, *Philosophical Investigations* (Oxford: Wiley Blackwell, 2009), 217.

as it were, and exposed as being essentially caught up in an unending process of constitution. Assuming this perspective, the world itself qua all-encompassing horizon proves to be the *result* of the foregoing constitution, which, however, cannot be simply equated with the constitution of single objects of experience in perception. Husserl underscores this point in the following way:

> The world of which I possibly speak, the world which I possibly consider, is something valid of my own sphere of validity (of actual or hidden holding-as-valid), and its sense is sense within myself, stemming from my own active or passive accomplishments.[51]

In order to understand correctly the meaning of this statement, it is crucial to appreciate the concept of validity Husserl is employing here. We should recall the Neo-Kantian insight, dating back to Lotze and reprised by Rickert and Lask, that being itself is a kind of validity.[52] Husserl appropriates the same notion of validity in his analyses of the 'positing' function of perceptual experience. Whenever we undergo a perceptual experience that culminates with the explicit positing of something as existing, we thereby establish a validity: the validity of, say, this desk as existent. The first establishment of such validity, which Husserl terms *Urstiftung*, however, entails "a horizon of continuing validity"[53] (*Fortgeltung*) which can be at any time reactivated, thus carrying out a *Nachstiftung* (post-establishment) which confirms and reinvigorates the certainty associated with the original *Stiftung*. My desk, whose validity as existent was established the fist time it manifested itself to me, continues to hold valid after I stop perceiving it, and whenever I return to my office its reappearance fills with intuitive content an anticipatory intention that was already in play. We should think of experience as an endless process of establishing and retrieving validities in constant negotiation with the prompts issuing from our perceptual field. In so doing, we disclose ever-new horizons and enrich those we already possess. Each newly established validity eventually merges into an already valid background and is integrated in the coherent whole of what we take as being the world. Occasionally, interferences and breaches occur in this process. What we took as valid proves to be mere illusion or to be different than we initially established. This leads to correction and partial reconfiguration of what counts as 'the

---

[51] Hua XXXIX, 118.   [52] See Chapter 1.   [53] Hua XXXIX, 1.

world,' but in no case does it affect our unwavering belief in the world's existence as the all-encompassing ground of what we take to be valid. Having a world, thus, does not simply mean having a collection of disconnected things that we partly experience and partly anticipate. It means mastering an encompassing horizon of spatio-temporal being that we know how to explore. In Husserl's words:

For us as subjects of a natural life there are not only things that we see (each of them with a horizon of familiarity regarding the unseen rear sides <whose manifestation> is eventually to be expected, however, as a mixture of determinate sense and horizon-sense), and on top of them those that we don't see, which are valid for us because we have seen them before and we still possess them as valid. Rather, in every waking moment of life a whole world is there for us, a world that reaches into the infinities of space and time (and which is structured in each of its details according to a real-categorial typical pattern).[54]

This world is, as Husserl mentions, the world of our natural, pre-scientific life. The infinite task of a phenomenological life-world ontology is the elucidation of all its underpinning a priori structures. The unfolding of this project, in line with the tenets of the Kantian liberation narrative, should fully clarify the sense in which we can possibly talk about a world and in so doing progressively justify the 'subjective' path that necessarily has to be taken for this purpose:

At this point, however, the constitutive analysis may proceed in its description and clarification of the genesis (questioning back into the essential primal establishings and their fundamental forms); it is certain that the title "world" – and specifically the world that is valid for us – is a *title for real and possible ego-acts*. 'Possibility' here refers on one hand to previous establishing through ego-acts in this specific sense, on the other hand to a free activity of disclosure of horizons based on the subjects' capacities, on their evidence: "I can carry forward my experiencing."[55]

This should not be taken to mean, however, that we can meaningfully construe the subjective process of world-constitution as the mere indefinite iteration of single processes of constitution of worldly existents, as one might erroneously think. The stretch of experiential life constituting a definite perceptual object has a beginning and an end in the stream of phenomenological time. True, its horizon refers to further stretches of

[54] *Ibid.*, 3.   [55] *Ibid.*, 4.

experiential life constituting perceptual validity in the same way. However, there is a certain, provisional completeness to the constitution of one single perceptual object. We can describe the process from its inception within the sphere of passivity up to our actual turning towards the affective salience in our perceptual field, which culminates in the full objectification and the concomitant establishment of a validity of being (*Seinsgeltung*). Contrariwise, we cannot conceive of world-constitution as a finite process with an identifiable point of inception and with a (provisionally) conclusive point of culmination in some type of objectifying apprehension. World-constitution is something we can only describe as always already underway. It is an intrinsically inception-less process, which admits of constant readjustment and modification as far as details are concerned, but never deviates from its necessary termination in the unbreakable certainty of an infinity of existing being. Accordingly, it does not culminate in some form of objectification in which the world-whole would be present to us after the manner of an existing worldly object. The world's pre-givenness as the backdrop of all actual establishment of validities in the sphere of givenness can be studied only precisely *qua* pre-givenness. The world's givenness is nothing over and above its thematized pre-givenness, which, in turn, is not just the preliminary stage of a process that would culminate with actual, full-blown perceptual manifestation. The world's thematized pre-givenness *is* the world's givenness, to the extent that the world is nothing but the infinite horizon of structured anticipations that entail the promise of unceasing manifestation. Husserl describes in a few brushstrokes the unique character of world constitution in the following passage:

The world is constituted as being – as the existing total unity [*All-Einheit*] of realities that exist in themselves. It is a constituted 'product' [*Gebilde*] in the streaming, world-constituting subjectivity. However, it is not a finished product to be equated with the products that we achieve in the naivety of our natural world-life. [Unlike the world,] these products became 'finished' through our production, and from then on they are readily available as being.[56]

The world is never 'ready' the way that an artifact actively produced according to a plan can be ready for use or the way that a perceptual

---

[56] *Ibid.*, 83.

object seized in active attention can be ready for further categorial or practical operations. Accordingly, the 'world-constituting' transcendental subjectivity cannot be possibly understood as some kind of transcendental demiurge molding a lump of clay into a statuette. That kind of subjectively planned production entirely presupposes the constitution of the world within transcendental subjectivity, and therefore it cannot be employed as a metaphor to shed light on it. Like Kant's transcendental ego in Simmel's rendition,[57] Husserl's transcendental subjectivity entirely coincides with its world-constituting function and should not be artificially separated from it. While as empirical human subjects we form and carry out plans, thereby modifying the world around us and producing new things, as transcendental subjects we constantly carry out world-constitution in a way that we are not in a position to steer according to plans and purposes. Husserl touches on this issue explicitly in a manuscript from the early 1920s. Here he compares the external world, which we originally acquire in outer experience, and the 'inner' world of consciousness, which discloses itself in the phenomenological reflection. The subjective sphere of immanence, unlike the objective sphere of transcendent things, is not a world in its own right existing merely alongside the world of experience and up for separate scrutiny: "Over the course of genesis, all immanent acquisition flows into worldly constitution; immanence merges and dissolves into [*geht auf*] its function of worldly constitution."[58]

At this point the attentive reader may have noticed that in most passages quoted above Husserl speaks of 'world' and of 'life-world' interchangeably. He actually refers mostly to just 'the world,' although, as we know, most of the manuscripts we quoted from belong in the bundle *Zur Weltanschauung* and have been published in the *Husserliana* volume devoted to the life-world. What does the addition of the prefix 'life' add to the term 'world'? Why coin a new term to talk about the world as a whole? Reconstructing the complex genesis of the concept of life-world in Husserl's thought and measuring out the broad spectrum of its meanings would exceed the scope of this chapter.[59] For our present purpose it is sufficient to say that the phrase 'life-world' is first and foremost a *contrastive* term. Husserl employs it mostly in

---

[57] See Chapter 2. [58] Hua XXXIX, 22.

[59] For an excellent reconstruction see the entry *Lebenswelt* in Gander, *Husserl-Lexikon*.

contrast to the idealized world of mathematical physics in order to emphasize how the latter is not *the real world* but rather a construction (albeit a fully legitimate and motivated one) fashioned by a definite set of intellectual operations. We shall explore this fundamental meaning in the next section.

Another context in which 'life-world' is employed as a contrastive term is that of culture. Husserl speaks of *the* one all-encompassing life-world in contrast to the multiple worlds of historical cultures or the special worlds created by selective interests (for instance, when I am doing mathematics, I am immersed in a self-contained world of numbers, operations, etc.).[60] The philosophical payoff of this contrast is, as we will see in greater detail in the next chapter, a distinctive openness to the plurality of cultures paired with a forceful rejection of cultural relativism and the prospect of a universal humanistic culture.

---

[60] On special worlds and attitudes see S. Luft, *Subjectivity and Lifeworld in Transcendental Phenomenology* (Evanston, IL: Northwestern University Press, 2011), 42. In his discussion Luft discusses the German term *Sonderwelt*, which, however, Husserl almost never uses. The only occurrence I was able to find is in Hua IX, 503 where he speaks of *ideale Sonderwelten* (ideal special worlds), presumably referring to ideal dimensions such as those of numbers, geometrical shapes, or music (notes, intervals, etc.) and insisting that they are, too, part of 'the world' (read: the life-world). In a recent paper Nicolas De Warren underscores the contrast between the life-world and special worlds in order to reject the notion that one can unqualifiedly identify the life-world with the world of culture. While the world of culture consists in a plurality of special worlds defined by horizons of interest (e.g., the world of sports, the world of politics, etc.), "the *Lebenswelt*, on the contrary, is neither a world defined by a special interest, nor a world defined by a general or universal interest." For this reason: "It would be wrong to conceive of the life-world as a universal cultural or social structure that all possible societies have in common." N. De Warren, "La Crise de la raison et l'énigme du monde," in F. De Gandt and C. Majolino (eds.), *Lectures de la* Krisis *de Husserl* (Paris: Vrin, 2008), 23–44. Here 35. Put this way, however, the contrast is overstated. Husserl speaks repeatedly of a universal *Seinsinteresse*, or naive interest in being, that underlies all of our transactions in the world within the natural attitude (see, for instance, Hua VIII, 98; 110; 159–160; 306). The life-world as the world in which we live our natural lives, is thus indeed the correlate of an overriding, universal interest. De Warren is right that the universal interest in being is nothing like the special interests underlying special worlds, in that it is mostly unthematic and pervasive. But the life-world can nonetheless be defined in terms of a kind of universal interest, which, among other things, also clarifies why all subordinated cultural worlds have an interest-structure. Since the life-world is organized around an interest, the interests underlying special worlds can be interpreted as branching off from the one, unchanging interest in being that defines the life-world.

However, even in this case Husserl's terminology retains its characteristic fluidity. While *the* life-world is mostly employed as a *singulare tantum*, Husserl uses the term in the plural here and there[61] to designate the subjectively shaped environments in which human and animal groupings live their communal lives. In these contexts Husserl is much more interested in the emphasis on the *life* component in the phrase life-world. Thinking this point through is paramount to understanding the import of the notion of life-world as indicating the world's being *aus dem Leben*, that is, growing out of life and harboring the growth of further life within itself.

While the special world of a certain culture or even the world of human culture overall do not coincide with the life-world as the *ground*

---

[61] See, for instance, Hua XXXIX, 198; 530; 540. The fluidity of Husserl's usage of the term life-world often puzzled and sometimes even irritated scholars. David Carr, for instance, deems Husserl's concept of life-world problematic and even inconsistent. This is because, he argues, "Husserl has assembled under one title a number of disparate and in some senses even incompatible concepts." D. Carr, "Husserl's Problematic Concept of Lifeworld," in L. Embree and D. Moran, *Phenomenology: Critical Concepts in Philosophy*, vol. 1 (London: Routledge, 2004), 359–374. Here 360. In particular, Carr sees a "[d]iscrepancy between lifeworld as cultural world and lifeworld as world of immediate experience," in that "the cultural community is not something perceived, like a thing or a body" (368). In Carr's view, "[s]uch terms as 'pre-predicative,' 'immediate,' 'intuitively given' are clearly out of place" if applied to the world of culture (367). The problem with Carr's argument is that if it is meant to highlight an *internal* difficulty within the horizon of Husserl's thought then it rests on a *pars pro toto* fallacy. Carr wrongly equates sensory perception (*pars*) and perception in general (*toto*). From Husserl's phenomenological perspective, however, there would be nothing wrong with saying that cultural objects and communities (alongside values, norms, etc.) are or can be intuitively perceived. If perception is defined as original givenness, then when I am contemplating a cultural object or observing the customs of a foreign cultural community, and provided I have a full grasp of the meaning of the cultural object or custom at issue, I am having a genuine perceptual experience. Consider the following anecdote: "On his deathbed in 1918, the art-collector Alexander Schnütgen was presented with a crucifix. After he inspected the object held before him, he expertly declared 'fourteenth century' and immediately died." Valentin Groebner, *Defaced: The Visual Culture of Violence in the Late Middle Ages* (New York: Zone Books, 2004), 88. Quoted in De Warren, "Pamina's Eyes, Tamino's Gaze." For Schnütgen the cultural value or set of values unambiguously identifying the crucifix as an artifact from the fourteenth century were *perceptually* present and not merely interpreted or hypothesized. If the Husserlian concept of perception as original, intuitive givenness is correctly understood, then there is absolutely no tension or difficulty in assembling under the concept of lifeworld both the world of sensory perception and the world of culture.

of all culture (including scientific culture), such a consideration of the world of culture is helpful to develop a guiding thread for understanding Husserl's life-world. In the culturally formed world of humans, we encounter a wide variety of objects (both empirical and ideal) that we recognize as growing out of the life of individuals and communities. Artifacts, legal systems, institutions, and religious ceremonies are among the objects whose existence is fundamentally entwined with that of humans who brought them about. In the natural attitude, however, such objects only constitute 'half' of the world, so to speak. The other half is that of nature, that is, the totality of what is prior to all cultural formation, including the 'stuff' that we use to create cultural objects (wood for artifacts, stones and sand for buildings, etc.). Clusters of cultural objects linked together by a coherent set of goal-oriented intentions, in turn, constitute special worlds, such as the world of a religious movement or the world of a certain musical niche. People partaking of such worlds know themselves as partaking of a flow of 'life' that precedes and surpasses them. What about the world as a whole? To what extent can it be designated a *life*-world?

As we explained in detail in the foregoing chapter of this book, the phenomenological reduction and the ensuing discovery of transcendental subjectivity open up the field of phenomenology to the totality of what is. It sets the basis for recognizing that it is not artifacts and specifically cultural objects alone that are fundamentally entwined with subjectivity. Rather, in keeping with the analysis of the world as a structure of experientially established validity, the world as a whole is a world entwined with life, a world grown out of it. This, of course, is not merely human life but the overarching transcendental life encompassing humans, conscious animals, and their respective worlds. It is transcendental life that carries out transcendental constitution in the sense defined above. Transcendental life, as we saw, "merges and dissolves into [*geht auf*] its function of worldly constitution"[62] as the ongoing establishment, retrieval, and dismissal of validities. In this respect, 'life-world' coincides with transcendental constitution. There is no such thing as a pre-existing world *and* a life that happens to live in it or a pure life that creatively spins the world out of itself, as it were. Rather, transcendental life is at bottom nothing but this world-in-the-making (it *geht auf* in it), and the world is nothing but this life-world,

---

[62] Hua XXXIX, 22.

that is, this totality of established being that is constantly in a process of disassembling, reassembling, and reconfiguring as the movement of transcendental life unfolds from one generation of empirical subjects to the next. This process makes for an increasing 'thickness' of the life world as newly established products of ongoing transcendental constitution flow into the totality of what henceforth shall count as 'world' and are handed down to future transcendental subjects.

Within the nexus of progressing experience belonging to each individual and each communalized humanity, the handing down [*Tradieren*] – one-sided at first, then reciprocal – produces a progressively unitary, an ever richer and extended pre-givenness. In this way, the world, which is always already world for all, constantly hands down the enrichments of individuals and groups to further individuals and groups.[63]

Following the suggestion entailed in these lines, we can state that the life-world in which we live is a much more complex and richer ground of established validities than the life-world in which, say, ancient Romans lived. However, some of the established validities that were part of their own life-world are now lost, and we can only retrieve them as having once been valid. In this respect, we can very well say that we live in *the same* life-world in which the ancient Romans lived, if we consider the life-world's abiding structure of pre-givenness with its a priori constituents. In another respect, however, our life-world is different from the ancient Roman life-world. This is because the actual horizon of validities in our life-world is inevitably other than theirs. This sheds light on the life-world's fundamental historicity, which does not amount to completely unpredictable variability, but to the constant coming and going of validities within a framework of abiding certainty in the world's being. In sum, while it is indeed mandatory to distinguish between the life-world and culture, the observation of culture provides the clue to understanding in what sense we can speak of the life-world as a world flowing out of life. Once we switch from the natural to the phenomenological attitude, the entwinement of what counts as world and life (which is patent in the sphere of human culture) is revealed to be universal. Here, life is transcendental life, and world constitution is not active creation as is the case with cultural products but is, rather, a

---

[63] *Ibid.*, 54.

complex play of activity and passivity in which transcendental life completely exhausts (*geht auf*) its potential and its meaning.

The life-world as the source of nature and its relationship with the life-world as the source of culture in *The Crisis of the European Sciences and Transcendental Phenomenology*

After painting a broad picture of Husserl's life-world as phenomenology's articulation of the 'world as a whole' sought by Neo-Kantian philosophers and *Lebensphilosophen* alike, it is now appropriate to spend some time clarifying how the life-world relates to the specific domains of the natural and the human sciences. I presented part of the analysis pertaining to nature in Chapter 5 in the context of Husserl's critique of Rickert. It is sufficient to recall that Husserl, in his confrontation with the Neo-Kantian understanding of nature as a purely logical notion, points out that we actually never encounter mere nature in our everyday life. Nature is obtained by way of an abstractive impoverishment of experienced reality, whereby all predicates of significance are excluded. Moreover, the subjective appearance of these objects is set aside and they are considered exclusively as the substrates of their objective properties.

Husserl's treatment of nature and its relationship with the life-world is famously embedded in his late reflection on the collapse of European culture in his incomplete masterpiece *The Crisis of the European Sciences and Transcendental Phenomenology* (1935–1936). His argument in this work is that the West lost its way because it grew increasingly oblivious to the genuine task of philosophy and of the empirical sciences that once branched off from it. In particular, natural science forgot its status of being an activity carried out by living human subjects, and instead of ennobling and serving humanity it turned into a threat for humanity's self-understanding. As a matter of fact, Husserl had been reflecting on these issues since the late 1910s. In Chapter 5, I mentioned in passing his emphasis on the perpetual risk of specialized research, the "mechanization of method,"[64] in his *Natur und Geist* lecture in 1919. In these lectures this issue is merely touched upon for introductory purposes. Subsequently, however, it gains increasing centrality, becoming Husserl's chief concern in the last years of his life. The core of Husserl's charge against the *historical development* of natural science, however, is clearly

[64] *Ibid.*

formulated as early as 1921 in a research manuscript preparatory to the *Erste Philosophie* lecture. Husserl's language here is particularly revealing of his full appropriation of *Weltanschauung* motifs, and the reference to Fichte's popular work *Anweisungen zum seligen Leben* (1806) confirms his newfound appreciation for the Neo-Kantian tradition:

The universal theoretical interest was <originally> only a branch and an organ of the universal *practical* interest. Science is power, and science makes you free, and freedom through scientific reason is the way towards "bliss," i.e., the way towards an authentically fulfilling human life, towards a new humanity, which dominates its world with the power of authentic science and through this power transforms itself into a world of reason. This is the fundamental thought of the "Enlightenment"; this thought sustains modern science in its entirety and functions as its driving force. However, the great science, which subsequently came to fruition, created for the intellect a world, which apparently dissolves the driving thoughts stemming from practical reason. Instead of opening wide for man the gates of genuine freedom and offering its empowering tools, science seemingly transforms man itself in a complex of facts bereft of freedom. Science seemingly subordinates man to a meaningless world-machinery. It explains man in terms of a merely subordinated machine in the world-machinery. Instead of providing man with scientific "directions towards a blessed life" [*Anweisungen zum seligen Leben*] [...] science turns nature and freedom into an incomprehensible antinomy.[65]

This passage is an ideal prelude to the main preoccupations and lines of inquiry in *Crisis*. Husserl alludes to what he considers a distinctive feature of Western thought and an innate tendency of cognitive activity as such. Knowing is originally a practical activity whose goals and limits are established by the given practical situation of the cognitive agents. However, the practice of knowledge can progressively branch off from the practical interests that initiated it and become an end in itself. Knowledge can be pursued as a contemplative activity and set goals of its own standing in some tension with those of practical life. We could talk here about an intrinsic *centrifugal* movement characterizing cognitive activity, which over the course of time pushes knowledge away from its gravitational center in everyday praxis.[66] This movement is at the same time liberating and dangerous. It is liberating to the extent that

---

[65] Hua VIII, 230–231. Husserl is obviously alluding to Fichte's popular work *Anweisungen zum seligen Leben* (1806).

[66] A phenomenological account of *why* it is the case that knowledge tends to become emancipated from the practical interests wherein it originally emerges would be

A transcendental-phenomenological worldview

it opens up the field of rationality to indefinitely expanding inquiry. It is dangerous to the extent that autonomous knowledge necessarily has a feedback on praxis. In the best-case scenario, this feedback results in enhancement and elevation of the foregoing praxis to a higher stage of rationality and responsibility. This is the kind of feedback on praxis Husserl envisions for his phenomenology. In the worst-case scenario, however, the feedback results in a conflict and even a denial of the ideals and demands characterizing pre-theoretical praxis. This is, in short, what Husserl imputes to modern science. Therefore, it is only by way of going back to the original movement of emancipation of knowledge in Western history and tracing its crucial shifts that autonomous knowledge, viz. science, can be reset on a track of positive feedback on human praxis that characterized, at least in theory, its pre-modern formulation.

Husserl's guiding example to illustrate this process of emancipation is the evolution of the practice or 'art' of measuring land into Euclidean geometry. This is because geometry clearly has a direct bearing on modern natural science. Measuring land is a kind of cognitive activity that necessarily requires acquaintance with basic spatial shapes and with the possibility to assign numerical values to the space of experience. However, the degree of exactitude required by the practice of measuring land, say, for the sake of adjudicating a dispute between landowners is relatively low. The legal land-measurer in ancient times does not need to operate with exact rectangles and with sophisticated measuring tools. The practice of appraising polygonal shapes and measuring lengths remains bound to imperfect empirical appearances and to the relatively low standards of truth sufficient in everyday life.

Geometry is born when the contemplation and measuring of shapes is undertaken for its own sake.[67] The focus of the newborn geometer is no

---

quite complex and exceed the scope of this chapter. I have attempted to outline how such an account would have to proceed in "The Mark of Beginnings: Husserl and Hegel on the Meaning of Naiveté," in F. Fabbianelli and S. Luft (eds.), *Husserl und die klassische deutsche Philosophie* (Dordrecht: Springer, 2014), 255–264.

[67] One of the most powerful documentations of this unheard-of change of focus and the mystifying effect it had on the populace in ancient Greece can be found in Aristophanes' *Clouds* (vv. 200–205). Here is the exchange between the protagonist Strepsiades and a student at the Academy:

(Strepsiades notices a strange array of ludicrous scientific instruments) . . .

Strepsiades: What's this for?
Student: Geometry.
Strepsiades: Geometry? What's that?

longer on the approximate space of perceptual experience but on an *idealized* space made of exact figures and completely deprived of the superabundant wealth of perceptual qualities. This change of focus requires a previous abstraction of the spatial dimension from the concrete bodies of experience, whose inexact geometrical properties are always infused with sensory and practical-aesthetic properties. The first two steps leading to the birth of geometry are thus (1) *abstraction* of the spatial dimension from the fullness of the experienced world and (2) *idealization* of the geometrical shapes thus obtained. With these two steps, in Husserl's words, "we attain what is denied us in empirical praxis – 'exactness' – for there is the possibility of determining the ideal shapes in absolute identity, of recognizing them as substrates of absolutely identical and methodically, univocally determined qualities."[68]

These two moves allowed geometry in particular and quantifying mathematical thinking in general[69] to yield impressive discoveries and reach a significant degree of sophistication. Moreover, like all knowledge that has become autonomous, geometry had a feedback on the praxis from which it emerged. Centuries later, at the dawn of modern science, geometry was not only a well-established discipline with its specialists, its textbooks, and so on. It was also an applied science assisting various kinds of technology and lending its conceptual arsenal to the work of craftspeople in the most disparate areas. When Galileo Galilei (1564–1642), the spearhead figure of modern science for Husserl, started delineating the basis of the scientific revolution, the 'applicability' of geometry to the empirical world was already taken for granted. The original operations of abstraction and idealization that gave rise to the objects of geometry in the first place were no longer vivid in the historical memory of Western philosophers. For Galileo, the fact

Student:	It is the science of measuring the land.
Strepsiades:	I see, to measure our plots for the landlords?
Student:	No, to measure the land generally.
Strepsiades:	Lovely! What a very democratic mechanism.

Aristophanes, *Clouds*, trans. Peter Meineck (Indianapolis, IN: Hackett, 2000), 16–17.

[68] *Crisis*, 27.
[69] As Husserl points out parenthetically: "Geometry represents for us here the whole mathematics of space-time" (*ibid.*). Another example could be the art of weighing, which obviously has different standards when it is employed for the sake of trade on the marketplace and when it is practiced purely for the sake of theory.

that idealized geometry can be 'applied' to the empirical world and that it allows us to overcome all relativity when it is applied, determining empirical objects in a reliable and predictive fashion, becomes of paramount importance. A groundbreaking guiding thought dawns on Galileo: "*Must not something similar be possible for the concrete world as such?*"[70] In other words, if the method of abstraction and idealization works for the univocal determination of spatial properties in empirical bodies, would it not be possible to extend this method to the totality of what is?

The observation of nature in experience yields the certainty of an "overall style"[71] of the world. This is a *causal* style, which allows for approximate predictions regarding the 'behavior' of different objects in different circumstances. Every natural occurrence stands in some causal relation with other natural occurrences in its surroundings. Galileo's plan is to expand the strategy of idealization that proved effective with geometrical shapes and apply it to the totality of empirical being. In order for this to happen, however, a dire problem has to be overcome. Unlike spatial shapes, the sensible qualities characterizing empirical objects do not allow for direct idealizing mathematization. Therefore, the third step in the genealogy of modern science and the ensuing naturalism is that of an "indirect mathematization"[72] of the sensible qualities characterizing physical bodies in their concreteness (3). This move to indirect mathematization of sensible qualities is the third step if considered with respect to the emancipation of knowledge from praxis to the investigation of the empirical world. However, it is the first or the inaugural step with respect to the historical development of modern natural science.

The reason why the mathematization of sensible qualities must be indirect is that they do not admit of a straightforward numerical determination in the way that shapes do. The experience that a certain rod is longer than another rod can be directly translated into the exact language of numerical relations, say, by way of measuring both rods with a third rod that we take as our standard and determining how many times the length of the standard rod is contained in the shorter and in the longer rod. Contrariwise, the experience that a certain rod is of a brighter shade of red compared to another rod cannot be translated into numerical language directly by way of adopting a third red rod and determining that, say, one rod is only twice as red as the standard

[70] *Ibid.*, 33.   [71] *Ibid.*, 31.   [72] *Ibid.*, 34.

rod while the other is a good three times redder. This is evidently impossible. The vagueness and approximation of sensible qualities is intrinsic. Another way of looking at this intrinsic vagueness is to say that while sensibly intuited geometric properties can be experienced as approximations of an ideal shape (the vaguely round shape of a pond 'points towards' a perfect circle), sensible qualities do not approximate any ostensible ideal quality. Given a certain shade of red there is no 'ideal red' that the shade points towards in and of itself.[73]

Therefore, the mathematization of such qualities envisioned by Galileo for the sake of a total geometrical idealization of the world "is thinkable only in the sense that the specifically sensible qualities ('plena') that can be experienced in the intuited bodies are closely related in a quite peculiar and *regulated* way with the shapes that belong essentially to them."[74] Introducing this thought, Husserl wants the readers to become aware of its "strangeness,"[75] which for those coming centuries after Galileo is hardly perceivable. True, there are, as Husserl reports, some sensible qualities that appear to be directly related to the shapes of the bodies to which they attach, such as the length of a string and the pitch and tone of the sound it produces. And it is also true that by way of introducing the notion of an infinite determinability of the approximately determined geometric qualities of empirical bodies applied geometry injects a previously unknown dimension of infinity into the sensible world as a whole. Neither of these two observations, however, directly proves the "mathematizeability" of *all* sensible properties. What Galileo has at this point is only the awareness of an all-encompassing causality that allows for approximate induction and the *hypothesis* that the method of mathematization originally designed for spatial shapes can be meaningfully extended to the total causal nexus of nature. Note that, unlike the original mathematization of shapes carried out in geometry, the mathematization of sensible 'plena' does not rest on a previous abstraction. It is not by way of abstracting the dimension of sensible qualities from the concreteness of experienced bodies that we set the conditions for their mathematization. The inaugural movement

---

[73] See François de Gandt, *Husserl et Galilée: Sur la crise des sciences européennes* (Paris: Vrin, 2004), 59. "One cannot depart from the empirical and sensible gradualness of colors and smells. On the contrary, the optimum of the contours possesses a sense independently of the given perception, it can be treated in and of itself."

[74] *Crisis*, 35.   [75] *Ibid.*, 37.

of modern science goes from the successful mathematization of shapes to the hypothesis of a possible mathematization of the *total causal nexus* of nature. It is only to the extent that sensible qualities belong in this total causal nexus that they are *indirectly* involved in the mathematization.

As a matter of fact, Galileo did not recognize the status of his project of mathematizing the 'plena' of experience as resting on a hypothesis, and, with the aid of theological-metaphysical beliefs, he took this hypothesis immediately for an absolute truth (he famously considers mathematics the language in which God wrote the great book of the universe). Husserl, on the contrary, wants his readers to appreciate and take seriously the hypothetical status of the assumption undergirding the project of modern science:

[T]he Galilean idea is a *hypothesis*, and a very remarkable one at that; and the actual natural science throughout the centuries of its verification is a correspondingly remarkable sort of verification. It is remarkable because the hypothesis, in spite of its verification, continues to be and is always a hypothesis; its verification (the only kind conceivable for it) is an endless course of verifications. It is the peculiar essence of natural science, it is a priori its way of being, to be unendingly hypothetical and unendingly verified.[76]

For Galileo and the first modern scientists, this hypothesis is immediately translated into a new *method*; "it was the matter for the passionate praxis of inquiry"[77] geared towards the establishment of new and increasingly precise measurements. These, in turn, are cast in mathematical formulae, and these formulae rapidly become the focal point of the newborn modern science. "In other words, if one has the formulae, one already possesses, in advance, the practically desired prediction of what is to be expected with empirical certainty in the intuitively given world of concretely actual life."[78] Reflecting on the meaning of these formulae and their relation to the intuitive world whose causal comportment they are designed to predict, Husserl points out that the increasing sophistication of algebra and of algebraic methods progressively create a "superficialization,"[79] or emptying of meaning. To the extent that, for instance geometrical shapes and relations are univocally associated with numbers, and, eventually, after the invention of analysis, with free variables symbolized by letters, the original intuitive

[76] *Ibid.*, 41–42.   [77] *Ibid.*, 40.   [78] *Ibid.*, 43.   [79] *Ibid.*, 44.

relation of these ideal entities to the dimension of space is progressively lost. We thus get to the fourth and definitive step on the way to the establishment of modern science: (4) *formalization*. With formalization the idealized entities of geometrical-mathematical thinking are replaced by the symbols figuring in the formulae. Such symbols facilitate calculations and the creation of new formulae. However, they obliterate the dimension of intuitive experience, to which they nonetheless must retain some obscure connection in order for the formulae to 'rub against' the empirical world that they are designed to make predictable. Over the course of time, natural scientists no longer need to take into view the bold hypothesis put forward by Galileo. The impressive power of formalized methods for the treatment of nature gives rise to increasingly technicized and non-reflective research praxis. To reiterate Lask's unfriendly but well-taken remark, modern natural science becomes more and more blasé about its methods.[80]

Up to this point, we traced, following Husserl's analysis in the second part of *Crisis*, the intentional shifts characterizing the birth of modern science. However, we have not encountered naturalism yet. It is with the next step that naturalism comes onto the scene. While Husserl hastens to point out that this next step is already undertaken in Galileo's work, it is important to keep it conceptually distinct from the three foregoing steps. If this distinction were not possible, then it would be impossible to criticize and reject naturalism *while at the same time* acknowledging and respecting the work of the natural sciences as Husserl ubiquitously does. The fifth step (or the first and last step with respect to the genesis of naturalism qua worldview) is "the surreptitious substitution of the mathematically substructed world of idealities for the only real world, the one that is actually given through perception, that is ever experienced and experienceable – our everyday life-world."[81]

This step can be further broken down into two steps: (5.1) the hypostatization of the formalized idealities of geometrical thinking and (5.2) the substitution of such hypostatized idealities for the objects of intuitive experience. As for (5.1), the tradition of hypostatizing idealities is as old as Plato's philosophy and long pre-dates the development of geometrical thinking as a formalized method for natural scientific inquiry. However, from a Platonic perspective, hypostatized idealities inhabit a world of their own, one of which the intuitive world of

---

[80] See Chapter 3.   [81] *Crisis*, 48–49.

experience is a mere copy. The innovative and previously hardly conceivable step is (5.2), in which the world of experience is not simply demoted to a copy but is entirely supplanted. In Galileo's philosophy, the world of experience is declared an entirely subjective slideshow of secondary qualities, as opposed to the great book of the real universe, which God wrote in the language of mathematics. Following this fifth step, in Husserl's famous words, "we take for true being what is actually a method."[82]

The supplanting of the life-world operated by modern natural science in its naturalistic development immediately translates into a problem of value:

> If the intuited world of our life is merely subjective, then all the truths of pre- and extrascientific life that have to do with its factual being are deprived of value. They have meaning only insofar as they, while themselves false, vaguely indicate an in-itself which lies behind this world of possible experience and is transcendent in respect to it.[83]

The fact that Husserl mentions the problem of value at this point is decisive in order to underscore a point that remains unaddressed in the analysis leading up to this conclusion. The intuited world of experience is not only a perceptual world made of inexact shapes, sensible 'plena,' and an overall causal style. It is first and foremost a world of value and significance, a world cultivated over the course of generations and viewed by subjects in light of human purposiveness. All of this is automatically undermined the moment that the world of experience, in which alone human praxis plays itself out, is declared merely subjective and therefore ultimately illusory. At this point, it is apt to recall the characterization of pure nature developed by Husserl (and Lask) in earlier chapters. Nature was characterized as what remains of the world

---

[82] *Ibid.*, 51. This distinction reiterates almost literally Ernst Mach's distinction between *Untersuchungsgegenstände* and *Bestimmungsweisen*, that is, objects of investigation and modes of determining these objects. For Mach, the abstract entities of mathematical physics fall in the second category; they are modes of determining the objects of investigation of natural science. These objects, in Mach's philosophy, are nothing but the appearances manifesting themselves in our consciousness. Husserl, of course, does not subscribe to Mach's phenomenalism and, in keeping with his concept of intentionality, maintains a distinction between the appearances of a natural object and the natural object itself.

[83] *Ibid.*, 54.

once we abstract from all predicates of significance and from all subjective appearances. We can then say that there is something like a zero step (0) in the history of natural science, a preliminary abstraction that precedes in principle the abstraction of geometry (1) focusing on pure shapes. This is the abstraction of pure nature as such from the totality of the culturally formed world in which we live. Such abstract nature is not yet the mathematized nature of modern natural science, but it is the domain of being in which modern natural science carries out its intentional shifts of meaning. It is indeed with Galileo and his successors that the abstraction of pure nature as the thematic totality for natural-scientific inquiry is explicitly thematized and achieved. However, we must make an effort to see the conceptual separability of this step (0) from all subsequent theoretical operations (1–5.2). While mathematized nature is a cultural production through and through, intuitive nature is transcendentally presupposed in all conceivable cultural productions, including modern natural science. Mathematized nature, however, is legitimately 'drawn out' of intuitive nature and it is, so to speak, a cultural product *cum fundamentum in re*. For Husserl, to mathematize nature is not an arbitrary activity, which Westerners just happened to engage in. To mathematize nature is to follow a path of inquiry suggested by the things themselves, to the extent that they display isolable quantitative features and recurring causal patterns in their interaction. What is problematic in Husserl's eyes is that the original mathematizing operations were forgotten as the methods of natural science grew increasingly familiar to new generations of apprentices. Thus, as we saw, mathematical constructions supplanted the actual beings encountered in our everyday life, *not only in their dimensions of significance and subjective outlook but also in their purely natural-intuitive core*. To put it differently, Husserl does not merely counterpose the mathematized world of natural science and the world of significant objects in our everyday life. He counterposes the meaningful objects encountered in the culturally formed human world and the meaning-free stratum of nature that inheres in these objects, as we saw in Chapter 5. In a further step, he contrasts intuitive nature qua abstract, albeit fully intuitive, layer in the human world and mathematized nature as a cultural product drawn out of intuitive nature via a number of intentional shifts that we attempted to trace in his masterpiece *Crisis*.

This point is so important that it occupies almost exclusively Husserl's work in his manuscripts surrounding *Crisis*. In an illuminating text from the early 1930s Husserl makes the following remarks concerning the status of nature as an abstract dimension in the totality of the experienced life-world:

The totality of what is [*Allheit des Seienden*] qua world has as its underlying ground [*Untergrund*] the existing nature [*seiende Natur*]. But this must not be misunderstood. As if nature were constituted as a valid universe for itself; as if, so to speak, we humans only occasionally had the idea of doing something with natural objects, to give natural matter a form according to our goals. We humans, as humans, are subjects who act according to goals, we always already have goals and in all our acts we pursue, achieve, expand, etc., certain goals. *Nature is an abstraction*, and all experiencing activity restricted to nature (explication, etc.) is precisely a restriction in the service and for the sake of human striving, of goal-directed striving. The world with all its already completed purposive products [*Zweckgestalten*] is always already a field for goal-directed activities, for goals to be conceived and attained in view of the future horizon.[84]

In another manuscript from the same group, he specifies how we should think about nature as the abstract core (*Kern*) underpinning concrete life-worldly being. His remarks fit nicely with the discussions in Chapter 5 of this book concerning the criteria for demarcation of different scientific fields:

The abstraction of a '*nature*' is possible in the same way in which the abstraction of geometrical space is possible (although obviously the latter kind of abstraction is subordinate to the first kind of abstraction). This abstraction delimits a self-contained structural a priori by way of creating in what is possibly factual [*im möglichen Faktum*] the ground for a self-contained science in complete independence from the a priori belonging to the concrete world with its dimensions of significance and to the rest of the world in general, including the abstractly excluded sphere of personal subjectivity. Obviously, independence is meant here in the sense of abstraction. On the contrary, when we pursue the a priori of the concrete world of experience, we are not dealing with a structure of this kind to be considered independently.[85]

Husserl's suggestion of an analogy with geometry is extremely helpful. In the same way in which, say, plane geometry deals with a delimited sphere of spatial phenomena by way of excluding from its theoretical

---

[84] Hua XXXIX, 326–327.   [85] *Ibid.*, 264.

purview other aspects of space, such as the third dimension, nature becomes a delimited sphere for inquiry to the extent that it is abstractly isolated from the fully concrete a priori of the world of experience.[86] This perspective allows Husserl to call into question the rationale behind carrying out the abstractive operations that establish nature as a self-enclosed domain of being and to ask about the authentic aims, both epistemic and practical, underpinning the project of modern natural science.

To conclude this section, it is worth noticing that the distinction between the intuitive nature underpinning the life-world and the mathematized nature created by modern natural science sets Husserl apart from his Neo-Kantian associates. Although, as we saw above, they all agreed that 'nature' is not an absolute being but a product of the synthetic-categorial activity of the subject, none of them recognized a different, autonomous meaning to *intuitive* nature. For the Neo-Kantians (with the exception of Lask), 'nature' and 'the subject matter of modern natural science' are synonymous. Dualism between nature and culture, in Rickert's sense, was therefore inevitable. Considering just Rickert's account of it, the Kantian Copernican deed may have freed the West from naturalism, but it left Westerners wondering how the idealized world described by natural science could possibly be *the same* world in which they live their historical and purposeful lives. Being assured that both nature and culture somehow have their origin in our categorial capacities is certainly not enough explanation. One chief merit in Husserl's distinction is to clarify the ambiguity inherent in the concept of nature after the advent of modern natural science and, thus, prepare the terrain for a renewed understanding of human subjectivity as the agent responsible for the natural-scientific endeavor.

In the next and final chapter I will address the salient features of a worldview inspired by Husserl's transcendental phenomenology of the life-world as he envisions it in his manuscripts. This worldview's proximity to the Kantian liberation narrative will become increasingly manifest, though some further points of divergence will surface, too.

---

[86] For a discussion of plane geometry as an abstract discipline see Chapter 5.

8 | Ethical and cultural implications in Husserl's phenomenology of the life-world

> Perhaps it will even become manifest that the total phenomenological attitude and the *epoché* belonging to it are destined in essence to effect, at first, a complete personal transformation, comparable in the beginning to a religious conversion, which then, however, over and above this, bears within itself the significance of the greatest existential transformation which is assigned as a task to mankind as such.
>
> Edmund Husserl[1]

After reconstructing the *Natur* versus *Geist* debate and exploring Husserl's contribution to it, we saw that his late notion of life-world engages some of the deepest philosophical preoccupations of his time. In particular, we highlighted that the life-world is the ground of both nature and culture, and that this insight bears important consequences pertaining to the problem of worldview as defined in Chapter 7. By way of conclusion, it is now time to articulate the general outlook of the phenomenological worldview yielded by the scientific investigation of the life-world within the phenomenological attitude. The perspective hereby assumed is worth reiterating: my argument is neither that the life-world somehow *is* a worldview, nor that Husserl's late phenomenology is all about worldview, but, rather, that a phenomenological investigation of the life-world *yields* a worldview, namely, a phenomenological worldview, which Husserl hoped would replace naturalism and positivism.

The opening quote above is a very appropriate place to begin. It is arguably one of the most famous passages in *Crisis*, and it is often produced as evidence of Husserl's allegedly newfound existential pathos in the last years of his life. However, the language of personal transformation and religious conversion (*Umkehr*) has never been

---

[1] *Crisis*, 137.

taken as seriously as it should. What exactly is a religious conversion? And what kind of personal transformation does it bring about? And, finally, what does this have to do with philosophical technicalities such as the *epoché* and the phenomenological attitude?

Let us remember that Husserl had the experience of a religious conversion earlier in his life. He converted to Christianity from Judaism under the influence of Masaryk in Vienna.[2] Although Husserl does not seem to have ever been a particularly fervent religious spirit, the conversion to Christianity had a profound impact on his personal life,[3] such that it would be unfair to characterize his later decision to be baptized as a matter of mere social convenience.[4] It is therefore likely that the paradigm for his understanding of 'religious conversion' is precisely his own conversion experience, that is, a specifically Christian conversion experience.

An excursus into the psychological and existential intricacies of Christian conversion would be out of place in the present context. However, one central aspect deserves to be mentioned as a guiding thread for looking at Husserl's understanding of the phenomenological attitude as a religious conversion. Famously, the Greek word for conversion in early Christianity is *metanoia* (from the verb μετανοεῖν). We can find it, for example, in St. Paul's epistle to the Romans (12:2) where he exhorts the community, saying: "Do not be conformed to this world, but be transformed by the renewal of your mind (*meta-noeite*)." Christian conversion in St. Paul's account is thus primarily a renewal of mind or a change of conception that transforms the convert by way of introducing an anti-conformist perspective on the world. The convert does not merely add one more belief (notably, the belief in the divinity of Christ) to the list of the beliefs she already held. Rather, the convert looks at the exact same things of previous acquaintance in a new way, one that is thoroughly informed by the novel religious

---

[2] K. Schuhmann, *Husserl-Chronik: Denk- und Lebensweg Edmund Husserls*, *Husserliana Dokumente*, vol. 1 (The Hague: Nijhoff, 1977), 10.

[3] See *ibid.*, Husserl's description to Metzger: "The powerful impact of the New Testament on the twenty-three-year-old developed into an impulse to find the way to God and to an authentic life through a rigorous philosophical science."

[4] At that time Husserl was still connected with the University of Berlin, where he had worked with the famous mathematician Weierstraß. However, he received his baptism in a Lutheran church in Catholic Vienna, where he was hearing Brentano's lectures on psychology. *Ibid.*, 15.

perspective.[5] I would like to suggest that this is largely the same structure of personal transformation Husserl has in mind with respect to the phenomenological attitude. By way of unearthing the transcendental dimension inherent in human subjectivity and revealing the ongoing dynamic of transcendental world-constitution, the phenomenological attitude transforms our way of thinking about ourselves as subjects in the world. In the phenomenological attitude, we are still seeing the same things and living through the same experiences, but we do so with a new sense of self dignified by the discovery of the non-reducible transcendental dimension of subjectivity.

The analogy between the switch to the phenomenological attitude and the logic of Christian conversion can be spelled out in one further direction. The change of mind that defines Christian *metanoia* is not a sudden insight or the merely intellectual adherence to a set of beliefs. Rather, *metanoia* matures within a new kind of praxis, including the exposure to the life of the Christian community, the attendance to religious services, and the involvement in charitable activities. Religious praxis thus precedes and founds religious conversion. It is religious praxis that throws a new set of values into relief, thus preparing the terrain for the actual conversion to such newly visualized values. Moreover, after the conversion it is the perseverance in this kind of praxis that aliments and preserves faith. Similarly, I contend, the kind of *theoretical praxis* that Husserl carries out in his manuscripts and lectures precedes and grounds the full embrace of the phenomenological perspective. It is only by way of constantly revisiting certain lines of thought leading up to phenomenology, and by way of continuing to *do* phenomenology, that the self-transformation Husserl envisioned for individuals and for humankind at large becomes a practical possibility.

In the two sections of this final chapter I want to explore the transformative power of phenomenology and, in particular, of the phenomenological analysis of the life-world both at the individual and at the intersubjective levels. This will involve commenting on a number of crucial notions of Husserl's late phenomenology, including the controversial concepts of teleology and cultural universalism.

---

[5] A *locus classicus* for a phenomenological description of Christian conversion is Martin Heidegger's early lectures on the phenomenology of religion in 1919. M. Heidegger, *The Phenomenology of Religious Life* (Bloomington: Indiana University Press, 2004).

The ethical impact and the transformative power of Husserl's life-world analyses

Husserl's manuscripts on the life-world offer a remarkable reading experience. They have an almost mesmerizing effect on the reader, who is exposed to phenomenology's being first and foremost a kind of practice that involves a demanding training of the apprentice's eye. In them, we see Husserl often reiterating the same lines of analysis time and again, starting off with what might seem a delimited issue and then progressively expanding his focus to encompass the total horizon in which the initial issue is embedded. These manuscripts are an exercise in what is perhaps the most difficult of all philosophical tasks: learning to *visualize* the world as a whole, before jumping to theorize about it.

Visualizing the world as a whole is for Husserl a transformative intellectual experience. (1) To the extent that the world as a whole is more than mere nature, it is an experience that enables one to relativize the meaning of nature and to integrate the investigation of nature into broader humanistic concerns. (2) To the extent that the world as a whole is what it is only as the total horizon of experiencing transcendental subjectivity,[6] learning to visualize the world as a whole implies learning to visualize subjectivity as a whole standing in its transcendental function. (3) Lastly, and this will be the theme of next section, to the extent that it makes us sensitive to dimensions of the world that lie beyond the limited horizons of what we are familiar with, learning to visualize the world as a whole bears important consequences for a universalistic view of humankind.

To begin with the first issue, the result of Husserl's analysis of nature squares with the understanding of nature characterizing one of the heroes in the Kantian liberation narrative: Fichte. In his popular writings from 1800 onwards, particularly in the last section of his acclaimed book *Die Bestimmung des Menschen* (1800), Fichte worked to replace the mechanistic conception of nature articulated by French Enlightenment thinkers, with a novel view in which nature is nothing but *the raw material for human action*, which awaits to be molded according to our innermost goals and aspirations.[7] Leaving aside the

---

[6] As we mentioned above, in the phenomenological perspective, the world is a "title for actual and possible ego-acts" (Hua XXXIX, 4).

[7] It should be added that for Fichte (and for Husserl, too) such goals and aspirations are not entirely haphazard as one might be tempted to assume. Rather, they are dictated from a universal moral imperative, which issues its commands to all

specifics of Fichte's philosophy, which is notoriously quite complex, let us limit ourselves to mention that a large number of passages from Husserl's manuscripts promote a remarkably similar conception of nature as one of the key achievements of the phenomenological perspective. This passage follows in Husserl's text the considerations about the abstractness of pure nature expounded in the foregoing chapter, and it illustrates his conception adamantly:

What connects humans is the world of validity [*Geltungswelt*] common to them all. In this world of validity the nature common to all humans [*allmens-chlich*] – if we think of the world as already constituted in a unitary fashion – is the essential core that essentially undergirds all layers of the common world. The existing world is the general ground of human existence [*Dasein*], or, better, it is the perpetual horizonal universe of materials, on which we humans purposefully act and shall act in the future. *The world that already is [die schon seiende Welt] is the universal matter for the world that ought to be and shall be according to this ought [die seinsollende und sollensmäßig sein werdende Welt].* It is the universe of that with which we shape the new [. . .] The existing world <is> material for the world that shall be in the future; a world that ought to be and that is up to us to bring about.[8]

Husserl seems to believe that assuming a panoramic perspective on the human world with the aid of the phenomenological method almost automatically 'activates' certain ethical imperatives, whose compelling force the phenomenologist is bound to perceive. For Husserl, awakening to the infinity of the life-world in which all our human activity, including natural-scientific theorizing, unfolds means awakening to the infinity of the values that animate our actions. In his *The Vocation of Man*, Fichte expressed metaphorically the same conviction:

humans and is ultimately rooted in the divine will. It is worth mentioning that Husserl gave *Übungen* on *Die Bestimmung des Menschen* and other Fichtean popular works, and in 1917 he offered a series of lectures on Fichte's ideal of mankind to the soldiers returning from the front. These lectures are available in Hua XXV, 267–293 and have been translated into English as Husserl, "Fichte's Ideal of Humanity [Three Lectures],' trans. J. Hart, *Husserl Studies* 12 (1995): 111–133. For an extensive discussion of their philosophical significance see J. Hart, "Husserl and Fichte: With Special Regard to Husserl's Lectures on 'Fichte's Ideal of Humanity'," *Husserl Studies* 12 (1995): 135–163 and my "Fenomenologia dell'ideale. Husserl lettore di Fichte nelle Lezioni del 1917," *Annuario Filosofico* 22 (2006): 401–421. For references to Husserl's *Übungen* on Fichte see K. Schuhmann, *Husserl-Chronik: Denk- und Lebensweg Edmund Husserls, Husserliana Dokumente*, vol. 1 (The Hague: Nijhoff, 1977), 75.
[8] Hua XXXIX, 327–8.

I cast a glance on the present relations of men towards each other and towards Nature, on the feebleness of their powers, the strength of their desires and passions. A voice within me proclaims with irresistible conviction – "It is impossible that it can remain thus; it must become different and better."[9]

In a kindred spirit, Husserl writes that "our acting life [*Aktleben*]" should be understood "as directed towards the pre-given world, in order to shape it purposefully and turn it into a world infused with value [*wertvoll*]."[10] He continues this line of thought explaining that "living in the world amounts to living towards a world infused with value, while the already existing world is always partly valuable, partly bereft of value, and partly valueless (indifferent)."[11]

These thoughts might strike a contemporary reader as naive at best and as seriously deficient at worst. How could Husserl really believe that an armchair survey of the world as a whole would suffice to awaken ethical responsibility and even provide grounding for the values that should guide humanity towards its constitutive *telos*? In precisely the same span of years, would not a survey of the world as a whole rather evoke ominous visions of revenge and total domination in the nationalistic majority of Husserl's fellow countrymen? Moreover, what are these values Husserl constantly refers to? Is he thinking of a more or less complete list of definite values? Does he have a convincing argument about their universality?

Admittedly, Husserl's project of ethical regeneration for Europe based purely on the phenomenological contemplation of the life-world and its a priori constituents raises a number of questions. However, similar questions could be raised with regard to any *purely philosophical* attempt to promote actual ethical renewal, and they would possibly touch on the intrinsic limits of philosophy when it comes to a substantial *motivation* (as opposed to mere descriptive elucidation) of human ethical behavior. In this regard, Husserl's aspirations are perhaps no more and no less naive than those of any other great philosopher in history who struggled with the same issues. In addition, the fact that Husserl's talk of universally human values remains vague is regrettable. One reason for this vagueness might be that in the Neo-Kantian context of his time reference to values was common currency in philosophy.

---

[9] J. G. Fichte, *The Vocation of Man*, translated by W. Smith (Chicago, IL: Open Court, 1906), 113.
[10] Hua XXXIX, 314.   [11] *Ibid.*, 315.

Husserl may not have felt obliged to spell out in detail the values putatively common to all humans, given the overall agreement among professional philosophers that such values were in fact given. Furthermore, we should remember that Husserl's approach to these issues is descriptive, that is, he is not engaging in an imaginary argument with the moral nihilist who denies that there are universal values or with the post-structuralist genealogist who believes that what we call 'values' only express relations of power, and the like. Those who seek arguments for these positions, pro or against, will most likely be disappointed by what Husserl has to offer. A different, more productive attitude regarding Husserl's work on these issues is recommended. I suggest that we should approach Husserl's descriptions in the following spirit: it is hardly deniable that we do have *experiences* of value in our everyday life, that regardless of the concrete responses to values for different human groups and individuals we do consider certain values to be *experienced* in fundamentally the same way by all humans (for instance, we seem to be able to recognize broadly virtuous behavior across cultural differences),[12] and that sufficiently reflective people do experience a disproportion between the world as it is and the world as it ought to be. Husserl's work is oriented to provide good descriptions of these experiences and not to provide answers to moral skeptics. Good descriptions should, in turn, increase our awareness and put us in a position to pursue willingly what, in Husserl's eyes, we had already been pursuing all along, albeit confusedly.

This being said, Husserl was certainly not naive enough to believe that turning one's phenomenological regard towards the life-world's infinity would *automatically* bring to light a definite and discrete set of values fit for the ethical orientation of humankind. Instead, what he firmly believes phenomenology *does* automatically bring about for its human practitioners is a novel self-understanding based on the transcendental interpretation of their subjectivity. Recall that this, for

---

[12] In a manuscript Husserl comments: "Some human virtues of friendship, loyalty, justice, and so forth, stand out from the particular form that they received through particular habits and prove to be a human kernel that may be found in very different nations as a universally human (*allgemeinmenschlich*) character of all 'civilized' populations." E. Husserl, *Die Krisis der europäischen Wissenschaften und die transzendentale Phänomenologie. Ergänzungsband: Text aus dem Nachlaß 1934–1937, Husserliana*, vol. 29 (Dordrecht: Kluwer, 1993), 42–43. Hereafter Hua XXIX.

Husserl, is not phenomenology's primary task (which is a purely theoretical elucidation of the a priori structures of any consciousness whatsoever), but, we could say, it is its most important side effect for the
world of human culture. Husserl insists repeatedly on the transformative power characterizing phenomenology, whose foremost
achievement is making one aware of one's transcendental status as a
world-constituting agent. If humans 'understand themselves transcendentally' (a phrase that recurs ubiquitously in Husserl's late work), they
are drawn out of the 'world-machinery' of mathematically interpreted
nature and become open to a novel understanding of their place in the
world:

> Through phenomenology, I reveal the transcendental sense of I, Us, and
> World. In so doing, I am not only open to my ultimate truth, but also, through
> this knowledge, I am at the same time individually other than the one I was
> before.[13]

This is another point where Husserl departs from the Neo-Kantian
version of the Kantian liberation narrative. In Rickert's interpretation,
Kant's critical philosophy affirms the centrality of a 'subject in general'
as the ideal carrier of the categories and the point of convergence of all
synthetic functions of the intellect, but at the same time it construes
human subjectivity as on a par with all further empirical being.
Husserl's phenomenological reduction does something more radical.
It transfers 'the transcendental' right to the heart of a human's experiencing life as a hidden (*verhüllt*), but at any time revealable (*enthüllbar*),
dimension that each of us can discover as our innermost self.[14]

Adequate understanding of the doctrine of transcendental world-
constitution, in turn, should find an echo in our practical self-
understanding. In light of this doctrine, the 'truth' about subjectivity is
not its appearance under the ruling apprehension of the naturalistic
attitude, according to which the psyche is just the accompanying phenomenon of certain physiological bodies.[15] Rather, revealing the

---

[13] Hua XXXIX, 215.
[14] See Hua XV, 389. Incidentally, Rickert understood this difference very well and
   attacked Husserl's conception of transcendental subjectivity on various
   occasions. See, for instance, MPU, 117 n. 3.
[15] Contemporary talk of the "psychic properties" of physical systems (first and
   foremost animal bodies) seems to be very much in line with the position Husserl
   intends to overcome.

transcendental-constitutive function of subjectivity through the *epoché* means revealing that subjectivity is through and through *operative*; it is an unceasing stream of operativeness in the two shapes of passive self-constitution and active object-constitution. This realization, in keeping with the Platonic-Aristotelian conviction that what acts is superior to or more noble than what is acted upon, opens up for the human being a scientifically grounded possibility to acknowledge one's and one's fellow humans' dignity over all empirical being, including every other human being's own body. Husserl adumbrates this view in a dense paragraph from a manuscript:

To the extent that the "transcendentally awakened" I, following the "guiding thread" of worldliness converted into a "transcendental phenomenon," reveals systematically his innermost transcendental being and that of transcendental subjectivity as a whole [...] [it] creates "productively" a new and endless horizon and a new kind of knowledge as self-knowledge of the transcendentally phenomenologizing I. This, however, entails also knowledge of the being of transcendental individuality in general in its infinite horizonality for itself, [horizonality] "produced" anew through a new "production." This horizonality is the infinity of evident transcendental interpretation, which the phenomenologizing I sets to work, thereby having the endless horizon of what is yet to be accomplished before its eyes. Generally, this horizon remains hidden for further transcendental subjects (except the phenomenologically awakened [ones]), that is, hidden through its worldliness.[16]

The *prima facie* obscure language used in this passage only partially overshadows the philosophical significance of the perspective Husserl is attempting to articulate. The 'transcendentally awakened' human subject is sensitive to other human subjects' transcendental dimension and to their impoverished self-understanding while they abide by the sphere of 'worldliness.' However, the world seen in its transcendental light reveals itself to be nothing but the arena in which humanity is called to wake up to its authentic status, and in so doing self-consciously pursue its path of enlightenment and "humanization."[17]

In spite of Husserl's paternalistic tone at times, it should be remarked that the worldview he articulates in these passages does not covertly entertain the wish for an impossible world in which all human beings would somehow become phenomenologists. Husserl would probably be happy to settle for less, that is, for a world in which the findings made

[16] Hua XV, 390.   [17] See *ibid.*, 391, 589; Hua XXXIX, 312.

possible by the phenomenological reduction were familiar to the general public and respected at least to the same degree that the findings of the natural sciences are respected in our contemporary world. Needless to say, one does not need to familiarize oneself with the intricacies of phenomenological inquiry in order to flourish as a human being. However, in Husserl's view, one does need to have some scientifically grounded sense of the transcendental meaning of her subjectivity in order not to succumb to the self-debasing influences of naively embraced naturalism. Flights into mysticism or religious enthusiasm will not do because Western civilization was born under the guiding star of Greek science. Therefore, educated Westerners will only be able to embrace wholeheartedly (that is, without being constantly tormented by the specter of doubt) doctrines and ideas that present themselves in a scientific guise.

That the dignity of subjectivity over all further being is the most important insight yielded by the phenomenological attitude and the reflection of the life-world is documented in numerous passages of Husserl's corpus where he talks about the *Seinsdignität*, or ontological dignity of subjectivity. Let me quote just two for the sake of exemplification:

The leading thought of idealism [. . .] <is> that subjectivity precedes objectivity in ontological dignity (*Seinsdignität*) and that all objectivity (all worldly being) is only being that flows from subjectivity's innermost passive and active sources. No ontology, if it is thought through consistently according to its eidetic correlations (*Wesenskorrelationen*), fails to lead to this insight as an apodictically evident one (not a metaphysical construction).[18]

   Reality, as much as ideality, has a subordinated ontological dignity (*untergeordnete Seinsdignität*). The preeminent ontological dignity (*übergeordnete Seinsdignität*) is that of subjectivity with *ego-cogito-cogitatum*.[19]

Interestingly, Husserl's conception of dignity is entirely coincident with Kant's, who, as Oliver Sensen recently proved, draws from the Ancient Roman tradition dating back to Cicero's *De Officiis* and conceives of dignity as a relational ontological property and not as an absolute, non-relational value inherent in human beings. As Sensen puts it: "Kant conceives of dignity as sublimity (*Erhabenheit*) or the elevation of something over something else. Ontologically 'dignity' refers to a

---

[18] Hua VIII, 215.   [19] Hua XIV, 257.

relational property of being elevated, not to a non-relational value property. 'X has dignity' is another expression for 'X is elevated over Y' or 'X is higher than Y'."[20] In particular, for Kant, "human beings are distinguished from the rest of nature by having capacities (e.g. reason, freedom) that put human beings at a distance from immediate natural determination."[21] However, note that, unlike Kant, for Husserl the dignity of human beings does not rest merely on their rationality and freedom as two characteristics to be isolated from a natural psychic basis common to both humans and animals, but rather on human subjectivity taken as a whole, i.e., including the 'passive sources' mentioned above. It is subjectivity as a whole (including de-naturalized sensibility, instincts, drives, habits, inclinations, and passive comportment) that carries out transcendental world-constitution. Rationality and freedom (or, better, rationality, viz. freedom) are indeed the two highest dimensions of subjectivity but their native soil is in sensibility and instinct and these 'lower' dimensions partake of subjectivity's ontological dignity over nature, too.[22]

---

[20] O. Sensen, "Kant on Human Dignity," *Kant-Studien* 100 (2009): 309–331. Here 310.

[21] *Ibid.*, 313.

[22] My gratitude to an anonymous referee for insisting on the necessity to address this issue, which (contrary to what the referee suggested) marks a significant difference between Husserl and Kant. Incidentally, Husserl's insistence on the dignity of *subjectivity as a whole*, and not just rationality, does include non human animals, who are, as much as humans, transcendental subjects. Husserl speaks explicitly of animals as "transcendental animal subjects (*transzendentale Tiersubjekte*)" (Hua XXIX, 87) and insists that animals are "no machines, but, rather, personal beings (*personal seiende Wesen*)" (Hua XV, 61). Moreover, we "do not experience animals as completely foreign living beings [. . .] The animals of one species have their characteristic being-there-for-one-another and with-one-another, they have their characteristic generative nexus, which (from an internal point of view) for them means an inner unity among themselves. They stand in relationships of empathy, they understand one another according to their species, they are familiar and unfamiliar to one another on the basis of instinct and experience – this is how we understand them, we experience them, at least in case they are animals belonging to 'higher' species" (Hua XV, 622–623). Whether this legitimately sets the basis for a phenomenological foundation of animal rights, as, for instance, Ullrich Melle has argued in recent talks, is an issue I cannot and do not intend to adjudicate in this book. However, as far as we know, it seems that (for entirely empirical reasons) only humans are capable of *realizing* their dignity, and that of animal subjects, with the aid of philosophy and phenomenology.

The next and concluding section is devoted to shedding further light on Husserl's concept of humankind and his endeavors to render this concept intuitive. In this context we shall also attempt to clarify the sense in which he talks about a teleology in history.

Husserl's cultural universalism

The concept of humanity plays a pivotal role in the tradition of transcendental philosophy. Famously, in Kant's ethical and historical works, references to humankind have a key normative function. In his practical philosophy, humankind is the ultimate standard by which we are supposed to evaluate the moral worth of our actions. It is also the object deserving our utmost respect, to the point that the respect we owe to individual rational beings rests entirely on the respect we owe to humankind at large. This is especially clear in the most quoted formulation of the categorical imperative in *Grounding for the Metaphysics of Morals*: "So act that you use *humanity*, whether in your own person or in the person of any another, always at the same time as an end, never merely as a means."[23] In Kant's philosophy of history, humankind as a whole is presented as the true subject of reason, that is, as the entity which alone can bring to full realization the demands of rationality, granted that these demands only find imperfect fulfillment in the lives of individuals.

The advent of Romanticism in post-Kantian Europe and its emphasis on national communities marked an important shift from Kant's original conception; however, rather than a wholesale rejection of 'humanity,' this shift can be interpreted as an attempt to recast this notion in a historically and geographically qualified sense. It could be further argued that a materialistically modified version of Kant's notion of humanity eventually resurged in the philosophy of Marx. A few decades after Marx, the German Neo-Kantians did not have a unified model of humanity, but they variously subscribed to available versions of this idea. Some thinkers such as Cohen and Natorp cherished a social-democratic understanding of humanity, whereas the seeds of nationalism could be seen in the work of other figures, such as the representative of the Southwestern school Bruno Bauch.

---

[23] I. Kant, *Groundwork of the Metaphysics of Morals* (Cambridge University Press: Cambridge, 1997), 38 (Ak. 429). My italics.

Husserl, who was by his own admission an apolitical thinker,[24] did nonetheless produce a number of manuscripts devoted to politically sensitive issues such as cultural differences and intercultural understanding. Husserl's unstated goal in these manuscripts can be formulated in a way that befits his broader philosophical commitments: rendering the idea of humankind intuitive. While in Kant and his Neo-Kantian followers the notion of 'humankind' is a theoretical construction that underlies certain argumentative strategies in practical philosophy,[25] Husserl works strenuously to clarify how this notion can be formed concretely starting from the finite and restricted perspective of culturally embedded historical individuals. Visualizing humankind as a whole, in Husserl's view, should prepare the terrain to see its teleology, that is, the inner tendency inherent in humankind's historical path. It is worth mentioning in advance that when Husserl talks about teleology in history he means *goal-orientedness*. His belief about humankind being oriented towards a goal does not entail any claim about the actual attainment of this goal. Husserl does not believe that humanity has a set 'destiny' of some sort and that it is inevitably marching towards that destiny, regardless of the actual decisions and inclinations of individual human beings. The teleology of humankind Husserl envisages is consistent with potential deviation from humankind's presumptive goal, and in this sense it is very distant form Hegelian and Marxist claims about a set direction in human history, be it towards freedom in an ethical state or towards a classless society, respectively.

Husserlian teleology should be understood along the lines of Aristotle's claim that all human beings seek happiness as their ultimate goal. This does not rule out the possibility that they make themselves and others very unhappy in the attempt. It is thus entirely possible that they end up even moving away from what nonetheless remains their teleological end. For Husserl, history at large displays the same tendency that characterizes individuals. This is a tendency towards the creation of enduring conditions for a harmonious and meaningful existence, conditions that can only be achieved with the aid of rational, self-critical deliberation. Societies should then be seen as moving

---

[24] See letter to Metzger, in E. Husserl, *Briefwechsel*, vol. 4, *Die Freiburger Schüler* (Dordrecht: Kluwer, 1994), 407–414. English translation by E. Kohák in E. Husserl, *Shorter Works*, 360–364.

[25] To reiterate the language of Chapter 3: it is a constitutive concept of the ethical standpoint.

teleologically (in the above sense) towards the establishment of life-conditions that befit and promote rational deliberation and self-critique.

In this sense, what makes Western civilization particularly significant is that in Husserl's view it is the only civilization whose very birth occurred under the auspices of philosophy, that is to say, of the discipline specifically devoted to rational deliberation and self-critique.[26] However, the fact that an individual explicitly sets for himself the goal of being rational and self-reflective does not assure anything about whether he will live up to his good intentions. Likewise, the fact that a civilization was born out of the ideals of philosophy does not at all imply that such civilization is morally or intellectually superior to other civilizations, and Husserl never seems to suggest that. However, if we accept that rational deliberation and self-critique for the enactment of a harmonious, meaningful life are essential traits of all humans, then the fact that one specific civilization made these traits explicit and even shaped itself around them in the first place is definitely a historically relevant fact, one that is bound to have an impact on every civilization that encounters the West.

Husserl's manuscripts dealing with the notion of humanity almost always begin with a description of one's so-called home-world (*Heimwelt*). This is because all human beings necessarily begin their life in some type of home-like environment: "The lowest stage is man in his home in the narrowest sense, no matter how primitive or 'cultivated'

---

[26] Of course, whether philosophy was the only or even the predominant factor for the birth of Western culture is up for debate and should be adjudicated historically. Husserl does not have the slightest hesitation that this is the case. This whole point ultimately depends on how broad a notion of philosophy one is willing to adopt. If we consider, say, Buddhism or Confucianism to be philosophies, then Husserl's particular interest for the West becomes unwarranted. If we want Husserl's perspective to remain more coherent, it would be advisable to adopt a narrower concept of philosophy, one that considers the use of logical and conceptual methods and the orientation towards universal truth, the *sine qua non* in order for a discipline to be legitimately called 'philosophy.' After all, it is not at all obvious that 'philosophy' must be considered a sort of honorific title, and that resisting to call sophisticated and deep forms of human wisdom such as Confucianism or Buddhism 'philosophy' necessarily amounts to demoting them in some way. Perhaps it is more lamentably Eurocentric to believe that we are somehow ennobling Eastern thought by calling it 'philosophy,' than to concede that the designation 'philosophy' indicates a specifically Western tradition of thought. This, however, would be the theme for another book.

a man is."[27] The decisive elements in order for an environment to be characterized as home are essentially two: proximity and normality. If we look at normality from the point of view of its habituation over time, we can then talk about 'familiarity' as the habituated normality in a context of proximity.

Talk of proximity in the home-world does not exclusively refer to perceptual proximity but, more broadly, to practical proximity, that is, to all things and people that are within one's practical reach – things to be acted upon and people to interact with. Practically proximate things and people, in turn, have a definite style; they behave in ways that the subject of a home-world has learned to anticipate from early childhood. This defines a sphere of normality. In this sphere life unfolds in an overall undisturbed fashion, which, as Husserl puts it, is

[t]he type of a coherent and entirely normal life, of a life that possesses constantly its normal practical horizon, a practical field, a field of 'predict-ability,' of practical possibility with foreseeable consequences, characterized by the awareness of 'being able to.'[28]

The horizon of practical proximity, or near-world (*Nahwelt*), is essentially surrounded by a far-world (*Fernwelt*).[29] For the person living in the home-worldly attitude, the inaccessible far-world surrounding the near-world is apprehended as a mere *continuation* of the near-world, as a world characterized by the same *style* as the near-world. In this sense, the home-world does not coincide with the near-world, as one might be tempted to think. The home-world includes distance (both perceptual and practical), but this distance is anticipated as being simply a contin-uation of proximity.

Proximity in the home-world is organized in a way that could be construed metaphorically in terms of concentric spheres: household, family, friends, village, county, region, homeland. Each of these spheres has its typicalities, that is, its normal style, which includes occasional anomalies. These anomalies, however, are *normal* anomalies, that is, anomalies that have themselves a familiar style and familiar ways of being overcome. The sudden death of a family member is an anom-alous event in the normal unfolding of a family's life, at least in most developed countries. However, there are typical ways in which other family members will face this event and cope with it according to

[27] Hua XXXIX, 153.   [28] Hua XV, 210.   [29] See Hua XXXIX, 329; 175–176.

established practices of grief. Over time, the normal unfolding of family life will be restored; alternatively, new scenarios may open up (the family might break apart, etc.) and become, in turn, familiar over time.

In the alternation of undisturbed normality with the occasional presentation of familiar anomalies, home-worlds offer to individual human beings the first environment for cultural maturation. This is where the individual learns what it means to be part of various groupings consisting of other individuals. Husserl stresses repeatedly that to be human is essentially to be part of some human grouping, and living in a home-world allows individuals to progressively understand themselves as members of a number of interconnected groups, from the original nucleus of their household all the way up to their *nation*. Forming the idea of nation means reaching the widest horizon of social awareness achievable in the context of one's home-world prior to all contact with foreign home-worlds.

The description of home-worlds up to this point was conducted according to a kind of methodological restriction similar to the one employed for the description of pure nature in Chapter 5. As a matter of fact, home-worlds do not exist in complete isolation. Living in a home-world always already entails being in some way aware that there are *foreign-worlds* (*Fremdwelten*) and that these worlds count as home-worlds for other groups of people. In an abstractly impoverished description of home-worlds, however, foreign home-worlds are indistinguishable from what we previously called the 'far-world,' that is, the empty horizon of practical inaccessibility implicitly anticipated to be a mere continuation of the near-world of practical proximity. This abstractive impoverishment is helpful in realizing what happens when a *concrete encounter* with a foreign home-world occurs. The foreign world comes into relief from the empty space of the far-world and gains its distinctive contours. Thereby, a fundamental modification for the members of both worlds begins:

I and we learn to recognize foreigners as subjects of a foreign world, which they experience coherently from within the life of their community. In correlation with this world, as the practical life-world and as world in general that is valid for them, they are people of different experiences, with a different natural environment, different life-goals, and all kinds of different convictions, different habits, different practical behavior, different traditions. Recognizing that there are other home-worldly communities [*Heimgenossenschaft*], who live and behave differently, who understand "the" world differently, who have *de facto* a different cultural world valid for them and not for us, my own world expands for me (and for my own home-worldly community).[30]

The concrete encounter with a foreign community transforms the individual's notion of home-world from a *singulare tantum* into a *plurale tantum*. There is no such thing as *the* home-world surrounded by a horizon of foreignness; there are only home-worlds, in the plural, which amount to ways in which the one world, common to us all, is apprehended according to historically contingent traditions. Herein lies the first specific element of transformation brought about by the encounter with a foreign cultural world: *the* one world comes into relief as different from just *our* world, that is, what counts as world within the restricted sphere of validity of a singular human community. This gives to the home-worldly community both a new horizon of meaning to be explored (the common world, which remained previously unseen) and full awareness of what they now recognize to be *their* world as opposed to another people's world. Husserl continues his description:

A foreign human group [*Menschentum*] constitutes itself, a foreign humanity [*Menschheit*], as a foreign people, for example. Precisely this constitutes for me and for us "our own" home-worldly community, the community of our people in relation to our cultural surrounding world as the world of our human validities, those specific to us. Therefore I have [. . .] a modification of my and our experience of the world and of the world itself. We, my people and the other people, are in "the" world, and each of us has a surrounding world characteristic of their people (with its unpractical horizon). 'Surrounding world' separates from 'world.'[31]

The split of surrounding world and 'the' world in Husserl's description clarifies the origin of both nationalism and the possibility of a universal human culture. Once 'we' realize that our home world is just one among many, a set of new questions regarding our national validities and practices arises. Which ones capture aspects of 'the' world as such, and are thus shareable with other people? Which ones are just idiosyn-cratic ways of looking at the world that do not come to friction with what is 'actually' the case for everyone? These questions can be per-ceived as threatening and instigate zealous resistance. This is where nationalism begins. On the other hand, even the extreme case of

[30] Hua XV, 214.   [31] *Ibid.*

nationalism testifies to a transformation that is already underway, that is, a home-world encountering a different home-world must necessarily revise its self-understanding in some relation to the foreign home-world, no matter how hostile this relation may be. No room is left for the *singulare tantum* of an isolated home-world. In this context, Husserl talks about a transformation in the home-worlds' respective histories. Both home-worlds transition from a merely national history to a genuinely political history:

The life of a nation in a unitary internationality results in a development to a historicity of a new kind: the political. Political historicity now pertains to this nation and to all nations living in international co-existence. Each nation has its own historicity, originally grown in the context of its generational lineage. By entering in a life-connection with a second nation and its national historicity, it initiates a process of transformation of national historicity into political historicity. This causes a certain unification of the different political historicities in a higher-level historicity.[32]

Although the encounter with a foreign world is a radically new event and a turning point in the history of a hitherto isolated home-world, Husserl indicates that if the members of an isolated home-world can understand a foreign world as foreign and eventually move to appropriate some of that world's validity, this is essentially because the foreignness of the foreign worlds is ultimately not so radical as one might be inclined to think. First, people of a foreign world are from the very start understood as human beings, that is, as subjects having the same basic human "needs"[33] and living in a world that, like one's home-world, was shaped over the course of generations in order to meet those needs. Second, experiences of foreignness and the necessity of interpretive efforts to cope with foreignness already occur within the sphere of one's home-world. Husserl mentions differences in social classes, for instance, the difference between growing up in a middle-class family as opposed to growing up in an aristocratic family.[34] The middle-class type perceives the world of the aristocrat as foreign and incomprehensible. A good deal of interpretive effort and, ideally, of actual living in the world of aristocracy would be required in order for the middle-class person to become familiar with the world of aristocracy and, so to speak, to incorporate it in what counts as *her own* home-world.

---

[32] Hua XXIX, 10.   [33] Hua XXXIX, 312.   [34] *Ibid.*, 161.

Similarly, we can progressively appropriate a completely foreign cultural world and, in so doing, form an actual cultural unity with our own
home-world. Husserl uses the example of China to illustrate this point:

Understanding a Chinese person presupposes understanding one's home-
world in the present, and it presupposes life in a circle of familiar people in
one's home-world. In the same way in which as a child I was educated into my
generative human world, if I want to understand the Chinese person and the
Chinese world, I have to be educated <into it>. By way of actively living into
[*hineinleben*] the foreign world, I have to acquire its characteristic apperception, in whichever way and as much as this is possible. This would amount to
becoming more and more a Chinese person among Chinese – while remaining
German and not losing my German surrounding world. The same goes for the
Chinese in my own world. I should get to the point of appropriating the
concrete Chinese life-world [*Lebensumwelt*], including the living past entailed
in it. Subsequently, I would have to appropriate also the living horizon of
the future, which, in its streaming, also belongs in the Chinese world. This
would then become the foundation to enable the reconstruction of "historical" traditions and the construction of an understandable Chinese history –
fully understandable from the Chinese point of view. Obviously, this is not
entirely possible; however, it is not possible in the same way in which it is not
entirely possible for me to appropriate in its full concreteness the type of the
Junker, etc.[35]

The fact of possible mutual understanding can only be explained
because "through all incomprehensibilities runs the unity of a traditionality – a unity of the surrounding world with its typical structure, which
is partly familiar and partly still in the making via appropriation."[36]
The line of traditionality running through, say, the home-world of the
German middle-class and the German aristocracy in Husserl's time was
definitely richer and more conspicuous than the very thin line of traditionality running through the German and the Chinese home-worlds
considered in their entirety. At a minimum, the level of traditionality
shared by two separate home-worlds can be limited to the mutual
recognition of belonging to the human race and being involved, perceptually and practically, with the same environing things. This, however,

[35] *Ibid.*, 162–163. It would be interesting to know whether Husserl was thinking
here of Matteo Ricci, S. J. (1552–1610) and his famous journey to China. The
idea of becoming Chinese among the Chinese can be found in his correspondence
and journals.
[36] *Ibid.*, 161.

would be the starting point for further interaction and for progressive increment of what henceforth will be a common traditionality.

For the sake of rendering the idea of humankind intuitive, we should imagine the encounter between two mutually foreign home-worlds iterated indefinitely. The contrast between 'the one world' and the *plurale tantum* of national home-worlds would grow increasingly sharper, while the wealth of validities appropriable for everyone would grow significantly. New lines of shared traditionalities would come into relief as variants of one and the same overarching traditionality common to all humans. Moreover, and most importantly, the conditions would be set for the appearance of an entirely new line of traditionality, that is, the traditionality of 'science' or 'philosophy' as the theoretical enterprise designed to investigate the newfound dimension of all things, 'the one world' common to all historical nations.[37]

From this point of view, it is possible to conclude this chapter by shedding some light on the basic idea inherent in Husserl's notion of a teleology intrinsic to humankind. In short, according to Husserl, humankind is moving teleologically to full awareness of inhabiting one and the same world ("the Earth"), and waking up to its practical and theoretical responsibility for this world and for its own position in it. It is moving towards a universally human world-culture. Husserl underscores that this movement only became conspicuous in recent times, thanks to groundbreaking developments in politics, science, and communication. The following passage, which is one of the few in Husserl's entire corpus where he refers to a specific time-venue in history, offers a particularly clear picture of the teleological movement he takes to be unfolding in human history:

Since roughly the second half of the nineteenth century, thanks to the organization of power in national states, humankind constitutes a maximally extended practical community, that is, a totality of ego-subjects for whom a real possibility of immediate or mediate reciprocal understanding and of practical social action is given. This is the case in a way that does not admit of the possibility of further expansion to include new subjects. In other words, human beings are now united through a communal practical surrounding world, that is, the earthly world (world in the sense of world-history). Such a

---

[37] Husserl underscores that philosophy is the only human cultural activity that "comes onto the scene bereft of all tradition, in order to create a tradition in the first place" (Hua VIII, 320).

maximal practical community constitutes a practical total community, a personal universe, a human world. Before the nineteenth century, multiple human worlds, multiple human total communities lived on Earth [. . .] and not just one.[38]

Different cultures began their historical trajectory in the restricted sphere of their isolated home-worlds. They eventually moved to encounter one another and to form international bonds. Following Husserl's suggestion, by the end of the nineteenth century, virtually no cultural home-world on the planet had remained stationary at the level of national historicity. All human nations encountered one another at some point and are now part of an all-encompassing total history. As we pointed out above, intercultural encounters necessarily ignite a revision of self-understanding for the members of a previously isolated home-world. Upon encountering a foreign world, its members come to realize that 'their' home-world is not "simply a piece of a 'true' world,"[39] of which every human groups just happens to possess a separate fragment. After the encounter, the inhabitants of each home-world experience it as a vantage point on *the* world, that same world that is accessible from other vantage points and that can be explicitly addressed as a theme for theoretical and practical consideration. Repeated intercultural encounters strengthen the awareness of the existence of one and the same world common to all humans and spawn attempts to articulate what should count as our common world in ways that can be shared by all humans regardless of their initial cultural provenance. From this point of view, the birth of Greek philosophy is an important step on the way towards the full unification of humankind. Philosophy, in Husserl's narrative, is nothing but the professionalization of hitherto extemporaneous attempts to articulate *the one* world common to all and is thus the discipline spearheading, at least ideally, humanity's journey towards its earthly *telos*.[40]

---

[38] Hua XIV, 215–216.   [39] Hua XXXIX, 203.

[40] Commenting on these issues in a recent paper, Dermot Moran has argued that "[p]hilosophy [. . .] allowed the Greeks to recognize their world-view as a local or national world-view (*Weltanschauung*)" and that this "leads the Greeks to make the crucial distinction between a 'world-representation' (*Weltvorstellung*) and the 'world in itself'." D. Moran, "Even the Papuan is a Man and Not a Beast: Husserl on Universalism and the Relativity of Cultures," *Journal of the History of Philosophy* 49/4 (2011): 463–494. Here 481. This characterization mistakes the effect (philosophy) for the cause (the separation of national home-world and the

These considerations on the teleological direction of history towards a planetary community square in substance with the picture of human history Kant offered in his rightly famous essay *Idea for a Universal History with Cosmopolitan Intent* (1784). However, there are a few aspects that distinguish Husserl's position from Kant's.

First, Kant's teleological view of history is based on the conviction that rationality cannot come to full fruition in the lives of individuals. The real locus where the innermost demands of reason can be possibly met must therefore be humankind at large in its historical progression. Contrariwise, for Husserl, the teleology inherent in human history is nothing but the large-scale continuation of a tendency towards a life in reason that manifests itself first and foremost in subjects considered singly. In the same way in which individual subjects seek to overcome the one-sidedness of their contingent perceptual position and continue to inspect the things in their surroundings until they reach an optimal grasp that harmonizes with the rest of their experience, subjects strive to achieve a harmonious and meaningful life as persons, at both the individual and the intersubjective levels. This requires the establishment of enduring convictions and dispositions that are not based merely on one's contingent cultural situation, but on rigorous self-examination and actively acquired self-understanding. Thus, it is not by transferring the possible realization of reason's demands from the individual to humanity at large that a teleological consideration of history becomes

one world). Husserl's point is rather the opposite. The intercultural encounters that happened at the time of the Greek colonization of the near East brought to light the relativity of cultures and their contrast with the one world common to all humans. Only on the basis of this experience could philosophy come about as the intellectual activity geared towards conceptual determination of the one true world. If philosophy qua specifically Greek cultural product were the *source* of the distinction between the one world and the contingent cultural worlds, then this distinction would rely entirely on a contingent cultural product whose existence cannot be further accounted for. Claims to universality for philosophy would be completely unwarranted. It is only because for Husserl the specific subject matter of philosophy (the one true world as opposed to contingent cultural worlds) comes to light in every intercultural encounter, no matter how fleeting and unthematic its appearance may be, that philosophy can lay claim to universality. Philosophy takes upon itself the task of investigating thematically and rigorously that object (the one world) that is bound to peep out, albeit marginally and mostly unnoticed, in every encounter between different cultures. Thus, every conceivable culture can in principle become philosophical to the extent that it can decide to partake in this task, whose meaning is in principle accessible to every conceivable culture that had an encounter with any other conceivable culture.

possible but, rather, by bringing to light the inner dynamics of self-realization governing the experience of each single subject.

Second, Kant insists that teleology is not a constitutive concept of history. Human history merely *admits of* a teleological consideration without, however, necessarily requiring it.[41] If we look at human history from a teleological viewpoint, Kant argues, we will be able to develop a meaningful narrative about it, though in so doing we should be aware that this is a deliberately chosen perspective and not a mere 'description' of what human history is in itself. This aspect in Kant's essay is obviously consistent with the tenets of his critical philosophy. Husserl's understanding of teleology is, in this regard, much stronger than Kant's. Teleology for Husserl is not merely a perspective that we may or may not choose to assume to describe human history. As he points out in his critical remarks to Simmel's *Das Problem der historischen Zeit*,[42] Husserl understands the teleological movement of human history to be one of its essential constituents, flowing from the subjective movement towards a harmonious and meaningful life under the guidance of reason. Failing to see the teleology operative in human history is thus for Husserl failing to catch hold of one of the key ontological specifics of human persons. A teleological consideration of history is therefore not only possible but also required.

Third and last, Husserl does not spell out in detail the characteristics of the international culture of reason that he takes humanity to be moving towards. He does not describe how such culture might look from a social and political point of view. However, in his descriptions, he seems to insist that the realization of the human world-culture would not imply a leveling down of all cultural differences and national traditions. In his ideal narrative, home-worlds realizing a part of the broader tradition of humankind understand themselves as functional *members* of mankind, but they can only do so if they maintain their national identity and thus preserve the *specificity* of their contribution to the whole. In keeping with the key insights of his mereology, Husserl does not believe in a total fusion of horizons in which the constituent national horizons would dissolve. On the contrary, upon encountering each other, national

---

[41] Bernward Grünewald argues correctly that, for Kant, "philosophical history is not a foundation, but just a reflective consideration of empirical history." B. Grünewald, *Geist – Kultur – Gesellschaft: Versuch einer Prinzipientheorie der Geisteswissenschaften auf transzendentalphilosophischer Grundlage* (Berlin: Duncker & Humblot, 2009), 171.

[42] See Chapter 6.

home-worlds should understand themselves as functional parts in the organic whole of humanity, to which they can now deliberately contribute. Full integration of previously isolated home-worlds into the overarching whole of humanity requires viewing each of them as one unique way of apprehending the one world, which, in turn, does not manifest itself elsewhere than in the indefinitely open manifold of culturally embedded world-apprehensions. In other words, in the same way in which the manifold profiles of perceptual objects do not blend into one single profile in order to let the object itself appear, home-worlds should not blend into one monochrome international culture in order to let the one universally shared world come into view. In Husserl's ideal narrative, a genuine international universal culture should be precisely as the phrase "inter-national" suggests. It would preserve national specificities, but these would be productively coordinated on the basis of the one world constituted jointly by all cultures.

To conclude this section, it is appropriate to recall that Husserl was well aware of the tense relationships between European nations in his time, and, as we saw, he was very vocal in denouncing a crisis in Western culture. This must be taken into account in order to assess correctly the status of the analyses just presented and not to mistake them for ahistorical wishful thinking. The register of Husserl's description is and remains, even in the sphere of history and culture, eidetic. This means that 'teleology' is intended to describe what should count as one of the essential traits of humanity as such, and not just the factual progression or regression of human history. Certainly, he takes his cue from historical facts such as the birth of philosophy in ancient Greece and the international connectedness of cultural worlds in the late nineteenth century. However, these facts are considered as examples and indicators of ideal validities whose actual realization in the contingent development of history can be significantly imperfect. Nonetheless, for Husserl, unveiling the teleology ideally inherent in human history with the aid of eidetic 'rationalization'[43] is a philosophically and culturally significant activity, one that, in Kant's spirit, may even "contribute" directly to the attainment of humanity's *telos*.[44]

---

[43] See Chapter 5.
[44] See Kant's *Ninth Proposition* in I. Kant, "Ideas for a Universal History with a Cosmopolitan Aim," *Anthropology, History and Education* (Cambridge University Press, 2007), 107–120. Here 118.

Recapitulation and conclusion

As we approach the conclusion of the book, let me briefly recapitulate the outcomes of the last two chapters. We began in Chapter 7 by suggesting that Husserl's late phenomenology of the life-world reveals its true meaning if interpreted in the context of the Kantian liberation narrative. We then articulated the Kantian liberation narrative: Kant sets the basis to overcome naturalism as the worldview dominating the West after the scientific revolution. Interestingly, this narrative proved to be largely shared by both the Neo-Kantians and the life-philosophers, who otherwise disagree significantly on philosophical issues. We then turned to consider the important notion of *Weltanschauung* and presented the controversy between those who consider worldviews to be the *terminus ad quem*, or final goal, of philosophic thinking and those who interpret them as the *terminus a quo*, that is the hidden existential source of philosophy. Husserl's take on *Weltanschauung* was one of initial skepticism, and subsequently of progressive appropriation. He began rejecting the notion of worldview as threatening the scientificity of philosophy; however, he eventually recognized the force of worldviews, and, in particular, of naturalism. He then set out to articulate a phenomenological worldview characterized by a deconstructive genealogy of naturalism (*pars destruens*) and a positive affirmation of the operative, world-constituting nature of transcendental subjectivity (*pars construens*). This included a thorough description of our consciousness of the world as the totality in which all our theory and praxis are embedded and the historical reconstruction of the intentional shifts operated by modern science as presented in Husserl's *Crisis*. We identified five steps: (1) abstraction of spatial qualities; (2) idealization of pure shapes; (3) indirect mathematization of the sensible qualities; (4) formalization; (5.1) hypostatization of the formalized idealities; (5.2) substitution of these hypostases for the concrete life-world. We then pointed out that the entire trajectory of modern natural science rests on a preliminary move, or step (0), that is the abstraction of pure nature from the concrete, culturally formed world of significance in which our lives unfold.

Once the misunderstandings of naturalism are dispelled, the way is clear for a reconsideration of culture-formation as the innermost vocation of subjectivity. Husserl believes that the transcendental analysis of the life-world as the total horizon of human life has a transformative power in that it restores the dignity of subjectivity over mere nature, that naturalism undermined. Finally, the panoramic surveys of the life-world's infinity enacted in Husserl's manuscripts offer resources to render the Enlightenment notion of 'humankind' intuitive. Rather than operating with an abstract normative concept of humankind, Husserl analyzes concretely how this concept is formed in and through the encounters between previously isolated national 'home-worlds.' For Husserl, the encounter between home-worlds and the ensuing experience of one and the same world apprehended in different ways delineate a teleology in the historical development of humankind. In Husserl's deliberately ideal or eidetic narrative, human history moves towards a world-culture in which a harmonious life of self-responsibility and reason may be possible. Phenomenology thus joins forces with other philosophical trends to defend a humanistic worldview in opposition to naturalism.

In conclusion, it is legitimate to reflect on the specificity of Husserl's humanism. Is it any different from Neo-Kantian humanism and the life-philosophical exaltation of history? In order to answer this question we have to return briefly to the important remark that humanism is a sort of *per se* accident of transcendental phenomenology and not its essential core. Phenomenology, as we saw, understands itself as an eidetic discipline, that is, a discipline oriented towards *rationalization via contemplation of pure possibilities*. To the extent that phenomenology studies the essential configurations of pure consciousness in its correlation with essential configurations of the world, it is indifferent to the empirical *fact* of human consciousness in the historical world. In Husserl's self-understanding, the essential configurations unearthed by phenomenology would hold valid for any possible consciousness experiencing any possible world. Husserl's humanism is thus essentially what we could phrase a *de-centered* humanism.[45] Its centerpiece is not the ideal of 'man' as the highest end but the contemplation of essential possibilities of consciousness and its preeminence over the natural world. This allows Husserl to maintain a healthy critical distance from the human world and to avoid the enticements of a naively celebratory attitude towards the *fact* of culture, whose C he is never inclined to capitalize. Husserl does not in the slightest resemble

[45] My gratitude to Claudio Majolino for suggesting the effective phrase "umanesimo decentrato" in a long and illuminating conversation on these issues.

Cocteau's character, whom Sartre rightly chastises, who contemplates the world from an airplane and proclaims: "Man is amazing!"[46] On the contrary, he would agree with Sartre that "man is constantly in the making."[47] This involves an unreserved acknowledgment of the contingency of history and the finitude of the cultural manifestations appearing in it. However, unlike Sartre, Husserl's eidetic analysis of consciousness in the life-world unearths essential possibilities that undergird this 'being-in-the-making' and that can even be actively assumed as rational guidelines for the unending self-shaping of human history. For instance, the *essential possibility* of humankind developing into a world-culture is, indeed, inscribed in the very fabric of a rational consciousness intentionally directed towards a world and empathetically connected to other rational consciousnesses. The actual development of history, however, can turn against this essential possibility and make it impossible as a *real possibility* for the actually existing subjects. However, the eidetic de-centering of humanism carried out in Husserl's transcendental phenomenology has a beneficial effect: it prevents humanistically oriented thinking from letting its validity depend on the contingent vicissitudes of history. The traditional humanist defending the ideal of man as the ultimate end is likely to see this ideal irrevocably crushed, say, in front of Auschwitz. The de-centered humanist schooled in Husserlian phenomenology knows that essential possibilities having been contemplated as such are indefinitely available to orient and reorient human history even in its darkest and most hopeless moments, when all belief in humanity is likely to crumble. Husserl expresses this view in a touching passage from a letter to the Canadian philosopher Winthrop Pickard Bell:

It is very gratifying that there are still lively people on this gloomy planet: Were there none, I nevertheless would not despair, but would build them up eidetically for myself, firmly convinced that purely formed ideas must give rise to lively people who accord with them.[48]

---

[46] J.-P. Sartre, *Existentialism is a Humanism* (New Haven, CT and London: Yale University Press, 2007), 51–52.
[47] *Ibid.*
[48] BW III, 16–17. Quoted in M. Brainard, "'For a New World': On the Practical Impulse of Husserlian Theory," *Husserl Studies* 23/1 (2007): 17–31. Here 18.

Conclusion

I would like to return to Husserl's statement that phenomenology is a "*scientific* life-philosophy [. . .] having as a fundamental scientific theme the concrete universal life and its life-world."[1] This is the passage that best summarizes the interpretation of Husserl's transcendental phenomenology I tried to articulate and whose philosophical dimensions I endeavored to spell out.

Husserl had a tendency to attribute to his phenomenology a variety of conflicting philosophical tags. In *Ideas I*, for instance, he boasts: "we are the genuine positivist"[2] just a few pages after bashing positivism for being blind to the autonomous validity of ideas. In *Einleitung in die Philosophie* (1922), he argues that phenomenology is simultaneously "the perfection [*Vollendung*] of rationalism and [. . .] the perfection of empiricism."[3] Ubiquitously in his work he professes that phenomenology is a form of transcendental idealism, while at the same time insisting that his own brand of idealism is actually the most radical form of realism, to the extent that it dispels all conflations of the transcendence of nature with the immanence of consciousness. By calling transcendental phenomenology a scientific life-philosophy, however, Husserl was doing more than just adding another item to his list of paradoxical self-brandings. As a matter of fact, while all aforementioned tags refer to very broad currents in Western philosophy in general, 'scientific life-philosophy' refers specifically to the philosophical controversy about the natural and the human sciences in Husserl's time. Husserl is offering a definitive determination of the position of his phenomenology in relation to Rickert and the Southwestern school on the one hand and to Dilthey and Simmel on the other. He is claiming that phenomenology is able to harmonize two traditionally divergent desiderata in post-Kantian German philosophy: scientificity and proximity to life. To be scientific in philosophy

---

[1] Hua XXXII, 140. [2] Ideen I, § 20. [3] Hua XXXV, 288.

291

does not mean, as Rickert would have it, to restructure the inchoate manifestations of life according to conceptual perspectives intrinsically alien to it. Rather, to be scientific in philosophy means to bring to faithful conceptual expression the transcendental structures and dynamics of life, which are responsible for the constitution of a world. It is helpful to recall here that by 'life' Husserl and the life-philosophers do not mean the biological processes governing the existence of an organism, but rather experiencing subjectivity itself, to the extent that experiencing subjectivity is not a mere mirror or a *tabula rasa*, but a vital and dynamic principle. *Life itself* is the transcendental, and all the categories and principles that philosophy endeavors to spell out conceptually must be drawn directly *from* it.

Furthermore, it is noteworthy that in his declaration of allegiance to life-philosophy Husserl immediately mentions the main issue of his late work: the life-world in its correlation with universal constituting life. The notion of life-world is thus part and parcel of Husserl's critical appropriation of life-philosophical themes in his confrontation with Dilthey and Simmel. One could argue that the identification of the life-world as a theme for phenomenology allows Husserl to stabilize the meaning of life-philosophy and correct certain lamentable irrationalistic tendencies in it. As I tried to show in the foregoing chapters, Husserl's discovery of the life-world leads to a reformulation of the relationship between nature and *Geist* in way that does not rely on overly simplistic oppositions, as is the case, for instance, with Dilthey. In a sense, if the main drawback of modern natural science is that it "turns nature and freedom into an incomprehensible antinomy,"[4] then the type of life-philosophy envisaged by Dilthey does not seem to offer viable resources to *overcome* the antinomy. It just restates the antinomy from the point of view of free and creative *Geist*, rather than from the point of view of nature. The discovery of the life-world opens up a new perspective, according to which both nature and *Geist* are constituted and thus refer back to an original experience of the world, which is accessible to phenomenological inquiry. The distinction between nature and *Geist* remains legitimate,[5] but it is embedded in a broader

---

[4] Hua VIII, 230–231.

[5] I am thankful to Nicolas De Warren for insisting on the necessity to include a discussion of the life-world, in order to assess the validity of my claim that Husserl's characterization of phenomenology as a scientific life-philosophy is

dimension of being, the life-world, in the framework of which the two ontological spheres prove to be mutually clarifying, rather than opposed. Actual phenomenological descriptions of the life-world and its relation to culture and nature can be significantly expanded and improved, and it is a fact that Husserl did not manage to develop them beyond the preliminaries. Husserl, however, indicated a promising avenue of research that does not infringe upon the prerogatives of

central to his late work. Unfortunately, I cannot agree with his remark that Husserl's view of history in the *Crisis* text is characterized by "the absence of this life-philosophy perspective, as we might call it, according to which history is an expression of life" and that "the view of history in the *Crisis* [...] consists in deconstructing, as it were, the very distinction between nature and spirit." De Warren, review of Andrea Staiti, *Geistigkeit, Leben und geschichtliche Welt in der Transzendentalphänomenologie Husserls, Husserl Studies* 28 (2010): 161–166. Here 166. The immediate connection of the life-philosophical character of phenomenology and the life-world theme in Husserl's quote seems to reveal that there is no ostensible difference between phenomenology qua scientific life-philosophy and phenomenology qua ontology of the life-world as presented in *Crisis*, unless one were able to prove that Husserl's notion of life-world in 1927 is significantly different from Husserl's notion of life-world in 1936. In light of the newly published materials in Hua XXXIX, spanning over three decades, such difference seems extremely implausible. True, in *Crisis* Husserl does not rehearse his descriptions of transcendental life as found in his 1920s lectures and manuscripts, and he moves directly to examine historical sedimentation and its impact on the self-understanding of Western science. However, this seems to provide evidence that he is *presupposing* the validity of his groundwork towards a phenomenology of constitutive life, rather than disavowing it. How else, otherwise, could we understand his claim that past intellectual achievements such as Galilean science are still accessible in their foundational dimension from the present, that they can be reactivated, subjected to rational scrutiny and taken up responsibly by subjects living centuries later? It seems that a life-philosophical framework like the one offered in Chapter 6, according to which transcendental life is an intersubjective unity that constitutes history, is unavoidable if we are to make sense of Husserl's claims in *Crisis*. Furthermore, some disambiguation of the term 'deconstruction' in the phrase 'deconstructing the distinction between nature and spirit' would be required in order to take a stance on De Warren's second claim. If by 'deconstructing the distinction' we mean 'undermining the distinction,' then this cannot possibly be Husserl's intention. Undermining the distinction between nature and spirit is precisely the main danger associated with the naturalism Husserl sets out to combat. Why would undermining the distinction of nature and spirit in the name of the life-world be preferable to undermining this distinction in the name of mathematically constructed nature? If by 'deconstructing the distinction' we mean, as I take De Warren to mean, 'deconstructing the Cartesian construal of the distinction' in order to show that nature and spirit are not opposed but rather interconnected layers in the one encompassing life-world, then I hope that Chapter 8 shed further light on De Warren's remark.

empirical inquiry but that, at the same time, bears far-reaching implications for the sciences' self-understanding and for the picture of the world that they contribute to propagating.

Husserl's phenomenology famously evolved through a series of beginnings. Some of them were major breakthroughs, like the one he attained in *Logical Investigations*, and some of them were just small beginnings, as Husserl designated the one offered in *Crisis*. Be they major or small, beginnings are always characterized by the introduction of a new perspective that elicits further work. Husserlian scholarship seems to have evolved in a similar way, following partly the publication of Husserl's unpublished materials and partly the concerns stemming from other philosophical traditions.

　With this book, I hope to have offered some kind of new beginning (of whatever size) for our understanding of Husserl and the German philosophy of his time. However, if I was able to prove at least that reading Husserl in the context of his confrontation with the Neo-Kantians and the *Lebensphilosophen* is a rewarding philosophical experience and a *sine qua non* to understand his late work, I can consider my primary goal achieved.

Bibliography

Aristophanes. 2000. *Clouds.* Indianapolis, IN: Hackett.

Bambach, Charles. 1995. *Heidegger, Dilthey and the Crisis of Historicism.* Ithaca, NY: Cornell University Press.

Beiser, Frederick. 2011. *The German Historicist Tradition.* Oxford University Press.

Biemel, Walter (ed.). 1968. "Der Briefwechsel Dilthey-Husserl." *Man and World* 1/3: 428–446.

Boehm, Rudolf. 1968. *Vom Gesichtspunkt der Phänomenologie.* The Hague: Nijhoff.

Böhm, Franz. 1933. *Ontologie der Geschichte.* Tübingen: Mohr Siebeck.

Brainard, Marcus. 2002. *Belief and Its Neutralization: Husserl's System of Phenomenology in Ideas I.* Albany, NY: SUNY Press.

— 2007. "'For a New World': On the Practical Impulse of Husserlian Theory." *Husserl Studies* 23/1: 17–31.

Brentano, Franz. 1995. *Psychology from an Empirical Standpoint.* New York: Routledge.

Campbell, Scott. 2012. *The Early Heidegger's Philosophy of Life: Facticity, Being, and Language.* New York: Fordham University Press.

Carr, David. 2004. "Husserl's Problematic Concept of Lifeworld," in L. Embree and D. Moran, *Phenomenology: Critical Concepts in Philosophy,* vol. 1. London: Routledge: 359–374.

Costa, Vincenzo. 2006. "L'esperienza dell'altro: per una fenomenologia della separazione," in A. Ferrarin (ed.), *Passive Synthesis and Life-world – Sintesi passiva e mondo della vita.* Pisa: ETS: 109–125.

Crowell, Steven G. 2001. *Husserl, Heidegger and the Space of Meaning: Paths toward Transcendental Phenomenology.* Evanston, IL: Northwestern University Press.

— 2010. "Transcendental Logic and Minimal Empiricism: Lask and McDowell on the Unboundedness of the Conceptual," in S. Luft and R. Makkreel (eds.), *Neo-Kantianism in Contemporary Philosophy.* Bloomington: Indiana University Press: 150–174.

D'Amico, Robert. 1981. "Husserl on the Foundational Structures of Natural and Cultural Sciences." *Philosophy and Phenomenological Research* 42: 5–22.

de Gandt, François. 2004. *Husserl et Galilée: sur la crise des sciences européennes*. Paris: Vrin.

de Mul, Jos. 2004. *The Tragedy of Finitude: Dilthey's Hermeneutics of Life*. New Haven, CT and London: Yale University Press.

De Warren, Nicolas. 2006. "On Husserl's Essentialism." *International Journal of Philosophical Studies* 14/2: 255–270.

2008. "La Crise de la raison et l'énigme du monde," in F. de Gandt and C. Majolino (eds.), *Lectures de la* Krisis *de Husserl*. Paris: Vrin : 23–44.

2009. *Husserl and the Promise of Time: Subjectivity in Transcendental Phenomenology*. Cambridge University Press.

2010. "Pamina's Eyes, Tamino's Gaze: Husserl's Phenomenology of Image-consciousness Refashioned," in Carlo Ierna, Hanne Jacobs, and Filip Mattens (eds.), *Philosophy, Phenomenology, Sciences – Essays in Commemoration of Edmund Husserl*. Dordrecht: Springer: 303–332.

Dewalque, Arnaud. 2010. "A quoi sert la logique des sciences historiques de Rickert?", *Les Études philosophiques* 1: 44–66.

Dilthey, Wilhelm. 1924. *Ideen über eine beschreibende und zergliedernde Psychologie*, in W. Dilthey, *Die geistige Welt. Einleitung in die Philosophie des Lebens. Erste Hälfte: Abhandlungen zur Grundlegung der Geisteswissenschaften, Gesammelte Schriften*, vol. 5. Göttingen: Vandenhoeck & Ruprecht: 139–240.

1924. *[Über vergleichende Psychologie.] Beiträge zum Studium der Individualität*, in W. Dilthey, *Gesammelte Schriften*, vol. 5. Göttingen: Vandenhoeck & Ruprecht: 241–316.

1924. *Das Wesen der Philosophie*, in W. Dilthey, *Gesammelte Schriften*, vol. 5. Göttingen: Vandenhoeck & Ruprecht: 339–416. Trans. S. A. Emery and W. T. Emery, *The Essence of Philosophy* (Chapel Hill: North Carolina University Press, 1969), 66 ff.

1927. "Der Aufbau der geschichtlichen Welt in den Geisteswissenschaften," in W. Dilthey, *Der Aufbau der geschichtlichen Welt in den Geisteswissenschaften, Gesammelte Schriften*, vol. 7. Göttingen: Vandenhoeck & Ruprecht: 79–291.

1960. *Weltanschauungslehre. Abhandlungen zur Philosophie der Philosophie, Gesammelte Schriften*, vol. 8. Göttingen: Vandenhoeck & Ruprecht.

1969. *The Essence of Philosophy*. Chapel Hill: North Carolina University Press.

1982. *Grundlegung der Wissenschaften von Menschen, der Gesellschaft und der Geschichte. Ausarbeitungen und Entwürfe zum zweiten Band der Einleitung in die Geisteswissenschaften (ca. 1870–1895), Gesammelte Schriften*, vol. 19. Göttingen: Vandenhoeck & Ruprecht.

2002. *The Formation of the Historical World in the Human Sciences*, in W. Dilthey, *Selected Works*, vol. 3. Princeton University Press: 100–311.

2010. "Ideas for a Descriptive and Analytic Psychology," in W. Dilthey, *Selected Works*, vol. 2, *Understanding the Human World*. Princeton University Press: 115–210.

2010. "[On Comparative Psychology.] Contributions to the Study of Individuality," in W. Dilthey, *Selected Works*, vol. 2, *Understanding the Human World*. Princeton University Press: 211–284.

Dodd, James. 2005. "Reading Husserl's Time Diagrams from 1917/18." *Husserl Studies* 21/2: 111–137.

Ebbinghaus, Hermann. 1896. "Erklärende und beschreibende Psychologie." *Zeitschrift für Psychologie und Physiologie der Sinnesorgane* 9: 161–205.

Farges, Julien. 2010. "Philosophie de l'histoire et système des valeurs chez Heinrich Rickert." *Les Études philosophiques* 1: 25–44.

Farrell Krell, David. 1992. *Daimon Life: Heidegger and Life-Philosophy*. Bloomington: Indiana University Press.

Fichte, Johann Gottlob. 1906. *The Vocation of Man*. Trans. W. Smith. Chicago, IL: Open Court.

Fellmann, Ferdinand. 1983. *Gelebte Philosophie in Deutschland*. Freiburg and Munich: Karl Alber.

Friedman, Michael. 2000. *A Parting of the Ways: Carnap, Cassirer and Heidegger*. La Salle, IL: Open Court.

Gadamer, Hans-Georg. 1989. *Truth and Method*. New York: Crossroad.

Gander, Hans-Helmuth. 1988. *Positivismus als Metaphysik. Voraussetzungen und Grundstrukturen von Diltheys Grundlegung der Geisteswissenschaften*. Freiburg and Munich: Alber.

(ed.). 2010. *Husserl-Lexikon*. Darmstadt: WBG.

Geiger, Moritz. 1930. *Die Wirklichkeit der Wissenschaften und die Metaphysik*. Bonn: F. Cohen.

Glatz, Uwe B. 2001. *Emil Lask: Philosophie im Verhältnis zu Weltanschauung, Leben und Erkenntnis*. Würzburg: Königshausen & Neumann.

Gordon, Peter. 2010. *Continental Divide: Heidegger – Cassirer – Davos*. Cambridge, MA and London: Harvard University Press.

Groebner, Valentin. 2004. *Defaced: The Visual Culture of Violence in the Late Middle Ages*. New York: Zone Books.

Grünewald, Bernward. 2009. *Geist – Kultur – Gesellschaft: Versuch einer Prinzipientheorie der Geisteswissenschaften auf transzendentalphiloso-phischer Grundlage*. Berlin: Duncker & Humblot.

Hart, James. 1995. "Husserl and Fichte: With Special Regard to Husserl's Lectures on 'Fichte's Ideal of Humanity'." *Husserl Studies* 12: 135–163.

Heidegger, Martin. 2004. *The Phenomenology of Religious Life.* Bloomington: Indiana University Press.

Heisenberg, Werner. 1999. *Physics and Philosophy.* New York: Prometheus Books.

Holzey, Helmut. 2010. "Neo-Kantianism and Phenomenology: The Problem of Intuition," in Sebastian Luft and Rudolf Makkreel (eds.), *Neo-Kantianism in Contemporary Philosophy.* Bloomington: Indiana University Press: 25–40.

Husserl, Edmund. 1954. *Ideen zu einer reinen Phänomenologie und phänomenologischen Philosophie. Zweites Buch: Untersuchungen zur Konstitution, Husserliana,* vol. 4. The Hague: Nijhoff.

1954. *Die Krisis der europäischen Wissenschaften und die transzendentale Phänomenologie. Eine Einführung in die phänomenologische Philosophie, Husserliana,* vol. 6. The Hague: Nijhoff.

1957. *Logische Untersuchungen. Erster Band: Prolegomena zur reinen Logik, Husserliana,* vol. 18. The Hague: Nijhoff. Trans. J. N. Findlay, *Logical Investigations,* vol. 1 (London: Routledge, 1970).

1959. *Erste Philosophie (1923/24). Zweiter Teil: Theorie der phänomenologischen Reduktion, Husserliana,* vol. 8. The Hague Nijhoff.

1962. *Phänomenologische Psychologie. Vorlesungen Sommersemester 1925, Husserliana,* vol. 9. The Hague: Nijhoff.

1963. *Cartesianische Meditationen und Pariser Vorträge (1931), Husserliana,* vol. 1. The Hague: Nijhoff.

1970. *The Crisis of the European Sciences and Transcendental Phenomenology: An Introduction to Phenomenological Philosophy.* Evanston, IL: Northwestern University Press.

1973. *Zur Phänomenologie der Intersubjektivität. Texte aus dem Nachlaß, Zweiter Teil: 1921–1928, Husserliana,* vol. 14. The Hague: Nijhoff.

1973. *Zur Phänomenologie der Intersubjektivität. Texte aus dem Nachlaß. Dritter Teil: 1929–1935, Husserliana,* vol. 15. The Hague Nijhoff.

1977. *Ideen zu einer reinen Phänomenologie und einer phänomenologischen Philosophie. Erstes Buch: Allgemeine Einführung in die reine Phänomenologie. Erster Halbband: Text der 1.–3. Auflage – Nachdruck, Husserliana,* vol. 3/1. The Hague: Nijhoff.

1977. *Phenomenological Psychology: Lectures Summer Semester 1925.* Trans. J. Scanlon. The Hague: Nijhoff.

1981. *Shorter Works.* University of Notre Dame Press.

1982. *Ideas Pertaining to a Pure Phenomenology and to a Phenomenological Philosophy. First Book: General Introduction to a Pure Phenomenology, Collected Works,* vol. 2. Dordrecht: Kluwer.

1986. *Aufsätze und Vorträge (1911–1921)*, Husserliana, vol. 25. Dordrecht: Kluwer.

1987. *Vorlesungen über Bedeutungslehre. Sommersemester 1908*, Husserliana, vol. 26. Dordrecht : Kluwer.

1989. *Ideas Pertaining to a Pure Phenomenology and to a Phenomenological Philosophy. Second Book: Studies in the Phenomenology of Constitution, Collected Works*, vol. 3. Dordrecht: Kluwer.

1993. *Die Krisis der europäischen Wissenschaften und die transzendentale Phänomenologie. Ergänzungsband: Text aus dem Nachlaß 1934–1937*, Husserliana, vol. 29. Dordrecht: Kluwer.

1994. *Briefwechsel*, vols. 1–9. Dordrecht: Kluwer.

1995. "Fichte's Ideal of Humanity [Three Lectures]." Trans. James Hart. *Husserl Studies* 12: 111–133.

1996. MS A VI 16/25a, ed. U. Melle, in T. Nenon and L. Embree (eds.), *Issues in Husserl's* Ideen II. Dordrecht: Kluwer: 1–8.

2001. *Natur und Geist. Vorlesungen 1927*, Husserliana, vol. 32. Dordrecht: Springer.

2002. *Einleitung in die Philosophie. Vorlesungen 1922/23*, Husserliana, vol. 35. Dordrecht: Springer.

2002. *Natur und Geist. Vorlesungen Sommersemester 1919*, Husserliana Materialien, vol. 4. Dordrecht: Springer.

2002. *Zur phänomenologischen Reduktion. Texte aus dem Nachlass (1926–35)*, Husserliana, vol. 34. Dordrecht: Springer.

2004. *Einleitung in die Ethik. Vorlesungen Sommersemester 1920 und 1924*, Husserliana, vol. 37. Dordrecht: Springer.

2005. *Einführung in die Phänomenologie der Erkenntnis. Vorlesung 1909*, Husserliana Materialien, vol. 7. Dordrecht: Springer.

2008. *Die Lebenswelt. Auslegungen der vorgegebenen Welt und ihrer Konstitution. Texte aus dem Nachlass (1916–1937)*, Husserliana, vol. 39. Dordrecht: Springer.

Ierna, Carlo, Hanne Jacobs, and Filip Mattens (eds.). 2010. *Philosophy, Phenomenology, Sciences – Essays in Commemoration of Edmund Husserl*. Dordrecht: Springer.

Jalbert, John E. 1988. "Husserl's Position between Dilthey and the Windelband-Rickert School of Neo-Kantianism." *Journal of the History of Philosophy* 26: 279–296.

Kant, Immanuel. 1997. *Groundwork of the Metaphysics of Morals*. Cambridge University Press.

1998. *Critique of Pure Reason*. Cambridge University Press.

2002. Prolegomena to Any Future Metaphysics that will be able to come forward as a Science, in I. Kant, *Theoretical Philosophy after 1781*. Cambridge University Press: 50–169.

2007. "Ideas for a Universal History with a Cosmopolitan Aim," in I. Kant, *Anthropology, History and Education*. Cambridge University Press: 107–120.

Karlsruhen, Thomas. 2001. "Simmel's Evolution der Kantischen Voraussetzungen des Denkens." *Simmel Studies* 11: 21–52.

Kern, Iso. 1962. "Die drei Wege zur transzendentalphänomenologischen Reduktion in der Philosophie Edmund Husserls." *Tijdschrift voor filosofie* 24: 303–49.

1964. *Husserl und Kant: Eine Untersuchung über Husserls Verhältnis zu Kant und zum Neukantianismus*. The Hague: Nijhoff.

Kim, Jaegwon. 2005. *Physicalism or Something Near Enough*. Princeton University Press.

Kreiter, Berend. 2007. "Philosophy as *Weltanschauung* in Trendelenburg, Dilthey, and Windelband," unpub. Ph.D. thesis, Vrije Universiteit Amsterdam. http://dare.ubvu.vu.nl/bitstream/1871/10750/1/dissertatie. CRC.19032007.pdf.

Kuttig, L. 1987. *Konstitution und Gegebenheit bei H. Rickert: Zum Prozess der Ontologisierung in seinem Spätwerk, eine Analyse unter Berücksichtigung nachgelassener Texte*. Essen: Die Blaue Eule.

Landgrebe, Ludwig. 1982. *Faktizität und Individuation. Studien zu den Grundfragen der Phänomenologie*. Hamburg: Meiner.

2005. "Husserl's Departure from Cartesianism," in Rudolf Bernet, Donn Welton, and Zavota Gina (eds.), *Edmund Husserl: Critical Assessments of Leading Philosophers*, vol. 1. New York: Routledge. 134–176.

Lask, Emil. 1923. *Fichtes Idealismus und die Geschichte*, in E. Lask, *Gesammelte Schriften*, vol. 1. Tübingen: Mohr Siebeck.

1923. *Die Logik der Philosophie und die Kategorienlehre*, in E. Lask, *Gesammelte Schriften*, vol. 2. Tübingen: Mohr Siebeck: 1–282.

1924. *Notizen zur Einteilung der Wissenschaften*, in E. Lask, *Gesammelte Schriften*, vol. 3. Tübingen: Mohr Siebeck: 257–293.

1924. *Zum System der Wissenschaften*, in E. Lask, *Gesammelte Schriften*, vol. 3. Tübingen: Mohr Siebeck: 239–257.

Lembeck, Karl-Heinz. 2003. "Begründungsphilosophische Perspektiven: Husserl und Natorp über Anschauung." *Phänomenologische Forschungen*: 97–108.

Lohmar, Dieter. 2005. "Die phänomenologische Methode der Wesensschau und ihre Präzisierung als eidetische Variation." *Phänomenologische Forschungen*. 2005: 65–91.

2006. "How are Formal Sciences Possible? On the Sources of Intuitivity of Mathematical Knowledge according to Husserl and Kant." *The New*

Yearbook for Phenomenology and Phenomenological Philosophy 6: 109–126.

Lotzte, Hermann. 1879. *System der Philosophie – Zweiter Theil: Drei Bücher der Metaphysik.* Leipzig: Hirzel.

Luft, Sebastian. 1998. "Husserl's Phenomenological Discovery of the Natural Attitude." *Continental Philosophy Review* 31/2: 153–170.

    2006. "Natorp, Husserl und das Problem der Kontinuität von Leben, Wissenschaft und Philosophie." *Phänomenologische Forschungen.* 2006: 99–134.

    2010. "Reconstruction and Reduction: Natorp and Husserl on Method and the Question of Subjectivity," in S. Luft and R. Makkreel (eds.), *Neo-Kantianism in Contemporary Philosophy.* Bloomington: Indiana University Press: 59–91.

    2011. *Subjectivity and Lifeworld in Transcendental Phenomenology.* Evanston, IL: Northwestern University Press. 2011.

Luft, Sebastian, and Rudolf Makkreel (eds.). 2010. *Neo-Kantianism in Contemporary Philosophy.* Bloomington: Indiana University Press.

Mahnke, Dietrich. 1917. *Der Wille zur Ewigkeit: Gedanken eines Deutschen Kriegers über den Sinn des Geisteslebens.* Halle: Niemeyer.

Majolino, Claudio. 2010. "La Partition du réel: remarques sur l'eidos, la phantasia, l'effondrement du monde et l'être absolu de la conscience," in Carlo Ierna, Hanne Jacobs, and Filip Mattens (eds.), *Philosophy, Phenomenology, Sciences – Essays in Commemoration of Edmund Husserl.* Dordrecht: Springer: 573–660.

Makkreel, Rudolf. 2010. "Wilhelm Dilthey and the Neo-Kantians: On the Conceptual Distinction between *Geisteswissenschaften* and *Kulturwissenschaften,*" in Sebastian Luft and Rudolf Makkreel (eds.), *Neo-Kantianism in Contemporary Philosophy.* Bloomington: Indiana University Press: 253–271.

Melle, Ullrich. 1991. "The Development of Husserl's Ethics." *Études phénoménologiques* 7/13–14: 115–135.

Moran, Dermot. 2011. "Even the Papuan is a Man and Not a Beast: Husserl on Universalism and the Relativity of Cultures." *Journal of the History of Philosophy* 49/4: 463–494.

Moyar, Dean (ed.). 2010, *Routledge Companion to Nineteenth Century Philosophy.* New York: Routledge.

Muslow, Martin. 2005. "Zum Methodenprofil der Konstellationsforschung," in Martin Muslow and Marcelo Stamm (eds.), *Konstallationsforschung.* Frankfurt am Main: Suhrkamp: 74–97.

Muslow, Martin, and Marcelo Stamm (eds.). 2005. *Konstallationsforschung.* Frankfurt am Main: Suhrkamp.

Natorp, Paul. 1917/18. "Husserls 'Ideen zu einer reinen Phänomenologie'."
Logos 7. 224–246. Reprinted in Hermann Noack (ed.), *Husserl*
(Darmstadt: WBG, 1973).
——. 2004. *Plato's Theory of Ideas: An Introduction to Idealism.* Sankt
Augustin: Academia.
Naugle, David. 2002. *Worldview: The History of a Concept.* Grand Rapids,
MI and Cambridge: Eerdmans.
Nenon, Tom, and Lester Embree (eds.). 1996. *Issues in Husserl's* Ideen II.
Dordrecht: Kluwer.
Rickert, Heinrich. 1920. *Die Philosophie des Lebens: Darstellung und Kritik
der philosophischen Modeströmungen unserer Zeit.* Tübingen: Mohr
Siebeck.
——. 1924. *Die Probleme der Geschichtsphilosophie. Eine Einführung.*
Heidelberg: Carl Winters.
——. 1934. *Grundprobleme der Philosophie. Methodologie, Ontologie,
Anthropologie.* Tübingen: Mohr Siebeck..
——. 1934. "Kennen und Erkennen. Kritische Bemerkungen zum theoretischen
Intuitionismus." *Kant Studien* 39: 139–155.
——. 1962. *Science and History: A Critique of Positivist Epistemology.*
Princeton, NJ: Van Nostrand.
——. 1986. *The Limits of Concept Formation in Natural Science.* Cambridge
University Press.
——. 1999. "Die Heidelberger Tradition und Kants Kritizismus (Systematische
Selbstdarstellung)," in Heinrich Rickert, *Philosophische Aufsätze.*
Tübingen: Mohr Siebeck: 347–411.
——. 1999. "Die Methode der Philosophie und das Unmittelbare," in Heinrich
Rickert, *Philosophische Aufsätze.* Tübingen: Mohr Siebeck: 107–151.
——. 1999. *Philosophische Aufsätze*, ed. Reiner Bast. Tübingen: Mohr
Siebeck.
——. 1999. "Thesen zum System der Philosophie," in Heinrich Rickert,
Philosophische Aufsätze. Tübingen: Mohr Siebeck: 319–324.
——. 1999. "Vom Begriff der Philosophie," in Heinrich Rickert, *Philosophische
Aufsätze.* Tübingen: Mohr Siebeck: 3–36.
——. 1999. "Vom System der Werte," in Heinrich Rickert, *Philosophische
Aufsätze.* Tübingen: Mohr Siebeck: 73–105.
——. 1999. "Wissenschaftliche Philosophie und Weltanschauung," in
Heinrich Rickert, *Philosophische Aufsätze.* Tübingen: Mohr Siebeck:
325–346.
Rodi, Frithjof. 2003. "Dilthey und die Kant-Ausgabe der Preußischen
Akademie der Wissenschaften. Einige editions- und lebensgeschichtliche
Aspekte," in F. Rodi, *Das strukturierte Ganze: Studien zum Werk von
Wilhelm Dilthey.* Weilerswist: Velbrück Wissenschaft.

Rollinger, Robin. 1999. *Husserl's Position in the School of Brentano.* Dordrecht: Kluwer.

Sakakibara, Tetsuya. 1998. "The Relationship between Nature and Spirit in Husserl's Phenomenology Revisited." *Continental Philosophy Review* 31: 255–272.

Sandmeyer, Bob. 2009. *Husserl's Constitutive Phenomenology: Its Problem and Promise.* New York: Routledge.

Sartre, Jean-Paul. 2007. *Existentialism is a Humanism.* New Haven, CT and London: Yale University Press.

Scheler, Max. 1972. "Versuche einer Philosophie des Lebens: Nietzsche – Dilthey – Bergson," in M. Scheler, *Vom Umsturz der Werte: Abhandlungen und Aufsätze.* Berne and Munich: Francke: 310–339.

Schrödinger, Erwin. 1992. *What is Life?* Cambridge University Press.

Schuhmann, Karl. 1973. *Die Dialektik der Phänomenologie II: Reine Phänomenologie und phänomenologische Philosophie. Historisch-analytische Monographie über Husserls "Ideen I."* The Hague: Nijhoff.

1977. *Husserl-Chronik: Denk- und Lebensweg Edmund Husserls, Husserliana Dokumente,* vol. 1. The Hague: Nijhoff.

Senderowicz, Yaron. 2004. "Figurative Synthesis and Synthetic a priori Knowledge." *Review of Metaphysics* 57/4: 755–785.

Sensen, Oliver. 2009. "Kant on Human Dignity." *Kant-Studien* 100: 309–331.

Simmel, Georg. 1915. *Vom Wesen des historischen Verstehens.* Berlin: Ernst Siegfried Mittler und Sohn.

1916. *Das Problem der historischen Zeit.* Berlin: Verlag von Reuther u. Reichard.

1977. *The Problems of the Philosophy of History: An Epistemological Essay.* New York: The Free Press.

1980. "On the History of Philosophy," in Georg Simmel, *Essays on Interpretation in Social Science.* Totowa, NJ: Rowman & Littlefield: 198–204.

1980. "On the Nature of Historical Understanding." Trans. G. Oakes, in Georg Simmel, *Essays on Interpretation in Social Science.* Totowa, NJ: Rowman & Littlefield: 97–126.

1980. "The Problem of Historical Time," in Georg Simmel, *Essays on Interpretation in Social Science.* Totowa, NJ: Rowman & Littlefield: 127–144.

1993. *Kant und Goethe,* in Georg Simmel, *Gesamtausgabe,* vol. 8. Frankfurt am Main: Suhrkamp: 116–123.

1996. Hauptprobleme der Philosophie, in Georg Simmel, *Gesamtausgabe,* vol. 14. Frankfurt am Main: Suhrkamp: 7–157.

1997. Kant. Sechzehn Vorlesungen gehalten an der Berliner Universität, in Georg Simmel, *Gesamtausgabe*, vol. 9. Frankfurt am Main: Suhrkamp: 8–226.

1997. *Die Probleme der Geschichtsphilosophie. Eine erkenntnistheoretische Studie*, in Georg Simmel, *Gesamtausgabe*, vol. 9. Frankfurt am Main: Suhrkamp: 227–419.

1997. *Was ist uns Kant?* in Georg Simmel, *Gesamtausgabe*, vol. 5. Frankfurt am Main: Suhrkamp. 145–177.

1999. *Vom Wesen des historischen Verstehens*, in Georg Simmel, *Gesamtausgabe*, vol. 16. Frankfurt am Main: Suhrkamp. 151–179.

2003. *Das Problem der historischen Zeit*, in Georg Simmel, *Gesamtausgabe*, vol. 15. Frankfurt am Main: Suhrkamp. 287–304.

2010. *The View of Life: Four Metaphysical Essays with Journal Aphorisms.* University of Chicago Press.

Snow, Charles Percy. 1998. *The Two Cultures.* Cambridge University Press.

Sowa, Rochus. 2010. "Husserls Idee einer nicht-empirischen Wissenschaft von der Lebenswelt." *Husserl Studies* 26/1: 49–66.

Staiti, Andrea. 2006. "Fenomenologia dell'ideale. Husserl lettore di Fichte nelle Lezioni del 1917." *Annuario Filosofico* 22: 401–421.

2009. "Systematische Überlegungen zu Husserls Einstellungslehre." *Husserl Studies* 25/3: 219–233.

2010. "Different Worlds and Tendency to Concordance: Towards a New Perspective on Husserl's Phenomenology of Culture." *The New Yearbook for Phenomenology and Phenomenological Philosophy* 10: 127–143.

2010. *Geistigkeit, Leben und geschichtliche Welt in der Transzendentalphänomenologie Husserls.* Würzburg: Ergon Verlag.

2012. "Human Culture and the One Structure: On Luft's Reading of the Late Husserl." *Comparative and Continental Philosophy* 4/2: 317–330.

2012. "The Pedagogic Impulse of Husserl's Ways into Transcendental Phenomenology: An Alternative Reading of the *Erste Philosophie* Lecture." *Graduate Faculty Philosophy Journal* 33/1: 39–56.

2012. "Unforgivable Sinners? Epistemological and Psychological Naturalism in Husserl's *Philosophy as a Rigorous Science.*" *Rivista Internazionale di Filosofia e Psicologia* 3/2: 147–160.

2013. "Heinrich Rickert," Stanford Encyclopedia of Philosophy: http://plato.stanford.edu/archives/win2013/entries/heinrich-rickert/.

2013. "The *Ideen* and Neo-Kantianism," in L. Embree and T. Nenon (eds.), *Husserl's* Ideen. Dordrecht: Springer: 71–90.

2014. "The Mark of Beginnings: Husserl and Hegel on the Meaning of Naiveté," in Faustino Fabbianelli and Sebastian Luft (eds.), *Husserl und die klassische deutsche Philosophie.* Dordrecht: Springer: 255–264.

Steinbock, A. 1995. *Home and Beyond: Generative Phenomenology after Husserl*. Evanston, IL: Northwestern University Press.

Tilitzki, Christian. 2002. *Die deutsche Universitätsphilosophie in der Weimarer Republik und Im Dritten Reich – Teil I*. Berlin: Akademie Verlag.

Ubiali, Marta. 2010. "Die Willensakte und der Umfang der Motivation: Eine Gegenüberstellung von Pfänder und Husserl," in Philippe Merz, Andrea Staiti, and Frank Steffen (eds.), *Geist–Person–Gemeinschaft: Freiburger Beiträge zur Aktualität Husserls*. Würzburg: Ergon: 241–267.

Vico, Giovambattista B. 1968. *The New Science: Revised Translation of the Third Edition 1744*. Ithaca, NY: Cornell University Press.

von Goethe, Johann Wolfgang. 1949. *Gedenkausgabe der Werke, Briefe und Gespräche 28. August 1949*, vol. 1. Zurich: Artemis Verlag.

von Schlegel, Friedrich. 1847. *The Philosophy of Life, and Philosophy of Language, in a Course of Lectures*. London: Henry G. Bohn.

Welton, Donn. 2002. *The Other Husserl: The Horizons of Transcendental Phenomenology*. Bloomington: Indiana University Press.

2003. "The Systematicity of Husserl's Transcendental Philosophy," in Donn Welton (ed.), *The New Husserl: A Critical Reader*. Bloomington: Indiana University Press: 255–288.

Willey, Thomas. 1978. *Back to Kant: The Revival of Kantianism in German Social and Historical Thought (1860–1914)*. Detroit, MI: Wayne State University Press.

Windelband, Wilhelm. 1914. "Immanuel Kant. Zur Säkularfeier seiner Philosophie," in W. Windelband, *Präludien: Aufsätze und Reden zur Philosophie und ihrer Geschichte*, vol. 1. Tübingen: Mohr Siebeck: 112–146.

1915. "Geschichte und Naturwissenschaft," in W. Windelband, *Präludien: Aufsätze und Reden zur Philosophie und ihrer Geschichte*, vol. 2. Tübingen: Mohr Siebeck: 136–160.

1915. "Kritische oder genetische Methode?," in W. Windelband, *Präludien: Aufsätze und Reden zur Philosophie und ihrer Geschichte*, vol. 2. Tübingen: Mohr Siebeck: 99–135.

1915. "Kulturphilosophie und transzendentaler Idealismus," in W. Windelband, *Präludien: Aufsätze und Reden zur Philosophie und ihrer Geschichte*, vol. 2. Tübingen: Mohr Siebeck: 279–294.

Wittgenstein, Ludwig. 2009. *Philosophical Investigations*. Oxford: Wiley Blackwell.

Wundt, Wilhelm. 1912. *Human and Animal Psychology*. Trans. J. E. Creighton and E. B. Tichener. London: George Allen.

Zijderveld, Anton. 2006. *Rickert's Relevance: The Ontological Nature and Epistemological Functions of Values*. Leiden and Boston, MA: Brill.

Index

a posteriori science, 152, 153
a priori science, 133, 152, 153, 155
absence, 30
abstraction, 33, 106, 122, 128, 154,
    155, 167, 192, 255, 256, 257,
    262, 288
    as impoverishment (*Abbau*), 103,
        142, 143, 192, 252, 279
    from values, 87, 142, 143, 260–261
    of spatial qualities, 156, 255, 288
action (*Aktion*), 101
    dominant action (*Hauptaktion*), 101
    "total acts" (*Gesamtakte*), 101
    un-accomplished action
        (*unvollzogen*), 102
analytic philosophy, 4, 5, 71
animals, 92, 183, 185, 249
    as transcendental subjects, 250, 274
anthropology, 71, 72, 76, 225
appearances, 141, 177, 188, 195, 254,
    260, 261
    appearance-reality distinction, 141
    unity of appearance, 141–142
Aristotle, 8, 41, 152, 276
attitude (*Einstellung*), 15, 82, 83, 97, 98
    change of attitude
        (*Einstellungswechsel*), 84, 105
    natural/phenomenological, 98, 108,
        190–191
    naturalistic/personalistic, 98, 100
    phenomenology and the constitutive
        function of changes of attitude, 108
    reflective versus straightforward
        (unreflective), 141
    theoretical/evaluative-volitional, 98,
        100
authenticity, 3, 55, 58, 116, 123, 139,
    148, 151, 167, 184, 197, 202, 216,
    225, 236, 253, 263, 265, 272

being
    absolute, 191, 263
    and meaning/value, 81, 127
    subjectivity, 272
    subjectivity and, 149–150
Beiser, Fredrick, 5
Bergson, Henri, 111
Berkeley, George, 92
biology, 54
    and life, 54, 80
    Dilthey and Simmel on biology, 54,
        80
Böhm, Franz, 43
    on history, 43, 46, 47–48, 49
    on ontology, 14, 20, 43, 44–46
    on subjectivity, 49–51
Brentano, Franz, 2, 91, 133, 137,
    176, 179, 202, 237, 265,
    295, 303

Campbell, Scott, 6
Carr, David, 249
Cassirer, Ernst, 5–6, 7, 19
categorial thought, 36, 45
    and unity, 38
    Böhm on categories, 44–45
    Lask on categories, 38–41
    ontology and, 43–44, 45
    Rickert on categories, 42
    Windelband on categories, 23
Christianity, 265, 266
    Christian conversion as grounded in a
        new praxis, 265, 266
    Christian conversion as *metanoia*,
        265, 266
classification of the sciences, 25, 42, 89,
    94, 140, 152, 165
    methodological (nature/history)
        versus material (nature/culture), 94

cognition, 9, 31, 32, 37, 44, 47, 57, 58,
83, 123, 134, 135, 190
copy-theory of cognition, 83, 85
Cohen, Hermann, 7, 19, 275
community, 17, 69, 112, 143, 166, 177,
189, 205, 206, 237, 249, 265, 266,
279, 280, 283, 285
comparative psychology, 75, 76
and history, 75, 76–77
Dilthey on comparative psychology,
227–228
Comte, Auguste
and positivistic social thought, 67
concepts
conceptual knowledge, 111,
119, 125
conceptuality of mechanistic
causality versus conceptuality of
motivation, 120
total concept, 154
consciousness
and immediateness, 128
and its preeminence over the natural
world, 289
and reflection, 127, 128, 247
logical versus sensuous, 124
pure consciousness as nexus of lived
experiences, 127
self-conscious, 272
stream of consciousness, 128, 131, 141
Crowell, Steven, 36, 39
culture
and its relation to science, 221
and traditionality, 282, 283
as community of subjects, 280–281
as the correlate of active (*leistende*)
subjectivity, 143
cultural differences, 270, 276, 286
cultural universalism, 266, 276–277
definition of, 143–144
intercultural encounter, 276, 284, 285
possibility of universal human
culture, 280

D'Amico, Robert, 6
Davos debate, the, 5–6
and the rift between analytic and
continental philosophy, 5
de Mul, Jos, 55, 71
de Tocqueville, Alexis, 93

De Warren, Nicolas, viii, 126, 130, 200,
202, 248, 249, 292, 293
Derrida, Jacques, 1, 2
Descartes, René, 8, 133, 139,
160, 220
descriptive psychology, 70, 74, 75, 76,
77, 176, 177, 179
and psychic life, 9–10, 14, 74–75
dignity, 236
Husserl on dignity, 272, 273,
274, 289
Kant on dignity, 226, 273
ontological dignity, 29, 273, 274
Dilthey, Wilhelm
approach to psychology, 75–76
distinction between inner and outer
experience, 15, 85, 90–92, 137
on nature, 69–70
on psychic life, 76–77
dogmatics, 233–234
Driesch, Hans, 54

Ebbinghaus, Hermann, 70, 71
ego
and affection, 181, 182
and nature, 182
as living agent, 103, 108
as monad, 188, 201
ego-motivation, 182
eidetic analysis, 128, 290
and eidetic generality, 128
and eidetic variation, 124
eidetic intuition, 112, 120, 121,
129, 239
and essential knowledge, 120, 121
and essential structures, 128, 130, 133
eidetic knowledge, 110, 116, 117, 118,
122, 128, 129
as conceptual-discursive rather than
intuitive-immediate, 117
as processual, 116, 117, 118, 122
eidetic science, 110, 119, 130
of consciousness, 126, 127–128, 129,
130–131
empathy
and monadic life, 191, 203
and recollection, 201, 202, 203, 204,
213, 217
as communalization of experience,
16–17, 191, 192

Taine, Hippolyte, 93
teleology
  and cultural universalism, 266
  and happiness, 62, 276
  and humankind, 18, 275, 276–277,
    283
  and the transcendental dimension of
    subjectivity, 11
  as ontological constituent of human
    persons, 131
  Kant's notion of, 286
time
  and empirical reality, 8, 27, 28, 48, 95
  and flux, 48, 63, 64
  and history, 48, 208
transcendence
  and intentionality, 190
  and subjectivity, 39, 176
  of nature, 291
transcendental ego, 15, 79, 107, 108,
    134, 173, 247
transcendental idealism
  and subjective realism, 291
transcendental logic, 124, 153
transcendental phenomenology, 3, 98,
    189, 220, 221
  as a scientific life-philosophy, 16, 291
  as project of renewal, 190, 265–266
  epistemology and, 222–223, 289
transcendental philosophy
  and intersubjectivity, 17, 222, 275
  and Kant, 2, 21, 32, 39, 45,
    109, 275
  as a transcendental theory of
    knowledge, 3
transcendental subjectivity, 82, 84, 108,
    110, 130, 201, 220, 221, 247, 250,
    267, 271, 272, 288
  and historical objectivity, 84
  as world-constituting, 245, 246, 247,
    266, 271, 274, 288
Trendelenburg, Friedrich Adolf, 91
two-worlds theory, 38
  Lask and, 38

validity, 37, 41, 49, 64, 66, 81, 95
  validity/value and being/reality,
    38–39, 95–96
value
  as the ground of culture, 260

values
  active valuation (*Wertung*), 144
  and ethics, 61–62, 268, 270
  and validity, 244–245
  as experienced, 127, 243
  Husserl on values, 166, 235, 266,
    269–270
  relatedness to value (Wertbeziehung),
    29–30, 144
  Rickert on values, 9, 30, 231
Vico, Giovambattista, 139

Windelband, Wilhelm
  and idiographic (historical) science
    vs. nomothetic science, 21–23, 93
  law and event, 28, 64
world
  and surrounding world (*Umwelt*),
    103, 149, 150, 168, 169, 175, 199,
    213, 280, 282, 283
  as foreign world, 279, 281,
    282, 284
  as home-world, 280–283, 284, 287
  as pre-given through universal
    experience, 142, 147–148, 182,
    243, 246–247, 269
  as theme of phenomenology, 17, 106
  awareness of world qua horizon
    (world-consciousness), 243–244
  historical world as opposed to natural
    world, 27, 55, 71, 174–177
  natural world as governed by
    spatio-temporality and
    causality, 32, 46, 159, 245
  possibility of knowledge of the world,
    164, 167
  Rickert on world-experience,
    164–165
  structure of homogeneity, 69, 164
  totality of the world (*das Weltganze*),
    146, 147
  world-as-a-whole vs. world-parts, 61,
    73, 146–147, 148, 223, 228,
    229, 231, 236, 241, 242,
    267, 269
  world-whole, 147, 148, 242, 246
world-view (*weltanschauung*), 17, 26,
    272, 284
  as opposed to science, 236
  as task of philosophy, 229, 252

Made in the USA
Middletown, DE
13 June 2023

32504258R00186